# Concentrated Corporate Ownership

A National Bureau
of Economic Research
Conference Report

# Concentrated Corporate Ownership

Edited by **Randall K. Morck**

**The University of Chicago Press**

Chicago and London

Randall K. Morck is the Stephen A. Jarislowsky Distinguished Professor of Finance at the University of Alberta, Edmonton.



The University of Chicago Press, Chicago 60637
The University of Chicago Press, Ltd., London

Printed in the United States of America
09 08 07 06 05 04 03 02 01 00 1 2 3 4 5
ISBN: 0-226-53678-5 (cloth)

Library of Congress Cataloging-in-Publication Data

Concentrated corporate ownership / edited by Randall K. Morck.
p. cm. — (A National Bureau of Economic Research conference report)
Includes bibliographical references and index.
ISBN 0-226-53678-5 (cloth : alk. paper)
1. Corporate governance. 2. Stock ownership. 3. Industrial concentration. I. Morck, Randall. II. Conference report (National Bureau of Economic Research).

HD2741.C64 2000
338.7—dc21

99-086549

♾ The paper used in this publication meets the minimum requirements of the American National Standard for Information Sciences—Permanence of Paper for Printed Library Materials, ANSI Z39.48-1992.

Since this volume is a record of conference proceedings, it has been exempted from the rules governing critical review of manuscripts by the Board of Directors of the National Bureau (resolution adopted 8 June 1948, as revised 21 November 1949 and 20 April 1968).

To Fyfe

# Contents

# Foreword

Over the past decade, the issue of corporate governance has commanded considerable attention in policy and academic circles. The issue is significant because of the modern corporation's role in societal wealth creation. Nevertheless, while the public debate over corporate governance reform has focused on the structure and performance of corporate boards of directors, legal and economic scholars have taken a much broader view of corporate governance and have sought to examine the complex interplay of legal, market, and organizational mechanisms designed to promote corporate accountability. Not surprisingly, as recognition of the broad array of factors implicating corporate governance has grown, so too has interest in examining corporate governance mechanisms in a comparative frame. This interest in enriching the debate over corporate governance by enlisting scholars from a number of different countries and disciplinary perspectives is the animating theme of this volume. It is particularly important that the corporate governance debate be broadened in light of the importance of understanding the impact of concentrated share ownership on the corporation—given that it is the dominant share ownership structure for publicly financed corporations located outside the United States.

The volume and the associated conferences were supported by a very generous grant to the Faculty of Law at the University of Toronto from the IMASCO Corporation of Canada. Purdy Crawford and Brian Levitt, IMASCO's chair and CEO, respectively, were instrumental in providing the necessary support and counsel to launch this project, and we are grateful for their visionary support. We are also indebted to Professor Randall Morck of the University of Alberta for his energetic and unflagging leadership of the project. Without his drive and commitment, this project would never have been brought to fruition.

Ronald J. Daniels

# Acknowledgments

This book was brought to press with the invaluable assistance, intellectual support, and hard work of many people. A deficient memory no doubt prevents me from thanking each individual who helped along the way, so I extend my apologies to those whose names I miss.

Ron Daniels was instrumental in the gestation of this volume as a joint effort by finance and legal scholars, and he greatly broadened and improved the book by bringing some of the world's leading legal scholars into the fold. Their ideas complement those of the first-rank financial economists who graciously lend their names to this volume. Ron, through the University of Toronto's Program on Corporate Governance, also provided the bulk of the financial support for the conferences and papers that ultimately led to this volume. In addition, his paper (joint with Ed Iacobucci) is a novel and highly useful contribution to our understanding of corporate ownership and economic institutions.

Martin Feldstein and Rob Vishny provided intellectual and moral support throughout this endeavor. Their advice on organizational matters, academic standards, and the integration of econometric work and public policy was critical at a number of junctures.

Although James Tobin was not involved directly in this project, he was nonetheless instrumental in pressing me, as a woolly minded undergraduate, to consider how the ownership of capital might matter, at the levels of both microeconomics and macroeconomics. His insight that mainstream economics was missing something important by treating capital ownership as irrelevant led me to a series of papers, which I unworthily coauthored with some of the intellectual giants of contemporary economics, about the importance of capital ownership by pension funds, corporate insiders, corporate raiders, foreign corporations, and wealthy individuals.

I am indebted to the authors of the papers contained in this volume for the great effort embodied in their contributions. This conference volume is perhaps unusual in that it contains many papers that unquestionably could have been published in top journals. Their authors sacrificed the prestige of those outlets to aid in the compilation of a volume that we all hope will stimulate research on the broader cross section of issues by illuminating their many hidden connections.

The discussants, whose thoughtful analyses profoundly improved several of the papers in this volume, were of enormous help. In many cases, where their suggestions have been incorporated in the papers they critiqued, these contributions may not be evident to the reader. Our better general understanding of some fundamental issues of corporate ownership is their lasting contribution.

Randy Kroszner provided exceptionally thoughtful and penetrating feedback as the National Bureau of Economic Research reviewer of the papers in this volume. An anonymous referee, commissioned by the University of Chicago Press, was also instrumental in greatly improving several papers. Finally, my discussions of a number of the papers in this volume with Andrei Shleifer led to highly useful suggestions.

Mike Percy, dean of the University of Alberta Business Faculty, in yet another sign of his continuing effort to promote finance research at that school, provided additional financial support that enabled the junior corporate finance professors there to participate in the Banff conference, which was penultimate to publication of this volume.

The professional staff of the National Bureau of Economic Research provided unsurpassable support at each stage of this project. Kirsten Foss Davis and her team of conference organizers made the two conferences that led to this volume, held in Toronto in January 1998 and in Banff in May 1998, pleasurable and complication free as well as intellectually stimulating. Jessica Rath, a member of that team, provided superb organization at the conference site in Banff. The writeup in the *National Bureau of Economic Research Reporter* by Lissa Davis provided invaluable high-profile publicity. Thanks to such publicity, many of the chapters in this volume became frequently cited well before publication. The chapter by Bebchuk, Kraakman, and Triantis was among the top ten most often downloaded papers of all time for the Social Sciences Research Network website. The chapter I coauthored with Stangeland and Yeung was featured in *Business Week* and in daily newspapers in Canada and Italy. Other chapters no doubt received accolades of which I am ignorant. Yet others will soon be recognized as fundamental contributions.

Helena Fitz-Patrick, coordinator of book publishing at the National Bureau of Economic Research, has patiently and painstakingly supervised the process of preparing the manuscripts for publication. Without her work, this volume would be but a shadow of itself. Geoffrey Huck took charge of the volume when control was passed to the University of Chicago Press. His enthusiasm and hard work are greatly appreciated, as is the overall support by the University of Chicago's Faculty Board of University Publications.

Finally, I thank my wife, Fyfe Bahrey, for her love and support, without which this volume would have been a more burdensome and less rewarding toil.

# Introduction

Randall K. Morck

## Background

Students of American business usually assume that large firms are owned by atomistic shareholders. This is a convenient assumption because it justifies a common premise in corporate finance, that firms should be run so as to maximize their value. La Porta, Lopez-de-Silanes, and Shleifer (1999) show that atomistic shareholders are, in fact, prevalent in only two countries, the United States and the United Kingdom. In most countries, corporate control is, for the most part, highly concentrated, and widely held firms are either unknown or the rarest of curiosities. Even in the United States, the current wave of corporate takeovers can be understood as a move toward greater ownership concentration, especially in leveraged buyouts (see Shleifer and Vishny 1997), and Holderness, Kroszner, and Sheehan (1999) show that ownership is more concentrated in the United States than had been commonly believed.

When an individual controls a firm, the assumption that the firm should be run so as to maximize its value conflicts with the more basic axiom of utility maximization. The first principles of microeconomics require that a shareholder with a control block run his firm so as to maximize his utility. The effect of utility-maximizing corporate governance by the controlling shareholder on the wealth of minority public shareholders is then an externality. We expect utility-maximizing holders of controlling blocks to use corporate resources to benefit themselves in both pecuniary and nonpecuniary ways. Pecuniary benefits might include actions that would increase the share price and so benefit minority shareholders, too, as in

Randall K. Morck is the Stephen A. Jarislowsky Distinguished Professor of Finance at the University of Alberta, Edmonton.

Shleifer and Vishny (1986). But they might also include such things as non-arm's-length transactions at artificial transfer prices between controlled companies and self-dealing via intercorporate loans or securities sales. Nonpecuniary benefits might include corporate hiring policies that discriminate against minorities the controlling shareholder dislikes (even when this raises labor costs) and the use of minority shareholders' money to lobby politicians for policies that disproportionately benefit the controlling shareholder, promote his social or political agenda, or entrench his economic position. Of course, these lists are not exhaustive.

Beginning with Berle and Means (1932), American financial economists have taken dispersed ownership as the norm and asked whether observed or alleged problems in the governance of U.S. firms might stem from their widely held ownership structures. As U.S. economists became aware of the peculiar nature of U.S. corporate ownership, a number of authors, notably Porter (1998) and Roe (1991), argued that atomistic ownership is a competitive disadvantage for the United States and that more concentrated ownership might be a good idea. Others (notably Romano 1993) argue that the U.S. system of corporate governance is unfairly maligned and that other countries might consider promoting less concentrated corporate ownership. Certainly, economic theory provides equally ample resources for constructing models in which concentrated corporate ownership is either good or bad.

The studies presented in this volume are not designed to promote one side or the other of this debate. Rather, they are a mixture of theoretical and empirical studies chosen to highlight the issues that arise in such a discussion and the empirical facts that such a discussion must harmonize.

## A Synopsis

Let the reader beware: this volume is unapologetically interdisciplinary. The paper by Brown, Mintz, and Wilson is on tax accounting. Those by Gompers and Lerner; Bebchuck and Zingales; Holderness and Sheehan; and Morck, Stangeland, and Yeung approach concentrated ownership from a financial economics perspective. Bebchuk and Kahan; Bebchuk, Kraakman, and Triantis; Daniels and Iacobucci; Mahoney; and Rock and Wachter all present contributions from a law and economics perspective. Where issues in one field may not be clear to students of another, the papers err on the side of making explanations too elementary. Thus, some papers may seem overly pedantic on some points, but this is to make them comprehensible to students of other fields. Also, the contributions from economists, lawyers, and tax accountants reflect the research and writing styles of those different disciplines. Finally, the papers are organized by topic rather than by discipline. The purpose of this is to encourage a cross-fertilization of ideas, for concentrated corporate ownership is a fundamentally important but neglected area of several disciplines, not just one.

The first set of papers deals with the determinants of concentrated corporate ownership structure. Gompers and Lerner (chap. 1) consider ownership structure at the venture capital stage, Bebchuk and Zingales (chap. 2) discuss initial public offerings, Daniels and Iacobucci (chap. 3) relate bank financing to concentrated ownership, and Brown, Mintz, and Wilson (chap. 4) consider tax factors that might concentrate corporate ownership.

The paper by Paul Gompers and Joshua Lerner examines the ownership structure of U.S. firms at the venture capital stage in the 1900s. Gompers and Lerner specifically focus on new ventures sponsored by established nonfinancial corporations and new ventures sponsored by independent venture capital funds. Independent venture capital funds generally organize the ownership structure of new ventures as partnerships. Nonfinancial corporations tend to fund new ventures as corporate projects or, in some cases, within divisions established to foster new products.

The potential and problems inherent in venture capital investment by established nonfinancial corporations are illustrated by an extended case study of the Xerox Corporation and its venture capital division, Xerox Technology Ventures (XTV), which was modeled on pure venture capital funds. One venture that XTV backed was Documentum, which marketed an object-oriented document-management system. XTV brought in outside entrepreneurs to critique Xerox's activities in this area. Those outside entrepreneurs determined that Xerox was misdirecting its efforts and led an effort to convert its knowledge into marketable products rapidly. Had Xerox sold out in an initial public offering (IPO), the authors estimate, its net internal rate of return on Documentum would have been about 56 percent.

Xerox could not bring itself to divest its control of such enterprises. Despite stellar performance by XTV, Xerox management terminated it and replaced it with Xerox New Enterprises (XNE), which was to retain control of new ventures and to avoid involving outsiders in them. The case study suggests that corporate-backed new ventures can succeed and draw on the backer's expertise in related areas but that corporate head offices may be unable to tolerate the degree of autonomy that venture capital funds allow entrepreneurs to have.

Gompers and Lerner explore these issues using a large database of U.S. venture capital investments. They find corporate investments to be no less successful than independent investments, especially when there is a strategic fit between the backer corporation and the start-up. They also find corporate-backed investments without such strategic fits to have a decidedly shorter average duration. They conclude that a strong strategic link is critical to the success of new ventures backed by nonfinancial corporations.

The paper by Lucian Bebchuk and Luigi Zingales considers the ownership structure that emerges from the IPO process. Bebchuk and Zingales show that private optimality may give rise to ownership structures that are not socially optimal. Surprisingly, they show this to be true even when a value-maximizing entrepreneur makes the choice of ownership structures at the IPO stage. A key assumption is that the market for minority shares is perfectly competitive while that for controlling blocks is not. Thus, the entrepreneur may prefer to sell to atomistic shareholders because he cannot appropriate a sufficient amount of the surplus from a block trade. Selling to atomistic shareholders therefore maximizes his private wealth, even though this is socially suboptimal. Since the transfer of ownership imposes different externalities on atomistic shareholders and a potential future blockholder, the IPO price does not simply capitalize the expected value from a potential subsequent purchase of a control block. Bebchuk and Zingales argue that empirical evidence from control-block sales in the United States is consistent with that country having a higher incidence of atomistic corporate ownership than is socially optimal. This paper complements Bebchuk (1999), which discusses whether an IPO should preserve a control block.

The contribution of Ronald Daniels and Edward Iacobucci asks why diffuse ownership structures came to characterize large U.S. firms and critically considers Roe's (1991, 1994) hypothesis that diffuse ownership in the United States resulted from the political economic history of that country. According to Roe, small banks and other interest groups took advantage of a general popular distrust of concentrated economic power in the United States and lobbied successfully for restrictions on equityholdings by large financial intermediaries and on large financial intermediaries per se. Daniels and Iacobucci point out that Canadian banks historically held very little equity in nonfinancial corporations despite the fact that, until 1967, Canada had no laws against banks owning shares. They add that other financial intermediaries, such as insurance companies, had equally little to do with ownership concentration in Canada. In fact, most concentrated corporate ownership in Canada consists of control blocks held by very wealthy families, often through multilayered holding companies.

Daniels and Iacobucci go on to criticize Morck (1996), in which I argue that concentrated corporate ownership might concentrate political rent seeking and thereby lead to concentrated market power. In particular, they take issue with my suggestions that wealthy families (or their managers) can act more discretely than the managers of widely held companies and that wealthy families are more credible partners in favor trading with politicians than are the managers of widely held companies, whose powers end at retirement. Daniels and Iacobucci see no reason why an ability to keep secrets should rise with ownership concentration and point out that the managers of narrowly held firms also retire. They suggest instead that a controlling shareholder can use his public firm's resources to lobby for policies that benefit him alone (or firms he owns fully). Of course, the minority shareholders must pay for part of this rent seeking. (For a discussion of the way in which pyramids of holding companies magnify wealthy families' rent-seeking power outside the United States, see Morck, Stangeland, and Yeung, chap. 11 in this volume.)

Daniels and Iacobucci also argue that, by increasing retained earnings, market power lessens the need for external financing and thereby increases ownership concentration. Since Canada erected high tariff barriers for the first several decades of its existence, market power may have fostered ownership concentration rather than the reverse. They further point out that value-increasing deconcentration is rendered unnecessarily difficult by Canada's equal opportunity rules, which require block sales to be extended, at the same price, to all shareholders on a pro rata basis.

Robert Brown, Jack Mintz, and Thomas Wilson study how taxation affects the decision to remain private or go public. They show how Canadian tax law encourages firms to remain private because of a special capital gains exemption and special favorable treatment of retained active business income. They further submit that, relative to U.S. tax law, Canadian tax law discourages individuals from selling shares. These factors explain, in part at least, their empirical finding that a much greater share of private wealth is held in private companies in Canada than in the United States. Along with the Canadian exemption for intercorporate dividends and the wider use of dual class equity in Canada, this preference for private firms may explain the more complex corporate structures, often allowing private companies to control public ones, that characterize Canadian business.

The second set of papers, by Holderness and Sheehan (chap. 5), Mahoney (chap. 6), Rock and Wachter (chap. 7), and Bebchuk and Kahan (chap. 8), considers the consequences of a concentrated ownership structure in terms of the abilities of majority and minority shareholders to expropriate wealth. These papers have a primarily legal focus and are concerned with various issues that arise in the corporate governance of firms with concentrated ownership.

The paper by Clifford Holderness and Dennis Sheehan explores the argument of Fama and Jensen (1983) that, if majority owners were entirely free to expropriate money from minority shareholders, there would very soon be no minority shareholders. One interpretation of this hypothesis is that poor legal and institutional protection of minority shareholders in the United States leads to economic selection that culls dominant shareholder ownership structures. Holderness and Sheehan take issue with the view that U.S. laws are relatively ineffective at constraining controlling shareholders. They point out that a shortage of case law is consistent with both a totally ineffective law and a totally effective law. They cite three broad empirical regularities as support for their revisionist views.

First, Holderness and Sheehan (1988) and Mikkelson and Partch (1989) find no evidence that majority-owned public firms are becoming rarer in the United States. Indeed, Holderness, Kroszner, and Sheehan (1999) find that managerial ownership in a large sample of public U.S. companies rose from 13 percent in 1935 to 21 percent in 1995. This is consistent with the earlier findings (in Holderness and Sheehan 1988) of no systematic difference in $q$-ratios for firms with control stakes exceeding 50 percent and paired diffusely held firms. (It is, perhaps, at odds with Barclay, Holderness, and Pontiff [1993], which finds high managerial ownership associated with high discounts from net asset value in a sample of U.S.-traded closed-end funds.) Contrast these U.S. findings with those of Morck, Stangeland, and Yeung (chap. 11 in this volume) that diffuse ownership is more commonplace in Canada subsequent to that country's free trade agreement with the United States.

Second, Holderness and Sheehan point out that, if minority shareholders were open to easy abuse, firms seeking public investors might commit to restraining their dominant shareholders. The authors find little evidence of this. Outside directors, staggered boards, cumulative voting, audit committees, and compensation committees are all rarer in controlled than in diffusely owned U.S. firms, suggesting more limited board independence. Majority-owned firms also tend to have very few other large shareholders, and their directors (other than the owner) have little or no stock and so have little or no direct interest in the public share price. Majority-owned firms have unusually low debt ratios, suggesting a more limited monitoring role for banks or large debtholders. Majority-owned firms go to public capital markets less frequently and so are presumably exposed to less scrutiny by them. Majority-owned firms also pay lower dividends than paired diffusely owned firms. Finally, no pattern of changes in the organizational features listed above can be discerned among firms that become majority owned or cease to be majority owned.

Third, U.S. minority shareholders gain on average when their holdings are bought out by the dominant shareholder. Moreover, Holderness and Sheehan point out that these gains are broadly similar to the gains that shareholders of widely held firms receive on similar reorganizations. The authors conclude that U.S. law may not be a perfect restraint on improper behavior by control-block owners but that it probably is a binding constraint on such behavior.

Mark Huson's comments on the paper by Holderness and Sheehan are insightful. He argues that a dearth of institutional checks on majority owners is not evidence of the existence of other checks, pointing out that nonlethal parasites survive better than lethal parasites. If majority owners are nonlethal parasites, the firms that they control ought to survive. He suggests that the dispersion of value discounts across majority-controlled firms might be more informative than an average value discount relative to diffusely owned firms. If some majority owners add to public shareholder value by, say, effective monitoring while others destroy value by, say, self-dealing, the averages suggest no effect. Huson also takes issue with using 50 percent as the threshold of control and adds that a finer classification of majority owners, into, say, heirs and founders, might also be interesting.

Paul Mahoney's paper models the interaction between majority and minority shareholders in close (privately held) corporations as a trust game. A shareholder in such a corporation in the United States can withdraw capital only with the consent of the majority of shareholders. This exposes the minority shareholder to opportunism by the majority shareholder. To avoid this, Hetherington and Dooley (1977) propose that minority shareholders be free to withdraw capital at will. Easterbrook and Fischel (1986, 1991) and O'Kelley (1992) point out that free exit might give rise to minority opportunism against the majority shareholder and argue that the exit rule should reflect a trade-off between majority and minority opportunism.

Mahoney uses his trust game model to show conditions under which majority opportunism does not "oppress" minority shareholders—the minority pays less for its stake because of the restrictions on exit. The trust game approach also suggests that, since a minority shareholder's withdrawal is at a judicially determined price, minority opportunism is not a credible threat unless judicial valuations are systematically biased. Given this, Mahoney explores other reasons for the survival of the majority-consent exit rule in the United States. He argues that abuse of minority shareholders by majority shareholders may well be effectively deterred in the United States by a combination of legal and nonlegal sanctions (such as family or social disapproval). Mahoney presents a detailed description of U.S. law in this area and argues that what some commentators have considered a greater degree of judicial intervention in close corporation governance is, in fact, nothing more than the application of a standard fiduciary duty principle to close corporations. Since, as manager, the majority shareholder can violate his fiduciary duty to the minority shareholder in the day-to-day operation of the firm, court attention must sometimes penetrate to that level.

The paper by Edward Rock and Michael Wachter is also about the laws governing majority oppression of minority shareholders in private corporations. But Rock and Wachter take a different approach. Rejecting the implicit comparison of close corporations to partnerships that supports much legal reasoning in this area, they propose an alternative analogy: the relationship between the majority and the minority shareholders in a close corporation is akin to an employment relationship with firm-specific human capital at risk.

Just as an employer and an employee both invest human capital in their relationship, the majority and minority shareholders both invest physical capital in a close corporation. Once the investment is made, both parties are locked in—by the sessility of firm-specific human capital in the employment relationship and by the laws restricting exit in a close corporation. This locked-in joint investment enforces a stable, long-term relationship by deterring opportunistic threats by the employee to quit or by the minority shareholder to "cash out."

If the majority shareholder is legally constrained to pay out only pro rata benefits, the inability of minority shareholders to cash out can be thought of as analogous to the "employment-at-will" doctrine. Rock and Wachter describe how employment contracts are best governed by this doctrine, whereby either party can terminate the employment relationship at will. This is because the cost of terminating the agreement, losing locked-in firm-specific human capital, deters opportunism. The authors argue that laws that lock in physical capital investments in close corporations serve the same purpose—to deter opportunistic threats to cash out.

The paper by Lucian Bebchuk and Marcel Kahan uses an adverse selection model in the style of Akerlof (1970) to illustrate clearly the difficulties that arise in determining a share value at which a controlling shareholder may freeze out minority shareholders. The model shows that, if the controlling shareholder can freeze out minority shareholders at the prefreezeout market price of their stocks, the prefreezeout market price is lower than what the minority shares would be worth were no freezeout possible. This is because the controlling shareholder will effect a freezeout when the market undervalues the minority shares but delay it when the shares are overvalued. Buyers of the minority shares capitalize the controlling shareholder's option to strategically time the freezeout into the share price, depressing it.

The fact that this option is valuable has important policy implications. The controlling shareholder has an incentive to gather and hoard information so as to increase the value of the option. He also has an incentive to skew capital investment toward projects that increase the information asymmetry between him and the minority shareholders, even negative net present value (NPV) projects. Finally, a freezeout option of this sort may create socially excessive incentives for wealthy people to become controlling shareholders.

The third set of papers in this volume—by Khanna and Palepu (chap. 9), Bebchuk, Kraakman, and Triantis (chap. 10), and Morck, Stangeland, and Yeung (chap. 11)—examines the political economy of concentrated corporate ownership.

Tarun Khanna and Krishna Palepu consider corporate groups in India, examples of stock pyramids with cross-holdings. They explain that monitoring firms in such groups is problematic for two reasons.

First, they point to a perceived lack of transparency in corporate groups. One factor in this lack of transparency is the apparent ease with which Indian group firms can shift income between each other via related-party transactions at artificial transfer prices or intercorporate lending at nonmarket interest rates. Another is the equity cross-holdings among publicly traded group firms that block corporate control challenges and between public and private group firms that exacerbate transparency problems.

Second, the close connections between the families that control corporate groups and India's political elite may make monitoring group firms pointless. Khanna and Palepu explain that, until 1991, the Indian government instructed banks, almost all of which are state run, to maximize loans to the industrial sector, to refrain from divesting shares, and to support management. A series of bizarre laws made it very difficult for creditors to shut down failing firms, prevented competition among banks, and virtually guaranteed bank financing to government-approved entrepreneurs. Finally, banks themselves were not monitored. These factors conspired to mire India's industrial firms in political rent seeking. Khanna and Palepu write of "financial preemption," whereby businesses used political lobbying to deny financing to other businesses, and of "industrial embassies" maintained by prominent businesses in New Delhi. Since corporate groups can realize greater economies of scale in lobbying than independent firms can, they presumably benefited disproportionately from government largesse. Although some of this dysfunctional government policy has been cleaned up during the 1990s, the authors conclude that Indian corporate governance is still deficient.

Khanna and Palepu then present evidence consistent with Indian financial institutions being poor monitors and foreign financial institutions being good monitors. They also show that foreigners are relatively reluctant to invest in firms in corporate groups, especially groups that engage in frequent intercorporate intragroup financial transactions. This is consistent with transparency being an issue to foreign investors in India. Since emerging economies such as India are increasingly courting foreign investors, these results are clearly important.

The paper by Lucian Bebchuk, Reinier Kraakman, and George Triantis distinguishes true majority ownership from minority-block ownership that bestows complete control. Mechanisms to achieve the latter include stock pyramids, cross-holdings, and dual class equity structures, all of which are commonplace in large firms outside the United States. The authors discuss each in turn and then argue that these structures are likely to create agency costs an order of magnitude larger than those associated with true majority shareholders or with highly leveraged capital structures. Using very simple mathematics, the paper builds detailed treatments of agency problems associated with capital investment project choice, scope of operations, and control transfers.

Bebchuk, Kraakman, and Triantis concede that wealthy families with a reputation for fair dealing may be able to extend their control via such ownership structures. This should be especially true in economies with weak legal systems and is therefore consistent with work by Khanna and Palepu (1997) that shows superior performance by Indian and Chilean firms in family-controlled stock pyramids.

Bebchuk, Kraakman, and Triantis then compare ownership structures that allow holders of minority blocks complete control with highly leveraged capital structures. Both allow control to be exerted with a relatively small stake, but high leverage is critically different (and better) in two ways. First, concerns about mezzanine financing and leveraged-buyout (LBO) shell companies aside, debtholders have priority rights to corporate cash flows. Second, creditors protect their interests by encumbering the debtor with restrictive covenants and other contractual obligations. Although they carefully hedge their bets, the authors suggest that sophisticated shareholders would prefer to invest in leveraged (minority-block-controlled) firms because debt might counter some of the agency problems associated with stock pyramids and the like. This hypothesis is consistent with the finding of Daniels, Morck, and Stangeland (1995) that firms in the Hees-Edper corporate group, the largest in Canada, have unusually high leverage.

The final paper, by Randall Morck, David Stangeland, and Bernard Yeung, investigates the relation between wealth concentration and economic growth across countries. My coauthors and I show that countries in which inherited billionaire wealth is large relative to GDP grow more slowly than do other countries at similar stages of development, with similar investment rates, and with similarly educated workforces. In contrast, countries in which self-made billionaire wealth is large grow faster than do otherwise similar countries.

My coauthors and I propose several possible explanations for our finding, using simple models where necessary. Since many large heir-controlled firms are members of stock pyramids, we argue that the extreme separation of ownership from control that occurs in such structures may impede corporate performance. We further argue that stock pyramids multiply the rent-seeking power of the wealthy families that control them and that these families might use their political clout to impede financing for entrepreneurial firms. We also argue that established billionaire families have a vested interest in preserving the economic status quo and so might try to frustrate innovation. Any or all of these factors could possibly slow economic growth.

To delve further into these explanations, we examine samples of narrowly and widely held Canadian firms. Firms controlled by wealthy heirs underperform other U.S. and Canadian firms the same age and size. In contrast, firms controlled by self-made entrepreneurs outperform their benchmarks. Heir-controlled firms also have lower labor-to-capital ratios than other firms the same age and size and in the same industries, consistent with other firms having more restricted access to capital. Heir-controlled firms also spend less on research and development (R&D), consistent with a satisfaction with the economic status quo. High barriers against foreign direct investment are also associated with countries with large inherited wealth.

We use the term *Canadian disease* to denote widespread corporate control by entrenched wealthy families via stock pyramids etc., which slows economic growth. We argue that Canada's economic growth may be impeded because its wealthy families restrict corporate control to relatives, use political connections to divert capital away from competitors, and avoid investments (such as R&D) that might upset the economic status quo. We suggest that, if the Canadian disease is prevalent throughout the world, it might explain our basic finding linking inherited billionaire wealth to slow economic growth.

Finally, we note that the Free Trade Agreement between Canada and the United States rendered Canada's markets more competitive at a stroke. This event is especially useful because it was unexpected. The pro–free trade Conservative government had called an election to get a mandate for free trade, and was trailing badly in the polls, but, to everyone's surprise, was returned with a majority. The share prices of heir-controlled Canadian firms fell relative to industry benchmarks on the news that free trade would go ahead, while those of companies controlled by self-made entrepreneurs rose. Under free trade, the fraction of Canadian firms that are widely held rose, and the labor-to-capital ratios of heir-controlled firms converged to their benchmarks. We argue that globalization might therefore be an effective treatment.

## Concentrated Ownership

It is surprising how pervasive the assumption of diffuse ownership is in finance, law, accounting, and economics. Virtually everything we teach our students stems from this assumption. This tends to be almost as true outside as within the United States, for the most important standard textbooks in these fields are American.

Positive NPVs are a sensible capital budgeting test in a widely held firm. Concentrated ownership calls for a more carefully crafted test—reflecting effects on related corporations, effects on the utility levels of controlling shareholders and the value of public shares, and other things. At present, we have little guidance about how to operationalize capital budgeting decisions in firms with concentrated ownership.

Cumulative abnormal stock returns measure shareholder value creation and are used to distinguish good corporate governance from bad in many empirical studies. But microeconomics tells us that the owners of control blocks in large corporations should maximize their utility, not the value of the shares they hold. This does not render studies of abnormal returns uninformative where corporate ownership is not diffuse. But it does mandate more care in basing normative conclusions about economic efficiency or the optimality of various outcomes on such studies. We know little about these issues.

Asset-pricing models, such as the capital asset–pricing model, the arbitrage pricing theory, and their numerous relatives, are all built on the assumption that investors are highly diversified. Where concentrated ownership is prevalent, the most critical controlling shareholder in each firm may be quite undiversified. Since this investor has control rights that let him influence corporate governance, capital budgeting, and numerous other aspects of corporate decision making, the firm's stock price surely must reflect his utility maximization as well as the portfolio value–maximizing behavior of diversified investors. Perhaps corporate groups of the sort described by Khanna and Palepu; Bebchuk, Kraakman, and Triantis; and Morck, Stangeland, and Yeung provide a countervailing effect by rendering controlling shareholders more diversified. We have little idea what an asset-pricing model should look like in a country where most or all firms have large undiversified controlling shareholders, control pyramids, etc. Despite their immediate importance in most countries, these problems have received remarkably scant attention from academics so far.

The studies gathered in this volume do not answer all, or even most, of the questions that surround concentrated corporate ownership. Our hope is that, by their incompleteness, they will encourage scholars in law, finance, and economics to pursue such questions more deeply. Certainly, its sweeping importance throughout the world, and in the United States, too, means that a constructive debate about the implications of concentrated corporate ownership for corporate and investor decision making will attract worldwide attention. It may also lead to a reconsideration of public policy in many countries.

## References

Akerlof, George. 1970. The market for lemons: Quality uncertainty and the market mechanism. *Quarterly Journal of Economics* 84:488–500.

Barclay, Michael, Clifford Holderness, and Jeffrey Pontiff. 1993. Private benefits from block ownership and discounts on closed end funds. *Journal of Financial Economics* 32:263–91.

Berle, A. A., and G. C. Means. 1932. *The modern corporation and private property.* New York: Macmillan.

Bebchuk, Lucian. 1999. A rent-protection theory of corporate ownership and control. NBER Working Paper no. 7203. Cambridge, Mass.: National Bureau of Economic Research.

Daniels, Ron, Randall Morck, and David Stangeland. 1995. High gear: A case study of the Hees-Edper corporate group. In *Corporate decision making in Canada,* ed. Ron Daniels and Randall Morck. Calgary: Industry Canada/University of Calgary Press.

Easterbrook, Frank, and Daniel Fischel. 1986. Close corporations and agency costs. *Stanford Law Review* 38:271–301.

———. 1991. *The economic structure of corporate law.* Cambridge, Mass.: Harvard University Press.

Fama, Eugene F., and Michael C. Jensen. 1983. Separation of ownership and control. *Journal of Law and Economics* 26, no. 2 (June): 301–26.

Hetherington, J. A. C., and Michael P. Dooley. 1977. Illiquidity and exploitation: A proposed statutory solution to the remaining close corporation problem. *Virginia Law Review* 63:1–75.

Holderness, Clifford G., Randall S. Kroszner, and Dennis P. Sheehan. 1999. Were the good old days that good? Changes in managerial stock ownership since the Great Depression. *Journal of Finance* 54, no. 2 (April): 435–69.

Holderness, Clifford, and Dennis Sheehan. 1988. The role of majority shareholders in publicly held corporations: An exploratory analysis. *Journal of Financial Economics* 20:317–46.

Khanna, Tarun, and Krishna Palepu. 1997. Why focused strategies may be wrong for emerging markets. *Harvard Business Review* 75, no. 4:41–51.

La Porta, Raphael, Florencio Lopez-de-Silanes, and Andrei Shleifer. 1999. Corporate ownership around the world. *Journal of Finance* 54, no. 2:471–517.

Mikkelson, Wayne, and M. Megan Partch. 1989. Managers' voting rights and corporate control. *Journal of Financial Economics* 25:263–90.

Morck, Randall. 1996. On the economics of concentrated ownership. *Canadian Business Law Journal* 26:63–75.

O'Kelley, Charles R., Jr. 1992. Filling gaps in the close corporation contract: A transactions cost analysis. *Northwestern University Law Review* 87:216–53.

Porter, Michael E. 1998. *The competitive advantage of nations.* New York: Free Press.

Roe, Mark. 1991. A political theory of American corporate finance. *Columbia Law Review* 91, no. 10:10–71.

———. 1994. *Strong managers, weak owners: The political roots of American corporate finance.* Princeton, N.J.: Princeton University Press.

Romano, Roberta. 1993. *Foundations of corporate law.* Oxford: Oxford University Press.

Shleifer, Andrei, and Robert W. Vishny. 1986. Large shareholders and corporate control. *Journal of Political Economy* 95:461–88.

———. 1997. A survey of corporate governance. *Journal of Finance* 52, no. 2: 737–83.

# I

# The Origins of Ownership Structure

1

# The Determinants of Corporate Venture Capital Success
## Organizational Structure, Incentives, and Complementarities

Paul A. Gompers and Josh Lerner

The structure of private equity organizations—in particular, the reliance on limited partnerships of finite life with substantial profit sharing—has been identified as critical to their success. Jensen (1993) and Shleifer and Vishny (1997b), among others, have attributed the rapid growth of private equity organizations to the ways in which their design addresses moral hazard and information-asymmetry problems. These claims, however, have received little empirical scrutiny.

This paper addresses this omission by comparing investments made by traditional venture capital organizations with those of venture funds sponsored by corporations. These corporate funds have similar missions and are staffed by individuals with backgrounds resembling those in independent organizations. But the organizational and incentive structures in corporate funds are very different: most are structured as corporate subsidiaries and have much lower incentive-based compensation. In this respect, corporate funds differ dramatically from both independent venture organizations and funds associated with commercial and investment banks. (Many bank-affiliated funds retain the autonomous partnership structure

Paul A. Gompers is associate professor of business administration at the Harvard Business School and a faculty research fellow of the National Bureau of Economic Research. Josh Lerner is professor of business administration at the Harvard Business School and a research associate of the National Bureau of Economic Research.

The authors thank VentureOne for making this project possible through generous access to their database of venture financings. The authors also thank conference and preconference participants (especially Randall Morck, Krishna Palepu, Michael Weisbach, Luigi Zingales, and two anonymous reviewers) and the Harvard Business School lunchtime finance workshop for helpful comments. Rob Bhargava and Amy Burroughs provided research assistance; Sanjeev Verma contributed to the design of this project. The authors thank the Harvard Business School's Division of Research for financial support.

employed by independent venture organizations, albeit with a lower share of the profits accruing to the venture investors.)

Thus, the contrast between corporate and independent venture funds provides a natural test case for examining the effect of organizational structure on investment performance. The arguments regarding the importance of the structure of independent private equity organizations suggest that corporate programs would prove less successful. Either their process of selecting or overseeing investments would be distorted, or else the programs would prove unstable. It may be, however, that corporate programs enjoy benefits that offset some of these costs. A lengthy literature on complementarities in the strategy literature argues that corporations can benefit from closely related activities (for a review and formalization, see Athey and Stern [1997]). Corporations may be able to select better ventures using the information from their related lines of business or may add greater value to the firms once the investments are made.

Before turning to the empirical analysis, we consider the experience of Xerox Technology Ventures, which illustrates both these points. This corporate venture fund compiled excellent financial returns between 1988 and 1996 by aggressively exploiting the technology and knowledge of the corporate parent. Nonetheless, the corporate parent dissolved the fund before the ending date originally intended. The case highlights the fact that—contrary to both popular wisdom and academic arguments—corporate venture programs can still be successful without the traditional partnership structure. The case also suggests, however, some of the difficulties that these efforts encounter and the apparent importance of having a strong linkage between the fund's investment focus and the corporate parent's strategic focus.

We then consider the more general evidence. Using the VentureOne database of private equity financings, we examine over thirty thousand investments in entrepreneurial firms by venture capital programs. The mix of firms in which corporate venture funds invested is little different than that of traditional organizations.

The first set of tests relates to the performance of firms financed by corporate venture capitalists as opposed to those funded by independent funds. If the structural features of the independent funds are critical, we should expect that their investments would perform better. The corporate funds, hampered by poor incentives and management interference, would be unable to select or oversee firms effectively. If corporations can exploit complementarities with their existing lines of business while evaluating or assisting portfolio firms, however, their investments may actually perform better. This should be particularly true for corporate investments in very similar businesses. It is unclear whether corporations will pay more or less than other investors in these cases: it may be that the corporate investor will be willing to pay more than other investors owing to the indirect benefits that it alone enjoys.

When we examine the empirical evidence, we find that, far from being outright failures, corporate venture investments in entrepreneurial firms appear to be at least as successful (using such measures as the probability of the portfolio firm going public) as those backed by independent venture organizations. This appears to be particularly true for investments in which there is strategic overlap between the corporate parent and the portfolio firm. It is harder to assess the relative returns that independent and corporate venture organizations enjoy. Corporations are likely to benefit from indirect gains (e.g., strategic alliances and greater understanding of industry trends) as well as direct financial returns.[1] While corporate venture capitalists tend to invest at a premium to other firms, this premium appears to be no higher in investments with a strong strategic fit where these benefits are likely to be greatest.

We then consider the duration of the programs themselves. We consider two potential reasons why corporate programs might be short-lived. First, it may be that corporations need to employ such programs only during periods of severe technological discontinuity. After such periods of rapid change pass, the programs are no longer needed. If programs were generally designed to address short-run technological discontinuities, it should be the strategic programs that have the shortest duration. A second possibility is that large corporations find it difficult to duplicate the autonomy and the high-powered compensation schemes offered in independent venture funds. As a result, key personnel may depart once they establish a track record and relationships with outside investors.

The empirical evidence suggests that corporate programs are much less stable than those of independent funds. The programs frequently cease operations after only a few investments. We show that the instability is particularly great in corporate funds whose investments do not have a strong strategic focus. This result is hard to reconcile with the first hypothesis.

In short, the evidence seems to underscore the importance of the complementarities hypothesis outlined above. Portfolio companies receiving funds from corporate investors with a well-defined strategic focus enjoy greater success. Investments are made at a premium, but this may reflect the indirect benefits that the corporation receives. Corporate programs with a well-defined strategic focus also appear to be as stable as traditional independent venture organizations. Among the corporate funds without a

1. Of course, these programs may also be associated with costs to the firms as well, such as distraction from the primary mission of the organization. These are difficult for us to assess, except possibly through the measure of program longevity discussed below.

strong strategic focus, we see significantly less success in investments and less stability than among the focused funds.

We end with a more general discussion of the implications. It may be that—contrary to the emphasis in the finance literature—the structure of corporate venture funds is not a critical barrier. Rather, the presence of a strong strategic focus may be critical. Alternatively, the corporate programs without a strong strategic focus may also have particularly weak incentive schemes and other problematic structural characteristics.

This paper is related to an extensive corporate finance literature about the relation between organizational structure and corporate performance (reviewed, e.g., in Jensen [1993]). More specifically, a set of papers has examined the structure of financial institutions and investment performance. Among these are studies of the performance of initial public offerings underwritten by investment banks that are and are not affiliated with commercial banks (Kroszner and Rajan 1994), the performance of loans underwritten by savings-and-loan institutions structured as mutual and stock organizations (Cordell, MacDonald, and Wohar 1993), and the effect of mutual fund performance on investment choices and returns (Chevalier and Ellison 1997). As far as we are aware, however, no paper has analyzed the effect of the limited-partnership structure on investment performance.

This paper is also related to a body of literature on private equity partnerships more generally. These writings suggest reasons to be both positive and skeptical about the importance of the partnership structure. On the one hand, a set of articles documents that investments by private equity organizations are associated with real changes in the firms that they fund, measured on both an accounting (Muscarella and Vetsuypens 1990) and a financial (Brav and Gompers 1997) basis. Moreover, the structure of private equity groups—whether measured through the sensitivity of compensation to performance (Gompers and Lerner 1999) or the extent of contractual restrictions (Gompers and Lerner 1996)—appears to be responsive to the changing investment mix and characteristics of the funds. On the other hand, it appears that other factors (e.g., relative supply and demand conditions for private equity funds [Gompers and Lerner 1996]) can also affect the structure of partnerships. Furthermore, certain features of partnerships apparently can lead to pathological outcomes. For instance, policies allowing venture capitalists to distribute shares in stock, designed to maximize investors' choices regarding the liquidation of their positions, have been exploited by some private equity groups to inflate returns and to boost their compensation (Gompers and Lerner 1998). This paper raises questions about the necessity of the partnership structure employed by independent private equity funds.

The organization of this paper is as follows. In section 1.1, we briefly summarize the history of corporate venture capital funds. Section 1.2 discusses the case of Xerox Technology Ventures. Section 1.3 describes the data set. The empirical analysis is presented in section 1.4. Section 1.5 concludes.

## 1.1 The History of Corporate Venture Capital Investment

The first corporate venture funds began in the mid-1960s, about two decades after the first formal venture capital funds.[2] The corporate efforts were spurred by the successes of the first organized venture capital funds, which backed such firms as Digital Equipment, Memorex, Raychem, and Scientific Data Systems. Excited by this success, large companies began establishing divisions that emulated venture capitalists. During the late 1960s and early 1970s, more than 25 percent of the Fortune 500 firms attempted corporate venture programs.

These efforts generally took two forms, external and internal. At one end of the spectrum, large corporations financed new firms alongside other venture capitalists. In many cases, the corporations simply provided funds for a venture capitalist to invest. Other firms invested directly in start-ups, giving them a greater ability to tailor their portfolios to their particular needs. At the other extreme, large corporations attempted to tap the entrepreneurial spirit within their organizations. These programs sought to allow entrepreneurs to focus their attention on developing their innovations while relying on the corporation for financial, legal, and marketing support.

In 1973, the market for new public offerings—the primary avenue through which venture capitalists exit successful investments—abruptly declined. Independent venture partnerships began experiencing significantly less attractive returns and encountered severe difficulties in raising new funds. At the same time, corporations began scaling back their own initiatives. The typical corporate venture program begun in the late 1960s was dissolved after only four years.

Funds flowing into the venture capital industry and the number of active venture organizations increased dramatically during the late 1970s and early 1980s. An important factor accounting for the increase in money flowing into the venture capital sector was the 1979 amendment to the "prudent man" rule governing pension fund investments; also important

2. This history is based in part on Fast (1978), Gee (1994), and Venture Economics (1986), among other sources.

The origin of the formal venture capital industry in the United States dates back to the formation of American Research and Development in 1946. (Venture capital can be defined as equity or equity-linked investments in young, privately held companies, where the investor is a financial intermediary who is typically active as a director, an adviser, or even a manager of the firm.) A handful of other venture funds were established in the years after the pioneering fund's formation, but the annual flow of money into new venture funds was quite modest in the first three decades of the industry.

was the lowering of capital gains tax rates in 1978. Prior to 1979, the Employee Retirement Income Security Act limited pension funds from investing substantial amounts of money in venture capital or other high-risk asset classes. The Department of Labor's clarification of the rule explicitly allowed pension managers to invest in high-risk assets, including venture capital. Fueled by these eased restrictions and a robust market for public offerings, fund-raising by independent venture partnerships recovered in the early 1980s. Corporations were also once again attracted to the promise of venture investing in response. These efforts peaked in 1986, when corporate funds managed $2 billion, or nearly 12 percent of the total pool of venture capital.

After the stock market crash of 1987, however, the market for new public offerings again went into a sharp decline. Returns from and fund-raising by independent partnerships declined sharply. Corporations scaled back their commitment to venture investing even more dramatically. By 1992, the number of corporate venture programs had fallen by one-third, and their capital under management represented only 5 percent of the venture pool.

Interest in corporate venture capital climbed once again in the mid-1990s, both in the United States and abroad. Once again, much of this interest was stimulated by the recent success of the independent venture sector: that is, the rapid growth of funds and their attractive returns. These corporate funds have invested directly in a variety of internal and external ventures as well as in funds organized by independent venture capitalists. (Venture Economics estimates that corporate investors accounted for 30 percent of the commitments to new funds in 1997, up from an average of 5 percent in the period 1990–92 [estimates compiled from various issues of the *Venture Capital Journal*].)

This brief discussion makes clear that corporate involvement in venture capital has mirrored (perhaps even in an exaggerated manner) the cyclic nature of the entire venture capital industry over the past three decades. At the same time, numerous discussions suggest that certain basic non-cyclic issues also have a significant effect on corporate venture capital activity.

In particular, it appears that the frequent disillusion of earlier corporate venture programs was due to three structural failings. First, these programs suffered because their missions were not well defined (Fast 1978; Siegel, Siegel, and MacMillan 1988). Typically, they sought to accomplish a wide array of not necessarily compatible objectives: from providing a window on emerging technologies to generating attractive financial returns. The confusion over program objectives often led to dissatisfaction with outcomes. For instance, when outside venture capitalists were hired to run a corporate fund under a contract that linked compensation to financial performance, management frequently became frustrated about their failure to invest in the technologies that most interested the firm.

A second cause of failure was insufficient corporate commitment to the venturing initiative (Hardymon, DiNino, and Salter 1983; Rind 1981; Sykes 1990). Even if top management embraced the concept, middle management often resisted. Research-and-development (R&D) personnel preferred that funds be devoted to internal programs; corporate lawyers disliked the novelty and complexity of these hybrid organizations. In many cases, new senior management teams terminated programs, seeing them as expendable "pet projects" of their predecessors. Even if they did not object to the idea of the program, managers were often concerned about its effect on the firm's accounting earnings. During periods of financial pressure, money-losing subsidiaries were frequently terminated in an effort to increase reported operating earnings.

A final cause of failure was inadequate compensation schemes (Block and Ornati 1987; Lawler and Drexel 1980). Corporations have frequently been reluctant to compensate their venture managers through profit-sharing ("carried-interest") provisions, fearing that they might need to make huge payments if their investments were successful. Typically, successful risk taking was inadequately rewarded and failure excessively punished. As a result, corporations were frequently unable to attract top people (i.e., those who combined industry experience with connections to other venture capitalists) to run their venture funds. All too often, corporate venture managers adopted a conservative approach to investing. Nowhere was this behavior more clearly manifested than in the treatment of lagging ventures. Independent venture capitalists often cut off funding to failing firms because they want to devote their limited energy to firms with the greatest promise. Corporate venture capitalists have frequently been unwilling to write off unsuccessful ventures, lest they incur the reputational repercussions that a failure would entail.

## 1.2 The Case of Xerox Technology Ventures (XTV)

These general observations can be illustrated through a case study. The Xerox Corporation originated as a photography-paper business called the Haloid Company.[3] The Haloid Company's entrance into what would later become its principal business came in 1947, when it and the Battelle Memorial Institute, a research organization, agreed to produce a machine based on the recently developed process named *xerography*. Invented by the patent lawyer Chester Carlson, xerography involved a process by which images were transferred from one piece of paper to another by means of static electricity. Rapid growth and a redirection of the company's emphasis toward xerography characterized the Haloid Company in the 1950s. In 1961, in recognition of the spectacular growth of sales engendered by the first plain-paper copier, the firm was renamed the Xerox Corporation.

3. The first sixteen paragraphs of this section are based on Hunt and Lerner (1995).

In response to IBM's entrance into the copier field in the late 1960s, Xerox experimented with computers and with designing an electronic office of the future. It formed Xerox Computer Services, acquired Scientific Data Systems, and opened its Palo Alto Research Center (PARC) in California. These efforts were only the beginning of the copier giant's effort to become a force in the computer industry. Throughout the 1970s, Xerox completed several acquisitions in order to further its project for an "architecture of information." Unfortunately, in assembling these noncopier companies and opening PARC, Xerox created a clash of cultures. Differences between its East Coast operations and its West Coast computer people would severely affect the company.

The focus for much of this division was PARC. In the 1970s, PARC was remarkably successful in developing ingenious products that would fundamentally alter the nature of computing. The Ethernet, the graphic user interface (the basis of Apple Computer's and Microsoft's Windows software), the "mouse," and the laser printer were all originally developed at PARC. The culmination of much of PARC's innovation was its development of the Alto, a very early personal computer. The Alto's first prototype was completed in 1973, and later versions were placed in the White House, Congress, and various companies and universities. Nonetheless, the Alto project was terminated in 1980.

Inherent in the Alto's demise was Xerox's relationship with PARC. Xerox did not have a clear-cut business strategy for its research laboratory, and, in turn, many of PARC's technologies did not fit into Xerox's strategic objectives. For instance, the Alto's ability to adapt to large customers' computer systems was inconsistent with Xerox's strategy of producing workstations compatible only with its own equipment.

The establishment of XTV was driven by two events in 1988. First, several senior Xerox managers were involved in negotiating and approving a spin-off from Xerox, ParcPlace, which sought to commercialize an object-oriented programming language developed at PARC in the 1970s. The negotiation of these agreements proved to be protracted and painful, highlighting the difficulty that the company faced in dealing with these contingencies. More important, in this year a book documenting Xerox's failure to develop the personal computer, *Fumbling the Future* (Smith and Alexander 1988), appeared. Stung by the description in the book, Xerox chairman David Kearns established a task force with the mandate of preventing the repetition of such a failure to capitalize on Xerox innovations.

The task force reviewed Xerox's history with corporate venture programs. Xerox had invested in venture-backed firms since the early 1970s. For instance, it had joined a variety of venture capitalists in investing in Rolm, Apple, and a number of other firms. While the investments were successful financially, they were made on an ad hoc basis. In the early 1980s, Xerox established two venture funds with an external focus. These did not prove particularly successful, largely owing to disputes within the firm about appropriate investments. The task force, in member (and future XTV president) Robert Adams's words, rapidly "concluded that we needed a system to prevent technology from leaking out of the company" (Armstrong 1993). The committee focused on two options: (1) to begin aggressively litigating those who try to leave with new technologies and (2) to invest in people trying to leave Xerox. Owing to variations in employee noncompetition law across states (and particularly the weak level of protection afforded by the California courts), it was unclear how effective a policy of aggressive litigation would be. Furthermore, such a policy might reduce Xerox's ability to recruit the best research personnel, who might not want to limit their future mobility.

On the basis of the task force's recommendation, Kearns decided to pursue a corporate venture capital program. He agreed to commit $30 million to invest in promising technologies developed at Xerox. As he commented at the time, "XTV is a hedge against repeating missteps of the past" (Armstrong 1993). He briefly considered the possibility of asking an established venture capital firm to run the program jointly with Xerox but decided that the involvement of another party would introduce a formality that might hurt the fledgling venture.

Modeling XTV after venture organizations had several dimensions. The most obvious was the structure of the organization. While this was a corporate division rather than an independent partnership (like most venture organizations), the XTV partners crafted an agreement with Xerox that resembled typical agreements between limited and general partners in venture funds.

The spinout process was clearly defined in the agreement in order to ensure that disputes did not arise later on and to minimize the disruption to the organization. The XTV officials insisted on a formal procedure to avoid the ambiguity that had plagued earlier corporate ventures. The agreement made clear that the XTV partners had the flexibility to respond rapidly to investment opportunities, something that independent venture capitalists typically possess. They essentially had full autonomy when it came to monitoring, exiting, or liquidating companies. The partners were allowed to spend up to $2 million at any one time without getting permission from the corporation. For larger expenditures, they were required to obtain permission from XTV's governing board, which consisted of Xerox's chief executive officer, chief financial officer, and chief patent counsel.

Similar to independent venture organizations (but unlike many corporate programs), the program also had a clear goal: to maximize return on investment. The XTV partners felt that the ambiguous goals of many of the 1970s corporate venture programs had been instrumental in their downfall. They hoped to achieve a return on investment that exceeded both the average returns of the venture capital industry and Xerox's corporate hurdle rate for evaluating new projects.

Not only was the level of compensation analogous to that of the 20 percent carried-interest that independent venture capitalists received and the degree of autonomy similar, but XTV operated under the same ten-year time frame employed in the typical partnership agreement. Under certain conditions, however, Xerox could dissolve the partnership after five years.

The analogy to independent venture organizations also extended to the companies in which XTV invested. These were structured as separate legal entities, with their own boards and officers. XTV sought to recruit employees from other start-ups who were familiar with managing new enterprises. The typical CEO was hired from the outside on the grounds that entrepreneurial skills, particularly in financial management, were unlikely to be found in a major corporation. XTV also made heavy use of temporary executives who were familiar with a variety of organizations.

The independence of management also extended to technological decision making in these companies. The traditional Xerox product—for instance, a copier—was designed so that it could be operated and serviced in almost any country in the world. This meant not only constraints on how the product was engineered but also the preparation of copious documentation in many languages. These XTV ventures, however, could produce products for "leading-edge" users, who emphasized technological performance over careful documentation.

Like independent venture capitalists, XTV intended to give up control of the companies in which they invested. Transferring shares to management and involving other venture capitalists in XTV companies would reduce Xerox's ownership of the firm. Their goal was that, over the long run, after several rounds of financing, Xerox would hold from 20 to 50 percent equity stake. XTV sought to have under a 50 percent equity stake at the time a spinout firm went public. In this way, it would not need to consolidate the firm in its balance sheet (i.e., it would not need to include the company's equity on its balance sheet, which would reduce Xerox's return on equity). The Xerox lawyers had originally wanted only employees to receive "phantom stock" (typically, bonuses based on the growth in the new units' performance). Instead, XTV insisted that the employees receive options to buy real shares in the venture-backed companies, in line with traditional Silicon Valley practices. The partners believed that this approach would have a much greater psychological effect as well as a cleaner capital structure to attract follow-on financings by outside investors.

Between 1988 and 1996, the organization invested in over one dozen companies. These covered a gamut of technologies, mostly involving electronic publishing, document processing, electronic imaging, workstation and computer peripherals, software, and office automation. These not only successfully commercialized technology lying fallow in the organization but also generated attractive financial returns.

One successful example of XTV's ability to catalyze the commercialization of technological discoveries was Documentum, which marketed an object-oriented document-management system. Xerox had undertaken a large number of projects in this area for over a decade prior to Documentum's founding, but had not shipped a product. After deciding that this was a promising area, XTV recruited Howard Shao and John Newton, both former engineering executives at the Ingress Corporation (a relational database manufacturer), to lead the technical effort.

Shao spent the first six months assessing the state of Xerox's knowledge in this area—including reviewing the several three-hundred-plus-page business plans prepared for earlier proposed (but never shipped) products—and assessing the market. He soon realized that, while Xerox understood the nature of the technical problems, the company had not grasped how to design a technologically appropriate solution. In particular, the Xerox business plans had proposed building document-management systems for mainframe computers rather than for networked personal computers (which were rapidly replacing mainframes at many organizations). With the help of the XTV officials, Shao and Newton led an effort rapidly to convert Xerox's accumulated knowledge in this area into a marketable product. Xerox's accumulated knowledge—as well as XTV's aggressive funding of the firm during the Gulf War period, when the willingness of both independent venture capitalists and the public markets to fund new technology-based firms abruptly declined—gave Documentum an impressive lead over its rivals.

Documentum went public in February 1996 with a market capitalization of $351 million.[4] XTV was able to exit a number of other companies successfully, whether through an initial public offering, a merger with an outside firm, or a repurchase by Xerox (at a price determined through arm's-length bargaining). A conservative calculation (assuming that Xerox sold its stakes in firms that went public at the time of the initial public offering rather than later, after prices had substantially appreciated, and valuing investments that Xerox has not yet exited or written off at cost, less a 25 percent discount for illiquidity) indicates that the $30 million fund generated capital gains of $219 million. Given the 80/20 percent split established in the XTV agreement, the proceeds to Xerox should have been at least $175 million, those to the three XTV partners at least $44 million.

The same assumptions suggest a net internal rate of return for Xerox (i.e., after fees and incentive compensation) of at least 56 percent. This compares favorably with independent venture capital funds begun in 1989, which had a mean net return of 13.7 percent (an upper-quartile fund begun in that year had a return of 20.4 percent) (Venture Economics 1997).

4. The next two paragraphs are based on public security filings and press accounts.

These calculations of Xerox's internal rate of return (IRR) do not include any ancillary benefits generated by this program for the corporation. For instance, some observers argued that high-expected-value projects that might otherwise not have been funded through traditional channels (owing to the high risk involved) were increasingly funded during this period, apparently out of the fear that they would otherwise be funded by XTV and prove successful.

Despite these attractive returns, Xerox decided to terminate XTV in 1996, well before the completion of its originally intended ten-year life.[5] The organization was replaced with a new one, Xerox New Enterprises (XNE), which did not seek to relinquish control of firms or to involve outside venture investors. The XNE business model called for a much greater integration of the new units with traditional business units. The autonomy offered to the XNE managers and their compensation schemes were much closer to that afforded in a traditional corporate division. As such, XNE appears to represent a departure from several of the key elements that the XTV staff believed were critical to that company's success, such as a considerable degree of autonomy and high-powered incentives.

The experience of Xerox Technology Ventures has several implications for corporate venture capital programs more generally. First, the case makes clear that, contrary to the suggestions in writings by both venture capitalists and financial economists, corporate venture capital programs need not fail. As noted above, Xerox's financial returns were exceedingly favorable when compared to returns from comparable independent venture funds. Second, XTV's successes—such as Document Sciences and Documentum—were concentrated in industries closely related to the corporate parent's core line of business (document processing). This suggests that the fund's strong strategic focus was important in its success. Finally, the Xerox Corporation was unable to commit to a structure akin to that of a traditional venture capital partnership. Despite efforts by XTV's founders to model the fund as closely as possible after a traditional venture partnership, the fund was still dissolved early. This experience underscores the challenges that these hybrid organizational forms face.

## 1.3 The Data Set

We now turn to a more systematic assessment of the experience of corporate venture programs. Before doing so, however, we discuss the VentureOne database used in this analysis. VentureOne, established in 1987, collects data on firms that have obtained venture capital financing. The database includes firms that have received early stage equity financing

5. This paragraph is based on information from the Xerox website and Turner (1997).

from venture capital organizations, corporate venture capital programs, and other organizations.

The companies are initially identified from a wide variety of sources, including trade publications, company web pages, and telephone contacts with venture investors. VentureOne then collects information about the businesses through interviews with venture capitalists and entrepreneurs. Among the data collected are the names of the investors, the amount and valuation of the venture financings, and the industry, history, and current status of the firm. Data on the firms are updated and validated through monthly contacts with investors and firms.[6] VentureOne then markets the database to venture funds and corporate business development groups (for a detailed discussion of the database, see Gompers and Lerner [2000]).

We supplemented the VentureOne data when necessary. Information on some firms in the VentureOne sample was missing, such as an assignment to one of the 103 VentureOne industry classes or information on the firm's start date. We examined a variety of reference sources to determine this information, including the *Corporate Technology Directory* (Corporate Technology Information Service 1996), the *Million Dollar Directory* (Dun's Marketing Services 1996), *Ward's Business Directory of U.S. Private and Public Companies* (Gale Research 1996), the *Directory of Leading Private Companies* (National Register Publishing Company 1996), and a considerable number of state and industry business directories in the collections of Harvard Business School's Baker Library and the Boston Public Library. We also employed several electronic databases: the Company Intelligence and Database America compilations available through LEXIS's COMPANY/USPRIV library and the American Business Disk CD-ROM directory.

The investors in the VentureOne database were diverse. They included individuals, institutions (e.g., pension funds), traditional independent venture funds (e.g., Kleiner, Perkins, Caufield, and Byers), and funds sponsored by corporations, financial institutions, and government bodies. In order to understand the effect of organizational structure, in many of the analyses presented below we concentrate on two types of funds: independent venture partnerships and corporate funds. As discussed above, we eliminated other hybrid venture funds, such as those affiliated with commercial and investment banks, because many of these closely resembled traditional venture organizations.

In order to identify independent and corporate venture capital organizations, we used an unpublished database of venture organizations assem-

6. Information about the financing of private firms is typically not revealed in public documents, and investors and entrepreneurs may consider this to be sensitive information. VentureOne seeks to overcome this reluctance by emphasizing that its database also helps firms obtain financing. In particular, firms can alert investors whether they intend to seek further private financing or intend to go public in upcoming months.

bled by the Venture Economics Investors Services Group. Venture Economics is a unit of the Securities Data Company that tracks the venture capital industry. The organization was known as Capital Publishing when it was established in 1961 to prepare a newsletter on federally chartered small business investment companies (SBICs). Since 1977, the company has maintained a database on venture partnerships, a database that includes over two thousand venture capital funds, SBICs, and related organizations. The Investors Services Group database is used in the preparation of directories, such as the Venture Economics annual *Investment Benchmark Performance.* The database is compiled from information provided by venture capitalists and institutional investors. We excluded from either classification a variety of private equity investors, including individuals, SBICs, funds sponsored by banks and other financial institutions, and funds associated with financial subsidiaries of nonfinancial corporations (such as General Electric Capital). In order to determine whether a company was a nonfinancial corporation, we consulted the firm directories noted above to determine the main lines of business in the year of the investment. By so doing, we sought to draw as sharp a contrast as possible between corporate and independent funds.

In some cases, it was difficult to ascertain whether an investor was a corporate venture organization. Some U.S. and several European companies invest in companies through traditional venture capital partnerships. For example, Eastman Kodak not only makes direct equity investments, but also invests through a partnership called Aperture Partners, in which it is the sole limited partner. While we were able to identify many of these cases, we may have missed some. In other cases, independent venture organizations also cater to corporate investors. A prominent example is Advent, a Boston-based organization that organizes comingled funds for financial investors and other funds for single corporate limited partners. From the VentureOne database, it is usually difficult to determine whether the private equity group is investing its traditional partnerships or one of its corporate funds.

Finally, for the corporate venture capital investments, we characterized the degree of fit between the corporation and the portfolio firm. To do this, we examined the corporate annual reports of the parent firm for the fiscal years 1983, 1989, and 1994. We classified investments as to whether there was a direct fit between one of the corporation's lines of business highlighted in the annual report closest to the year of the investment and the portfolio firm, whether there was an indirect relation, or whether there was no apparent relation at all. In the analyses below, we denoted investments as having a strategic fit only if there was a direct relation between a line of business of the corporate parent and the portfolio firm. The results are robust to expanding the definition to include indirectly related transactions as well: for example, when a corporate fund invests in a firm that is a potential supplier to or customer of the corporate parent. Not all investments were classified. In some cases, we were not able to determine the relation. In others, we could not obtain the proximate annual reports. In particular, it was difficult to obtain the 1983 and 1989 annual reports for many of the foreign firms.

We limited the analysis to investments in privately held firms between 1983 and 1994. While VentureOne has sought to "backfill" its database with information on earlier venture investments, its coverage of the 1970s and early 1980s is poor. Furthermore, we were concerned that the VentureOne methodology may have introduced selection biases. While the database does not include all venture investments between 1983 and 1994, we believe that it provides a reasonable view of the activity in the industry during this period.[7] We did not include investments made after 1994 because we wish to assess the outcomes of the investments: it may take several years until the fate of venture-backed firms is clear. We also eliminated a variety of investments that were outside the scope of this analysis, such as purchases of shares of publicly traded firms and other financings.

## 1.4 Empirical Analyses

We now analyze this sample empirically. After presenting an overview of the sample, we undertake analyses of the ultimate success of corporate and other venture investments as well as the duration of the venture investment programs themselves.

### 1.4.1 Summary Statistics

Table 1.1 provides an overview of the sample by year. After the deletions noted above, the sample consists of 32,364 investments. Investments by independent venture funds represent over half the total transactions in the sample. Corporate venture investments represent a much smaller share, about 6 percent. Because on average about four investors participate in each financing round, the number of rounds, 8,506, is significantly smaller. Below, we analyze patterns on both the investment and the round level.[8]

7. For an analysis of the comprehensiveness of the VentureOne database over time, see Gompers and Lerner (2000). We address concerns about selection biases by repeating the analyses below using only observations from 1988 to 1994, when VentureOne's coverage of the industry was much more comprehensive. The results are little changed.

8. The reader may note that the dollar amounts reported here are greater in some years than are the cumulative disbursements from venture capital funds reported elsewhere (e.g., Kortum and Lerner 1998). This reflects the fact that the VentureOne data represent total financings from all sources for privately held venture-backed firms rather than just funds from venture capital organizations.

**Table 1.1** **Distribution of the Sample, by Year**

| | Number of Investments | | | | |
|---|---|---|---|---|---|
| Year | Total | Corporate VC | Independent VC | Number of Rounds | Dollar Amount |
| 1983 | 1,841 | 53 | 1,013 | 436 | 2,219 |
| 1984 | 2,249 | 91 | 1,206 | 550 | 2,905 |
| 1985 | 2,593 | 139 | 1,382 | 625 | 2,910 |
| 1986 | 2,557 | 129 | 1,381 | 592 | 2,394 |
| 1987 | 2,675 | 152 | 1,397 | 642 | 3,065 |
| 1988 | 2,599 | 179 | 1,385 | 611 | 2,687 |
| 1989 | 2,866 | 202 | 1,490 | 720 | 3,069 |
| 1990 | 2,826 | 233 | 1,455 | 784 | 3,640 |
| 1991 | 2,890 | 249 | 1,472 | 757 | 3,207 |
| 1992 | 3,166 | 214 | 1,699 | 911 | 3,891 |
| 1993 | 3,118 | 198 | 1,586 | 931 | 4,532 |
| 1994 | 2,984 | 193 | 1,601 | 947 | 4,973 |
| Total | 32,364 | 2,032 | 17,067 | 8,506 | 39,492 |

*Note:* The table depicts the number of venture capital investments in the VentureOne sample by year between 1983 and 1994 as well as the number of financing rounds (a round may consist of several investments by different investors) and the aggregate amount of funding disbursed (in millions of 1994 dollars). Similar tabulations of the number of investments are presented for corporate and independent venture funds. VC = venture capital.

Table 1.2 provides a comparison of four categories of investment: the total sample, investments by corporate and independent venture capital organizations, and corporate investments where there was a strategic fit between the parent and the portfolio firm. In general, the corporate investments closely resemble those of the other funds:

*Status at Time of Investment.* Corporate funds tend to invest slightly less frequently in start-up and mature private firms. Instead, they are disproportionately represented among companies in the middle stages, such as "development" or "beta."[9]

*Location of Firm.* The sample disproportionately includes investments in firms based in California. This reflects VentureOne's greater coverage of this region, particularly in the early years (for a discussion, see Gompers and Lerner [2000]). While corporate venture investments as a whole are slightly more common in California than are other venture investments, corporate investments with a strong strategic fit are more frequent elsewhere.

9. For definitions of stages, regions, and industries, see the appendix.

**Table 1.2 Characteristics of Firms at the Time of Investment**

| | Entire Sample | Corporate VC Only | Corporate VC and Strategic Fit | Independent VC Only |
|---|---|---|---|---|
| Status at time of investment (%): | | | | |
| Start-up | 9.8 | 7.1 | 6.4 | 10.4 |
| Development | 30.5 | 33.6 | 35.9 | 31.2 |
| Beta | 4.1 | 5.5 | 6.4 | 4.1 |
| Shipping | 45.5 | 44.4 | 42.9 | 44.8 |
| Profitable | 7.6 | 6.9 | 5.6 | 7.3 |
| Restart | 2.4 | 2.5 | 2.8 | 2.3 |
| Location of firm (%): | | | | |
| All Western United States | 59.7 | 63.7 | 59.6 | 60.8 |
| California | 51.6 | 53.7 | 51.3 | 52.7 |
| All Eastern United States | 24.1 | 25.2 | 29.1 | 23.4 |
| Massachusetts | 12.8 | 14.0 | 16.5 | 12.6 |
| Industry of firm (%): | | | | |
| Medical | 25.5 | 25.9 | 24.2 | 24.2 |
| Computer hardware | 16.7 | 17.0 | 16.2 | 16.8 |
| Communications | 14.5 | 14.2 | 22.1 | 15.5 |
| Computer software on-line services | 15.1 | 15.1 | 14.0 | 16.2 |
| Other | 28.1 | 27.9 | 23.5 | 27.3 |
| Round of investment: | | | | |
| Mean | 2.4 | 2.8 | 2.9 | 2.4 |
| Median | 2 | 3 | 3 | 2 |
| Age of firm at time of investment: | | | | |
| Mean | 3.9 | 4.0 | 4.2 | 3.8 |
| Median | 3.0 | 3.3 | 3.4 | 2.8 |
| Amount invested in venture round: | | | | |
| Mean | 6.1 | 6.2 | 6.0 | 5.7 |
| Median | 4.3 | 4.5 | 4.7 | 4.2 |

*Note:* The sample consists of 32,364 investments in privately held venture-backed firms between 1983 and 1994. The table presents the stage of the firm's development at the time of the investment, the geographic location of the firm, the industry of the firm, the ordinal rank of the venture round, the age of the firm at the time of the investment (in years), and the amount of the investment in the financing round (in millions of 1994 dollars). Separate tabulations are presented for investments by corporate venture firms, corporate funds where there was a strategic fit between the parent and the portfolio firms, and independent venture funds. VC = venture capital.

*Industry of the Firm.* Venture capital investments tend to focus on a few high-technology industries. This is even more true for corporate venture investments with a strategic focus.

*Maturity of Firm and Investment Characteristics.* Corporate venture funds tend to invest in later and larger financing rounds and in slightly older firms than other venture funds.

### 1.4.2 Success of Investments

We now consider the success of the investments by the various types of venture organizations. The discussions of the importance of the independent venture organizations' partnership structure noted above suggest that these investors should have the greatest success. Meanwhile, potential complementarities with existing lines of business suggest that corporate investments may also perform well, at least those where there is a strong strategic fit.

The measurement of returns presents some challenging issues. Ideally, we would capture the direct and indirect returns to each class of venture investor. Unfortunately, because VentureOne does not compile the stake held by each investor, we cannot compute the direct financial returns for particular investors. Furthermore, it is difficult to identify the indirect benefits—for example, an insight that leads to a redirected research program in a corporate laboratory—that corporate venture investors receive, much less to quantify these benefits. As a result, we employ two less satisfactory but more tractable measures.

The first is the success of the firm receiving the funds. This is likely to be a reasonable measure for traditional venture groups. Venture capitalists generate the bulk of their profits from firms that go public. A Venture Economics (1988) study finds that a $1.00 investment in a firm that goes public provides an average cash return of $1.95 in excess of the initial investment with an average holding period of 4.2 years. The next best alternative as estimated by Venture Economics (1988), an investment in an acquired firm, yields a cash return of only $0.40 over a 3.7-year mean holding period. This measure is also likely to have some validity for corporate venture investors. If the venture fails, the key people and knowledge are likely to be scattered, and the benefits to the corporation are likely to be few. A more successful venture may or may not provide indirect benefits to the corporate parent but at least should have attractive financial returns.

We determine the status of the firms in spring 1998 from the VentureOne database. Table 1.3 presents the outcomes for four classes of investors as well as tests of the statistical significance of the differences between them. Firms backed by corporate venture groups are significantly more likely to have gone public than those financed by other organizations and are less likely to have been liquidated. These differences are particularly strong for investments in which there was a strategic tie between the corporate parent and the portfolio firm. These comparisons may be influenced, however, by differences between the firms backed by corporate and those backed by other venture investors.

To address this concern, we examine these patterns in a regression framework (see table 1.4). We estimate logit regressions, alternatively us-

**Table 1.3 Status of Firms in Spring 1998**

| | A. Status of Firms in Spring 1998 | | | |
|---|---|---|---|---|
| | Entire Sample | Corporate VC Only | Corporate VC and Strategic Fit | Independent VC Only |
| IPO completed | 31.1 | 35.1 | 39.3 | 30.6 |
| Registration statement filed | 0.7 | 0.2 | 0.3 | 0.7 |
| Acquired | 29.0 | 29.0 | 27.5 | 30.3 |
| Still privately held | 20.6 | 21.1 | 18.3 | 19.7 |
| Liquidated | 18.7 | 14.6 | 14.7 | 18.7 |

| | B. $p$-Value, Tests of Equality of Firm Status in Spring 1998 | | |
|---|---|---|---|
| | Probability of IPO | Probability of IPO, Registration, or Acquisition at > 2X Value | Probability Not Liquidated |
| Corporate VC vs. all others | .000 | .002 | .000 |
| Independent VC vs. all others | .043 | .557 | .796 |
| Corporate VC vs. independent VC | .000 | .005 | .000 |
| Corporate VC and strategic fit vs. independent VC | .000 | .000 | .006 |

*Note:* The sample consists of 32,364 investments in privately held venture-backed firms between 1983 and 1994. Panel A presents the status of the firms in spring 1998. Separate tabulations are presented for investments by corporate venture firms, corporate funds where there was a strategic fit between the parent and the portfolio firms, and independent venture funds. Panel B presents the $p$-values from Pearson $\chi^2$ tests of the equality of three outcomes (completion of an IPO; IPO or filing of a registration statement or acquisition at twice [in inflation-adjusted dollars] the post–money valuation at the time of the investment; and not being liquidated) in different subsamples. VC = venture capital. IPO = initial public offering.

ing each investment and each financing round as observations. We seek to explain the probability that the investment had gone public by spring 1998 or the probability that the firm had gone public, filed a registration with the U.S. Securities and Exchange Commission (a preliminary step before going public), or been acquired for a valuation of at least twice the post–money valuation of the financing.[10] As independent variables, we use the age of the firm at the time of the investment and the ordinal rank of the investment round. We also employ dummy variables denoting investments by corporate and independent venture capital funds, corporate venture

10. The results are also robust to the use of a third dependent variable, the probability that the firm has not been liquidated by spring 1998.

The *post–money valuation* is defined as the product of the price paid per share in the financing round and the shares outstanding after the financing round. In calculating the valuations, VentureOne converts all preferred shares into common stock at the conversion ratios specified in the agreements. Warrants and options outstanding are included in the total, as long as their exercise price is below the price per share being paid in the financing round.

**Table 1.4 Logit Regression Analyses of Firms' Status in Spring 1998**

| | Observations Are Investments | | | | | |
|---|---|---|---|---|---|---|
| | Did Firm Go Public? | | Did Firm Go Public, Register, or Have Favorable Acquisition? | | Observations Are Rounds: Did Firm Go Public? | |
| Age of firm at time of financing | −0.02 | −0.02 | −0.02 | −0.02 | −0.02 | −0.02 |
| | (5.52) | (0.50) | (6.17) | (6.13) | (2.47) | (2.50) |
| Round number | 0.13 | 0.13 | 0.13 | 0.13 | 0.17 | 0.16 |
| | (11.39) | (11.18) | (11.48) | (11.29) | (7.13) | (6.95) |
| Corporate venture investment? | 0.15 | −0.19 | 0.12 | −0.23 | 0.20 | 0.03 |
| | (2.54) | (1.31) | (2.15) | (1.64) | (2.87) | (0.31) |
| Independent venture investment? | −0.003 | −0.002 | 0.07 | 0.07 | 0.14 | 0.13 |
| | (0.09) | (0.07) | (2.54) | (2.56) | (1.92) | (1.82) |
| Corporate investment and strategic fit? | | 0.52 | | 0.57 | | 0.40 |
| | | (3.15) | | (3.55) | | (3.32) |
| Firm based in California? | 0.30 | 0.29 | 0.23 | 0.22 | 0.25 | 0.26 |
| | (9.29) | (8.96) | (7.44) | (6.98) | (3.96) | (4.04) |
| Firm based in Massachusetts? | 0.36 | 0.36 | 0.24 | 0.23 | 0.25 | 0.25 |
| | (7.83) | (7.75) | (5.26) | (5.04) | (2.77) | (2.71) |
| Firm is in development stage? | 0.44 | 0.42 | 0.38 | 0.35 | 0.37 | 0.36 |
| | (7.73) | (7.27) | (6.99) | (6.41) | (3.70) | (3.68) |

| | | | | | | |
|---|---|---|---|---|---|---|
| Firm is in beta stage? | 0.25 | 0.22 | 0.14 | 0.11 | 0.13 | 0.13 |
| | (2.83) | (2.50) | (1.60) | (1.24) | (0.70) | (0.69) |
| Firm is in shipping stage? | 0.38 | 0.36 | 0.30 | 0.28 | 0.33 | 0.34 |
| | (6.28) | (5.95) | (5.20) | (4.82) | (3.12) | (3.23) |
| Firm is in profitable stage? | 1.32 | 1.30 | 1.10 | 1.08 | 1.44 | 1.46 |
| | (17.08) | (16.61) | (14.77) | (14.27) | (10.52) | (10.65) |
| Firm is in restart stage? | −0.56 | −0.56 | −0.43 | −0.45 | −0.45 | −0.45 |
| | (4.20) | (4.19) | (3.64) | (3.71) | (1.70) | (1.68) |
| Log-likelihood | −14,743.6 | −14,252.0 | −15,477.4 | −14,973.7 | −3,694.4 | −3,688.9 |
| $\chi^2$-statistic | 2,409.9 | 2,362.4 | 2,065.5 | 2,025.7 | 609.0 | 620.1 |
| *p*-value | 0.000 | 0.000 | 0.000 | 0.000 | 0.000 | 0.000 |
| Number of observations | 24,515 | 23,740 | 24,515 | 23,740 | 6,445 | 6,445 |

*Note:* The sample in the first four regressions consists of 32,364 investments in privately held venture-backed firms between 1983 and 1994, in the fifth and sixth regressions 8,506 financing rounds of privately held, venture-backed firms between 1983 and 1994. The dependent variable in the first, second, fifth, and sixth regressions is a dummy variable that takes on the value of one if the firm had gone public by spring 1998. In the third and fourth regressions, the dummy takes the value of one if the firm had gone public, filed a registration statement, or been acquired at twice (in inflation-adjusted dollars) the post–money valuation at the time of the investment by spring 1998. Independent variables include the age of the firm at the time of the investment, the ordinal rank of the investment round, and dummy variables denoting investments by corporate and independent venture capital funds, corporate venture investments where there was a strategic fit with the portfolio firm, firms based in California and Massachusetts, the status of the firm at the time of the investment, the year of the investment (not reported), the industry of the firm (not reported), and a constant (not reported). All dummy variables take on the value of one if the answer to the posed question is in the affirmative. Absolute *t*-statistics are reported in parentheses.

investments where there was a strategic fit with the portfolio firm, firms based in California and Massachusetts, the status of the firm at the time of the investment, the year of the investment, the industry of the firm, and a constant.

The results are consistent with the univariate comparisons reported above. Corporate venture investments are significantly more successful than other investments. (In most of the regressions, independent venture investments are also more successful, although the effect is smaller in magnitude and statistical significance.) When the dummy variable denoting corporate venture investments with a strategic fit is added to the regressions, the corporate venture dummy variable becomes insignificant (and frequently negative). Corporate venture investments in general do not perform better, only those with a strategic fit. These results seem consistent with the complementarities hypothesis outlined above.

Our second proxy for the direct and indirect returns for corporate and other investors is the valuation assigned to the firm at the time of the investment. All else being equal, the higher the valuation (i.e., the higher the price paid per share), the lower the direct financial returns to the investor (subject to the caveats outlined in the discussion below). For each investment round for which data were available (about half the entire sample), we computed the pre–money valuation, the product of the price paid per share in the financing round, and the shares outstanding before the financing round.[11]

Table 1.5 presents the pre–money valuations for the four classes of investors tabulated above as well as tests of the statistical significance of these differences. Corporate venture funds do appear to pay significantly more, with a mean pre–money valuation of $28.5 million, as compared to an average of $18.1 million for the independent venture firms. Corporate investments in which there is a strategic fit are also priced at a premium, but the average price ($26.9 million) is lower than that of the other corporate investments.

Once again, we seek to corroborate these patterns through a regression analysis (see table 1.6). Following the approach of Gompers and Lerner (2000), we estimate a hedonic regression, seeking to explain the logarithm of the pre–money valuations (for a detailed discussion of this methodology, see that paper). Once again, we use each investment and each financing round as observations. As independent variables, we use the logarithm of the age of the firm at the time of the investment and the logarithm of the ordinal rank of the investment round. We also employ dummy variables denoting investments by corporate and independent venture capital funds,

11. As discussed at length in Lerner (1994), the pre–money valuation is a more appropriate dependent variable than the post–money valuation because it is independent of the amount invested in the firm during the current financing round. As Gompers (1995) discusses, the amount invested may vary with many considerations, including the fund-raising environment.

**Table 1.5** **Pre–Money Valuation at the Time of Financing**

| | A. Pre–Money Valuation at Time of Financing | | | |
|---|---|---|---|---|
| | Entire Sample | Corporate VC Only | Corporate VC and Strategic Fit | Independent VC Only |
| Mean | 20.1 | 28.5 | 26.9 | 18.1 |
| Median | 12.9 | 17.4 | 15.9 | 11.7 |

| | B. *p*-Value, Tests of Equality of Pre–Money Valuations | |
|---|---|---|
| | Mean | Median |
| Corporate VC vs. all others | .000 | .000 |
| Independent VC vs. all others | .000 | .000 |
| Corporate VC vs. independent VC | .000 | .000 |
| Corporate VC and strategic fit vs. independent VC | .000 | .000 |

*Note:* The sample consists of 32,364 investments in privately held venture-backed firms between 1983 and 1994. Panel A presents the mean and median pre–money valuation of the firms at the time of the financing. The pre–money valuation is defined as the product of the price paid per share in the financing round and the shares outstanding prior to the financing round. Separate tabulations are presented for investments by corporate venture firms, corporate funds where there was a strategic fit between the parent and portfolio firms, and independent venture funds. Panel B presents the *p*-values from *t*-tests and Wilcoxon rank-sum tests of the equality of the mean and median valuations in different subsamples. VC = venture capital.

corporate venture investments where there was a strategic fit with the portfolio firm, firms based in California and Massachusetts, the status of the firm at the time of the investment, the year of the investment, the industry of the firm, and a constant.

We find results similar to those in the univariate comparisons. Corporate venture investments are associated with between 18 and 30 percent higher valuations, while those by independent funds are associated with between 7 and 18 percent lower valuations. The dummy variable denoting corporate venture investments with a strategic fit is inconsistent in sign and never significant.

These results suggest two possible interpretations. First, traditional venture investors and entrepreneurs could be exploiting the relative inexperience of the corporate venture investors, persuading them to invest in overvalued transactions (see, e.g., AbuZayyad et al. 1997). Second, corporate investors are likely to enjoy some indirect benefits from their involvement with portfolio firms that independent venture firms do not enjoy. Standard bargaining models (e.g., Nash 1950) suggest that the additional surplus enjoyed by the corporation will lead to corporate venture capitalists investing at higher prices than others. In this way, some of the additional value created will be allocated to the smaller firm and its existing investors.

Disentangling these interpretations is difficult. Nonetheless, we are struck by the lack of a relation between the price premium paid and the

**Table 1.6** **Ordinary Least Squares Regression Analyses of the Pre–Money Valuation at the Time of the Financing**

| | Observations Are Investments | | Observations Are Rounds | |
|---|---|---|---|---|
| Logarithm of age of firm | 0.14 | 0.14 | 0.15 | 0.15 |
| | (11.32) | (11.26) | (6.01) | (6.00) |
| Logarithm of round number | 0.68 | 0.69 | 0.68 | 0.68 |
| | (49.43) | (48.94) | (24.09) | (24.04) |
| Corporate venture investment? | 0.18 | 0.26 | 0.30 | 0.27 |
| | (7.39) | (4.38) | (9.43) | (6.76) |
| Independent venture investment? | −0.07 | −0.07 | −0.18 | −0.18 |
| | (5.76) | (5.75) | (4.85) | (4.91) |
| Corporate investment and strategic fit? | | −0.09 | | 0.07 |
| | | (1.37) | | (1.22) |
| Firm based in California? | 0.20 | 0.20 | 0.14 | 0.14 |
| | (14.78) | (14.54) | (4.76) | (4.80) |
| Firm based in Massachusetts? | 0.06 | 0.06 | 0.03 | 0.03 |
| | (2.79) | (2.82) | (0.61) | (0.59) |
| Firm is in development stage? | 0.40 | 0.38 | 0.37 | 0.37 |
| | (14.08) | (13.30) | (7.01) | (6.99) |
| Firm is in beta stage? | 0.51 | 0.50 | 0.48 | 0.48 |
| | (13.24) | (12.81) | (6.11) | (6.10) |

| | | | | |
|---|---|---|---|---|
| Firm is in shipping stage? | 0.58 | 0.57 | 0.60 | 0.60 |
| | (18.86) | (18.26) | (10.28) | (10.30) |
| Firm is in profitable stage? | 1.10 | 1.09 | 1.15 | 1.15 |
| | (29.06) | (28.61) | (15.51) | (15.54) |
| Firm is in restart stage? | −0.85 | −0.84 | −0.72 | −0.72 |
| | (17.22) | (17.00) | (7.04) | (7.04) |
| Adjusted $R^2$ | 0.39 | 0.39 | 0.43 | 0.43 |
| F-statistic | 397.1 | 371.5 | 102.0 | 98.3 |
| *p*-value | 0.000 | 0.000 | 0.000 | 0.000 |
| Number of observations | 15,895 | 15,406 | 3,544 | 3,544 |

*Note:* The sample in the first two regressions consists of 32,364 investments in privately held, venture-backed firms between 1983 and 1994, in third and fourth regressions 8,506 financing rounds of privately held, venture-backed firms between 1983 and 1994. The dependent variable is the logarithm of the pre–money valuation of the firms at the time of the financing. The pre–money valuation is defined as the product of the price paid per share in the financing round and the shares outstanding prior to the financing round. Independent variables include the logarithm of the age of the firm at the time of the investment, the logarithm of the ordinal rank of the investment round, and dummy variables denoting investments by corporate and independent venture capital funds, corporate venture investments where there was a strategic fit with the portfolio firm, firms based in California and Massachusetts, the status of the firm at the time of the investment, the year of the investment (not reported), the industry of the firm (not reported), and a constant (not reported). All dummy variables take on the value of one if the answer to the posed question is in the affirmative. Absolute $t$-statistics are reported in parentheses. VC = venture capital.

degree of strategic fit. We suggest that this may reflect the fact that corporations are also more savvy investors in companies close to their existing lines of business. While the indirect benefits to the parent may be greater in these instances, resulting in a willingness to pay more, its understanding of the market is also likely to be better. As a result, the corporation may be less likely to invest in overpriced transactions in these cases. In areas outside the corporation's experience, overpaying for investments may be a more common phenomenon.

### 1.4.3 Duration of Programs

Finally, we consider the duration of the venture organizations. Table 1.7 presents several measures of the stability of these organizations. First, we examine the total number of investments in the sample. Similarly, we examine the time span (in years) between the first and the last investment in the sample by each venture organization. (A venture organization that made a single investment would be coded as having a time span of 0.)

Both these measures, however, are somewhat problematic. Many corporate venture programs have begun in recent years. As a result, they may have made only a few investments to date. This does not imply, however, that they will not continue to exist for a long time. To control for this "vintage effect," we create a third measure: the time between the first and the last investments by the venture organization in the sample expressed as a percentage of the time from the first investment by the venture organization to December 1994. Using this approach, both a long-standing venture group and a relatively recent program that remains active through the end of the sample period would be coded as 1.0.

Unlike the earlier analyses, we confine the analysis (and that in table 1.8 below) to independent and corporate venture funds. Some of the other investors are reported in an inconsistent manner, which would make this type of analysis potentially misleading. For instance, when only a small number of individuals invest, the more prominent ones are identified by name. When a large number invest, all are lumped together as "individuals."

Stark differences appear between the corporate and the independent funds. The corporations make a mean of 4.4 investments over 2.5 years, while the independent funds make 43.5 investments over 7.1 years. Even using the ratio of the active time span to the possible time span, the differences are dramatic: the average is 34.8 percent for the corporate funds, as opposed to 71.7 percent for the independent funds. The differences are less extreme, but still significant, for the corporate programs where there was a strategic fit in at least half the investments.

We then examine these patterns in a regression analysis (see table 1.8). The first two regressions employ all corporate and independent venture organizations in the sample as observations, the second set only those

**Table 1.7** **Duration of Investment Programs**

A. Duration of Investment Programs

| | Corporate and Independent VC Funds | Corporate VC Only | Corporate VC and Strategic Fit | Independent VC Only |
|---|---|---|---|---|
| Number of investments: | | | | |
| Mean | 22.3 | 4.4 | 9.8 | 43.5 |
| Median | 4 | 2 | 4 | 21 |
| Timespan: | | | | |
| Mean | 4.6 | 2.5 | 4.4 | 7.1 |
| Median | 3.8 | 1.0 | 4.2 | 8.0 |
| Ratio of active to possible time span (%): | | | | |
| Mean | 51.7 | 34.8 | 55.6 | 71.7 |
| Median | 58.7 | 21.8 | 71.5 | 90.4 |

B. *p*-Value, Tests of Equality of Investment Program Duration

| | Number of Investments | | Time Span | | Ratio of Active to Possible Time Span | |
|---|---|---|---|---|---|---|
| | Mean | Median | Mean | Median | Mean | Median |
| Corporate VC vs. independent VC | .000 | .000 | .000 | .000 | .000 | .000 |
| Corporate VC and strategic fit vs. independent VC | .000 | .000 | .000 | .000 | .001 | .000 |

*Note:* The sample consists of 19,099 investments by 855 corporate and independent venture funds in privately held firms between 1983 and 1994. Panel A presents the mean and median number of investments during the sample period by each venture organization, the time span between the first and the last investments by the venture organization in the sample (in years), and the time span between the first and the last investments by the venture organization in the sample expressed as a percentage of the time span from the first investment by the venture organization to December 1994. Separate tabulations are presented for investments by corporate venture firms, corporate venture funds where there was a strategic fit with the portfolio firm in at least half the investments, and independent venture funds. Panel B presents the *p*-values from *t*-tests and Wilcoxon rank-sum tests of the equality of the mean and median measures of duration in different subsamples. VC = venture capital.

**Table 1.8** **Double-Censored Regression Analyses of Duration of Investment Program**

| | All Corporate and Independent VC Funds | | Corporate and Independent Funds with ≥ 4 Investments | |
|---|---|---|---|---|
| Date of first investment | −0.05 | −0.05 | −0.0003 | 0.001 |
| | (10.15) | (9.69) | (0.07) | (0.28) |
| Corporate venture fund? | −0.32 | −0.39 | −0.11 | −0.16 |
| | (8.98) | (10.77) | (4.55) | (6.03) |
| Corporate investment and strategic fit? | | 0.35 | | 0.15 |
| | | (6.42) | | (3.95) |
| Constant | 103.85 | 96.77 | 1.47 | −1.45 |
| | (10.22) | (9.76) | (0.18) | (0.18) |
| Log-likelihood | −586.2 | −566.1 | −52.2 | −59.9 |
| $\chi^2$-statistic | 290.2 | 330.5 | 23.0 | 38.4 |
| *p*-value | 0.000 | 0.000 | 0.000 | 0.000 |
| Number of observations | 855 | 855 | 450 | 450 |

*Note:* The sample consists of 855 corporate and independent venture funds that invested in privately held firms between 1983 and 1994. The dependent variable is the time between the first and the last investments by the venture organization in the sample expressed as a percentage of the time from the first investment by the venture organization to December 1994. The first two regressions employ all observations, the second set only those organizations with four or more investments in the sample. Independent variables include the date of the venture organization's first investment (with an investment in May 1992 expressed as 1992.4 etc.), dummy variables denoting observations of corporate venture capital funds and of corporate venture funds where there was a strategic fit with the portfolio firm in at least half the investments, and a constant. All dummy variables take on the value of one if the answer to the posed question is in the affirmative. Absolute *t*-statistics are reported in parentheses. VC = venture capital.

organizations with four or more investments in the sample.[12] As a dependent variable, we use the ratio of the time span that the fund was active to the time span from its first investment to December 1994. Independent variables include the date of the venture organization's first investment, dummy variables denoting observations of corporate venture capital funds and of corporate venture funds where there was a strategic fit with the portfolio firms in at least half the investments, and a constant. Reflecting the fact that the dependent variable must fall between zero and one, we employ a double-censored regression specification.

Once again, the corporate venture programs have a significantly shorter duration. The dummy variable for corporate venture programs in which at least half the investments were strategic, however, has a positive coefficient of almost equal magnitude. While corporate programs without a stra-

12. In this way, we seek to examine whether groups that dissolve after only one or two investments drive the results or whether this is a more general pattern. The results are also robust to the use of other cut-off points.

tegic focus are very unstable, those with such a focus appear to have a longevity equivalent to more traditional independent funds, at least using this measure.

We consider two explanations for the shorter time span of the corporate investments. One possibility is that this is a response to technological change. An extensive literature on the economics of innovation has highlighted that new entrants often exploit technological breakthroughs in more innovative and aggressive ways than do the established incumbents and that these changes are often associated with dramatic shifts in market leadership.[13] In many cases, product leaders have rapidly lost their commanding position after many years of dominance. Academics have attributed these patterns to a rational reluctance on the part of existing industry leaders to jeopardize their current revenues and profits as well as to the myopic reluctance of many successful organizations to recognize that their leadership is waning. (In many instances, the continuing financial success of mature product lines masks the organizations' failure to introduce new products.)[14] Corporate venture capital programs may be a response to these short-run periods of technological discontinuity.[15] Once this transition period has passed, the corporation may dissolve the effort.

Alternatively, the instability may reflect the manner in which the corporate programs are designed. One important argument in favor of the decade-long partnership structure typically employed by independent venture funds is that it allows venture capitalists to make long-run investments without the fear of demands to liquidate their portfolios. (For a discussion of how such fears can affect the behavior of hedge fund managers, who typically do not have these protections, see Shleifer and Vishny [1997].) Corporate venture funds are typically structured as corporate divisions or affiliates without the protections afforded by a legal partnership agreement. Furthermore, field research suggests that corporate venture groups are often plagued by defections of their most successful investors, who become frustrated at their low level of compensation. These defections may also affect the stability of the groups. This view suggests that all corporate venture programs should be less stable.

It is a challenge to reconcile either hypothesis with the evidence. If programs were generally designed to address short-run technological discontinuities, it should be the strategic programs that were of the shortest dura-

13. Two academic studies documenting these patterns (there are also many other more anecdotal accounts) are Henderson (1993) and Lerner (1997).

14. For an overview, see Reinganum (1989).

15. For instance, the pharmaceutical industry was ill prepared for the biotechnology revolution in the early 1980s. Henderson and Cockburn (1996) show that the more successful firms responded by aggressively establishing outside relationships to access new ideas in response to this technological discontinuity. One avenue through which the firms built external relationships was corporate venture programs.

tion. This is clearly not the case. The structural view suggests that most corporate venture programs should be terminated rapidly, which is hard to reconcile with the success of programs with strong strategic objectives. One possibility is that the organizations without a clear strategic focus also tend to be the ones with a low degree of autonomy and low levels of incentive compensation. Thus, the limited duration of the funds without a clear strategic focus may be a proxy for the organizational structure employed by independent venture funds.

## 1.5 Conclusions

This paper has compared investments by corporate venture organizations with those of independent and other venture groups. Corporate venture investments in entrepreneurial firms appear to be at least as successful (using such measures as the probability of the portfolio firm going public) as those backed by independent venture organizations, particularly when there is a strategic overlap between the corporate parent and the portfolio firm. While corporate venture capitalists tend to invest at a premium to other firms, this premium appears to be no higher in investments with a strong strategic fit. Finally, corporate programs without a strong strategic focus appear to be much less stable, frequently ceasing operations after only a few investments, but strategically focused programs appear to be as stable as independent venture organizations. The evidence is consistent with the existence of complementarities that allow corporations to select and add value to portfolio firms effectively, but it is somewhat at odds with the suggestion that the structure of corporate funds introduces distortions.

The paper suggests that the presence of a strong strategic focus is critical to the success of corporate venture funds. This subset of corporate funds appears to have been quite successful, despite having very different structures from traditional funds. This finding appears to challenge the emphasis in the finance literature on the importance of the partnership structure employed by independent private equity funds. But, as alluded to in section 1.4 above, it may well be that corporate programs without a clear strategic focus are also the ones with a low degree of autonomy and low levels of compensation. To distinguish between these hypotheses comprehensively, we would need to have information on the compensation schemes and organizational structures employed by these groups. This paper has only skimmed the surface of this issue, and this is a rich area for further exploration, which we hope to undertake in future research.

The analysis raises several puzzles that cannot be answered with the existing data. We end by highlighting two of these. First, why do corporations set up programs that appear likely to be unsuccessful? In the sample, for instance, we see repeated examples of funds being established that do not have a clear relationship to the corporate parent's lines of business. Certainly, in many cases, carefully thought through proposals appear to have been modified during the review process in ways that are likely substantially to reduce their likelihood of success. Understanding these processes and placing them in the context of the broader literature on the problems that can beset corporate decision making are interesting areas for future research.

Second, is there an optimal mixture between internally funded corporate research and outside ideas accessed through initiatives such as corporate venture programs? Some high-technology corporations, such as AT&T and IBM, have historically funded internal research laboratories at high levels. Other high-technology giants, such as Cisco Systems, have relied on acquisitions and strategic investments to identify and access product and process innovations. The "make-or-buy" decisions that corporate R&D managers face is an important but little-researched issue.

## Appendix

### *Definition of Firm Categorizations*

The definitions provided below have been adapted from VentureOne (1998).

#### Investment Stages

*Start-up:* Company with a skeletal business plan, product, or service development in preliminary stages.

*Development:* Product or service development is under way, but the company is not generating revenues from sales.

*Beta:* For companies specializing in information technology, the beta phase is when the product is being tested by a limited number of customers but not available for broad sales. For life sciences companies, beta is synonymous with a drug in human clinical trials or a device being tested.

*Shipping:* The product or service is being sold to customers, and the company is deriving revenues from those sales, but expenses still exceed revenues.

*Profitable:* The company is selling products or services, and the sales revenue yields a positive net income.

*Restart:* A recapitalization at a reduced valuation, accompanied by a substantial shift in the product or marketing focus.

**Industry Groups**

*Computer hardware:* Firms whose primary lines of business are personal computing, minicomputers or workstations, mainframe computers, CAD/CAM/CAE systems, data storage, computer peripherals, memory systems, office automation, source data collection, multimedia devices, and computer networking devices.

*Computer software:* Firms whose primary lines of business are compilers, assemblers, and systems, application, CAD/CAM/CAE/CASE, recreational and home, artificial intelligence, educational, multimedia software, and on-line services.

*Communications:* Firms whose primary lines of business include modems, computer networking, fiber optics, microwave and satellite communications, telephone equipment, pocket paging, cellular phones, radar and defense systems, television equipment, teleconferencing, and television and radio broadcasting.

*Medical:* Firms whose primary lines of business include biotechnology, pharmaceuticals, diagnostic imaging, patient monitoring, medical devices, medical lab instruments, hospital equipment, medical supplies, retail medicine, hospital management, medical data processing, and medical lab services.

**Regions**

*Eastern United States:* Firms whose headquarters are located in Connecticut, Delaware, the District of Columbia, Maine, Maryland, Massachusetts, New Hampshire, New Jersey, New York, Pennsylvania, Rhode Island, Vermont, and West Virginia.

*Western United States:* Firms whose headquarters are located in Alaska, Arizona, California, Colorado, Hawaii, Idaho, Montana, Nevada, New Mexico, Oregon, Utah, Washington, and Wyoming.

## References

AbuZayyad, Tarek, Thomas J. Konick, Josh Lerner, and Paul C. Yang. 1996. GO Corporation. Case 9-297-021, Teaching Note 5-298-153. Harvard Business School.

Armstrong, Larry. 1993. Nurturing an employee's brainchild. *Business Week,* 23 October, 196.

Athey, Susan, and Scott Stern. 1997. An empirical framework for testing theories about complementarity in organizational design. Working paper. Massachusetts Institute of Technology, Sloan School of Management.

Block, Zenas, and Oscar A. Ornati. 1987. Compensating corporate venture managers. *Journal of Business Venturing* 2:41–52.

Brav, Alon, and Paul A. Gompers. 1997. Myth or reality? The long-run underperformance of initial public offerings: Evidence from venture capital and nonventure capital–backed companies. *Journal of Finance* 52:1791–1821.

Chevalier, Judith A., and Glenn D. Ellison. 1997. Risk taking by mutual funds as a response to incentives. *Journal of Political Economy* 105:1167–1200.

Cordell, Lawrence R., Gregor D. MacDonald, and Mark E. Wohar. 1993. Corporate ownership and the thrift crisis. *Journal of Law and Economics* 36:719–756.

Corporate Technology Information Services. Various years. *Corporate technology directory.* Woburn, Mass.

Dun's Marketing Services. Various years. *Million dollar directory.* Parsippany, N.J.

Fast, Norman D. 1978. *The rise and fall of corporate new venture divisions.* Ann Arbor, Mich.: UMI Research.

Gale Research. Various years. *Ward's business directory of U.S. private and public companies.* Detroit.

Gee, Robert E. 1994. Finding and commercializing new businesses. *Research/Technology Management* 37 (January/February): 49–56.

Gompers, Paul A. 1995. Optimal investment, monitoring, and the staging of venture capital. *Journal of Finance* 50:1461–89.

Gompers, Paul A., and Josh Lerner. 1996. The use of covenants: An analysis of venture partnership agreements. *Journal of Law and Economics* 39:463–98.

———. 1998. Venture capital distributions: Short- and long-run reactions. *Journal of Finance* 53 (December): 2161–83.

———. 1999. An analysis of compensation in the U.S. venture capital partnership. *Journal of Financial Economics* 51 (January): 3–44.

———. 2000. Money chasing deals? The impact of fund inflows on private equity valuations. *Journal of Financial Economics* 55, no. 2:281–325.

Hardymon, G. Felda, Mark J. DeNino, and Malcolm S. Salter. 1983. When corporate venture capital doesn't work. *Harvard Business Review* 61 (May–June): 114–20.

Henderson, Rebecca. 1993. Underinvestment and incompetence as responses to radical innovation: Evidence from the photolithographic alignment equipment industry. *Rand Journal of Economics* 24:248–70.

Henderson, Rebecca, and Iain Cockburn. 1996. Scale, scope, and spillovers: The determinants of research productivity in drug discovery. *Rand Journal of Economics* 27:32–59.

Hunt, Brian, and Josh Lerner. 1995. Xerox Technology Ventures: March 1995. Case 9-295-127, Teaching Note 9-298-152. Harvard Business School.

Jensen, Michael C. 1993. Presidential address: The modern industrial revolution, exit, and the failure of internal control systems. *Journal of Finance* 48:831–80.

Kortum, Samuel, and Josh Lerner. 1998. Does venture capital spur innovation? NBER Working Paper no. 6846. Cambridge, Mass.: National Bureau of Economic Research.

Kroszner, Randall S., and Raghuram G. Rajan. 1994. Is the Glass-Steagall Act justified? A study of the U.S. experience with universal banking before 1933. *American Economic Review* 84:810–32.

Lawler, E., and J. Drexel. 1980. *The corporate entrepreneur.* Los Angeles: Center for Effective Organizations/University of Southern California, Graduate School of Business Administration.

Lerner, Josh. 1994. The importance of patent scope: An empirical analysis. *Rand Journal of Economics* 25:319–33.

———. 1997. An empirical examination of a technology race. *Rand Journal of Economics* 28:228–47.

Muscarella, Chris J., and Michael R. Vetsuypens. 1990. Efficiency and organizations structure: A study of reverse LBOs. *Journal of Finance* 45:1389–1414.
Nash, John F. 1950. The bargaining problem. *Econometrica* 18:155–62.
National Register Publishing Co. Various years. *Directory of leading private companies, including corporate affiliations.* Wilmette, Ill.
Reinganum, Jennifer R. 1989. The timing of innovation: Research, development, and diffusion. In *The handbook of industrial organization,* ed. R. Schmalensee and R. D. Willig. New York: North-Holland.
Rind, Kenneth W. 1981. The role of venture capital in corporate development. *Strategic Management Journal* 2:169–80.
Shleifer, Andrei, and Robert W. Vishny. 1997a. The limits of arbitrage. *Journal of Finance* 52:35–55.
———. 1997b. A survey of corporate governance. *Journal of Finance* 52:737–83.
Siegel, Robin, Eric Siegel, and Ian C. MacMillan. 1988. Corporate venture capitalists: Autonomy, obstacles, and performance. *Journal of Business Venturing* 3: 233–47.
Smith, Douglas K., and Robert C. Alexander. 1988. *Fumbling the future: How Xerox invented, then ignored, the first personal computer.* New York: Morrow.
Sykes, Hollister B. 1990. Corporate venture capital: Strategies for success. *Journal of Business Venturing* 5:37–47.
Turner, Nick. 1997. Xerox inventions now raised instead of adopted by others. *Investors' Business Daily,* 28 January, A6.
*Venture Capital Journal.* Various issues. Newark, N.J.: Venture Economics.
Venture Economics. 1986. Corporate venture capital study. Newark, N.J. Typescript.
———. 1988. *Exiting venture capital investments.* Newark, N.J.
———. 1997. *Investment benchmark reports—venture capital.* Newark, N.J.
———. Annual. *Investment benchmark performance.* Newark, N.J.
VentureOne. 1998. *VentureOne 1997 annual report.* San Francisco.

## Comment Michael S. Weisbach

The paper by Paul Gompers and Josh Lerner is one of the first to study corporate venture programs. It starts with speculation from the literature that corporate venture capital funds will underperform other venture capital programs. This underperformance would presumably occur because of agency problems inside corporations that discourage high-powered incentives and risk taking inside corporate venture capital units as well as because of a lack of a well-defined mission for the venture capital division (making money or providing technology to the rest of the firm?). To counter this point, Gompers and Lerner point out that corporate venture capital programs have some advantages from complementarities with the firm's existing assets that potentially offset some of these disadvantages.

The goal of the paper is to evaluate empirically whether the literature's

Michael S. Weisbach is the I.B.E. Distinguished Professor of Finance at the University of Illinois at Urbana-Champaign.

speculation about the relative performance of corporate venture capital funds is correct. The two offsetting factors that make this a potentially interesting empirical exercise are the agency costs discussed by the literature and the complementarities between the investments and the firm's assets. One issue that I have with this approach is that Gompers and Lerner do not spell out exactly what one would expect to observe in the data a priori. Both effects are undoubtedly present in some cases and are not mutually exclusive. In addition, sample-selection issues are not really discussed in the paper—if all programs are undertaken only if the net expected profitability (including expected agency costs and/or complementarities) is positive, it is not clear what the relative profitability of programs that corporate and independent programs actually undertaken would be.

The first part of the paper presents a case study of Xerox's capital division, Xerox Technology Ventures. This case makes interesting reading, and the authors describe how this division of Xerox was outrageously profitable, in large part because of investments in a company called Documentum. What is not clear to me is why the case is included in the paper. It was clearly a positive outlier, but, if all that the authors wanted to demonstrate was that there were positive outliers, I would recommend some kind of plot of all the data. Such a plot would give the reader a feel for how likely such a positive outlier is. Sometimes case studies provide useful lessons not easily conveyed by conventional empirical work; however, I do not see that such lessons are learned here.[1] I would encourage the authors to provide a better explanation of why they included the case in their study.

The main empirical findings of the paper were as follows: First, corporate investments, particularly "strategic" ones, go public more often than do independent venture capital investments (39.3 percent for corporate strategic investments, 35.1 percent for all corporate investments, and 30.6 percent for independent venture capital investments). Second, corporate investments have higher "pre–money valuations" than do independent venture capital investments. (*Pre–money valuation* refers to the valuation of the firm at the time the investment is made, equal to the product of the price paid per share times the number of shares outstanding prior to the investment.) Third, corporate venture capital programs have shorter durations than independent venture capital funds.

My overall reaction is that I liked the paper. It is on an important topic that the authors clearly know well. I learned a lot from it. I just wish that I could have learned more and feel that I will in subsequent work on the topic.

In terms of the specific results presented in the paper, I would caution

1. One paper that does use case studies effectively is Lerner and Merges (1998). In the discussion at the conference, Krishna Palepu pointed out that this case does serve as a counterexample to the arguments in the literature and, as such, serves a useful purpose for this reason.

the reader about interpreting the higher initial public offering rate for corporate investments as meaning higher profitability. One agency problem common in corporations is that they are likely to be overly conservative in their investments. Compared to independent venture capital funds, they probably are not going to undertake as risky investments and also are likely to undertake higher-quality investments. The authors do control (probably as well as they can given the available data) for the maturity of the companies in which the programs invest. Nonetheless, it seems likely that their measures are fairly crude proxies for the expected profitability of the companies. One possibility that the authors cannot really rule out is that the corporate venture programs invest in pricier but higher-potential companies but do not either add more value through their monitoring or make more money on their investments.

The comparison between corporate and independent venture capital programs also ignores other benefits that go to the corporations sponsoring the programs. For example, I recently had a speaker in my M.B.A. class who works in this industry. He told the class that you should never take money from Microsoft—they will just steal your idea and do the same thing inside their own company! The point is that Microsoft makes its money not directly through its investments but through the effect of those investments on the profitability of Microsoft's other assets.

In addition, the paper argues that the companies "invest at a premium." The authors imply that this result means that the companies overpay for their investments. I am not sure that this interpretation is appropriate. It seems to me that the corporate valuations must be scaled by something like assets or earnings for this measure to make sense. This result, like the previous one, is consistent with the possibility that the corporate venture programs simply invest in higher-quality start-up companies than do independent venture capital funds. I think that this is an interesting interpretation and that it deserves some discussion in the paper. I would also like to encourage the authors to think about the general issue of how one would distinguish between a fund that makes higher-quality investments ex ante and one that does a better job of monitoring once it has made the investments.

In conclusion, I think that the paper opens up a whole series of interesting questions about corporate venture capital. I found it a bit frustrating that the questions on the topic that I thought were the most interesting really are not discussed in this paper. For example, Why do companies have some research projects done internally, some through contracts with an external firm, and some through "hybrid" contracts like a corporate venture capital program? Why are the contracts in corporate venture capital programs structured the way they are? What organizational forces limit the scope of corporate venture capital? To what extent are agency problems inside the sponsoring company responsible for the short lives of these programs? Does the corporate form induce excess conservatism in the investments they make? To what extent are corporate venture programs used for the expansion of managerial power inside the sponsoring company? One hopes that the authors will address some of these questions in future work.

## Reference

Lerner, Josh, and Robert P. Merges. 1998. The control of technology alliances: An empirical analysis of the biotechnology industry. *Journal of Industrial Economics* 46, no. 2 (June): 125–56.

2

# Ownership Structures and the Decision to Go Public
## Private versus Social Optimality

Lucian Arye Bebchuk and Luigi Zingales

It is generally accepted among academic economists and lawyers that the ownership structure chosen at the initial public offering (IPO) stage is efficient. The costs and benefits of the chosen ownership structure—the argument goes—are reflected in the price the owner can fetch for her shares (Jensen and Meckling 1976). Consequently, the owner of a private firm taking it public will fully internalize the costs and benefits of her choice. Ergo, the ownership structure chosen at the IPO stage is socially efficient. This view has served as the foundation for much of the positive and normative work in corporate finance.

This paper shows that the ownership structure chosen by a value-maximizing entrepreneur at the IPO stage might differ from the socially optimal one. Interestingly, we show this while retaining all the standard assumptions: efficient markets populated by rational agents who maximize the total value of their payoffs.

Lucian Arye Bebchuk is the William J. Friedman and Alicia Townsend Friedman Professor of Law, Economics, and Finance at Harvard Law School and a research associate of the National Bureau of Economic Research. Luigi Zingales is professor of finance at the Graduate School of Business of the University of Chicago and a research associate of the National Bureau of Economic Research.

This paper is a revision, containing new results, of a manuscript circulated earlier as "Ownership Structures: Private versus Social Optimality." The authors thank Reuven Avi-Yona, Victor Brudney, Francesca Cornelli, Szuszanna Fluck, Merritt Fox, Henry Hansmann, Oliver Hart, Louis Kaplow, Bo Li, and workshop participants at the American Law and Economics Association meeting, the Canadian Finance Association meeting, the Western Finance Association meeting, the Harvard Economics Department, the Harvard Law School, and Tel Aviv University. Lucian Bebchuk benefited from the financial support of the National Science Foundation and the Harvard Law School's John M. Olin Center for Law, Economics, and Business. Luigi Zingales benefited from financial support from the Center for Research in Security Prices.

The reason for the identified inefficiency is an externality that the choice of ownership structure has on potential buyers of control. In fact, the initial choice of ownership structure will have important effects on the welfare of the initial owner, the dispersed shareholders, and the potential buyer. Of course, a rational entrepreneur will fully internalize the effects that the ownership structure will have on her future wealth. Moreover, she will fully internalize the effects that the ownership structure will have on the dispersed shareholders because, in an efficient market, those effects are reflected in the IPO price. But the initial owner will not internalize the effects of the ownership structure on the surplus captured by potential buyers (as long as the potential buyer is still willing to buy). This will create a wedge between the choices that are optimal from the initial owner's point of view and the choices that are socially efficient. As we argue, the magnitude of this wedge is a function of the degree of competition in the market for corporate control. In a perfectly competitive market for corporate control, the wedge will disappear, and the privately optimal choice of ownership structure coincides with the socially efficient one.[1]

Specifically, our model includes three ways in which the initial choice of ownership structure affects potential buyers of control. First, this choice will influence whether a transfer of control will take place, affecting both the likelihood of a control transfer and the circumstances under which it will occur. The likelihood and circumstances of control transfer, in turn, affect the expected surplus that potential buyers can be expected to capture.

Second, in those control transfers that will take place, the initial distribution of ownership will influence the division of surplus between the initial shareholders and the control buyer. This, again, will affect the expected surplus of potential future buyers.

Third, should a control transfer take place, the initial distribution of ownership might affect the value of the company under the control buyer. For example, if the initial ownership is dispersed and the control buyer wants to move to a more concentrated ownership (because that would be a more efficient structure), such a change might be difficult to accomplish. This, yet again, might affect the surplus that a potential control buyer can expect to capture.

To demonstrate our thesis, we focus on one important choice that initial

1. The idea that private choices made by those who set up a company might differ from the socially optimal ones was first introduced by Grossman and Hart (1980). Grossman and Hart, however, take as given the choice of ownership structure (dispersed ownership in their case), and they focus on the choice of the dilution factor in takeovers. Subsequent work on the divergence between private and social optimality in the setting up of a company also takes the ownership structure as given and focuses on choices concerning the rules governing control transfers (see, e.g., Bebchuk and Kahan 1990; and Bebchuk 1994). In contrast to the existing work, we endogenize the choice of ownership structure, and we analyze the divergence between private and social optimality in making this basic choice.

owners make. Specifically, we analyze the initial owner's choice between a privately held (PR) company, in which the company remains private and the initial owner retains complete ownership of the firm's cash-flow rights, and a publicly owned (PU) company, in which the initial owner retains control of the firm but sells some of the firm's cash-flow rights to public investors. This is the choice that an owner faces in deciding whether to go public.[2]

Because of the three general effects noted above, the privately optimal choice between a PR and a PU structure generally differs from the socially optimal one. Not only do we demonstrate the existence of such a distortion, but we also explore its likely direction. Much of our analysis is devoted to identifying the conditions under which this distortion will be in the direction of PR structures and the conditions under which it will be in the direction of PU structures.

Our results indicate which empirical evidence would be needed to determine the direction of the identified distortions. Some such evidence already exists, and combining our results with that evidence suggests that, in the United States, the distortion is likely to be in the direction of an excessive incidence of going public. As is well known, the incidence of IPOs (adjusted for population) is larger in the United States than in other advanced economies (see La Porta et al. 1997). While this large incidence of IPOs is generally taken to be a socially optimal outcome, our results suggest the possibility that this incidence is excessive. We should emphasize, however, that much more empirical work, along the lines suggested by our analytic conditions, would be needed before firm conclusions on the direction of the distortion can be reached.

Our analysis is also shown to have policy implications for the legal rules governing the sale of control blocks. We analyze how the equal opportunity rule, the main contender to the market rule prevailing in the United States, affects the direction of the distortion. More important, we identify a regulatory approach for sales of control blocks that could in principle eliminate the identified distortions. We show that, if legal rules were to ensure that sales of control blocks neither benefit nor harm minority shareholders, then the choice between PR and PU would not be distorted. We examine whether and how rules could be designed to accomplish such a result.

There is a large literature on the costs and benefits of a PU structure as compared with those of a PR structure (see, e.g., Jensen and Meckling 1976; Shleifer and Vishny 1986; Holmström and Tirole 1993; Zingales

2. Bebchuk (1999)—which we discuss briefly in our concluding remarks—analyzes potential distortions in another important choice made by the initial owner. Specifically, that paper studies the choice, in the event that the initial owner chooses to go public, between a structure with a controlling shareholder and a structure without a controlling shareholder.

1995; Burkart, Gromb, and Panunzi 1997; Bolton and von Thadden 1998; and Pagano and Roell 1998). This literature largely assumes that initial owners will choose the most efficient structure and focuses on identifying the factors that influence initial owners' choices.[3] In contrast, our model focuses on a consideration that drives a wedge between initial owners' choice and social optimality.

Section 2.1 of the paper describes the framework of analysis. Section 2.2 demonstrates the existence of a distortion. Section 2.3 derives conditions that help us identify the direction of this distortion. Section 2.4 discusses possible extensions of the model. Section 2.5 discusses the model's policy implications for the rules governing control transfers. Section 2.6 concludes.

## 2.1 The Framework

We consider an initial owner, $I$, who owns all the shares of a firm and decides whether she should maintain the company as a privately held (PR) concern or take it public (PU) by selling a fraction $\alpha$ of her cash-flow rights. In the latter case, we assume that she always retains a majority of voting rights and, hence, control of the company.[4] Since, through the use of dual class stocks and stock pyramids, $I$ can retain control while selling an $\alpha$ much greater than 50 percent, we let $\alpha$ vary between zero and one.

The problem is interesting only if there is a difference between the value that an individual investor attributes to a company's shares and the value of a controlling block. Let $Y_I$ be the value of the verifiable cash flow produced by the company, that is, the value that a risk-neutral outside investor will pay for the company's cash flow. Let $B_I$ be the difference between the value of the company for the incumbent ($V_I$) and the value of the verifiable cash flow ($Y_I$): $B_I = V_I - Y_I$. For convenience, we refer to $B_I$ as the private benefits of control to $I$ even though $B_I$ also includes the costs of control.[5]

We make the conventional assumption that the values of $V_I$, $Y_I$, and $B_I$ are affected by the fraction $\alpha$ of cash-flow rights that the initial owner sells to outside shareholders. The total value of a company ($V_I$) will be affected by the fraction $\alpha$ for various reasons. On the one hand, going public may reduce value because of the transaction costs involved in the process (Rit-

3. A notable exception is Pagano (1993). Pagano argues that the number of public companies may be excessively low from a social point of view because the initial owner bears all the costs of listing but reaps only part of the gains of increased diversification opportunities that she provides other owners.

4. In future work, we plan to analyze private vs. social optimality in the choice between going public while retaining control (PU) and moving further to dispersed ownership.

5. Note that this definition is more general than the one commonly used in the literature. $B_I$ includes both the private benefits of control and the costs associated with control. For instance, $B_I$ can be negative if the initial owner is very risk averse.

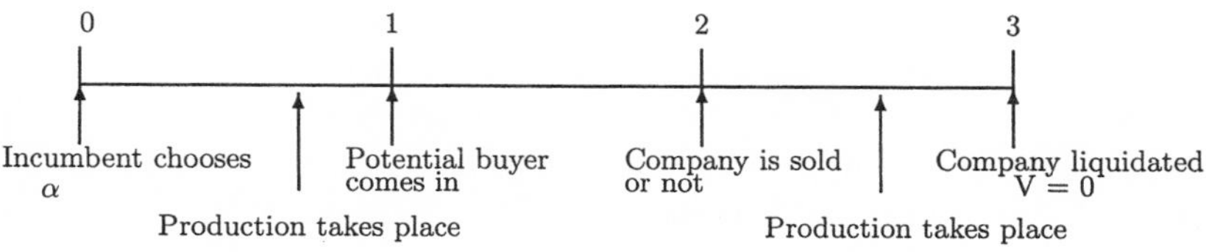


**Fig. 2.1 Timing of the events**

ter 1987) and, more important, because of the agency costs thereby created (Jensen and Meckling 1976).[6] On the other hand, going public may increase the value of a company by spreading risk, by increasing the amount of information for compensating employees (Holmström and Tirole 1993), or by preventing a large shareholder from interfering with the company's management (Burkart, Gromb, and Panunzi 1997).

We define $1 - \alpha_I^*$ as the optimal fraction of cash-flow rights that the incumbent should retain:

$$V_I^* = V_I(\alpha_I^*) = \max_{\alpha_I \in [0,1]} V_I(\alpha_I).$$

We make no assumptions about the value of $\alpha_I^*$. In other words, consistent with Demsetz (1983), we do not assume that the efficient level of ownership is necessarily 100 percent, and we allow for the optimal $\alpha$ to vary from case to case. We also make no assumptions about the shape of the function $V_I(\alpha)$. We do not even assume that $V_I(\alpha)$ is a continuous function. In particular, we want to allow for the possibility of a discontinuity at $\alpha = 0$. In fact, there are some fixed costs associated with the decision to go public, costs that will be borne independently of the fraction $\alpha$ sold to outside investors, provided that $\alpha > 0$.

The timing of the events is summarized in figure 2.1. At time 0, an initial owner, *I*, makes a choice between maintaining complete ownership or moving to a controlling-shareholder structure by selling a fraction $\alpha$ of her shares to the public.

Between time 0 and time 1, the company operates and produces value. At time 1, a potential buyer of control, *N*, emerges and can purchase the company. At time 2, control may be transferred. Between time 2 and time 3, there are again value-producing operations. At time 3, the company is dissolved.

Note that a critical element of our analysis is that, when making the

6. In principle, the initial owner could design incentive contracts that would reproduce the effects of ownership, eliminating the agency costs associated with an increase in $\alpha$. In practice, however, such a contract would succeed in eliminating the agency costs only by undoing the sale through a contract. Therefore, if the incumbent owner wants to dispose of a fraction of cash-flow rights, she will have to bear the increased agency costs.

time 0 choice between PR and PU, the initial owner will pay attention to the possibility that a potential buyer will emerge at time 1. This seems to us quite plausible in light of the evidence on the substantial frequency of control changes in firms that have gone public.[7]

The potential buyer, who emerges at time 1, has a different valuation of the company, $V_N = B_N + Y_N$.[8] The buyer's valuation may differ from that of the incumbent for many reasons. Different owners may have different managerial ability and thus produce different levels of cash flow. They might also have different synergies with the company or be more or less risk averse. Therefore, they might differ not only in their total valuation, $V_N$, but in its components as well. Consistently, we define $1 - \alpha_N^*$ as the optimal fraction of cash-flow rights that the new buyer should retain:

$$V_N^* = V_N(\alpha_N^*) = \max_{\alpha_N \in [0,1]} V_N(\alpha_N).$$

Note that the initial owner is not able to change her ownership level just after the first production period. This assumption is meant to capture the fact that the timing of the arrival of the potential buyer is uncertain and, therefore, that, if the initial owner wants to pre-position the ownership structure, she faces the risk of having a suboptimal ownership structure in at least one production period.

While the market for minority shares is perfectly competitive, the market for controlling blocks is not. Therefore, when the owner sells a fraction $\alpha$ of her shares to dispersed shareholders, she will receive the expected value of those shares. By contrast, when she trades her large block with another party interested in control, she will not be able to appropriate all the surplus from the trade. This assumption of an imperfectly competitive market for corporate control seems to be a realistic one. Suppose, for example, that some private benefits derive from a synergy with another company owned by a potential acquiring party. This is something very specific to the particular buyer, and, in this situation, it seems unlikely that a seller could extract all the surplus.[9]

7. The empirical evidence indicates that controlling blocks in publicly traded companies are transferred rather frequently. For example, Holderness and Sheehan (1988) find that, in a group of 114 New York and American Stock Exchange companies each of which had a shareholder owning a majority interest, there were twenty-one sale-of-control transactions in the four-year period between 1978 and 1982. Similarly, Caprio, Floreani, and Radaelli (1994) look at the frequency of the transfer of control blocks on the Milan Stock Exchange, where most companies have a controlling block (Zingales 1994). They report that, in the 1970s, 35 percent of the companies experienced a control-block transfer; during the 1980s, the same figure was 33 percent. Similarly, Pagano, Panetta, and Zingales (1998) show that firms experience an unusually high level of control sales in the three years following an IPO.

8. For simplicity, we assume that, if $I$ and $N$ are risk averse, this affects only the function $B$. Otherwise, we treat them as risk neutral.

9. An alternative rationale might be that the acquisition of a company requires large financial resources, which are available generally only to a few wealthy individuals. Therefore, the sale of a company cannot always be conducted as a competitive auction.

We assume that the incumbent will get a fraction $1 - \theta$ of the total surplus captured by the buyer and the incumbent combined. This can be formalized as the outcome of a bargaining game in which, with probability $0 < \theta < 1$, $N$ has the right to make a take-it-or-leave-it offer and, with probability $1 - \theta$, the opportunity belongs to $I$. The main thrust of the results is not sensitive to the particular bargaining model chosen so long as the incumbent does not capture all the buyer's surplus (i.e., $\theta \neq 0$).

Initially, we assume that whoever is in control of the company in period 2 will move to the optimal $\alpha$. In particular, if $\alpha = 0$ and $\alpha^* > 0$, then the controller will sell additional shares. If $\alpha > 0$ and $\alpha^* = 0$, we assume that the controller will freeze out minority shareholders at the current value of the shares, that is, paying $\alpha Y(\alpha)$.[10] As we show in section 2.4.2 below, dropping this assumption introduces another source of divergence between private and social optimality.

We also assume that the discount rate is equal to zero and that the buyer is not liquidity constrained.[11] Finally, we assume that all the parameters are common knowledge.

## 2.2 Divergence between Private and Social Optimality

In this section, we show the existence of a divergence between the ownership structure that maximizes the proceeds of the initial owner at the IPO stage and the socially efficient ownership structure (i.e., the ownership structure that a benevolent social planner facing the same problem as the initial entrepreneur will choose). In order to achieve this objective, we first need to illustrate how the choice of ownership structure influences whether a transfer of control will take place and the price at which it will take place.

### 2.2.1 Conditions for a Transfer

The first step involves identifying when control will be transferred from $I$ to $N$ as a function of the cash-flow rights sold by the incumbent ($\alpha$). If $N$ gets control, he will capture $V_N^* - \alpha Y_N$. By contrast, if $I$ retains control, she will get $V_I^* - \alpha Y_I$. Thus, a transfer will take place if and only if

(1) $$V_N^* - V_I^* > \alpha[Y_N(\alpha) - Y_I(\alpha)].$$

In what follows, we drop the subscripts $I$ and $N$ unless the context requires otherwise. Let $\Delta V^* = V_N^* - V_I^*$ and $\Delta Y(\alpha) = Y_N - Y_I$. Then the condition for a transfer is

(2) $$\Delta V^* > \alpha \Delta Y(\alpha).$$

10. For an analysis of the optimal freezeout rule, see Burkart, Gromb, and Panunzi (1998).

11. Implicitly, we also assume that the incumbent is not liquidity constrained in the sense that she can finance all positive net present value projects with internal funds or riskless debt. We make the assumption in order to avoid the additional complication associated with the capital structure decision (see Israel 1992).

The left-hand side represents the total value generated by the change in control, while the right-hand side is the effect of the transfer on minority shareholders. Thus, condition (2) simply says that a transfer of control will take place if it generates value in excess of what is captured by minority shareholders.

Note that, when $\alpha = 0$, there will be a transfer of control whenever it is socially efficient (i.e., whenever it generates value $\Delta V^* > 0$). Thus, the value of the company in the second period will always be $\max\{V_N^*, V_I^*\}$.

As shown in Bebchuk (1994), however, when $\alpha > 0$, some efficient transfers will be prevented, and some inefficient transfers will take place. Specifically, an efficient transfer will be blocked when

$$0 < \Delta V^* < \alpha\Delta Y(\alpha),$$

and an inefficient transfer will occur when

$$\alpha\Delta Y(\alpha) < \Delta V^* < 0.$$

As a result, when $\alpha > 0$, the value of the company in the second period will not always be equal to $\max\{V_N^*, V_I^*\}$ but will be a function of $\alpha$. We refer to this second-period value as $V_2(\alpha)$.

### 2.2.2 The Socially Optimal Incidence of PU

Since we assumed a discount rate of zero, the social planner maximizes the sum of the value of the company in the two periods. This is given by

$$\max_{\alpha\in[0,1]} W(\alpha) = V_I(\alpha) + E\{V_2(\alpha)\}. \tag{3}$$

Let $\alpha^{FB}$ be the solution to program (3). Then, for a given distribution of potential buyers, we can define

$$PU^{FB} = \{I : \alpha^{FB} > 0\} \tag{4}$$

as the set of incumbents for whom it is socially optimal to have a PU structure rather than a PR one. Note that $\alpha^{FB}$ can well be different from $\alpha^*$ because of the effect of $\alpha$ on $V_2$.

### 2.2.3 The Initial Owner's Choice

The initial owner chooses $\alpha$ to maximize her profits ($\Pi$), not the social welfare ($W$). The difference between the two is represented by the expected gain captured by the buyer, which enters the social planner's objective function but not that of the initial owner. Thus,

$$\Pi = W - G_N, \tag{5}$$

where $G_N$ is $N$'s expected gain from the transfer. $G_N$ is the source of the potential divergence between the social and the private optimization. $N$'s expected gain can be written as

$$(6) \qquad G_N = \text{prob[transfer]}E[\text{expected gains to } N\,|\,\text{transfer}].$$

Thus, the initial owner cares not only about the effect of α on $W$ but also about its effect on $G_N$.

2.2.4 The Effect of α on the Surplus Captured by the Buyer

Under PR, the surplus captured by the buyer is simply

$$G_N^{PR} = \theta E[\Delta V^* | \Delta V^* > 0]\text{prob}\{\Delta V^* > 0\}.$$

Under PU, the surplus captured by the buyer is

$$G_N^{PU} = \text{prob}\{\Delta V^* - \alpha\Delta Y(\alpha) > 0\}$$
$$\cdot\ \theta E[\Delta V^* - \alpha\Delta Y(\alpha) | \Delta V^* - \alpha\Delta Y(\alpha) > 0].$$

We are interested in studying how the choice of ownership structure affects the surplus captured by the buyer. Thus, we want to study the difference between $G_N^{PU}$ and $G_N^{PR}$. This difference can be written (assuming $\text{prob}\{\Delta V^* - \alpha\Delta Y(\alpha) = 0\} = 0$) as

$$(7) \quad \Delta G_N(\alpha) = -\theta\alpha E[\Delta Y(\alpha) | \Delta V^* > 0 \cap \Delta V^* - \alpha\Delta Y(\alpha) > 0]$$
$$\times\ \text{prob}\{\Delta V^* > 0 \cap \Delta V^* - \alpha\Delta Y(\alpha) > 0\}$$
$$-\ \theta E[\Delta V^* | \Delta V^* > 0 \cap \Delta V^* - \alpha\Delta Y(\alpha) < 0]$$
$$\times\ \text{prob}\{\Delta V^* > 0 \cap \Delta V^* - \alpha\Delta Y(\alpha) < 0\}$$
$$+\ \theta E\{[\Delta V^* - \alpha\Delta Y(\alpha)] | \Delta V^* \leq 0 \cap \Delta V^* - \alpha\Delta Y(\alpha) > 0]\}$$
$$\times\ \text{prob}\{\Delta V^* \leq 0 \cap \Delta V^* - \alpha\Delta Y(\alpha) > 0\}.$$

The first term represents the expected effect that a move to PU would have on $N$'s surplus in all those circumstances in which a control transfer would take place under both PU and PR. This effect can be either positive or negative, depending on whether the expected effect of a control transfer in those circumstances on minority shares is negative or positive. When a control transfer raises the value of minority shares, the presence of minority shares leaves $N$ with less surplus under PU than under PR. In contrast, when a control transfer reduces the value of minority shares, the presence of minority shares would enable $N$ to extract more surplus under PU than under PR.[12]

The second term represents the expected surplus that $N$ would lose from a move from PR to PU owing to the fact that the move would block some (efficient) transfers that would take place under PR. The third term repre-

12. In Zingales (1995), the effect of a move to PU on $N$'s surplus is always negative because of his assumption that a control transfer always benefits the minority shareholders. We study a more general setting, one in which minority shareholders can either benefit or lose from a control transfer, and, in this setting, the considered effect is ambiguous.

sents the expected surplus that $N$ would gain from the move from PR to PU owing to the fact that the move would lead to some (inefficient) control transfers that would not take place under PR.

### 2.2.5 Private versus Social Optimality

From equation (5), it is easy to see why the socially efficient level of $\alpha$ may diverge from the privately optimal one. In particular, given $I$ and $N$, we have the following proposition:

PROPOSITION 1. *I will choose PU even though PR is socially optimal if and only if* $\Delta G_N < W(\alpha) - W(0)$ *for some* $\alpha$. *Vice versa, I will choose PR even though PU is socially optimal if and only if* $\Delta G_N > W(\alpha) - W(0)$ *for all* $\alpha$.

PROOF. See the appendix.

Note that a necessary condition for $\Delta G_N < W(\alpha) - W(0)$ for some $\alpha$, given that $W(\alpha) < W(0)$ for all $\alpha$ (i.e., PR is socially optimal), is $\Delta G_N < 0$ for some $\alpha$. Similarly, a necessary condition for $\Delta G_N > W(\alpha) - W(0)$ for all $\alpha$, given that $W(\alpha) > W(0)$ for some $\alpha$ (i.e., PU is socially optimal), is $\Delta G_N > 0$ for some $\alpha$.

The intuition is as follows. If the choice between PR and PU affects the expected surplus captured by the potential buyer, it drives a wedge between the social and the private optimum. In particular, if a positive $\alpha$ decreases the expected surplus extracted by the buyer to a sufficient extent, it will distort the initial owner's choice in favor of going public (excessive PU). On the other hand, if a positive $\alpha$ increases the expected surplus captured by the rival to a sufficient extent, it will distort the decision of the initial owner against going public (excessive PR).

Having established the possibility of a divergence, we can now explore the direction and the magnitude of this divergence. This is the subject of the next section.

## 2.3 The Direction of the Distortion

### 2.3.1 The Importance of $\Delta Y$

The source of the externality that generates the divergence between private and social incentives is the effect that a control transfer has on minority shareholders. When $\Delta Y(\alpha) = 0$, there is no externality, and thus there is no divergence. This idea is formalized in the following proposition:

PROPOSITION 2. *If* $\Delta Y(\alpha) \equiv 0$ *(i.e., if* $Y[\alpha]$ *is the same for any possible controlling shareholder), then* $\Delta G_N \equiv 0$, *and the privately optimal choice between PU and PR is socially optimal.*

PROOF. If $\Delta Y(\alpha) = 0$, then $G_N^{PR} = G_N^{PU}$, so $\Delta G_N(\alpha) = 0$. Then the conclusion follows directly from proposition 1.

$\Delta Y(\alpha)$ is the effect of a sale of control on minority shareholders. Thus, it will be zero only if minority shareholders are completely unaffected by the transaction. There are both theoretical and empirical reasons to doubt that this is the case. Theoretically, minority shareholders' value might well be affected by a control transfer owing to a change in either $V$ or $B$ (or both) because, under the existing corporate law rules, there is no mechanism that shields minority shareholders from the economic effects of a control transfer on their shares.

Empirically, $\Delta Y(\alpha)$ can be estimated. Barclay and Holderness (1991), for instance, find that block trades that lead to a change in control generate an abnormal return of 18 percent for minority shareholders.[13] This figure represents only the unanticipated component of the externality. Nevertheless, it suggests that, on average, the externality is positive in the United States. It also suggests that the size of the externality imposed on minority shareholders by control transfers is far from trivial. The blocks analyzed by Barclay and Holderness (1991) represent about 30 percent of the companies' stock. Therefore, just the unanticipated component of the externality represents about 13 percent of the value of a firm.[14]

In sum, under current corporate law rules, $\Delta Y(\alpha)$ should not be expected to be generally equal to zero and thereby eliminate all distortions. Nevertheless, proposition 2 is useful in attempting to determine what rules can eliminate the externalities of control transfers. We return to this issue in section 2.5 below. For now, we assume that $\Delta Y(\alpha) \neq 0$ and explore its consequences.

### 2.3.2 The Relation between $\Delta Y$ and $\Delta V$

An important role in determining the direction of the distortion is played by the correlation between the effect that a change of control has on total value and its effect on the value of minority shareholders:

Proposition 3. *If $\Delta Y(\alpha)$ and $\Delta V^*$ have opposite signs for all $\alpha$, I, and N, then $\Delta G_N(\alpha) > 0$ for all $\alpha$, I, and N, and the potential distortion is in the direction of an excessive incidence of PR.*

Proof. The only interesting case is that in which $\Delta V^* > 0$ and $\Delta Y(\alpha) < 0$. When $\Delta V^* > 0$ and $\Delta Y(\alpha) < 0$, the first term in (7) is nonnegative (positive when the probability term is positive and zero when the probability term is zero). $\Delta V^* > 0$ and $\Delta Y(\alpha) < 0$ also imply that $\Delta V^* - \alpha \Delta Y > 0$. Thus, all transactions that will take place under PR will also take place under PU. This implies that the second term in (7) is zero. Finally, given $\Delta V^* - \alpha \Delta Y(\alpha) > 0$, the last term in (7) is positive when the probability is

13. This figure is obtained by averaging the 19 percent return obtained by the forty-one firms that were subsequently taken private and the 8.1 percent return obtained by the forty-five firms that experienced changes in control while remaining publicly traded.

14. A similar study conducted by Caprio, Floreani, and Radaelli (1994) for the Italian market comes to similar conclusions.

positive and zero when the probability is zero. Thus, if there is any chance of a transaction under PU, it must mean that the sum of the probability terms in the first term and in the third term is positive and, thus, that either the first term or the third term is positive.

$\Delta Y(\alpha)$ and $\Delta V^*$ are likely to have opposite signs when legal constraints on self-dealing transactions are weak and different controlling shareholders can generate different synergies. In this case, a controlling shareholder with more synergy (higher $V$) will also be the one with a greater business relationship with the acquired company and, thus, the one who is able to extract more value from the company (lower $Y$) through self-dealing transactions.

A different scenario, and perhaps the one that is more likely to occur in the United States, is that in which $\Delta Y(\alpha)$ and $\Delta V^*$ have the same sign. In this case, we have the following proposition:

PROPOSITION 4. *If* $\Delta Y(\alpha)$ *and* $\Delta V^*$ *have the same sign for all* $\alpha$, *I, and N, and if prob*$\{\Delta V^* \leq 0 \cap \Delta V^* - \alpha\Delta Y(\alpha) > 0\} \equiv 0$, *then* $\Delta G_N(\alpha) < 0$ *for all* $\alpha$, *I, and N, and the potential distortion is in the direction of an excessive incidence of PU.*

PROOF. The third term in (7) is positive if the probability is positive and zero if the probability is zero. In addition, given that $\Delta Y(\alpha)$ has the same sign as $\Delta V^*$, which is positive in the first term in (7), the first term in (7) is negative. Finally, the second term is nonpositive by definition.

One scenario in which the conditions of this proposition are satisfied is that in which the private benefits of control are a given fraction of the firm's total value. Another scenario in which the conditions of this proposition are likely to hold is that in which the differences among the private benefits of different controlling shareholders are small. In this latter case, an acquirer with a higher $V$ will also have a higher $Y$. Thus, in countries where the private benefits of control tend to be small (as they are in the United States), the distortion is likely to be in the direction of excessive PU.

Since $V$ cannot be directly observed, any statement trying to identify the condition that is more likely to hold in a particular country is inevitably speculative. The value of cash flow to security holders ($Y$), however, can be observed. We can draw certain inferences from $\Delta Y$ regarding the relation between the signs of $\Delta Y$ and $\Delta V$:

PROPOSITION 5. *If in a control transfer* $\Delta Y(\alpha) > 0$, *then* $\Delta Y(\alpha)$ *and* $\Delta V^*$ *must have the same sign in that transfer.*

PROOF. Assume not. Then it should be possible that a transfer occurs where $\Delta Y(\alpha)$ is positive and $\Delta V^*$ is negative. But this implies that $\Delta V^* - \alpha\Delta Y < 0$, which makes a transfer impossible, contradicting the hypothesis.

When $I$ and $N$ agree to a transfer, it must be the case that either the transfer generates value $\Delta V^* > 0$ or it generates a negative externality on minority shareholders $\Delta Y(\alpha) < 0$; otherwise, there is no room for agreement. So, when we observe a transfer of control with $\Delta Y(\alpha) > 0$, we are guaranteed that $\Delta V^* > 0$ also.

Among other things, $\Delta Y(\alpha)$ is a function of the legal regime governing sale-of-control transactions. In particular, the following corollary of proposition 5 can be stated:

COROLLARY 1. *If corporate law rules ensure that minority shareholders never lose from control transfers, then $\Delta Y(\alpha)$ and $\Delta V^*$ will always have the same sign, and the distortion is in the direction of an excessive incidence of PU.*

One example of a rule that ensures that minority shareholders never lose from a control transfer is the equal opportunity rule, which gives minority shareholders the option to be bought out at the same price paid by the acquirer. We discuss this rule more extensively in section 2.4.1 below. Another rule that can achieve the same result is the right to sue majority shareholders in the case of a predatory acquisition (i.e., an acquisition that reduces $Y$).

This corollary is important in assessing the likely direction of the distortion in practice. For example, in countries where minority shareholder rights are well protected (as they are in the United States), the changes in total value and in minority shareholders' value are always in the same direction, and, as a result, the distortion is clearly in favor of PU. This conclusion highlights an interesting externality of any legislation aimed at improving the protection of minority shareholders. It is consistent with Roe's (1994) claim that populist legislation in favor of minority shareholders has forced the American system toward an excessive separation of ownership from control. Interestingly, however, the mechanism by which that excess takes place is different. In Roe (1994), the law directly forbids some players (specifically, financial institutions) from assuming the role of large shareholders. In our case, it is the protection of minority shareholders that makes it very convenient for the incumbent to disperse ownership.

While the discussion presented above suggests that $\Delta Y(\alpha)$ and $\Delta V^*$ are likely to have the same sign in the United States, it does not guarantee that their signs are always the same (as the conditions of proposition 4 would require). On the other hand, the existing empirical evidence indicates that, in the majority (but not necessarily in all) of the cases, $\Delta Y(\alpha)$ and $\Delta V^*$ do have the same sign in the United States.

### 2.3.3 The Expected Value of $\Delta Y$

Let us assume that both cases, that of proposition 3 and that of proposition 4, are possible and analyze what we can learn from the fact that, on average, $\Delta Y(\alpha)$ is positive:

PROPOSITION 6. *A necessary condition for $\Delta G_N$ to be negative, and thus for the distortion to be in favor of PU, is that the expected effect on minority shareholders of a value-enhancing transfer of control is positive ($E[\Delta Y(\alpha) \mid \Delta V^*$*

$> 0] > 0$). *A sufficient condition for $\Delta G_N$ to be negative, and thus for the distortion to be in favor of PU, is that the expected effect of a transfer of control on minority shareholders is positive* ($E[\Delta Y(\alpha) \mid \Delta V^* - \alpha \Delta Y(\alpha) > 0] > 0$).

PROOF. See the appendix.

The source of the distortion is that the surplus captured by the incumbent is modified by her choice of ownership structure. A necessary condition for her to benefit from going public is that, by going public, she succeeds in extracting a larger share of the rents. This occurs only if a transfer of control generates a positive externality on minority shareholders, which the incumbent can capture up front, in the price fetched at the IPO stage. This condition is exactly $E\{\Delta Y(\alpha) | \Delta V^* > 0\} > 0$.

The condition outlined above, however, is not sufficient because a change in the ownership structure also affects which transfer of control will take place. In particular, the fact that in a PU structure the incumbent does not own 100 percent of the cash-flow rights allows for the possibility that some transfer will take place even when $\Delta V^* < 0$ and $\Delta Y(\alpha) < 0$. Thus, the sufficient condition of proposition 6 requires that the positive externality exists even after we account for the changes in the set of control transfers that will take place.

Correspondingly, we have the following proposition:

PROPOSITION 7. *A necessary condition for $\Delta G_N$ to be positive, and thus for the distortion to be in favor of PR, is that the expected effect of a transfer of control on minority shareholders is negative* ($E[\Delta Y(\alpha) | \Delta V^* - \alpha \Delta Y(\alpha) > 0] < 0$). *A sufficient condition for $\Delta G_N$ to be positive, and thus for the distortion to be in favor of PR, is that the expected effect on minority shareholders of a value-enhancing transfer of control is negative* ($E[\Delta Y(\alpha) | \Delta V^* > 0] < 0$).

PROOF. See the appendix.

When a transfer of control generates a negative externality on minority shareholders, the amount of surplus that the incumbent can capture is reduced by going public. As a result, a necessary condition for the distortion to be in favor of PR is that the externality is on average negative. Again, this condition does not ensure the existence of a distortion because a PU structure changes the set of control transfers that will take place. The sufficient condition of proposition 7 requires that the negative externality exists even within the modified set of control transfers.

Barclay and Holderness (1991) show that, on average, the effect of a control transfer on the share price is positive. It is, then, legitimate to conclude that, on average, the expected value of a transfer of control on minority shareholders in the United States is positive. This suggests that the distortion in the United States is likely to be in the direction of excessive PU.

Two qualifications are warranted here. First, all firms in the sample used by Barclay and Holderness (1991) are firms that choose the PU structure. Thus, it might well be possible that, across the entire population of firms,

$E[\Delta Y(\alpha) \mid \text{transfer occurring}]$ is negative, but we observe only the ones for which $\Delta Y > 0$ because these firms are the most likely to go public. While possible, this hypothesis is rather unlikely for the United States given the great propensity of companies to go public there. The problem may be more relevant for other countries, where only a small fraction of companies choose to go public.

Second, the evidence discussed here comes only from the United States. We are aware of another paper that finds similar results in Italy (see Caprio, Floreani, and Radaelli 1994). It would be interesting, however, to investigate the effect of control transfers in different institutional environments, environments in which different rules for the protection of minority shareholders hold.

## 2.4 Extensions

### 2.4.1 The Equal Opportunity Rule

In many countries other than the United States, there exists a law requiring that the acquirer of a control block extend an offer at the same price to all shareholders—the equal opportunity rule (EOR). Even in the United States, where such a law does not exist, many companies insert a similar requirement in their corporate charter. Therefore, it is of practical relevance to understand the effects of an EOR on the direction of the distortion.

Corollary 1 has established that, if corporate law eliminates the possibility that $\Delta Y < 0$ in an acquisition, then the distortion is always in the direction of excessive PU. It is easy to see that this is exactly the effect produced by the EOR, provided that the incumbent's private benefits of control are nonnegative. In fact, under the EOR, minority shareholders get at least as much as $I$ (per share). Since $I$ will agree to a transfer only if she is better off, the minority shareholders (who, given that $B \geq 0$, will start from a lower price per share) will be made better off as well.[15] Thus, all transfers of control generate a positive externality. It follows that the EOR ensures that the divergence between private and social optimality is in the direction of an excessive use of PU. Thus, other things being equal, countries that have the EOR should have proportionally more companies going public.

### 2.4.2 Difficulties in Implementing a Freezeout in the Last Period

Thus far, we have assumed that whoever ends up in control at time 2 will be able to move to the optimal ownership level at no additional cost. In particular, we assumed that, if $\alpha > 0$, the period 2 controller would be able to buy out all minority shares at $\alpha Y(\alpha)$. However, as Burkart, Gromb,

15. Since we defined $B$ as the private benefits of control net of the risk-bearing costs, it is possible that $B$ is negative. In such a case, however, the incumbent will have an interest in selling shares at least to the point at which $B \geq 0$. Thus, for all practical purposes, we can assume that $B \geq 0$.

and Panunzi (1998) point out, when a move to complete ownership produces some efficiency gains, dispersed shareholders will not tender at $\alpha Y(\alpha)$. Even if we introduce the possibility of a freezeout, it is likely that a premium above $\alpha Y(\alpha)$ might be needed. It is, thus, important to consider what happens when a controlling shareholder faces a cost in moving toward the optimal ownership level.

To examine the implications of such difficulties, consider the extreme case in which a freezeout at time 2 is impossible. In this case, any $\alpha > 0$ chosen at time 1 becomes irreversible, whereas a choice of $\alpha = 0$ at time 1 can be modified at time 2. Under this assumption, an initial PU structure may impose a cost on whoever is in control at $t = 2$ by impeding a move to the optimal $\alpha$. This cost is going to be borne at least partially by $N$, and, therefore, it will not be fully internalized by $I$ in her initial decision.

If the distortion is in favor of PU to begin with (as we found to be somewhat more likely for the United States), this new factor will exacerbate that situation. However, if the initial distortion is against PU, this new factor will mitigate that situation. This is not at all surprising: in a world of second best, some distortion can actually improve welfare.

## 2.5 Policy Implications for the Rules Governing Sale-of-Control Transactions

The source of the divergence, we have seen, is that the choice of an initial ownership structure is influenced by the prospect of a future sale-of-control transaction. As we have seen before, both the market rule prevailing in the United States and the EOR prevailing in other countries generate some distortions in the choice of ownership. It is natural to wonder, then, whether it is possible to regulate sale-of-control transactions in a way that would eliminate the distortion in the choice of the initial ownership structure.

Such a regulatory approach can be identified but might be hard to implement. As we saw, the divergence between private and social optimality results from the fact that, under the existing rules for sale-of-control transactions, a transfer of control from $I$ to $N$ may impose a positive or negative externality on minority shareholders. This problem will disappear if we have an arrangement that ensures, in the event of a control transfer, that minority shareholders will end up with exactly $Y_I$. Bebchuk (1994) demonstrates that such an arrangement will ensure ex post efficiency—that is, control blocks will be transferred if and only if the transfer is efficient. Our analysis points out that such an arrangement will also lead to an ex ante efficient choice of ownership structure and, in particular, to an efficient incidence of control blocks.

As Bebchuk (1994) shows, there are two arrangements that ensure that minority shareholders always end up with a value of $Y_I$. Unfortunately, they both require that courts and minority shareholders have sufficient information. First, if courts have the same information concerning $Y_I$ as $I$ and $N$ are assumed to have, then a combination of appraisal rights and freezeout rights would produce the desired result. Under this arrangement, minority shareholders will have an appraisal right to redeem their shares for a value of $Y_I$ as estimated by the court, and $I$ will also have a freezeout right to buy out the minority shareholders prior to the transaction for a value of $Y_I$ as estimated by the court. If courts can observe $Y_I$ accurately, this arrangement would ensure that minority shareholders always get $Y_I$. But, if courts might err in estimating $Y_I$ (and in a direction that can be anticipated by $I$ and $N$), then this arrangement will not ensure that minority shareholders get an expected value of $Y_I$ in sale-of-control transactions.

Second, if minority shareholders have the same information concerning $Y_I$ and $Y_N$ as $I$ and $N$ are assumed to have, then a specialized voting arrangement can be used. Under this arrangement, a control transfer will require a vote of approval by a majority of the minority shareholders; furthermore, a majority of the minority shareholders will be able to approve a transaction in which they end up with less than $Y_N$ by, say, approving a payment from the company to $I$ or $N$. Under this arrangement, if minority shareholders know $Y_I$ and $Y_N$ as $I$ and $N$ are assumed to know, then all the transactions that are brought to shareholders for approval and that obtain such approval will be ones that provide the minority shareholders with a value equal to $Y_I$. Once again, it can be shown that, if minority shareholders might err in estimating either $Y_I$ or $Y_N$ (and in a direction that can be anticipated by $I$ and $N$), the sale-of-control transactions will still involve an expected externality with respect to minority shareholders.

## 2.6 Conclusions

This paper shows that the ownership structure chosen by a value-maximizing entrepreneur might differ from the one that is socially optimal. Focusing on the choice between PR and PU structures, we show how this choice might be distorted, and we identify conditions under which the distortion will be in the direction of an excessive and suboptimal incidence of going public.

The results of the model indicate which empirical evidence would be useful for determining the direction of the identified distortion. Some of the evidence already exists, and combining it with our results suggests that, in the United States, the distortion tends to be in the direction of an excessive incidence of going public. But more empirical work, along the lines suggested by our results, would be needed to reach firm conclusions about the direction of the distortions.

While our analysis has focused on the choice between PR and PU structures, our point about the divergence between private and social optimality also applies to the choice between a PU structure and a structure of dispersed ownership (DI). The choice between PU and DI might also have an external effect on potential buyers of control by influencing the conditions for a transfer and the buyer's surplus in a transfer. This external effect is analyzed in Bebchuk (1999), which shows that, when the corporate law system is lax and the private benefits of control are consequently large, a PU structure will enable the initial shareholders to extract more surplus from control transfers than will a DI structure. Therefore, when private benefits of control are large, publicly traded companies tend to have a PU structure (as is indeed the case), and they might choose a PU structure even if a DI structure is superior from a social point of view. Thus, the divergence between the private and the social optimality in the choice of ownership structure, which this paper has identified, is a general problem, one that should be recognized by students of corporate ownership structure.

## Appendix

### Proof of Proposition 1

For PU to be chosen even if PR is optimal, we must have that, while $W(0) > W(\alpha)$ for all $\alpha > 0$, there is an $\alpha$ such that $\Pi(0) < \Pi(\alpha)$. Substituting (5), this is equivalent to saying that there is an $\alpha$ such that $0 < W(0) - W(\alpha) < -\Delta G_N$.

For PR to be chosen even if PU is optimal, we must have that, while there is an $\alpha > 0$ such that $W(0) < W(\alpha)$, $\Pi(0) > \Pi(\alpha)$ for all $\alpha > 0$. Substituting (5), this is equivalent to saying that, for all $\alpha > 0$, $W(0) - W(\alpha) > -\Delta G_N$.

### Proof of Proposition 6

*Necessary Condition.* We can rewrite (7) as

$$\begin{aligned}
\Delta G_N(\alpha) = & -\theta\alpha E[\Delta Y(\alpha) | \Delta V^* > 0 \cap \Delta V^* - \alpha\Delta Y(\alpha) > 0] \\
& \times \text{prob}\{\Delta V^* > 0 \cap \Delta V^* - \alpha\Delta Y(\alpha) > 0\} \\
& - \theta\alpha E[\Delta Y(\alpha) | \Delta V^* > 0 \cap \Delta V^* - \alpha\Delta Y(\alpha) < 0] \\
& \times \text{prob}\{\Delta V^* > 0 \cap \Delta V^* - \alpha\Delta Y(\alpha) < 0\} \\
& - \theta E[\Delta V^* - \alpha\Delta Y(\alpha) | \Delta V^* > 0 \cap \Delta V^* - \alpha\Delta Y(\alpha) < 0] \\
& \times \text{prob}\{\Delta V^* > 0 \cap \Delta V^* - \alpha\Delta Y(\alpha) < 0\} \\
& + \theta E[\Delta V^* - \alpha\Delta Y(\alpha) | \Delta V^* \le 0 \cap \Delta V^* - \alpha\Delta Y(\alpha) > 0] \\
& \times \text{prob}\{\Delta V^* \le 0 \cap \Delta V^* - \alpha\Delta Y(\alpha) > 0\}.
\end{aligned}$$

Collecting terms, we obtain (assuming $\text{prob}\{\Delta V^* - \alpha\Delta Y(\alpha) = 0\} = 0$)

$$\text{(A1)} \quad \Delta G_N(\alpha) = -\theta\alpha E[\Delta Y(\alpha) | \Delta V^* > 0]\ \text{prob}\{\Delta V^* > 0\}$$

$$+ \theta E[|\Delta V^* - \alpha\Delta Y(\alpha)| \,|\, \Delta V^* \text{ and } \Delta V^* - \alpha\Delta Y(\alpha) \text{ have opposite signs}]$$

$$\times\ \text{prob}\{\Delta V^* \text{ and } \Delta V^* - \alpha\Delta Y(\alpha) \text{ have opposite signs}\}.$$

Since the second term in (A1) is always nonnegative, a necessary condition for $\Delta G_N(\alpha)$ to be negative is that the first term is negative, that is, $E[\Delta Y(\alpha)|\Delta V^* > 0]\text{prob}\{\Delta V^* > 0\} > 0$.

*Sufficient Condition.* Rewrite the last term in (7) as

$$\theta E[\Delta V^* | \Delta V^* \leq 0 \cap \Delta V^* - \alpha\Delta Y(\alpha) > 0]$$
$$\times\ \text{prob}\{\Delta V^* \leq 0 \cap \Delta V^* - \alpha\Delta Y(\alpha) > 0\}$$
$$-\theta\alpha E[\Delta Y(\alpha) | \Delta V^* \leq 0 \cap \Delta V^* - \alpha\Delta Y(\alpha) > 0]$$
$$\times\ \text{prob}\{\Delta V^* \leq 0 \cap \Delta V^* - \alpha\Delta Y(\alpha) > 0\}.$$

Collecting terms, we can rewrite $\Delta G_N$ as follows:

$$\text{(A2)} \qquad \Delta G_N(\alpha) = -\theta\alpha E[\Delta Y(\alpha) | \Delta V^* - \alpha\Delta Y(\alpha) > 0]$$
$$\times\ \text{prob}\{\Delta V^* - \alpha\Delta Y(\alpha) > 0\}$$
$$-\ \theta E[\Delta V^* | \Delta V^* > 0 \cap \Delta V^* - \alpha\Delta Y(\alpha) < 0]$$
$$\times\ \text{prob}\{\Delta V^* > 0 \cap \Delta V^* - \alpha\Delta Y(\alpha) < 0\}$$
$$+\ \theta E[\Delta V^* | \Delta V^* \leq 0 \cap \Delta V^* - \alpha\Delta Y(\alpha) > 0]$$
$$\times\ \text{prob}\{\Delta V^* \leq 0 \cap \Delta V^* - \alpha\Delta Y(\alpha) > 0\},$$

or

$$\text{(A3)} \quad \Delta G_N(\alpha) = -\theta\alpha E[\Delta Y(\alpha) | \text{transfer under PU}]$$
$$\times\ \text{prob}\{\text{transfer under PU}\}$$
$$-\ \theta E[|\Delta V^*| \,|\, \Delta V^* \text{ and } \Delta V^* - \alpha\Delta Y(\alpha) \text{ have opposite signs}]$$
$$\times\ \text{prob}\{\Delta V^* \text{ and } \Delta V^* - \alpha\Delta Y(\alpha) \text{ have opposite signs}\}.$$

The second term of (A3) is always nonpositive. Thus, $E[\Delta Y(\alpha)$ | transfer under PU]prob{transfer under PU} $> 0$ is sufficient to ensure that $\Delta G_N(\alpha) < 0$.

**Proof of Proposition 7**

*Necessary Condition.* Since the second term in (A3) is always nonpositive, a necessary condition for $\Delta G_N(\alpha)$ to be positive is that the first term is positive, that is, $E[\Delta Y(\alpha)$ | transfer under PU]prob{transfer under PU} $< 0$.

*Sufficient Condition.* Since the second term in (A1) is always nonnegative, $E[\Delta Y(\alpha) \mid \Delta V^* > 0]$ is sufficient to ensure that $\Delta G_N$ be positive.

## References


Barclay, M. J., and C. G. Holderness. 1991. Negotiated block trades and corporate control. *Journal of Finance* 46, no. 3:861–78.

Bebchuk, L. 1994. Efficient and inefficient sales of corporate control. *Quarterly Journal of Economics* 109:957–94.

———. 1999. A rent-protection theory of corporate ownership and control. NBER Working Paper no. 7203. Cambridge, Mass.: National Bureau of Economic Research.

Bebchuk, Lucian A., and Marcel Kahan. 1990. A framework for analyzing legal policy toward proxy contests. *California Law Review* 78, no. 5:1071–1135.

Bolton, P., and E. L. von Thadden. 1998. A dynamic theory of corporate structure. *Journal of Finance* 53, no. 1:1–25.

Burkart, M., D. Gromb, and F. Panunzi. 1997. Large shareholders, monitoring, and fiduciary duty. *Quarterly Journal of Economics* 112:693–728.

———. 1998. Why higher takeover premia protect minority shareholders. *Journal of Political Economy* 196:172–204.

Caprio, L., A. Floreani, and L. Radaelli. 1994. I trasferimenti del controllo di societa' quotate in Italia: Un' analisi empirica dei prezzi e dei risultati per gli azionisti di minoranza (Transfers of control of publicly traded companies in Italy: An empirical analysis of their impact on minority shareholders). Working paper. Universita' Cattolica, Department of Economics.

Demsetz, H. 1983. The structure of ownership and the theory of the firm. *Journal of Law and Economics* 26:375–93.

Grossman, S., and O. Hart. 1980. Takeover bids, the free rider problem, and the theory of the corporation. *Bell Journal of Economics* 11:42–69.

Holderness, C. G., and D. P. Sheehan. 1988. The role of majority shareholders in publicly held corporations: An exploratory analysis. *Journal of Financial Economics* 20:317–47.

Holmström, B., and J. Tirole. 1993. Market liquidity and performance monitoring. *Journal of Political Economy* 101:678–709.

Israel, R. 1992. Capital and ownership structures and the market for corporate control. *Review of Financial Studies* 5:181–98.

Jensen, M. C., and W. Meckling. 1976. Theory of the firm: Managerial behavior, agency costs, and capital structure. *Journal of Financial Economics* 3:305–60.

La Porta, R., F. Lopez-de-Silanes, A. Shleifer, and R. Vishny. 1997. Legal determinants of external finance. *Journal of Finance* 52, no. 3:1131–50.

Pagano, M. 1993. The flotation of companies on the stock market: A coordination failure model. *European Economic Review* 37:1011–1125.

Pagano, M., F. Panetta, and L. Zingales. 1998. Why do companies go public? An empirical analysis. *Journal of Finance* 53, no. 1:27–64.

Pagano, M., and A. Roell. 1998. The choice of stock ownership structure: Agency costs, monitoring, and liquidity. *Quarterly Journal of Economics* 113:187–225.

Ritter, J. R. 1987. The costs of going public. *Journal of Financial Economics* 19: 269–81.

Roe, Mark. 1994. *Strong managers, weak owners: The political roots of American corporate finance.* Princeton, N.J.: Princeton University Press.

Shleifer, A., and R. Vishny. 1986. Large shareholder and corporate control. *Journal of Political Economy* 94:461–88.
Zingales, L. 1994. The value of the voting right: A study of the Milan Stock Exchange. *Review of Financial Studies* 7:125–48.
———. 1995. Insider ownership and the decision to go public. *Review of Economic Studies* 62:425–48.

## Comment Merritt B. Fox

The ideal level of public ownership is determined by achieving the proper trade-off between private ownership's illiquidity and public ownership's agency costs of management. According to the traditional view, in a country with a highly developed capital market, such as the United States, each firm makes the socially optimal choice concerning its ownership structure. This is because its founding entrepreneur feels the full social effects of her choice when she decides what portion, if any, of her firm's shares should be sold to the public. In many other countries, however, institutional factors, such as weak legal protections for outside shareholders, limit the development of capital markets, and this in turn restricts entrepreneurial choice and results in too little public ownership.

In their paper, Lucian Bebchuk and Luigi Zingales enlarge our understanding of public versus private ownership by questioning this traditional view. They do so in the context of an entrepreneur's choice of ownership structure in a situation where, regardless of any public sale, she retains voting control of the firm during the current period but may sell this control at some point in the future. The paper makes three points of real importance to the study of both comparative corporate governance and transition economics. First, it shows that, under certain circumstances, a country with a highly developed capital market can have too much public ownership. This is because the entrepreneur's decision is distorted from a social point of view by the fact that, when a subsequent transfer of control increases the verifiable cash flow available to minority shareholders, these shareholders are the beneficiaries of a positive externality flowing from the transferee's improved management. Since the prospect of this externality increases share price at the time of the entrepreneur's initial public offering (IPO), the entrepreneur can capture a larger piece of the surplus generated by such a transfer by selling a larger portion of the firm at the time of the IPO.

Second, the paper shows how legal rules can affect this bias toward too

Merritt B. Fox is professor of law at the University of Michigan Law School. He is also co–area director for corporate governance at the William Davidson Institute at the University of Michigan Business School.

much public ownership. Specifically, an "equal opportunity" rule, whereby the acquirer of a control block must extend an offer at the same price to all shareholders, exacerbates the problem. The problem is also exacerbated by a legal structure that results in minority shareholders receiving, at the time of a freezeout by a new controlling shareholder, a premium for their shares above the value of these shares as pro rata claims on the firm's verifiable cash flows under the original entrepreneur's management.

Third, the paper enriches our understanding of the institutional factors that can lead to too little public ownership in countries with less well-developed capital markets. It is already well understood that weak protections for minority shareholders will have a negative effect on public ownership because fear that the entrepreneur will engage in such overreaching reduces the price at which shares can be sold. Bebchuk and Zingales, however, go beyond this usual analysis by considering the role of expectations concerning future control changes. Specifically, they show that, where the expected impact of a value-enhancing transfer of control on minority shareholders is negative (which is more likely to be the case in a country with weak minority shareholder protections), public ownership will occur even less often than has been previously understood. This is because, in such a situation, the transfer of control would on average create a negative externality on the minority shareholders. As a result, a lower level of public ownership will allow the entrepreneur to capture a larger share of the surplus created by the transfer and thus affect the division of rents between her and the transferee.

Bebchuk and Zingales's paper stimulates several observations, which are set out below. I parallel their notation throughout.

## The Welfare Effects of the Distortion

A closer examination of the social welfare effects of the distortion identified by Bebchuk and Zingales helps sharpen the policy implications of their analysis.

### A Simple One-Period Model with No Possibility of a Control Transfer

I start this examination by looking at a simple one-period model with no potential transfer of control. Thus, no potential for distortion exists. As in Bebchuk and Zingales's paper, the entrepreneur intends to keep voting control regardless of what ownership structure she chooses.

If the entrepreneur decides to keep the firm privately held (PR), that is, if $\alpha = 0$,

$$\text{(C1)} \qquad \mathrm{CE}(0) = S + Y(0) - D(0),$$

where CE($\alpha$) is the certainty equivalent value to the entrepreneur of the ownership structure she has chosen, $S$ is synergies and is not a function of $\alpha$ since the entrepreneur is assumed to retain voting control whatever $\alpha$ she chooses, $Y(\alpha)$ is identifiable cash flow available for pro rata distribution and is a negative function of $\alpha$, and $D(\alpha)$ is dollar measure of disutility from lack of diversification, which is also a negative function of $\alpha$.

If the entrepreneur decides to sell some of the firm's shares to the public, that is, if $\alpha > 0$,

$$\text{(C2)} \quad CE(\alpha) = S + R(\alpha) + (1 - \alpha)Y(\alpha) + \alpha Y(\alpha) - D(\alpha),$$

where $R(\alpha)$ is the "rip-off" factor (due to managerial shirking, direct diversions of cash flow and assets, and transactions in which management is interested), $R(\alpha)$ is a positive function of $\alpha$ (because the greater the public's share of identifiable cash flow, the less "rip-offs" involve just moving money from one of the entrepreneur's pockets to the other), and $\alpha Y(\alpha)$ is cash received from selling shares to the public. Equation (3) follows directly from equation (2):

$$\text{(C3)} \quad CE(\alpha) = S + \underbrace{\overset{+}{R(\alpha)} + \overset{-}{Y(\alpha)}}_{-} - \underbrace{D(\alpha)}_{+}.$$

As demonstrated by Jensen and Meckling (1976), the sum of $R(\alpha) + Y(\alpha)$ is a negative function of $\alpha$, reflecting the fact that reduction in verifiable income resulting from managerial rip-offs is greater than the utility that managers gain from these rip-offs. $D(\alpha)$, managerial disutility from lack of diversification, is also a negative function of $\alpha$ because the entrepreneur's sale of a larger portion of the firm's shares permits her to diversify a larger portion of her wealth. Thus, there is a trade-off between $R(\alpha) + Y(\alpha)$ and $D(\alpha)$. The entrepreneur maximizes her utility, represented by CE($\alpha$), by choosing $\alpha^*$, which optimizes this trade-off. The entrepreneur's choice is socially optimal because the investing public pays only for what it gets.

## The Consequences of Adding the Possibility of a Transfer of Control

Now introduce a second period and the possibility of a second owner. As Bebchuk and Zingales have shown, the initial entrepreneur will choose an $\alpha_1$ different from $\alpha^*$, and, because of this deviation, social welfare will not be maximized.

What are the consequences of this deviation? First, consider the first period. The effects of the deviation can be divided into its effect on the return on capital and its effect on the return on entrepreneurship. As for its effect on the return on capital, if $\alpha_1 > \alpha^*$, there is a bad trade-off between agency costs and diversification in the first period, resulting in $Y$

being below the optimal level. This lowers the return on capital and, hence, its supply. On the other hand, if $\alpha_1 < \alpha^*$, it raises $Y$ and actually increases return on capital. As for the effect of the deviation, first-period returns on entrepreneurship are diminished by a deviation in either direction since any deviation from $\alpha^*$ leads to an inefficient trade-off between diversification and agency costs. This, however, will be more than compensated for by the entrepreneur's gain in the second period because of the increased portion of second owners' rents that entrepreneurs capture.

Next consider the consequences of the deviation in the second period. Returns on capital are hurt by a deviation either way from $\alpha^*$. Some transfers that would decrease $Y$ will go through. Some transfers that would increase $Y$ will be blocked. The deviation increases the returns to entrepreneurship since it permits entrepreneurs to capture more of the potential control purchaser's rents. For the same reason, returns to being a potential control purchaser are hurt by the deviation.

### Policy Implications

This analysis has several policy implications. We may believe, for example, that entrepreneurship and second ownership are relatively inelastically supplied, that capital is relatively more elastically supplied, but that the amount of capital supplied in the economy is, for other reasons, suboptimal (i.e., that capital formation needs to be encouraged). In that case, we should be particularly concerned with a deviation if we think that $\alpha_1 > \alpha^*$ (i.e., that $\Delta G$ is negative) since that would lower the supply of capital. We should not be as concerned if $\alpha_1 < \alpha^*$ since that would increase the supply of capital without promoting significant other distortions in the economy. Thus, if we are somewhat uncertain as to whether $\alpha_1$ is greater than or less than $\alpha^*$, we should err on the side of a policy that discourages PU; that is, we should favor a policy that tends to reduce $\alpha_1$. On the other hand, we may believe that capital and second ownership are relatively inelastically supplied and that it is entrepreneurship that is both relatively more elastically supplied and, for other reasons, undersupplied. In that event, a deviation in either direction should not bother us since allowing the deviation increases the rents available to entrepreneurs, thus prompting an increase in the amount of entrepreneurship supplied, without promoting serious other distortions in the economy.

## Do $\Delta Y$ and $\Delta V$ Have the Same Sign?[1]

Bebchuk and Zingales state: "Another scenario in which the conditions of this proposition are likely to hold is that in which the differences among

1. $\Delta Y$ is the change in $Y$ from a sale of control, and $\Delta V$ is the difference between the value of controlling the firm to the control purchaser and that value to the entrepreneur.

the private benefits of different controlling shareholders are small. In this . . . case, an acquirer with a higher $V$ will also have a higher $Y$. Thus, in countries where the private benefits of control tend to be small (as they are in the United States), the distortion is likely to be in the direction of excessive PU" (section 2.3.2). The first two sentences are clearly true. As for the third sentence, however, all we really know is the status of the United States *relative to other countries*—that the private benefits from control are smaller in the United States than they are in other countries. We do not know that in the United States they are small *relative to* $V$. Yet it is the smallness of private benefits relative to $V$ that is necessary for the conclusion in the third sentence to follow. This observation is important because Bebchuk and Zingales's suggestion that the United States has too much public ownership rests on the assumption that $\Delta Y$ and $\Delta V$ have the same sign (see their proposition 4).

## Is $\Delta Y$ Positive?

Bebchuk and Zingales's proposition 6 shows that a sufficient condition for $\Delta G_N$ to be negative and hence for there to be a distortion in favor of PU is that the expected effect of a transfer of control on minority shareholders be positive. They conclude that this is the case in the United States. They base this conclusion on Barclay and Holderness (1991), which shows abnormal positive returns to changes in ownership blocks. Barclay and Holderness's study forms an uncertain foundation for such a conclusion. After all, their findings could well be the result of signaling. Outsiders might conclude from a control buyer's interest in the stock that they had previously underestimated $Y$, whoever might be in control. This seems quite possible given that much of the actual effect of changes in ownership on $Y$ would be anticipated in price well prior to the actual announcement of a control-transfer transaction.

## The Desirability of an Equal Opportunity Rule

In the extensions to their analysis, the authors consider the desirability of an equal opportunity rule whereby the acquirer of a control block is required to extend an offer at the same price to all shareholders. They conclude that such a rule would be bad policy in the United States, where they assume that $\Delta G < 0$. They show that an equal opportunity rule would increase $\alpha$ and thus, when $\Delta G < 0$, increase the deviation from social optimality.

It is worth noting, however, that, whatever the situation in the United States, an equal opportunity rule might be good for another country. This is because, in other countries, $\Delta G$ may be greater than zero since $\Delta Y$ and $\Delta V$ may have opposite signs. This is likely to happen where private benefits for control are large and thus, relative to $V$, vary more from one owner to another.

## Multiple-Period, Multiple-Owner Extension

Suppose that liquidation is many years off, that there will be several controlling owners, and that the discount rate is positive. Working back, starting with the penultimate owner, each owner would want to have $\alpha > \alpha^*$ in order to try to capture the rents of the owner after him. The deviations each period may be quite small, however, given that current-period efficiency must be traded off against gains that, at least in part, are far in the future. This raises the possibility that the problem of too much public ownership may not be of large magnitude.

## Extension: Freezeout by First Owner and Appraisal

Bebchuk and Zingales suggest that the tendency toward too much public ownership would be solved by a combination of giving the entrepreneur, prior to a control sale, a right to freeze out minority shareholders at a price equaling $Y_I$ (the verifiable cash flow available for pro rata distribution with the firm under the incumbent entrepreneur's management) and giving the shareholders appraisal rights at the same price. Their concern is that there might be a predictable bias by the courts in estimating $Y_I$. Such a bias, however, could be corrected by a change in the legal standard. The more interesting issue is the effect of uncertainty concerning this estimate even if the estimate is expected to be unbiased since courts will inevitably be uncertain in their estimates.

## References

Barclay, M. J., and C. G. Holderness. 1991. Negotiated block trades and corporate control. *Journal of Finance* 46, no. 3:861–78.

Jensen, M. C., and W. Meckling. 1976. Theory of the firm: Managerial behavior, agency costs, and capital structure. *Journal of Financial Economics* 3:305–60.

3

# Some of the Causes and Consequences of Corporate Ownership Concentration in Canada

Ronald J. Daniels and Edward M. Iacobucci

The June 1997 edition of *Canadian Business* ranks the top ten Canadian corporations in terms of growth. It states of its number-one performer, the Goldfarb Corporation, "Goldfarb's expansion strategy is founded on a few basic principles: First, look to invest in global companies. . . . *Second, own more than 50% of the company in order to consolidate and control the business.* Last, use Goldfarb's own marketing expertise." It states of its number-three performer, on the other hand, "Question: What turns a $395-million pipeline company into a $2.5 billion powerhouse in just three years? Answer: *losing the majority shareholder.* Ever since Olympia and York Developments Ltd. sold its 65% stake in IPL Energy Inc. of Calgary in 1992, IPL has grown with a vengeance. Instead of maximizing dividend payouts to satisfy cash-hungry O&Y, it has focused on expansion" ("Performance 500, Top 10" 1997, 137, 141; emphasis added). Mere pages apart, the magazine partially credits majority ownership with driving a successful company and blames majority ownership for restraining the performance of a potentially successful company. As this paper will discuss, there may be some truth to both opinions.

At least since the time of Adam Smith, commentators have expressed concern about the effect of separating those who own a corporation from those who manage it, an effect resulting from the adoption of a widely held ownership structure (Smith 1937, 700; Berle and Means 1933). The suggested problem is that, if those who manage do not have a personal

Ronald J. Daniels is dean of the Faculty of Law, University of Toronto. Edward M. Iacobucci is assistant professor of law at the Faculty of Law, University of Toronto.

The authors are grateful for comments from conference and preconference participants. Particular thanks are owed to George Triantis for his many helpful comments.

interest in the returns generated by the firm's assets, those assets will be utilized in a way that may be beneficial to the manager but not to the owners.

Berle and Means (1933), however, were more pessimistic, predicting not only that corporations not owned by their managers would underperform corporations owned by managers but also that these widely held corporations would eventually become the norm in developing industrial economies. The argument was simple. As an economy grows and firms strive for scale economies, entrepreneur-managers are not capable of raising money to finance the firm's growth on their own and thus are compelled to go to equity markets to finance expansion. In repeatedly going to equity markets, of course, the entrepreneur eventually loses control of the firm. Because of the unceasing demand for capital in a rapidly industrializing society, the economy will in time largely comprise widely held corporations, which, given their inadequate governance by disinterested managers, does not bode well for the efficiency of the economy.

It is apparent, however, that Berle and Means overstated the likelihood of an economy replete with widely held firms. While the widely held corporation is indeed the norm in the United States, firms controlled by very few shareholders remain predominant in other industrialized countries, such as Germany, Japan, and Canada. In Canada, for example, Morck and Stangeland (1994) report that just under 16 percent of the 550 largest corporations in Canada in 1989 were widely held in the sense that no single shareholder owned more than 20 percent of outstanding voting stock. Using the same definition, Demsetz and Lehn (1985) had found earlier that almost 50 percent of the largest 511 corporations in the United States were widely held.

We first provide a brief outline of the literature on corporate governance and ownership concentration.[1] Next, we examine legal issues that, as a positive matter, may have contributed to the concentrated ownership structure in Canada. We then examine the normative implications of these causal relations.

## 3.1 Concentration of Ownership and Corporate Governance

### 3.1.1 Problems with the Widely Held Corporation

The fundamental concern about the widely held corporation is that, since the manager has only an attenuated interest in the profits generated by the firm, she will act not to maximize those profits but rather to maximize her own private utility. The manager may not work hard (she may "shirk"), may divert corporate resources to herself (perhaps by overcon-

1. Much of the outline draws on Daniels and Halpern (1996).

suming material perquisites), or may otherwise invest corporate resources poorly (perhaps by investing to avoid risky undertakings that, even though they may be profitable, may endanger the risk-averse manager's job).

Jensen and Meckling (1976) formally developed a theory of the firm based on Berle and Means's (1933) concern about the separation of ownership and control. Clearly, one way to reduce the conflicts of interest between the shareholders and the managers—conflicts that lead to agency costs—is to increase the proportion of shares in the firm held by the manager. As the manager's interest in the firm's performance increases because of his increased shareholding, he is less likely to manage the corporation suboptimally. Other sources of disciplinary control over managers include takeovers and the market for corporate control (Manne 1965), executive compensation, product market discipline (Hart 1983), the managerial labor market (Fama 1980), and such outside stakeholders as creditors.[2] Finally, by establishing disclosure obligations or fiduciary duties, the law itself may exert pressure on managers.

### 3.1.2 Problems with Concentrated Ownership

If the only agency concern relevant to corporate governance were the divergence of interest between managers and nonmanagerial shareholders, an increase in managerial ownership would be an unambiguous boon to corporate efficiency. As the divergence in interest between managers and share owners is reduced, agency costs are reduced. As more recent scholarship has suggested, however, as ownership becomes more concentrated, countervailing pressures indicate that an overall reduction of agency costs will not necessarily result.

A manager will engage in undesirable agency behavior if the private benefits exceed the private costs of doing so. Increased concentration of ownership may lower the private costs of undesirable agency behavior, thus perhaps increasing the likelihood of managerial self-indulgence. The private costs of managerial diversion include the opportunity costs to the manager resulting from the suboptimal use of corporate resources, costs that increase as managerial ownership of the firm increases. This is Jensen and Meckling's (1976) line of argument. However, private costs also comprise any disciplinary costs that result from suboptimal management. These disciplinary costs will likely decrease as ownership increases, for two principal reasons related to the entrenchment of the controlling shareholder. First, as equity control increases, the controlling shareholder exerts greater control over the board of directors, thus increasing the likelihood of translation of its wishes into action and reducing the likelihood of disci-

2. For an overview of the issues related to executive compensation, see Iacobucci and Trebilcock (1996). For an overview of the relation between corporate governance and debt, see Triantis (1996) and Triantis and Daniels (1995).

pline from the board. Second, sources of discipline other than ownership, such as the market for corporate control (Stulz 1988), may be attenuated by increased managerial ownership.[3] If the private costs of managerial self-indulgence fall as ownership concentration rises, increased concentration may encourage agency problems between the controlling shareholder(s) and the minority shareholders.

#### 3.1.3 Evidence of Ownership Concentration and Performance

While a complete survey is beyond the scope of this paper, suffice it to say that the ambiguity of the theory of the effects of increased concentration is reflected in the empirical evidence.[4] Some studies have shown a curvilinear relation between concentration and ownership: as ownership concentration rises from very low levels, firm performance improves, but, as ownership continues to rise, firm performance falls off.[5] Other studies have indicated that the effect of concentration of share ownership on firm performance is negligible.[6] Still others have found a significant negative correlation between performance and concentrated ownership.[7]

### 3.2 The Determinants of Concentrated Ownership

Commentators have offered a variety of suggestions about the determinants of ownership concentration. Some have theorized that the economic nature of the particular firm may be a significant factor in determining ownership concentration. For example, Demsetz and Lehn (1985) contend

3. In Canada, where corporate shareholding concentration is high, there is empirical support for the claim that concentrated ownership reduces the likelihood of a hostile takeover. Of the 1,148 Canadian merger-and-acquisition transactions in the Venture database in 1989, only 7 resulted in management resistance or in the making of a competitive bid (Daniels and MacIntosh 1991, 889).

4. For a more complete survey of recent empirical studies, see Daniels and Halpern (1996).

5. Morck, Shleifer, and Vishny (1988), e.g., found that, as concentration continues to rise to very high levels, firm performance (as measured by Tobin's *Q*) eventually improves. An explanation for this result is that, once entrenchment is complete, increased ownership serves only to better align managerial and shareholder interests.

6. See, e.g., Jog and Tulpule (1996). Rao and Lee-Sing (1996) found that corporate concentration and performance were not correlated in Canada but that a weak, negative correlation existed in the United States. MacIntosh and Schwartz (1996) found ambiguous evidence: firms that had controlling shareholders had higher returns on assets and equity, no discernible effect on sales growth, and lower price-to-book ratios. Demsetz and Lehn (1985) found no correlation between concentrated managerial ownership and financial performance. Holderness and Sheehan (1988) found that performance as measured by Tobin's *Q* did not differ significantly between a sample of firms with a shareholder holding between 50 and 95 percent of equity and a matched sample of firms with diffuse holdings. They did find, however, that, if the control block was held by an individual as opposed to a corporation, performance as measured by Tobin's *Q* was lower than that of firms in the control group, although the difference was not significant.

7. Slovin and Sushka (1993), e.g., found that, when a CEO or founder with a significant shareholding died, there was, on average, a positive, abnormal return, a result consistent with entrenchment.

that share ownership concentration is positively related to the volatility of a firm's cash flow and the size of the firm. As cash-flow volatility rises, outside monitors cannot discern whether the managers or outside factors have determined firm performance. Inside monitoring by large shareholders attenuates this problem and reduces agency costs accordingly. As firm size increases, Demsetz and Lehn also argue, the price of a given fraction of equity rises, which reduces ownership concentration. While these and other factors may indeed be important in determining the structure of ownership, in this section we review various aspects of the Canadian legal regime that may help explain the concentrated nature of corporate ownership in that country. While we do not engage in rigorous testing of the hypotheses, we note some relevant empirical evidence.

### 3.2.1 Restrictions on Investment by Financial Intermediaries

Roe offers a political theory explaining concentration levels in the United States (Roe 1991, 1994). He suggests that political pressure from interest groups, such as small banks, combined with a general distrust of concentrated economic power, gave rise in the United States to laws designed to diminish the ability of large capital pools to invest in the equity of American corporations. Concentrated corporate ownership was correspondingly diminished: those entities controlling asset pools large enough to obtain control of corporations were legally prevented from doing so. Berle and Means's vision of an economy controlled by widely held firms emerged, not as an inevitable result of the economy's growth and economic forces, but as the result of political populism.

If Roe's theory correctly captures the American experience, then, but for the legal restrictions, American corporations would be owned by financial intermediaries controlling large pools of capital. If America's corporations would be widely held in any event, then the financial restrictions were not responsible. Thus, a prediction that one could infer from Roe's theory is that, in countries with a liberal legal attitude toward investment by financial intermediaries, ownership structure is more likely to be concentrated.

In Canada, the rules governing investment in corporate equity by banks have in fact been liberal. The first piece of general banking legislation in Canada contained no quantity restrictions on the holding of shares by banks but did provide that banks could not "either directly or indirectly . . . engage in any trade whatever . . . except in such trade generally as pertains to the business of banking."[8] While such a provision certainly could have been interpreted to limit the ability of banks to invest in corporate equity, courts have taken a liberal approach in interpreting the bounds

8. Bank Act, S.C., 1871, chap. 5, sec. 40. A similar limitation exists today: see S.C., chap. 46, sec. 409.

of "the business of banking." In *White et al. v. Bank of Toronto et al.*, for example, the Ontario Court of Appeal held that there was nothing in the Bank Act

> to suggest that a bank may not "deal in" the stock of its corporate debtor just as freely as it might deal in the stock of a corporation not its debtor or, for that matter in the bonds of the Dominion of Canada. . . . The conduct of modern business inevitably leads to an infinite variety of situations not the least complicated of which may occur in the carrying on in this country "of such business generally as appertains to the business of banking" and it seems to me that this has been recognized throughout the numerous decennial revisions of the Bank Act by the use of broad and general terms in describing what a bank may do.[9]

At the very least, banks were permitted to invest in corporations of which they were creditors, ostensibly in order to protect their investment in the debt rather than to make a profit on the security itself (Baxter 1968, 198). It was not until 1967 that quantitative restrictions on banks' equity investments were implemented.[10]

Thus, Canada was a country that did not place significant limitations on the ability of its banks to invest in Canadian equity. If Roe is right that such legal limitations contributed to widely held corporate ownership structures in the United States, then perhaps the absence of such limitations in Canada would have invited bank investment and more concentrated ownership.

Canada certainly does have more concentrated ownership, but, historically, banks' equity investments have not been significant. The level of securities held by Canadian banks as a percentage of total assets was around 7 percent in 1926, 7 percent in 1935, 5 percent in 1955, 5 percent in 1965, and 6.0 percent in 1980 (Daniels and Halpern 1996, 34).[11] In the 1990s, this level has not exceeded 1.5 percent (MacIntosh 1996, 181). Various explanations have been offered for this low level of investment by banks. Neufeld (1972, 113) claims that the disinterest in equity arose because of the need for large-scale government financing during the wars and the depression and because of losses suffered by the banks from financing railways. Jamieson (1953, 134–37) concludes that concern for stability and liquidity led banks to invest in government debt rather than corporate equity. Niosi (1982, chap. 1) claims that the inculcation of British financial practices in Canadian bankers led Canadian banks to place a premium on traditional debt financing rather than equity investment.

9. *White et al. v. Bank of Toronto et al.*, [1953] 3 D.L.R. 118 (Ont. C.A.), 125.

10. A change that followed the recommendations of the Royal Commission on Banking and Finance (1964).

11. As indicators of banks' investment in corporate equity, these figures are biased upward, given that they do not discriminate between corporate equities and other types of securities, such as municipal securities and corporate bonds and debentures.

For whatever reason, Canadian banks did not invest significantly in corporate equity. This observation may cast doubt on Roe's explanation of the American experience: in Canada, in any event, the absence of legal restrictions in the United States may not have had the binding effect that Roe ascribes to them. More germane to the present analysis, the legal differences between the United States and Canada with respect to rules governing banks' investments do not appear to have contributed to the concentration of ownership in Canada since banks were not the source of capital that allowed firms to grow while maintaining concentrated ownership structures.

A similar conclusion applies with respect to equity investment by insurance companies. In 1868, federal law treated investment by insurance companies as a matter to be set out in the companies' corporate charters,[12] and, in 1899, the statute was amended to permit all life insurance companies to invest in securities. In 1910, the Insurance Act limited equity investment to a maximum of 30 percent of any single firm—and then only if the firm met a seven-year dividend test of at least 4 percent.[13] Following the market crash of 1929, restrictions were tightened, limiting equity investment to 15 percent of total investments (Royal Commission on Banking and Finance 1964, 249). In 1965, the restrictions were relaxed again, and the limit became 25 percent of total investments.[14]

While the legal restrictions have varied over time, observers suggest that they were rarely binding, at least during the postwar period. Insurance companies had suffered significant losses during the depression and were also concerned about meeting regulatory liquidity standards (Hood and Main 1956, 478). Total industry investment in equity stood at about 3 percent of the value of the portfolio in 1964, and this did not change significantly with the introduction of the 25 percent rule in 1965, investment rising only to 5 percent by 1968. In more recent times, this percentage has remained well below the legal limit, at around 10 percent in the 1980s and up to 1991, although jumping to 19.7 percent in 1992 (MacIntosh 1996, 182).

While the experience with insurance investment has been more ambiguous than that with bank investment, it supports the conclusion that, over the years, "the traditional picture of Canadian finance, one of abstention [by Canadian financial intermediaries] from the founding, reorganization and control of non-financial corporations, has remained unchanged" (Niosi 1982, 63). The cause of concentrated ownership in Canada is unlikely to be found in the legal regime governing the investment portfolios of financial intermediaries.

12. An Act Respecting Insurance Companies, S.C. 1868, chap. 48.

13. Insurance Act, 1910, R.S.C., chap. 32, sec. 59.

14. An Act to Amend Certain Acts Administered in the Department of Insurance, S.C. 1964–65, chap. 40, sec. 5(9).

### 3.2.2 Banking Regulations

Canadian banks faced regulations that differed from those faced by American banks in other ways that may have contributed to a lower cost of debt for Canadian corporations and therefore allowed firm growth to rely more on debt than equity financing. There are at least two relevant differences in Canadian banking regulations. First, entry into banking in Canada is difficult. Under the Bank Act, only eight "Schedule I" banks are presently permitted to carry on business as full-service banks.[15] Second, Canadian banks are permitted to carry on business throughout Canada, without regard to provincial boundaries.[16] These rules imply that Canadian banks are large relative to the economy. In 1984, for example, there were 7,547 bank branches in Canada, with the 5 largest banks having over 1,000 branches each (Shearer, Chant, and Bond 1984, 225). In contrast, in the United States, there were 15,000 separate banks with a total of 39,000 branches, or an average of 2.6 branches per bank (Shearer, Chant, and Bond 1984, 225).

It may be that the structure of Canadian banking that resulted from these rules led to efficiencies in providing debt financing (Daniels and Halpern 1996). Canadian banks faced economies in monitoring that American banks, fettered by such restrictions on growth as limitations on interstate banking, did not realize. The large absolute size of Canadian banks permitted the spreading of the fixed costs of monitoring over a larger number of transactions. Moreover, the small number of banks in Canada enhanced the information supply among banks there, lowering screening and monitoring costs. On top of these economies relative to American banking, the law in Canada permitted greater bank input in the affairs of a borrower in financial distress. For example, Canadian courts have yet to embrace the doctrine of equitable subordination,[17] which allows courts to subordinate a lender's claims if the lender uses its control over the borrower to obtain an advantage at the expense of other creditors.[18] Given the lower costs to Canadian banks resulting from these differences, it may be that firm growth in the Canadian economy was permitted through debt financing to a greater extent than it was in the United States, a consequence of which was the maintenance of high-equity ownership concentration.

Cutting against the banking efficiency explanation of ownership con-

15. Bank Act (n. 3 above), sec. 14.

16. Ibid., sec. 15.

17. In *Canada Deposit Insurance Corp. v. Canadian Commercial Bank,* [1992] 3 S.C.R. 558, the Supreme Court of Canada expressly declined to consider whether the doctrine of equitable subordination exists in Canada.

18. For example, *In re American Lumber Co. v. Bergquist,* 5 Bankr. 470 (D. Minn. 1980) (equitable subordination applied to creditor who received new security interests in inventory and equipment from distressed borrower).

centration in Canada is the possibility that the same regulations that led to large banks in absolute and relative terms, and thus lower costs, may also have led to market power. With such high barriers to entry and so few significant Canadian banks, it may have been that, even if debt was less costly to the banks, an absence of competition prevented prices on debt to firms from being below those prevailing in the United States.

If it is true that efficiencies in Canadian banking relative to banking in the United States led to a lower cost of debt to firms and thus contributed to the concentration of ownership there, then Canadian firms would historically have had a higher debt-to-equity ratio than their American counterparts. We do not have any definitive empirical evidence that would allow us to answer this question.[19]

### 3.2.3 Protectionism

Historically, Canada has erected barriers to the free movement of goods and capital across its borders. Both these types of barriers may have contributed to the concentration of Canadian ownership.

A particularly relevant capital restriction penalized Canadian investment portfolios that had over 10 percent of their value in foreign assets.[20] Such a restriction may have given Canadian issuers market power[21] that allowed them to finance growth without relinquishing control (Daniels and Halpern 1996). For example, in the absence of market power, it may be that the sale of minority equity under a concentrated ownership structure that allows significant transfers of wealth from minority shareholders to the controller will fail to raise sufficient capital for a liquidity-constrained entrepreneur to finance a particular investment. On the other hand, in the presence of market power, investors may accept the lower returns associated with entrenchment, and sufficient funds will be available despite the risk of transfers. While we cannot explain why firms would prefer to take a discount on the shares from adopting an inefficient ownership structure, if the firms chose to do so, some degree of market power may have allowed liquidity-constrained firms to raise sufficient capital for a particular project despite an inefficient structure. Perhaps as evidence of this phenomenon, firms in Canada have often adopted dual class share structures, which, by concentrating control in a small minority of shares, are known to have significant potential for agency problems between the controlling shareholders and the noncontrolling shareholders.[22]

19. Preliminary work in comparative international capital structures does not reveal significant differences in firm leverage across the G7 (Rajan and Zingales 1994).

20. There were tax consequences with respect to retirement savings if a portfolio had over 10 percent of its assets in foreign investments (An Act to Amend the Income Tax Act, S.C. 1970–71–72, chap. 63, sec. 206). Since 1991, the threshold is 20 percent.

21. That is, the ability to earn supracompetitive returns when issuing equity.

22. As of December 1987, companies listing restricted shares constituted 15 percent of the total number of companies listed on the Toronto Stock Exchange (TSE) (Amoako-Adu, Smith, and Schnabel 1990, 39).

Canada has also historically imposed significant trade barriers. These may have had several effects on industry conducive to concentrated ownership. First, tariffs may have helped keep firms small given the relatively small size of the Canadian economy and the restriction of international trade (Harris 1984; Eastman and Stykolt 1967). As Demsetz and Lehn (1985) point out, the smaller a firm is, the lower the cost of a control block and thus the greater the likelihood of concentrated ownership. Thus, by fostering small firms, tariffs may have contributed to concentrated ownership.

Second, to circumvent the high tariffs on trade with Canada, foreign firms often established partially owned subsidiaries in Canada. Rather than owning these firms outright, which would have led to private companies, not to concentrated ownership structures in the sense of controlling and minority shareholders, the foreign firms had tax incentives to sell part of their equity to Canadians. For example, in the 1963 budget, withholding taxes on dividends were lower if Canadians owned at least 25 percent of the voting shares of a company (Daniels and Halpern 1996, 42). These incentives, along with the tariff barriers, may have contributed to the concentrated nature of Canadian corporate ownership.

A third reason why trade barriers may have led to increased concentration relates to market power. By limiting foreign competition, tariff barriers discouraged the development of competitive markets in Canada (Harris 1984; Eastman and Stykolt 1967). We argue in more detail in the next section that market power may contribute to concentrated ownership.

### 3.2.4 Market Power

There are two significant ways in which Canadian law has fostered the growth of market power[23] in its economy. First, Canada has historically been protectionist. The National Policy of 1879 established high tariffs and thus significant barriers to entry into the Canadian market for foreign producers, and tariffs since then have continued to protect Canadian firms from foreign competition (Harris 1984; Eastman and Stykolt 1967). Obviously, the 1989 Free Trade Agreement with the United States and successor agreements considerably opened trade and the likelihood of competition. Second, while a competition policy regime has been in place since 1889, the regime was virtually ineffective until the Competition Act of 1986.

The possible connections between market power and concentrated ownership are complex. Rather than viewing market power as a cause of concentrated ownership, a possibility that we discuss shortly, Morck has suggested that concentrated corporate ownership may lead to market power because of political rent seeking (Morck 1996). If the benefits exceed the

23. That is, the ability of firms to earn supracompetitive returns in their product markets.

costs, firms will lobby politicians to erect barriers to entry and other impediments to competition in order to increase their market power. Morck provides two reasons why firms with concentrated ownership are lower-cost rent seekers and, therefore, why they are more likely to have market power. First, more narrowly held firms may be able to operate in greater secrecy than their widely held counterparts. Second, the managers of narrowly held firms may be less likely to be terminated and therefore better able to repay politicians or bureaucrats in exchange for the erection of impediments to competition.

We are skeptical of Morck's claims.[24] Secrecy may or may not be important to rent seeking. For example, a corporation may wish to establish a reputation of reliably returning favors. On the other hand, a politician may want secrecy in order to preserve a reputation of integrity, but this will not always be true. For instance, a politician may wish to take public credit if the corporation promises to build a factory in her jurisdiction in exchange for an entry barrier. Even if secrecy is important, however, it is unclear how significant an advantage concentrated public firms have in this regard. Disclosure rules, such as in the case of campaign contributions, will publicize both a concentrated and a widely held firm's rent-seeking efforts equally. To the extent that public disclosure is not required, there may be a secrecy benefit for *privately* held firms that do not have to hold public meetings or issue annual reports, but it may not be significantly easier to keep secrets as ownership concentration increases in public corporations.

With respect to Morck's second point, it is not clear that managers of more narrowly held firms are more secure in their positions. Where the controlling shareholder and managers are different people, it may be that management has less security of tenure than at a widely held firm. Rational apathy on the part of shareholders may protect managers at a widely held firm from termination, while managers subject to intense monitoring by a controlling shareholder do not have such protection.

In any event, even if the threat of termination shortens significantly the widely held firm's horizons for rent seeking, it is unclear whether politicians and bureaucrats, who are subject to the whims of the political process, have particularly long horizons themselves. It strikes us as plausible to assume that rent-seeking deals are struck with a view to forthright consummation.

In our view, there may be a difference with respect to the *benefits* of rent seeking that establish ownership concentration as a potential cause of market power. As outlined above, control blocks of equity may give

24. We do, however, accept Morck's premise that rent seeking is an important determinant of market outcomes. For a thoughtful expression of reservations about the importance of rent seeking in practice in recent years, see Trebilcock (1999).

their owners the opportunity to realize a disproportionate share of the firm's profits. The controller will undertake an investment if the private benefits to it exceed the total costs, costs that are shared by both the controller and the minority shareholders. If the controller has an interest in activities outside the firm (such as ownership stakes in other firms) that could benefit from a particular form of rent seeking, it may use the firm's resources to invest in this rent seeking even if the total private benefits of the rent seeking are less than the total costs. The controller's interests outside the firm imply that it realizes a disproportionate share of the private benefits of rent seeking, while the costs are shared with the firm's shareholders.

Thus, as compared to a shareholder who has significant holdings but who is not entrenched, an entrenched controlling shareholder may invest more in rent seeking; rent seeking itself is an agency problem between the minority and the controller. Because of this agency behavior by the controlling shareholder, concentrated ownership may give rise to market power.

While ownership concentration may have an effect on market power, there is also a possibility that market power may have an effect on ownership concentration. The simple reason for this is that, as market power and the future profits from an enterprise rise, a lower degree of outside financing is required. In what follows, we assume, following Myers and Majluf (1984), that there is asymmetric information between a firm's insiders and outside investors. There is some information that is difficult to convey to the market, such as the ability of management, and there is an adverse selection problem about unobservable information: outsiders discount the likely prospects of the firm.

With market power and higher profits, firms may be able to finance future investment out of retained earnings. Because of asymmetric information between insiders and outside investors, such retained earnings may entail a lower cost of capital and thus may be the capital source of choice (Myers and Majluf 1984). Profitable firms—firms with market power—are better able to finance investment without selling equity. Hence, firms with market power are more likely to retain a concentrated ownership structure than competitive firms given that the former do not have to use outside financing to the same extent. Another reason why firms with market power may have more concentrated ownership is that a firm with prospects for significant profits is able to raise a given amount of capital selling a relatively low percentage of its total shares when it does go to equity markets. If an asymmetric information problem exists, therefore, market power and higher profits are likely to be correlated with a greater degree of ownership concentration.[25]

25. In his comment on our paper, George Triantis rightly points out that, by treating the cash available to the corporation as a function of market power, we do not account for the

To summarize, market power, ownership concentration, and the law are related in the following ways. Ownership concentration may encourage rent seeking, which may result in laws encouraging market power, such as tariffs. Laws that encourage market power by definition give rise to market power, which in turn may give rise to ownership concentration by allowing firms to minimize outside financing. These effects are reinforcing, solidifying the relation between ownership concentration, market power, and the law.[26]

### 3.2.5 Rigidity in Ownership Structure and the Equal Opportunity Rule

There may be rigidity in a concentrated ownership structure that heightens concern about inefficiently concentrated ownership structures. Even if it is efficient to evolve to a less concentrated ownership structure and the parties know that it is efficient to do so, once in place, an inefficiently concentrated ownership structure may be difficult to change. The law in Canada may exacerbate the problem by adherence to an "equal opportunity rule." We first explain the rigidity phenomenon and then review the legal problem.

By definition, there would be gains from lowering the concentration of an inefficiently concentrated firm: agency costs would be lower. However, even assuming now that there is no asymmetric information between the firm and outsiders (as in the previous section), the following factors may conspire to prevent the realization of those gains. First, the controlling shareholder realizes a disproportionate return to its shares as a result of agency behavior.[27] Second, minority shareholders and the controlling shareholder could collectively benefit from deconcentration and need each other to accomplish those gains; thus, the surplus from lowering agency costs will likely be shared between the controlling shareholder and the minority shareholders. Given these two factors, the controlling shareholder will require compensation for the private losses to it from forgone control benefits and will also likely require a share of the surplus created

prospect that cash flow itself may cause agency problems and lower profits. This is analytically similar to the problem we do address: concentrated ownership may itself cause agency problems. While reducing concentrated ownership through equity sales and reducing free cash flow through debt issuance may both reduce agency problems, asymmetric information may deter such sales in either case—the information discount may dominate the losses from agency costs.

26. There is evidence from Canada that is at least not inconsistent with the conjecture that competition-promoting policies will lower the concentration of ownership. While competition policy has existed in Canada for over a century, it was largely ineffective until the passage of the Competition Act in 1986. Moreover, in 1989, Canada entered into the Free Trade Agreement with the United States. Defining widely held firms as those with a float percentage above 90 percent, we find that the number of widely held firms on the TSE 300 has indeed risen since these competition-promoting developments. In December 1988, 29.0 percent of firms on the TSE 300 were widely held; in December 1997, 65.7 percent of firms were widely held.

27. Since the agency behavior is inefficient, however, the control benefits to the majority are smaller than the costs of these benefits to the minority.

by the deconcentration (the surplus being the recovered deadweight losses). If they could act as a collective unit, the minority shareholders could compensate the controller and still profit since the gains from deconcentration exceed the losses. However, there will likely be a significant collective action problem.

If concentration is excessive, deconcentration is a public good: all minority shareholders benefit from lower agency costs. Given this factor and the controlling shareholder's demand for a share of the surplus as well as compensation for lost control benefits, a minority shareholder is best off when it does not buy any of the controller's shares but the other minority shareholders collectively act to purchase some of the controller's shares. Since each minority shareholder is best off when the others act to purchase the shares, the purchase may not occur even though it is efficient. Once established, a concentrated ownership structure may be difficult to change even though it is efficient to do so and the parties know that it is efficient to do so.[28]

The law in Canada, exemplified by the law in Ontario, may compound the rigidity problem in the following respects. Section 1 of the Ontario Securities Act provides that the sale of any shares by a shareholder with sufficient holdings materially to affect control of the corporation, or, in any event, holding 20 percent or more of the voting securities of the corporation, is defined to be a "distribution." Under part 15 of the Ontario Securities Act, any trade that is a distribution must be accompanied by a prospectus. The sale of part of a control block in order to bring about lower concentration of ownership may be in part discouraged by the transactions costs that are particular only to control-block transactions.

Another potential legal impediment to efficient deconcentration is that Ontario courts and statutes have frowned on the payment of a premium to controlling shareholders when they sell part of their control blocks. In *Re CTC Dealer Holdings Ltd. and Ontario Securities Commission,* a corporation had a dual class share structure: there were about 3.5 million common shares with voting rights and about 80 million outstanding "class A" shares that did not have voting rights.[29] There was a "coattail" provision

28. The collective action problem described here is similar to that described by Grossman and Hart (1980) in the takeover context: shareholders subject to a takeover bid are best off if other shareholders tender into the bid. The problem of compensation for control benefits impeding efficient deconcentration is similar to Bebchuk's (1994) analysis of inefficiencies in the sale of corporate control. Bebchuk points out that an efficient sale of control may not take place if the potential buyer is unable to compensate the target's current owner for the lost benefits of private control; even a buyer that could increase the value of the firm may not buy it. The problem that we point out assumes that the buyer of part of control, the minority shareholders, could, acting collectively, compensate the controller for the lost benefits of private control and still profit from the increased value of the firm, but a collective action problem prevents them from doing so.

29. *Re CTC Dealer Holdings Ltd. and Ontario Securities Commission,* [1987] 37 D.L.R. (4th) 94 (Ont. H. Ct.).

in the corporation's articles that provided that, if a majority of the common shares were tendered into a takeover bid, the class A shares would convert to voting shares. A prospective buyer of control offered to buy 49 percent of the common shares from three members of the Billes family at a considerable premium relative to the stock market price, thus gaining effective control without triggering the coattail provision. The Ontario Securities Commission set aside the transaction on the grounds of public policy, holding that the deliberate attempt to sidestep the coattail was "grossly abusive" of the class A securityholders and of the equity market in general.

While this case clearly involved matters beyond the question of the legitimacy of a control premium, the commission and, in approving the commission's decision, the Ontario Court of Justice both viewed negatively the incumbent controlling shareholders' desire to realize the control premium themselves without sharing it with the class A shareholders. Justice Reid referred to the Billes family's clear wish to horde the control premium for itself as evidence supporting the commission's finding of an abuse.[30] In that case, the court clearly viewed a premium to controlling shareholders alone as unfair.

By adhering to the equal opportunity rule, Ontario statutes also discourage the payment of premia to controlling shareholders. If a purchaser will own 20 percent of the shares of a particular class after the transaction is completed, the transaction is a takeover bid under section 89 of Ontario Securities Act. Pursuant to section 97, a takeover bid must offer the same consideration to all shareholders in the same class. A large shareholder contemplating the purchase of shares from the majority cannot single out the majority for its offer but rather must extend it to all shareholders in the relevant class. Obviously, the payment of a premium to the controlling

30. Justice Reid stated for the court (ibid., 109):

> The Commission made it clear that the abuse it perceived was of two kinds: abuse of the Class A shareholders and of the marketplace itself. There was much evidence before it to support its conclusion that the offer was an abuse of the Class A shareholders. . . . The Commission was concerned that the Billeses had participated in the offer in order to serve their sole object, i.e., to get the maximum amount possible for their control position, and wholly ignored the interests of the Class A shareholders. . . .
>
> [T]he Commission heard evidence from Fred, the son of one of the founders, that neither he nor his brother or sister were concerned over the Class As being left out of the enormous premium they were to receive under the offer. The following evidence was considered important enough for the Commission to repeat it in its reasons at p. 82 . . . :
>
> Q. Am I correct in assuming that you, David and Martha wanted to maximize the control proceeds which you realized, if you were going to sell your shares of Canadian Tire.
>
> A. I believe that is correct.
>
> Q. Your concern for the well-being of the holders of the A shares did not extend to permitting them to participate in the control premium?
>
> A. That's correct.

shareholder alone is deterred by such a rule. Such deterrence under the takeover rules may be particularly problematic given that a shareholder most likely to be willing to pay a premium and compensate the controlling shareholder for lost control benefits is one with significant shareholdings. Only with significant shareholdings are the benefits of lower agency costs sufficiently realized by an individual purchaser such that it may be privately profitable to purchase part of the control block in order to reduce agency costs.[31] The equal opportunity rule may prevent payment of a premium by those shareholders most likely to overcome the free-rider problem in moving to a more efficient, less concentrated ownership structure.

The equal opportunity rule also applies to corporate buybacks where the firm purchases some of its own outstanding equity. Such a buyback could address the rigidity problem. If the firm itself purchases some of the controlling shareholders' equity, the collective action problem may be overcome. The firm acts as a representative of all shareholders, and the costs and benefits of the share purchase are thus shared on a pro rata basis. It will, however, remain the case that the controlling shareholder will demand a premium for its shares in order both to be compensated for lost control benefits and to share in the surplus from efficient deconcentration. The law in Ontario prevents such a premium.

According to section 89 of the Ontario Securities Act, any offer by an issuer of securities to redeem or acquire any or all of the outstanding shares of that issuer is an "issuer bid." An issuer bid is subject to many of the same rules as takeover bids, including the equal opportunity rule. Under section 97, the same consideration must be offered to all members of a class in an issuer bid. This effectively eliminates the possibility of reliance on a buyback to overcome the rigidity problem. The controller will demand a premium, yet the equal opportunity rule prevents an idiosyncratic premium. Given that the premium cannot be offered profitably to the class as a whole, the equal opportunity rule may deter efficient deconcentration through a buyback.

There are two circumstances in which the free-rider problem inherent in paying the controlling shareholder a premium may be overcome and therefore efficient deconcentration may occur: where there is a large minority shareholder and where there is a buyback. The equal opportunity rule prevents the payment of a premium to the controlling shareholder in precisely these circumstances. Thus, the rule may deter deconcentration even if it is efficient to move to a less concentrated ownership structure. The existence of this rule in Canada, but not in the United States, may perhaps contribute to the concentrated ownership structures in Canada,

31. Just as toehold stakes held by the raider in the takeover context may overcome the Grossman and Hart (1980) free-rider problem.

although we have no specific empirical evidence supporting or rejecting this hypothesis.[32]

## 3.3 Normative Implications

The various possible causal links between the law and ownership concentration have different normative implications. As discussed, there is no theoretically optimal corporate ownership structure. Widely held firms may face agency costs because of rogue managers, while more narrowly held firms may face agency costs because of rogue controlling shareholders. The following discussion remains neutral on the question of the optimal structure but does assess other normative implications of the relations between various laws and ownership structure.

Whether the rules governing financial intermediaries have affected ownership concentration levels in Canada is, as discussed, unclear. Financial intermediaries appear not to have invested in Canadian equity despite permissive regulations. In any event, even supposing that the legal regulation had an effect on ownership structure by permitting significant investment by financial intermediaries, this cause itself does not add anything to the question of the social desirability of the regulations. The question is simply whether concentrated ownership is desirable relative to widely held firms: if so, then the regulations were desirable in this respect; if not, then they were not desirable in this respect. We have no opinion on this matter.

The second causal factor discussed above argues in favor of the regulations in question. If a regulatory environment fostering large banks helped reduce the cost of debt to both banks and corporations in Canada, which led in turn to greater ownership concentration, then ownership concentration could perhaps be viewed as evidence of the efficiency of the Canadian banking system, at least relative to that in the United States. Whether ownership concentration was a desirable result in itself is a separate question; as a causal explanation of ownership concentration, however, the regulations may demonstrate their efficiency-enhancing properties.[33]

To the extent that they were a cause of ownership concentration, protectionist policies with respect to trade and capital flows may have served to distort the form of Canadian corporations away from the optimum. For example, tax incentives may have induced foreign corporations to estab-

32. Our analysis is based on rigidity of concentrated ownership structures once established. Bebchuk and Zingales (chap. 2 in this volume) show that the equal opportunity rule may encourage the establishment of a concentrated ownership structure as opposed to a private firm.

33. We do not have an opinion, however, about one aspect of the regulatory regime discussed: the doctrine of equitable subordination. While it contributes to a lower cost of debt, it may raise the cost of equity to an inefficient level.

lish potentially inefficient concentrated ownership structures for their Canadian subsidiaries rather than wholly owned subsidiaries. Moreover, the subsidiaries themselves may have been established only to circumvent tariffs. Such distortions argue against the protectionist regulatory regime that spawned them.

We argued that a lax regulatory attitude with respect to competition may have contributed to concentrated ownership in Canada and that concentrated ownership in Canada may have contributed to a lax regulatory attitude with respect to competition. The latter possibility perhaps suggests an additional reason for concern about concentrated ownership. The welfare effects of the former possibility are as follows. In the absence of asymmetric information, in establishing an ownership structure an entrepreneur would choose a level of ownership concentration that maximizes the value of the firm in order to maximize her private returns from the sum of future profits and the proceeds from the sale of equity. That is, she would choose a level of ownership that minimizes agency costs. If, however, there is asymmetric information such that outside investors discount the value of the equity, she may avoid equity financing in order to avoid her private losses associated with outsiders' discounting the equity. Asymmetric information combined with product market power, which allows the firm to raise a given amount of capital selling a smaller fraction of equity, may give rise to a concentrated ownership structure that does not minimize agency costs.

From a policy perspective, it is important to isolate the respective roles played by market power and information asymmetry in excessive ownership concentration. It is the asymmetry of information that leads the entrepreneur to minimize equity sales despite agency costs, while market power simply accommodates concentrated ownership. While minimizing asymmetric information problems, perhaps by establishing penalties for false disclosure, is clearly desirable from a policy perspective, there is no a priori reason to conclude that reducing market power will have a beneficial effect on the choice of corporate ownership since it will focus the entrepreneur's choice on choosing the ownership structure that maximizes the value of the firm.[34] Again, it depends on the unanswered question of the overall desirability of concentrated as opposed to atomistic ownership. As a positive matter, however, we would predict that tougher competition rules and liberalized trade would lead to a lower level of ownership concentration.[35]

The final aspect of Canadian law that we considered that may contrib-

34. In Ontario, see the Ontario Securities Act, pt. 23.

35. As noted above, there is evidence from Canada that is at least not inconsistent with the conjecture that competition-promoting policies will lower the concentration of ownership (see n. 26 above).

ute to concentrated ownership was the equal opportunity rule. By perhaps preventing efficient deconcentration of ownership, the rule may have harmful effects. There are competing considerations,[36] but our analysis here suggests a reason for repeal.

If the rule were to be abolished, it is important to recognize its sources. An equal opportunity rule is clearly established by the Ontario Securities Act, but, apparently, it also has independent support in the courts, as evidenced by *CTC Dealer Holdings.* By finding that a control premium was an abuse of noncontrolling shareholders, in *CTC Dealer Holdings* the court established a precedent that may hurt minority shareholders by deterring efficient deconcentration.

### 3.4 Conclusion

The law may have contributed to Canada's corporate ownership structure in a variety of ways. Our theoretical analysis, which would require empirical confirmation before any firm conclusions could be reached, suggests that some of these contributions were likely socially beneficial (e.g., relatively liberal banking regulations), some were likely neutral with respect to corporate ownership (e.g., liberal investment rules for financial intermediaries), and others were undesirable (e.g., protectionism). While there may be implications for specific laws to be culled from our analysis, we do not offer any answers to the basic question of whether there is too much concentrated ownership in Canada. For example, as a positive matter, we predict that, as market power in Canada declines because of international competition and competition law, so, too, will ownership concentration. Whether, as a normative matter, this would be a desirable development we cannot say.

## References

Amoaku-Adu, B., B. Smith, and J. Schnabel. 1990. The risk of dual classes of shares: Are there differences? *Journal of Economics and Business* 42:39–50.

Baxter, I. 1968. *The law of banking and the Canadian Bank Act.* 2d ed. Toronto: Carswell.

Bebchuk, L. 1994. Efficient and inefficient sales of corporate control. *Quarterly Journal of Economics* 109:957–94.

Berle, A., and G. Means. 1933. *The modern corporation and private property.* New York: Macmillan.

36. For example, Bebchuk (1994) describes how the equal opportunity rule may in some circumstances discourage inefficient sales of control, although it may also deter efficient sales of control in other circumstances.

Daniels, R., and P. Halpern. 1996. Too close for comfort: The role of the closely held public corporation in the Canadian economy and the implications for public policy. *Canadian Business Law Journal* 26:11–62.

Daniels, R., and J. MacIntosh. 1991. Toward a distinctive Canadian corporate law regime. *Osgoode Hall Law Journal* 29:863–933.

Demsetz, H., and K. Lehn. 1985. Managerial ownership of voting rights: Causes and consequences. *Journal of Political Economy* 93:1155–77.

Eastman, H., and S. Stykolt. 1967. *The tariff and competition in Canada.* Toronto: Macmillan.

Fama, E. 1980. Agency problems and the theory of the firm. *Journal of Political Economy* 88:288–307.

Grossman, S., and O. Hart. 1980. Takeover bids, the free-rider problem, and the theory of the corporation. *Bell Journal of Economics* 11:42–69.

Harris, R. 1984. *Trade, industrial policy, and Canadian manufacturing.* Toronto: Ontario Economic Council.

Hart, O. 1983. The market mechanism as an incentive scheme. *Bell Journal of Economics* 14:366–82.

Holderness, C., and D. Sheehan. 1988. The role of majority shareholders in publicly held corporations: An exploratory analysis. *Journal of Financial Economics* 20:317–47.

Hood, W. M., and O. W. Main. 1956. The role of Canadian life insurance companies in the post-war capital market. *Canadian Journal of Economics and Political Science* 22:467–80.

Iacobucci, E., and M. Trebilcock. 1996. *Value for money: Executive compensation in the 1990s.* Toronto: C. D. Howe Institute.

Jamieson, A. B. 1953. *Chartered banking in Canada.* Toronto: Ryerson.

Jensen, M., and W. Meckling. 1976. Theory of the firm: Managerial behavior, agency costs, and capital structure. *Journal of Financial Economics* 3:305–60.

Jog, V., and A. Tulpule. 1996. Control and performance: Evidence from the TSE 300. In *Corporate decision-making in Canada,* ed. R. Daniels and R. Morck. Calgary: University of Calgary Press.

MacIntosh, J. 1996. Institutional shareholders and corporate governance in Canada. *Canadian Business Law Journal* 26:145–88.

MacIntosh, J., and L. Schwartz. 1996. Do institutional and controlling shareholders increase corporate value? In *Corporate decision-making in Canada,* ed. R. Daniels and R. Morck. Calgary: University of Calgary Press.

Manne, H. 1965. Mergers and the market for corporate control. *Journal of Political Economy* 73:110–20.

Morck, R. 1996. On the economics of concentrated ownership. *Canadian Business Law Journal* 26:63–75.

Morck, R., A. Shleifer, and R. Vishny. 1988. Management ownership and market valuation: An empirical analysis. *Journal of Financial Economics* 20:293–315.

Morck, R., and D. Stangeland. 1994. Corporate performance and large shareholders: An empirical analysis. In Issues in corporate control and the performance of corporations, by D. Stangeland. Ph.D. diss., Faculty of Business, University of Alberta.

Myers, S., and N. Majluf. 1984. Corporate financing and investment decisions when firms have information that investors do not have. *Journal of Financial Economics* 13:157–226.

Neufeld, E. P. 1972. *The financial system of Canada.* Toronto: Macmillan.

Niosi, J. 1982. *The economy of Canada: A study of ownership and control.* 2d ed. Montreal: Black Rose.

Performance 500, top 10. 1997. *Canadian Business,* June, 135–87.

Rajan, R., and L. Zingales. 1994. What do we know about capital structure? Some evidence from international data. NBER Working Paper no. 4875. Cambridge, Mass.: National Bureau of Economic Research.

Rao, P. S., and C. Lee-Sing. 1996. Governance structure, corporate decision-making, and firm performance in North America. In *Corporate decision-making in Canada,* ed. R. Daniels and R. Morck. Calgary: University of Calgary Press.

Roe, M. 1991. A political theory of American corporate finance. *Columbia Law Review* 91:10–67.

———. 1994. *Strong managers, weak owners: The political roots of American corporate finance.* Princeton, N.J.: Princeton University Press.

Royal Commission on Banking and Finance. 1964. *Report.* Ottawa: Queen's Printer.

Shearer, R., J. Chant, and D. Bond. 1984. *The economics of the Canadian financial system.* 2d ed. Scarborough, Ont.: Prentice-Hall Canada.

Slovin, M., and M. Sushka. 1993. Ownership concentration, corporate control activity, and firm value: Evidence from the death of inside blockholders. *Journal of Finance* 48:1293–1321.

Smith, A. 1937. *Wealth of nations.* 1776 Cannan ed. New York: Modern Library.

Stulz, R. 1988. Managerial control of voting rights, financing policies, and the market for corporate control. *Journal of Financial Economics* 20:25–54.

Trebilcock, M. 1999. Lurching around Chicago: The positive challenge of explaining the recent regulatory reform agenda. In *Rationality in public policy: Retrospect and prospect: A tribute to Douglas G. Hartle,* ed. R. Bird, M. Trebilcock, and T. Wilson. Toronto: Canadian Tax Foundation.

Triantis, G. 1996. Debt financing, corporate decision making, and security design. *Canadian Business Law Journal* 26:93–105.

Triantis, G., and R. Daniels. 1995. The role of debt in interactive corporate governance. *California Law Review* 83:1073–1113.

## **Comment** George G. Triantis

Ronald Daniels and Edward Iacobucci describe various ways in which the concentrated ownership structures in Canada may be due to the organization of Canadian industry. The focus of my comments is on two of their claims: (1) Market concentration in many industries has produced higher profits, thereby allowing firms to finance their activities with retained earnings rather than external capital. (2) Concentration in the banking sector has produced efficiencies in lending, thereby reducing the cost of debt financing and enabling firms to finance by borrowing rather than diluting equity interests.

These two claims relate to the means by which a firm can finance its activities without issuing new stock: internal capital or debt finance. With respect to the former, Daniels and Iacobucci suggest that many Canadian firms enjoy market power that increases their retained earnings and hence

George G. Triantis is professor of law at the University of Chicago.

their pool of internal capital. In a world of imperfect information, the abundance of internal funds is a mixed blessing. It is efficient when the ability of a firm to tap equity markets is impeded by information asymmetry between its managers and investors (Myers and Majluf 1984). However, internal capital also insulates managers from the scrutiny and discipline of capital markets and enables them to appropriate free cash for self-interested activities (e.g., Easterbrook 1984; Jensen 1986). The determination of the optimal amount of internal capital depends on the firm's opportunity set, and it can be implemented to some degree by manipulating capital structure (e.g., Triantis 2000).

Daniels and Iacobucci treat the availability of retained earnings as exogenous: the cash available to the firm is determined by its profitability, which is a function of its market power. However, it ought to be viewed as an endogenous variable in the choice of capital structure. The analysis should consider that capital markets might entice or compel firms to commit to paying out earnings by taking on debt or paying dividends and to returning to capital markets for the funding of new projects. The issue then becomes the conditions under which the entrepreneur or controlling shareholder can internalize the efficiency gains from making such commitments.

Daniels and Iacobucci suggest that Canadian banks have achieved economies of scale and scope in screening, monitoring, and intervening in the affairs of their borrowers. As a result, the cost of bank loans may be lower in Canada than in the United States, encouraging firms to borrow rather than issue new equity. The more leveraged a firm is, the more concentrated will be its ownership. The argument is sound, but it may miss a more relevant point by focusing on concentration of stockholding rather than of control. While stockholders enjoy voting rights and the ability to enforce fiduciary duties, debtholders hold rights embedded in the covenant, default, acceleration, and enforcement provisions of their contracts with the firm. A breach of a covenant enables the debtholder to accelerate the maturity of the debt and, if it is not paid in full, to remove assets from the firm. Thus, the control rights of equity and debt vary in relative significance with the prevailing financial condition of the firm. Specifically, the managers of a financially distressed firm tend to be more responsive to the voice of their lenders than shareholders are. As a firm becomes more leveraged, the likelihood of financial distress increases, as does, consequently, the effective control of its lenders. Therefore, if it is true that Canadian firms have more concentrated ownership structures because they are more highly leveraged, this fact simply means that control rights are more likely to be held by lenders rather than shareholders. Indeed, the authors imply that, beyond the majority shareholders, control over Canadian firms is exercised aggressively by a concentrated group of highly skilled banks.

## References

Easterbrook, Frank H. 1984. Two agency-cost explanations of dividends. *American Economic Review* 74:650–59.

Jensen, Michael C. 1986. Agency costs of free cash flow, corporate finance, and takeovers. *American Economic Review* 76:323–29.

Myers, Stewart, and N. Majluf. 1984. Corporate financing and investment decisions when firms have information that investors do not have. *Journal of Financial Economics* 13:187–221.

Triantis, George G. 2000. Financial slack policy and the laws of secured transactions. *Journal of Legal Studies* 29:35–69.

4

# Corporations and Taxation
## A Largely Private Matter?

Robert D. Brown, Jack M. Mintz, and Thomas A. Wilson

Corporations may be "public" (widely held) or "private" (closely held). As has long been recognized in the industrial organization literature, beginning with Berle and Means (1932), the performance of widely held corporations may differ from that of those that are closely held for a variety of reasons (see, e.g., Jensen and Meckling 1976; and Demsetz 1983). Private corporations may be governed better than public firms since managers in public firms have greater incentives to "shirk" by enjoying nonpecuniary benefits (Williamson 1978), or controlling shareholders of public firms may make decisions that have negative consequences for new shareholders after an initial public offering (Bebchuk and Zingales, chap. 2 in this volume). On the other hand, owners of private businesses may be less willing to take on risk (owing to a lack of opportunities to diversify risk) or might face constraints in raising equity finance.

The purpose of this paper is to examine how taxation can influence businesses' choice between private and public status. In section 4.1, we begin with a review of the primary differences between U.S. and Canadian tax systems that might influence the extent to which corporations might be privately held. Our review suggests that the Canadian tax system may

Robert D. Brown is the Clifford Clark Visiting Economist in the Department of Finance, Ottawa, and a former senior partner of Price Waterhouse in Canada. Jack M. Mintz is president and CEO of the C. D. Howe Institute and the Arthur Andersen Professor of Taxation at the University of Toronto. Thomas A. Wilson is professor of economics and director of the Policy and Economic Analysis Program at the Institute for Policy Analysis, University of Toronto.

The authors thank Steve Murphy for research assistance. They thank Bruce Harris and Doug Scheetz of Price Waterhouse, Toronto, for reviewing the technical sections dealing with Canadian and U.S. tax provisions. They also thank Daniel Feenberg and an anonymous referee for helpful comments.

provide some inducement for corporations to be kept private. This arises from special favorable treatment given to certain private corporations, in particular, lower corporate income taxes on active business income retained in the corporation and a special capital gains tax exemption. U.S. tax law also encourages individuals to sell shares more readily than Canadian tax law does, and the Canadian exemption for intercorporate dividends, along with a less restrictive approach to the use of nonvoting shares, may create more complex corporate structures, allowing private companies to control public ones.

Then, in section 4.2, we examine a simple model to simulate the decision of entrepreneurs to go public. On the one hand, private ownership avoids any agency costs that arise by going public but may result in businesses failing to undertake sufficient investment owing to insufficient internal resources. On the other hand, a public offering of the firm can create opportunities to obtain capital at a cheaper price, although there may be an agency cost that is incurred since outside investors do not have full information to control the effort and risk-taking decisions of entrepreneurs. With this model, we can show that lower taxes on the return to investment in private firms, compared to the return on investment for public firms, encourage greater numbers of privately held companies. On the other hand, income and wealth taxes on entrepreneurs that reduce their ability to fund investments internally may encourage greater public offerings of businesses.

In section 4.3, we provide a simulation of the theoretical model described in section 4.2. We then review the data and find that there tends to be a much greater share of Canadian corporate wealth held in private companies in Canada than in the United States. This would be consistent with our simulation.

## 4.1 Canadian and U.S. Treatment of Private and Public Companies

In this section, we review a number of special features of the Canadian tax system, consider how these may influence the behavior of Canadian entrepreneurs and corporate shareholders, and contrast this with the corresponding tax treatment in the United States, with 1997 as the reference year. We then discuss whether—and how—particular Canadian tax issues may influence growing Canadian companies to remain private perhaps to a greater extent than they do in the United States. Comparisons of the size of the private corporate sectors in Canada and the United States are provided in the following section.

### 4.1.1 Canada Has Highly Progressive Personal Rates

The tax issues relating to corporate operations and ownership must be understood in the context of the overall tax system, including that affecting individuals. The average top rate of personal income tax—combined federal and provincial—in Canada is about 51 percent, in comparison to an average federal and state level of 43–44 percent in the United States. But the significant difference in Canada is that the Canadian rate structure is much more progressive at moderate income levels: these top rates are reached in Canada at a level of income of approximately U.S.$43,000, in contrast to an income level of over U.S.$250,000 for the top rate in the United States.

As a generalization, it would be somewhat more difficult in Canada than in the United States for investors to accumulate capital in the absence of certain provisions, reviewed below.

### 4.1.2 General Features of the Taxation of Business Income

In considering the tax position of smaller business enterprises, the following general features of the Canadian tax system are relevant (within each case, the corresponding position in the United States is noted).[1]

#### *Dividend Tax Credit*

Individual shareholders receiving dividends from Canadian corporations are entitled to the equivalent of a 25 percent dividend tax credit. The mechanics of this, which involve an integrated approach under federal and provincial tax regimes, require the amount of the dividends being "grossed up" by 25 percent for inclusion in the individual's taxable income, but with the individual receiving a dividend tax credit roughly equivalent to 20 percent of the amount of the grossed-up dividends. This effectively reduces the tax rate payable by individuals on Canadian dividend income, with the top personal tax rate falling to about 35 percent (combined federal and provincial tax) on such income, instead of the normal combined 51 percent. The gross up and the dividend tax credit are applied to essentially all dividends from taxable Canadian corporations and are not related to the actual corporate taxes paid by the corporation.

As noted below, the dividend tax credit has the effect of largely eliminating the double taxation of certain corporate source income received by Canadian-controlled private corporations and flowed out to their Canadian individual shareholders as dividends but serves as only a partial offset to the corporate tax paid when such dividends are paid out of fully taxed income by other Canadian companies (such as public companies). In the United States, in contrast, dividends are not subject to special treatment when received by individual taxpayers and bear full personal tax with no relief for the corporate tax on the income out of which they are distributed.

1. In this section, all dollar amounts given with respect to the Canadian tax system are in Canadian dollars except where otherwise noted, while amounts relating to the U.S. tax system are in U.S. dollars. At the time of writing, the exchange value of the Canadian dollar was approximately U.S.$0.70.

As discussed later, U.S. entrepreneurs do have the availability of subchapter S elections and limited-liability corporations (LLCs) to avoid the double tax on dividend income.

*Intercorporate Dividends*

In Canada, dividends received by one Canadian company from another taxable Canadian company are generally free of corporate tax. (Private corporations receiving portfolio dividends from other Canadian companies are liable to pay a special "antideferral" tax on these dividends: the tax is fully refundable to the company when this income is distributed to its shareholders as dividends.)

In the United States, the position is more complex, and significant taxes can be imposed on dividends received by one U.S. corporation from another. In brief terms, dividends can flow tax free between U.S. companies only if the one company has a substantial (frequently 80 percent) interest in the other: Dividends received by one U.S. corporation from another are included in taxable income to the extent of 30 percent if less than a 20 percent interest (votes or values) is held, are included in taxable income to the extent of 20 percent if the holdings is 20–80 percent, and are totally exempt if more than an 80 percent interest is held. Dividends flow tax free between companies that jointly file a consolidated return (generally requiring an 80 percent or greater interest [votes and value] being held by a U.S. parent in the group).

*Capital Gains*

Taxable capital gains are included in income in Canada to the extent of three-quarters of such gains, and capital losses in general can be offset only against taxable gains, not against ordinary income, with carryovers provided. At the corporate level, the effective combined federal and provincial tax on capital gains at the general rate of corporate income tax is roughly 32 percent, while, for individuals in the top rate bracket, the total personal tax on such gains would amount to about 38 percent. (Canadian-controlled private corporations [CCPCs] recognizing capital gains do pay a further "antideferral" tax on this income, fully refundable when the gain is distributed.)

In the United States, capital gains are fully taxable, but, for individuals, special tax rates apply to the amount of such gains. For corporations, capital gains are taxed as ordinary income, with the effective (federal and state) corporate rate being about 38 percent. For individuals in the United States prior to the 1997 tax changes, the effective federal top tax rate on capital gains would have amounted to about 28 percent. Under new rules adopted in 1997, the effective federal tax on longer-term capital gains (with respect to assets held at least eighteen months) is now 20 percent (10 percent for certain lower-income individuals), with a higher rate (28 percent) being applied to medium-term capital gains (with a one-year to eighteen-month holding period).

The legislation also provides that, after the year 2000, very long-term gains (on assets held over five years) will be taxed at a federal rate of only 18 percent (8 percent for certain lower-income individuals). Of course, most, but not all, states have personal income taxes that will raise the total effective tax on capital gains by an average of about 5 percentage points. The new U.S. rules mean that effective capital gains tax rates in Canada for individuals will be substantially above those in the United States. Both countries have incentive capital gains provisions for entrepreneurs: a special lifetime exemption of up to $500,000 in Canada, half rates on gains on certain "original issue" stock in the United States. Both measures are discussed below.

*Death Taxes*

Canada does not have any estate tax, succession duty, or gift taxes either at the federal or the provincial level. Instead, most capital assets are deemed to be realized at their fair market value at death (or on some inter vivos transfers), with the resulting gain or loss included in the deceased's final tax return. (There are "rollovers" of assets at the deceased's adjusted cost base available with respect to transfers to spouses and certain spousal trusts.)

In the United States, summarizing a complex tax picture, the estates of deceased individuals are subject to federal estate tax and, additionally, in many cases to state taxes (with a limited credit with respect to such state taxes available on the federal return). There is also a federal gift tax, integrated with the estate tax. Deferral of tax is available on transfers to spouses. However, for income tax purposes, assets transferred on the owner's death to a beneficiary generally have a basis equal to their fair value at that time, thus totally avoiding income tax on any accrued gain. U.S. federal rates of estate tax range from 18 up to 55 percent, subject to a general exemption of $625,000 (rising to $1 million over the next nine years).

As a judgmental generalization, the Canadian deemed realization at death is substantially less on medium-size and larger estates than the U.S. estate tax. However, in both countries, estate-planning techniques can reduce effective burdens, particularly on larger estates.

### 4.1.3 Favorable Tax Treatment for Small Business

In accordance with the practice in many countries, small business corporations in Canada receive a variety of special tax incentives and concessions. However, the difference is that, in Canada, such tax incentives are generally larger than elsewhere—Canada has one of the most favorable tax regimes, relative to the general tax system, for small business enterprises of any country in the world. Further, the Canadian incentives are distinguished by the fact that most of them are reserved exclusively for CCPCs, which can be of any size, as opposed to small corporations generally.

In this discussion, *Canadian-controlled* means that an enterprise is not controlled, directly or indirectly, by nonresidents of Canada. And the term *private company* simply refers to a company that does not have equity or debt securities traded on public markets (or that is controlled by a public company).

### 4.1.4 Tax Incentives for Private Business

The main specific provisions providing special treatment of private or smaller (the terms are far from synonymous) companies are noted below.

#### *Lower Corporate Rates*

CCPCs pay a combined federal and provincial tax rate of about 21 percent on the first $200,000 of active business income, in contrast to the general combined federal and provincial corporate tax rate of 43 percent. The reduction is achieved through the "small business deduction," which reduces the federal corporate income tax rate for CCPCs by 16 percentage points to 13.12 percent (with surtax) on this first slice of active business income, with most provinces also having lower rates for the same income, again confined to CCPCs. Total federal and provincial rates in 1997 vary from 18.12 percent in Newfoundland, Nova Scotia, and the Northwest Territories to 22.62 percent in Ontario. (Lower provincial rates are available in some provinces for manufacturing activities.) The $200,000 limit, along with some other incentives, must be shared among an associated group of companies.

#### *Tax Integration*

An important effect of the lower rate for small business in Canada is that shareholders of CCPCs benefit from having their corporate and individual income taxes more fully integrated than are the corporate and individual income taxes of shareholders of larger businesses. For CCPCs, the lower rate of federal and provincial income tax of about 21 percent on the first $200,000 of active business income (in contrast with the general combined corporate rate of about 43 percent) means that the corporate and personal taxes on such profits are roughly integrated when the after-tax corporate income is paid out to individuals and covered by the dividend tax credit. The result is an individual shareholder paying about the same total tax (corporate and personal) on distributed profits out of such income as if he or she had earned the income personally. There is also a complex regime for the taxation of income from property—investment income—that provides the same benefits of full integration for such income earned in a CCPC, regardless of amount.

The benefit of the lower rate of corporate tax on a CCPC's active business income of up to $200,000 is clawed back as the CCPC grows in size. The federal incentive starts to be recovered when the CCPC reaches $10 million of capital and is fully phased out when capital reaches $15 million: provincial incentives are also generally clawed back as the CCPC's income rises.

In the United States, the federal tax code provides for reduced corporate rates of tax for lower-income corporations: 15 percent for taxable income up to $50,000; 25 percent for taxable income from $50,000 to $75,000; 34 percent for taxable income from $75,000 to $10,000,000; and 35 percent for taxable income over $10,000,000. The benefits of the lower rates on the first $75,000 of income are clawed back as income exceeds $100,000, and the 1 percent tax reduction (a 34 percent corporate rate instead of the general 35 percent rate) is also recovered as income exceeds $15 million.

However, regardless of the level of income, U.S. corporations and their shareholders face a significant burden through the double taxation of corporate income since *no* relief is provided to individuals receiving dividends from such companies with respect to the corporate tax already paid. Accordingly, not only is the Canadian treatment of the business income of smaller corporations relatively more generous than that in the United States, but the full integration of corporate and personal taxes means that the distributed income of smaller Canadian corporations is not subject to a substantial tax penalty, as is the case in the United States. However, U.S. entrepreneurs have available special operating forms—the subchapter S election and the LLC (both discussed below)—to attain the equivalent benefits of full integration.

The ability of shareholder-managers of CCPCs to achieve a fully integrated tax is expanded through the administrative practice of allowing such companies to pay bonuses, almost without limit, to shareholder-managers so as to maintain active business income at or below the $200,000 annual threshold. The funds so bonused to shareholder-managers are subject to personal tax only and can be loaned back to the company if required in the business. The validity of bonuses paid to shareholder-managers is subject to a greater degree of review in the United States than in Canada, and, in general, such bonuses must be justified as being reasonable compensation for services provided.

The U.S. tax system does have features that allow for the equivalent of a full integration of corporate and personal taxes for private business operations. The first of these is the subchapter S elections. U.S. corporations with relatively simple share structures (one class of shares), having only U.S. individuals or other qualifying entities as shareholders (and having no more than seventy-five shareholders), and meeting other criteria are allowed to elect to have their income taxed only in the hands of their shareholders. Under this option, the corporation's income is not subject to corporate income tax but is required to be allocated currently to its individual shareholders. This treatment eliminates the double taxation of corporate income while still enabling the business to benefit from limited liability and other features of the corporate form of organization.

In addition, there has been a growing use of LLC entities—essentially organizations that have limited liability but lack some of the other characteristics of ordinary corporations—which are also treated as conduit vehicles for tax purposes: their income is not subject to corporate tax but is allocated to and taxed currently in the hands of its member-owners. The LLC has some advantage in flexibility over a subchapter S election, but both are widely used by U.S. entrepreneurs to carry on small and even large U.S. businesses. Compared to the Canadian CCPC, the LLC and subchapter S election have the advantage that there is no limit to the amount of business income that can be earned and flowed through to shareholders without any "double tax" penalty.

The Canadian CCPC does, however, have the advantage of a significant tax deferral for earnings retained in the business—qualifying business income up to $200,000 is taxed currently at a low rate, with further personal tax postponed until actual distribution.

*Capital Gains*

Canada has a unique feature allowing a $500,000 lifetime capital gains exemption to individuals on gains realized on shares of qualifying CCPCs (and on farm property). For this purpose, any CCPC with most of its assets used in an active business in Canada, without size limitation, qualifies its shareholders for this special exemption.

The United States also has a special tax regime applying to gains on the sale of certain small business companies. Only 50 percent of qualifying gains are included in income (and eligible for capital gain treatment), although 100 percent of losses are still recognized. This special treatment is available only to individuals (and certain other noncorporate entities) and applies only to gains realized on shares acquired on original issue from a corporation after 10 August 1993 and held for at least five years. Further, only shares in a corporation having assets of less than $50 million and meeting tests to demonstrate that it is almost exclusively engaged in an active trade or business (other than certain excluded activities, such as personal services, hospitality, banking, resource extraction, etc.) qualify as original issue shares.[2] The gain eligible for this exclusion is limited to the lesser of $10 million or ten times the investor's cost basis in the stock. The U.S. incentive is more favorable for larger gains than the Canadian exemption, but its application is much more restricted.

2. Guenther and Willenborg (1998) conclude that this favorable tax treatment has both increased the price at which shares of qualifying small businesses are sold in an initial public offering (IPO) and offered net benefits to the investors in such shares.

Investors in CCPCs are allowed a more generous treatment with respect to capital losses on shares or debt on CCPCs primarily carrying on an active business in Canada: in general, they can claim 75 percent of such losses (allowable business investment loss), not only against capital gains, but also against ordinary income (with no maximum). The U.S. tax rules contain a much more limited provision allowing investors to write off up to a $100,000 loss on their investment in a small business enterprise against ordinary income.

*Capital Tax*

A capital tax is imposed under the "large corporations tax" on companies in Canada, but there is an exemption for the first $10 million of taxable capital that effectively eliminates federal capital taxes for small business. Some provinces also impose general corporate capital taxes, but many exempt or provide lower rates of tax on capital below a certain threshold.

In the United States, there is no federal tax on corporate capital, while some states levy capital taxes at varying rates.

*Other Features*

The Canadian tax rules contain a variety of other special provisions targeted at smaller private companies: an enhanced scientific research and experimental development tax credit, available only to CCPCs within certain size limitations; a deferral of tax on stock options issued by small businesses to employees, with the result that no tax arises when the option is exercised, only when a gain on the stock acquired is realized; enhanced treatment for investors in labor-sponsored venture capital corporations with respect to investments in smaller businesses; measures that reduce the tax compliance burden on small corporations; provisions allowing smaller corporations to obtain "after-tax" financing on more favorable terms than other companies;[3] the right to use funds in registered retirement savings plans (RRSPs) to invest, within limits, in a CCPC.

In general, U.S. federal tax law contains relatively few other provisions benefiting smaller corporations as such, although some states provide limited concessions.

### 4.1.5 Both Countries Favor Smaller Companies

In Canada, there are a large number of tax incentives and special treatments available to private companies in general and to CCPCs in particular, including a substantially reduced corporate rate of tax on the first $200,000 of annual active business income, the full integration (absence of double taxation) on such business income plus all income from property,

3. This can be done by issuing preferred shares to banks and others on which the dividends to the recipient company are not taxable—up to a limit of $500,000 a year. For smaller companies with losses or without income taxed at full rates, this can offer financial savings.

and a $500,000 lifetime capital gains exemption to the owners of the shares of such companies.

The Canadian tax system does offer a limited dividend tax credit that offsets part of the burden of the double tax on corporate source income that would otherwise apply: the United States has no similar provision. On the other hand, owners of private U.S. enterprises have mechanisms available under U.S. tax law (subchapter S elections and LLCs) that also offer the advantages of integration and avoid the double taxation of corporate income, without limit, through allowing such income to be taxed only at the personal level.

The Canadian tax system does, however, have the substantial advantage of a deferral of personal tax on retained business earnings built up from the $200,000 a year amount of active business income eligible for the lower corporate rate—a benefit that is not available to LLCs or subchapter S companies in the United States. In the Canadian tax system, this deferral of personal tax can amount to 30 percent of pretax business income (the difference between the 51 percent top personal rate and the 21 percent corporate rate), or $60,000 a year (30 percent of $200,000). Over a ten-year period, this could result in a tax deferral of over $0.5 million—far larger than the corresponding amount in the United States.

There are, of course, important potential gains to be achieved through going public—including the possibility of obtaining additional funding at better rates, achieving a premium value relating to the easier transferability of ownership, and so on. With respect to tax issues, Canadian entrepreneurs have the advantage of a $500,000 lifetime capital gains exemption on their shares, while, in the United States, individuals may qualify for a 50 percent tax discount on the realization of long-term gains on original issue shares held in qualifying small businesses. The tax advantages of going public tend to be roughly similar in both countries, except possibly that the United States, with a better-developed capital market for smaller public enterprises, offers better returns to such enterprises that go public.

On balance, a critical difference may be the ability of CCPCs to build up significant retained earnings out of business income that has borne only a relatively low rate of corporate tax. This feature may therefore provide a modest inducement for Canadian CCPCs to remain private for a longer period than might similar U.S. companies operating under U.S. law.

### 4.1.6 Tax Treatment of Dividends and Capital Gains

In Canada, individuals pay about the same rate of personal tax in upper income brackets on dividends as on capital gains. In the United States, dividends are fully taxed as ordinary income, but capital gains are eligible for much more favored treatment, with a combined federal and state tax burden that may be below 25 percent (and possibly eligible for even more favored treatment on "original issue" stock).

The substantial tax advantage of receiving capital gains rather than dividends would tend to induce U.S. shareholders of U.S. private companies to prefer "cashing in" their gains through sale, rather than receiving distributed earnings. In Canada, the relative neutrality between the taxation of dividends and that of capital gains will tend to mean that there is less tax reason for entrepreneurs to realize accumulated earnings through sale (other than those gains qualifying for the $500,000 lifetime capital gains exemption).

### 4.1.7 Death Taxes Influence Holdings

Canada has a deemed realization of capital assets at death, while the United States has an estate tax that is generally more onerous. The fact that the Canadian tax system has a lower net burden at death on larger estates may mean slightly less pressure on older taxpayers to arrange for companies to go public and thus facilitate liquidity for investments in such enterprises. In the United States, the threat of death duties may influence owners of smaller enterprises to have their corporations go public to a greater degree than prevails under the Canadian system.

### 4.1.8 Complex Corporate Structures Facilitated in Canada

The absence of tax on dividends paid between Canadian companies could be a reason making for more complex corporate group structures in Canada, as there is no general tax penalty—as there would be in the United States—for holding blocks of dividend-paying shares (but less than complete ownership) in other companies. When combined with the greater acceptability in Canada of the use of nonvoting equity shares in the capital structures of public companies, complex corporate structures involving layers of corporations that permit family groups to maintain control with less than 51 percent of the economic interest in other enterprises can provide advantages to a few private corporations.

### 4.1.9 Summary

Overall, the general Canadian tax rules appear to provide, directly and indirectly, some moderate but appreciable inducements for Canadian entrepreneurs to have their corporations remain as private companies to a greater extent than would prevail in the United States. However, it is important not to overstate these inducements, which may in many particular cases be more than offset by nontax factors and other specific tax factors. Prospective reforms to the Canadian federal tax structure could reduce this incentive.[4] On the other hand, the province of Ontario plans to cut its

4. The Technical Committee on Business Taxation (1998) has recommended that the $500,000 capital gains tax be eliminated, coupled with a provision to allow capital gains for farms and CCPCs to be rolled over into registered savings plans.

small business corporate rate in half over the next seven years, which would increase the incentive.[5]

## 4.2 A Simple Entrepreneurial Model: The Choice between Private and Public

In this section, as a basis for the simulation offered in the next section, we consider a simple two-period model of an entrepreneur deciding whether to maintain a company under private (closely held) ownership or move to public (widely held) ownership.[6] If the company is private, the entrepreneur is the only owner and may not have sufficient resources to fund a desired level of capital. Should the company go public, the entrepreneur will have better access to financing investment but may incur an agency cost that adversely affects the profitability of the company. The agency cost is related to the inability of investors fully to monitor the entrepreneur's effort to achieve an efficient level of production and an appropriate level of risk for the firm.[7]

As discussed in the previous section, taxes affect the entrepreneur's decision to create a public company in several ways. First, the tax rates on dividend and capital gains income derived from the private and public firms account for the degree of integration between corporate and personal income taxes for each type of firm. Capital gains taxes at death and taxes on wealth transferred to heirs may also be important. Although estate taxes (and taxes on deemed realizations of capital gains) apply to wealth transfers, an equivalent effective tax rate on capital income can also include computations for estate taxes (Poterba 1997). Second, income from safe assets (bonds) is taxable at the personal income tax rate.[8] Third, any differential treatment of income received from private and public companies can be reflected in the individual tax rates. Fourth, estate and other taxes on accumulated wealth can reduce the amount of resources available to entrepreneurs for investment.

Each entrepreneur has an initial level of pretax wealth, $\hat{W}$, distributed uniformly over the index $[0, W^*]$. Accumulations of wealth prior to the initial period are subject to estate, income, and capital gains taxes at the

5. The 1998 Ontario budget would reduce the provincial corporate tax rate for CCPCs in eight steps from 9 to $4\frac{1}{2}$ percent in 2005.

6. The two-period model is meant to capture a lengthy time period since creating a public firm can result in significant sunk transaction costs.

7. The agent has private information about internal resources that is unavailable to the market. Those agents that go public would convey information about their wealth. The model could enable one to derive a signaling equilibrium that would result in a cost imposed on the high-quality firms that would give up profitable investments. We use a simpler model for understanding the role played by taxes.

8. Estate taxes can also fall on safe assets that are transferred to heirs. The tax rate on the return on safe assets can also be adjusted for the effect of estate taxes.

total effective rate $\tau$. Wealth can be invested in safe assets, $b \geq 0$,[9] earning the return $r(1 - t)$, $t$ being the effective tax rate on interest income. Alternatively, wealth can be invested in the corporation, $y \geq 0$. If the corporation is a private one, the entrepreneur will receive all the income from the firm plus the value of the original capital, $y$, received as a tax-free return of capital. Let $g(y, e) = f(y)\varphi(e)$ be the expected pretax income of the firm that is strictly concave in its arguments, capital, $y$, and effort, $e$, the latter supplied at the equivalent monetary constant cost of $c$ per unit.[10] At the end of the second period, the owner receives back the capital, $y$, plus the pretax income of the firm. Taxes paid on pretax income of the private corporation are levied at the rate $u$, which is the effective total tax rate incorporating corporate and personal income taxes on returns and potentially other taxes, such as estate taxes (this will be discussed further below in deriving effective tax rates on income).

If the firm is private, the entrepreneur's problem is to maximize consumption (end-of-period wealth) by choosing the level of investment, $y$, and effort, $e$:

$$\text{(1a)} \qquad \max W_p = \{\hat{W}(1 - \tau) - y\}[1 + r(1 - t)] + y + (1 - u)f[y]\varphi[e] - ce,$$

subject to

$$\text{(1b)} \qquad \hat{W}(1 - \tau) - y \geq 0.$$

The solutions for the optimal values, $y^*$ and $e^*$, to this problem are the following:

$$\text{(2a)} \qquad \partial W_p / \partial y = (1 - u)f_y\varphi - r(1 - t) \geq 0,$$

for $y^* \leq \hat{W}(1 - \tau)$, and

$$\text{(2b)} \qquad \partial W_p / \partial e = (1 - u)f\varphi_e - c = 0.$$

Equation (2a) states that the entrepreneur will invest in capital until the after-tax marginal product of capital is equal to the after-tax cost of capital, assuming that there are sufficient internal resources to invest in the firm (otherwise, the after-tax marginal product of capital is greater than

9. It is assumed that the entrepreneur is constrained from borrowing funds from outside investors either directly or indirectly through the business. Thus, there is no bankruptcy in the model since all returns are in the form of equity. Short-selling constraints are appropriate since agency costs could arise if entrepreneurs borrow funds that may not be repaid to outside investors. For a recent model incorporating such agency costs associated with the repayment of debt, see Hart and Moore (1998).

10. Income is uncertain, but, without limiting generality, we treat the variables in gross income as the certainty-equivalent value. Taxes treat gains and losses symmetrically, and there is no bankruptcy in the model since all finance is in the form of equity.

the cost of capital as the entrepreneur gives up good projects). Equation (2b) states that the after-tax marginal product of effort is equal to its cost. Note that there is a value of after-tax initial wealth, $\hat{W}'(1 - \tau)$, that is the point at which wealth is just sufficient to meet the demands for capital, $y$, and invest in no bonds. High-wealth entrepreneurs with wealth greater than $\hat{W}'(1 - \tau)$ will invest in both the firm and bonds. Low-wealth entrepreneurs with wealth less than $\hat{W}'(1 - \tau)$ will choose to invest only in the firm, with their investment constrained below the most profitable level of capital investment.

Should the firm become public, the entrepreneur sells off some of the wealth held in the firm, $E$, to outside investors, or "angels," prior to the determination of investment and effort decisions by the entrepreneur. Angels can observe investment levels but cannot monitor the entrepreneur's effort level. As derived below, the entrepreneur will let the firm become public only if there are insufficient resources available to maximize end-of-period wealth if the firm were to remain private. Thus, the gain to becoming public is achieving an effective lower cost of funds. The cost of becoming public is that the firm operates with an agency cost that arises from angels having imperfect information about the entrepreneur's willingness to supply effort that has an associated nonpecuniary cost that the entrepreneur would like to avoid.[11]

The value of equity sold to the angels is equal to $E$ and is composed of two components ($E = \alpha y + G$). The first is a share of capital investment, $\alpha y$, where $\alpha$ is a proportion of capital financed by the angels. The second is a goodwill payment, $G$, a lump-sum payment paid to the entrepreneur from the angels for a share of the economic rents earned by the private firm.[12] If the firm is public, the angels choose the share of capital investment they wish to hold, given the goodwill payment, $G$. The entrepreneur chooses the level of investment, contingent on the choice of $\alpha$ made by the angels. Therefore, if the firm goes public, the problem for the entrepreneur is solved by using subgame perfection—the entrepreneur's choices of effort and investment are made in reaction to the shareholders' choice of contract.

If the firm goes public, the taxes on income are the following. The entrepreneur's wealth is taxed at the rate $\tau$, and the return on bonds is taxed at

11. The model could be extended to include other economic reasons for going public, such as risk diversification or obtaining better management support than can be supplied by the angels (see Amit, Brander, and Zott 1997). These other economic factors affecting the status of business would play a role a determining the economic benefits and costs of going public.

12. We assume that the goodwill payment is predetermined as a Nash bargaining solution between the entrepreneurs and the angels regarding the distribution of "pure profits" or rents earned by the firm. Note that, at the maximum, $G$ cannot be set such that the present value of the firm's investment is negative, as shown in eq. (5) below. Otherwise, the choice of $G$ will depend on a bargaining outcome. In principle, $G$ could also be subject to a capital gains tax.

the rate $t$ for both the entrepreneur and the shareholders.[13] The entrepreneur and the angels pay tax on the firm's income at the rate $\theta$. Any special relief for capital gains taxes on shares held in the entrepreneur's firm would be captured in a lower value of $\theta$. We note that there may be important differences between the rate of taxes that the entrepreneur pays when the firm is held privately ($u$) and the rate paid when the firm is public. Generally, given some of the provisions of the U.S. and Canadian tax systems, we expect that private-company ownership has more preferential treatment, so $u < \theta$.

The entrepreneur's investment and effort decision is determined by maximizing end-of-period wealth, which is denoted as follows:

$$(3) \qquad W_s = \{\hat{W}(1 - \tau) - y + E\}[1 + r(1 - t)] + E + (1 - \alpha)(1 - \theta)f[y]\varphi[e] - ce.$$

The entrepreneurial choices of investment and effort are determined, respectively, as follows:

$$(4a) \qquad \partial Ws/\partial y = (1 - \theta)f_y\varphi - r(1 - t) = 0,$$

$$(4b) \qquad \partial Ws/\partial e = (1 - \theta)f\varphi_e - c/(1 - \alpha) = 0.$$

The important distinction between equations in (2) and (4) is that the share of profits earned by the entrepreneur, $(1 - \alpha)$, affects the entrepreneur's effort decision, reducing the desire to work. In this model, the agency cost of going public is related to the entrepreneur's effort decision, which affects the value of the firm—entrepreneurial effort cannot be directly compensated by the angels, who cannot monitor amounts provided. However, the higher the share of income ($\alpha$) paid to the angels, the lower is the incentive for work effort by the entrepreneur.[14]

When the firm is public, the angels maximize their end-of-period wealth, choosing $\alpha$, given that the entrepreneur chooses the optimal level of effort, $e^*$, and capital, $y^*$, to maximize the entrepreneur's end-of-period wealth from equation (3):

$$(5) \max V = \alpha\{y^*[\alpha] + (1 - \theta)(f[y^*[\alpha]]\varphi[e^*[\alpha]])\} - (1 + r(1 - t))E, \geq 0,$$

with $e^*$ and $y^*$ denoting the values that maximize the entrepreneur's wealth for given levels of $\alpha$.[15] The choice of $\alpha$ by the angels that solves the equations in (5) is the following (applying the envelope theorem):

13. Shareholders could have a different tax rate on bond income, but, to avoid unnecessary complexity, we ignore this difference for modeling purposes.

14. The comparative static effects, $\partial e/\partial\alpha$, can be shown to be negative—an additional share of income to the angels reduces effort by the entrepreneur.

15. Note that, in this problem, we do not incorporate a minimum participation constraint for the entrepreneur, who must earn income at least as great as some alternative investment

$$(6)\quad \partial V/\partial\alpha = \{(1-\theta)f\varphi - r(1-t)y\} + (1-\theta)\alpha f\varphi_e\,\partial e/\partial\alpha = 0.$$

For a maximum choice of $\alpha$ in (6), the after-tax income, net of the opportunity cost of investing capital in bonds in the first term, is balanced with the loss in the entrepreneur's effort in the second term.

From the above, we compare two outcomes for privately and publicly held firms in terms of the investment and effort decisions. For the public firm, the investment decision is determined at the point where the after-tax marginal product of capital is equal to its cost of capital ($[1-\theta]fy\varphi = r[1-t]$), but the effort decision is provided at an additional cost beyond the entrepreneur's marginal cost of supplying effort ($[1-\theta]f\varphi_y > c$). For the private firm, investment may not be determined at the cost of funds since the lack of internal resources may constrain the firm from achieving its full capacity, but the effort level is chosen at a lower cost on the basis of the entrepreneur's cost of providing effort.

Leaving aside taxes, the entrepreneur would not consider taking the firm public if there were sufficient internal resources to invest in capital—the agency cost associated with the entrepreneur's effort decision reduces potential income should the firm become public. Thus, the choice of going public critically depends on the internal resources of the entrepreneurs (as well as tax variables). High-wealth entrepreneurs, with $\hat{W}(1-\tau) > y^*$, would not go public, while low-wealth entrepreneurs would go public if the agency cost from a public offering is less than the gain from relaxing the entrepreneur's capital constraint.

With taxes, the decision whether to go public will be determined by the comparative statics of the model: (*a*) If income, capital gains, and estate taxes on the entrepreneur's return from investments in private firms are levied at a rate, $u$, that is less than the rate, $\theta$, for public firms, then there will be greater incentive for the firm to be privately held, as reviewed in section 4.1 above. This seems to be the representative case for Canada. (*b*) Estate, income, and capital gains taxes that reduce the initial accumulated wealth of entrepreneurs will encourage more firms to be publicly held. Since $\tau$ reduces the initial amount of wealth for investment, low-wealth entrepreneurs take on less investment and may be more willing to let the firm become public. (*c*) Any exemption for capital gains taxes or income earned on the basis of the status of the company (e.g., special incentives to sell shares for a public offering) reduces taxes on income held, creating an incentive for the firm to go public. As discussed in section 4.1, the United States does provide such an incentive for going public, while Canada provides capital gains incentives for private shares only.

(investment in bonds). Here, we assume that the angels do not have sufficient power to force the entrepreneur to give up all the excess returns associated with original ownership of the firm.

The model presented above provides a basis for evaluating how the tax system affects the choice of firms to be public or private.

## 4.3 Private and Public Companies: A Quantitative Review

This section assesses the relative importance of private and public corporations in Canada, with some comparative data for the United States. Data sources for Canada include the LEAP (Longitudinal Employment Analysis Program) database, developed by the University of British Columbia and Statistics Canada, and data derived from corporate taxation statistics from Revenue Canada and Statistics Canada. The data for the United States include balance-sheet data from the Federal Reserve Board and data from *Statistics of Income,* published by the Internal Revenue Service.

As noted in section 4.1 above, both Canada and the United States have special tax provisions that favor private companies. For Canada, CCPCs have a low rate of corporate tax on the first $200,000 of net income. This effectively creates full integration for distributed earnings and a significant deferral for reinvested earnings. In addition, each of a CCPC's shareholders can realize up to $500,000 of tax-free capital gains on the sale (or deemed sale) of his or her shares in the company.

In the United States, certain private companies may qualify for S status. If S status is elected, all shareholders of the private corporation are taxed on a partnership basis—thereby eliminating the double taxation of corporate source income that would otherwise occur.

Both systems have changed significantly over the postwar period. The special treatment of CCPCs in Canada dates from the 1971 income tax reforms. The lifetime capital gains exemption was introduced in 1985.

In the United States, prior to the major income tax reform of 1986, the advantages of S status were attenuated by personal marginal income tax rates well above corporate rates. This meant that corporations that reinvested a high share of earnings would not elect S status. The 1986 tax reform moved marginal personal rates below the corporate rate, effectively removing this disincentive for S status.[16]

As a result of these changes, the attractiveness of CCPC status in Canada and S status in the United States increased significantly after 1986.[17]

Table 4.1 presents current (1998) effective tax rates on private and public corporations in Canada and the United States on the basis of the features

16. Some small corporations may still find S status unattractive because of the low rates of corporate tax on the first $75,000 of income.

17. Subsequent changes in Canada—the limitation of the general capital gains exemption and its elimination in 1994—enhanced the attractiveness of the $500,000 exemption for CCPCs and farm property. In recent years, LLC status has become an alternative to S status in the United States.

**Table 4.1 Effective Tax Rates by Type of Corporation and Dividend-Payout Rates and the Decision to Go Public**

| | Effective Tax Rates | | |
|---|---|---|---|
| | Private | Public | Decision |
| *Canada (CCPCs)* | | | |
| 100 percent payout: | | | |
| Small CCPC | .48 | .63 | Stay private |
| Large CCPC | .63 | .63 | Go public |
| 50 percent payout: | | | |
| Small CCPC under CGE | .35 | .59 | Stay private |
| Small CCPC above CGE | .43 | .59 | Stay private |
| Large CCPC under CGE | .53 | .59 | Stay private |
| Large CCPC above CGE | .59 | .59 | Go public |
| Zero payout: | | | |
| Small CCPC under CGE | .21 | .56 | Stay private |
| Small CCPC above CGE | .39 | .56 | Stay private |
| Large CCPC under CGE | .43 | .56 | Stay private |
| Large CCPC above CGE | .56 | .56 | Go public |
| *United States (firms eligible for S status)* | | | |
| 100 percent payout | .44 | .66 | Stay private |
| 50 percent payout | .44 | .55 | Stay private |
| Zero payout | .44 | .45 | Go public |

*Note:* CGE = capital gains exemption.

of the two tax structures described in section 4.1 above. These rates represent the combined effect of corporate and personal income taxes and capital gains taxes at the personal level. Details regarding these calculations are presented in the appendix.

As is clear, the differences between the effective tax rate on a private corporation and the rate it would face if it were to go public vary with the dividend-payout ratio in both countries. In Canada, the effective rate also depends on whether the firm's income is under the small business deduction and on whether accrued capital gains would be covered by the lifetime capital gains exemption.

We have simulated the decision of a cash-constrained firm whether to go public under alternative dividend-payout ratios using an arbitrary quadratic function for the underlying revenue function described in section 4.2 above. The results are shown in the final column of table 4.1. Details are provided in the appendix.

Taxes can play a major role affecting the decision whether to go public. In Canada, a CCPC would not typically go public until two conditions are met: (*a*) the firm must have exhausted its small business deduction, and (*b*) the shareholders must have reached the point at which incremental capital gains are not sheltered under the lifetime capital gains exemption. The decision is also affected by the payout ratio: since capital gains are less important for higher-payout firms, a CCPC would go public when it fully exhausts the small business deduction.[18]

In the United States, for firms that could qualify for S treatment, the decision also depends on the payout ratio. The lower the payout ratio, the less important is the double taxation of dividend income. At a sufficiently low payout ratio, the tax advantages of S status are insufficient to offset the advantages to a cash-constrained firm of going public.

### 4.3.1 1994 Benchmark Comparison of Canada and the United States

Because of the changed tax incentives for the formation/election of CCPCs and S corporations, we decided to compare the situations of the two countries in 1994. This is the latest year for which certain data are available and is several years after the major tax changes that fundamentally altered incentives.

Figure 4.1 and table 4.2 provide a summary picture of the relative importance of private and public nonfinancial corporations in the two countries. Note that *private* here refers to *all* closely held nonpublic companies, not just CCPCs and S status companies.

Although the data are not strictly comparable, the difference in the relative importance of private companies between the two countries is striking. In Canada, private companies' share of total assets is higher than the public companies' share. In the United States, on the other hand, the market value of public companies' equity is two and a half times the market value of closely held companies.

One explanation of the difference is the much greater role of subsidiaries of foreign companies in Canada. Wholly owned subsidiaries of foreign companies (whether public or private) are classified as *other private* companies in Canada (i.e., private but not CCPCs).

Figure 4.2 and table 4.3 provide some insight on this issue. If we treat all corporations classified as *other private* as foreign subsidiaries and exclude their assets (and the assets in the *other* category) from the data, the relative share of private companies declines to 43 percent, and the share of public companies increases to 57 percent. The relative share of CCPCs is nevertheless substantially higher and the relative share of public companies lower than the relative shares of private and public corporations in the United States. Foreign subsidiaries explain part, but by no means all, of the difference between the two countries.[19]

Another way of examining the role of private corporations in Canada

18. Note that, in the table, the tax rate for a large CCPC refers to a firm whose small business deduction has been fully clawed back. This would occur at an asset level of $15 million.

19. Note that the comparison presented above no doubt understates the relative importance of closely held Canadian-controlled companies since some public companies are controlled by foreign companies and some of the other private companies are not subsidiaries of foreign companies.

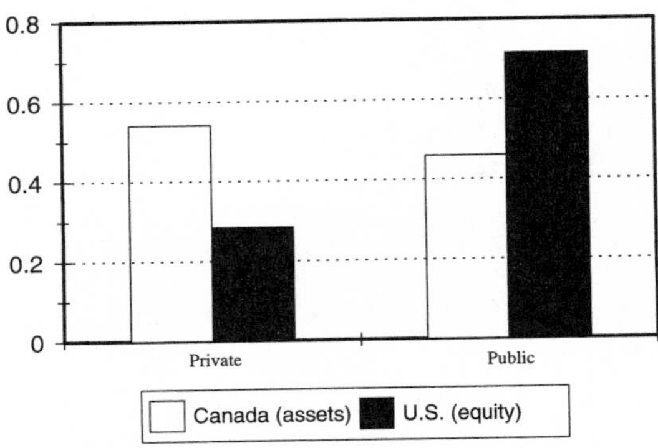


**Fig. 4.1 Share of nonfinancial corporations, Canada and the United States, 1994 (Canada, assets)**

**Table 4.2 Shares of Nonfinancial Corporations, Public versus Private, Canada and United States, 1994**

| | Private | Public |
|---|---|---|
| Canada (assets) | .541 | .459 |
| United States (equity) | .285 | .715 |

*Sources:* Canada: Statistics Canada, special tabulations of Canadian corporations by type, 1992–96. United States: Federal Reserve Board, unpublished balance-sheet data on market values of equities of closely held and public nonfinancial corporations, 1994.

and the United States is to compare the relative importance of CCPCs in Canada with that of S corporations in the United States. As noted above, changes in tax incentives in the mid-1980s should have stimulated the growth of both types of firms. This is confirmed in figures 4.3 and 4.4. In Canada, CCPCs increased in importance over the period 1984–93 (see fig. 4.3). The expansion of CCPCs was accompanied by a decline in the relative importance of unincorporated employers. Since proprietors and partnerships were not eligible for the $500,000 capital gains exemption, the most likely explanation of this trend is that many of these types of enterprises became incorporated.

In the United States, the growth of S corporations after 1985 was much more dramatic, as illustrated in figure 4.4. S corporations' share of total receipts increased from 5.1 percent in 1985 to 16.5 percent in 1994. Over the same period, the percentage of corporations that were S corporations more than doubled, from 22.1 percent in 1985 to 46.6 percent in 1994. The dramatic increase in S corporations appears to have leveled off after 1992.

The number and relative importance of S corporations in the United States grew more than the number and relative importance of CCPCs in

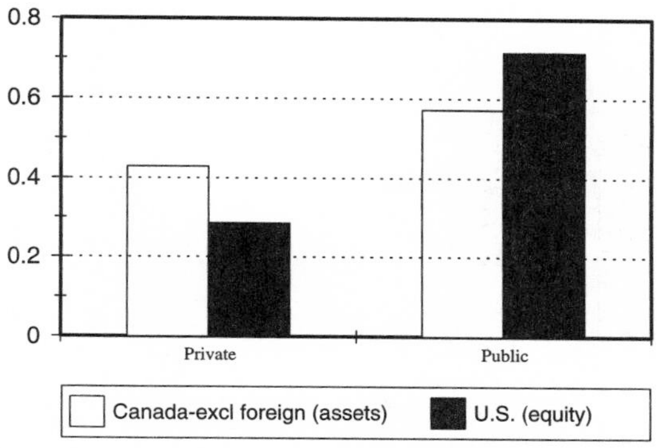


**Fig. 4.2 Share of nonfinancial corporations, Canada and the United States, 1994 (Canada, excluding foreign assets)**

**Table 4.3 Shares of Nonfinancial Corporations, Public versus Private, Canada and United States, 1994**

| | Private | Public |
|---|---|---|
| Canada (assets) | .438 | .572 |
| United States (equity) | .285 | .715 |

*Sources:* See table 4.1 above.
*Note:* Figures for Canada exclude foreign subsidiaries.

Canada over the period 1985–94. However, in 1994, CCPCs were a much more important category within Canada than S corporations were within the United States. CCPCs constituted 95 percent of Canadian corporations (vs. 47 percent for S corporations in the United States). Almost two-thirds of corporate employment in Canada was in CCPCs. These firms accounted for 32 percent of the assets of nonfinancial corporations and 47 percent of the income. In the United States, by contrast, S corporations accounted for 16.5 percent of receipts of all corporations and 8.1 percent of the assets of nonfinancial corporations.

Taken in conjunction with the aggregate data discussed above, these data indicate that S corporations represent a smaller share of the assets of privately held corporations in the United States than CCPCs' share of such assets does in Canada.

The relative importance of S corporations and CCPCs varies with firm size. Figure 4.5 and table 4.4 present data for CCPCs classified by employment size. Figure 4.6 and table 4.5 present data for S corporations classified by asset size. In Canada, CCPCs dominate the first four size classes, but their share of employment drops to 43 percent for the largest size class

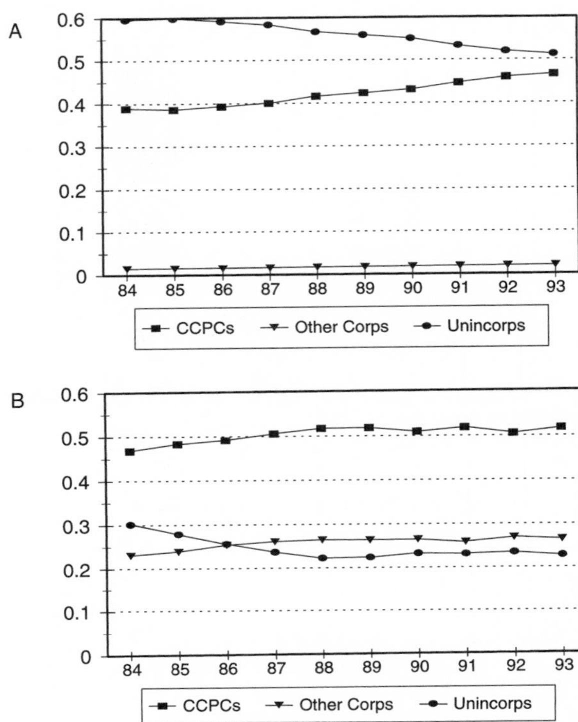


**Fig. 4.3 CCPCs, other corporations, and unincorporated firms, Canada, 1984–93:** ***A*, Number of companies; *B*, Share of employment**

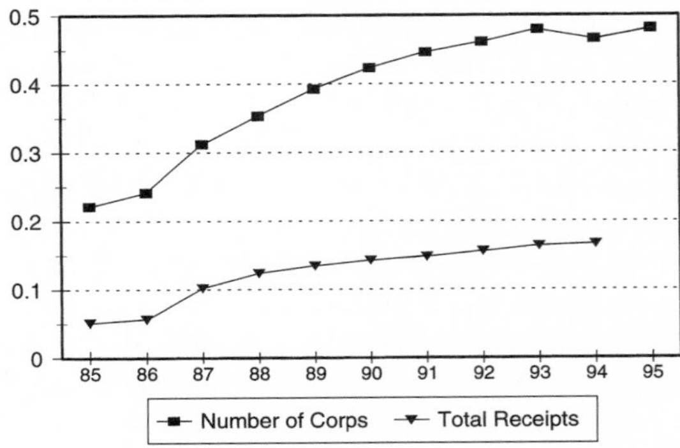


**Fig. 4.4 U.S. S corporations as a share of all corporations, 1985–94**

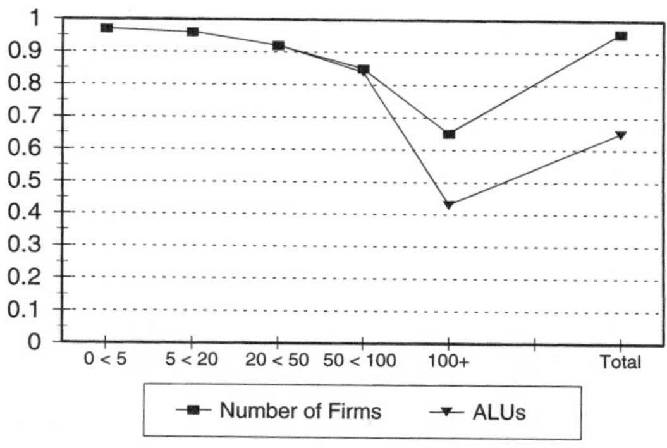


**Fig. 4.5 CCPCs' share of all incorporated firms by number of ALUs, Canada, 1992**

*Note:* An ALU is a standardized unit of labor input, measured by payroll divided by the average wage for each industry/province/size category.

**Table 4.4 CCPCs' Shares of All Incorporated Firms by Firm Size (level of employment), Canada, 1992**

| Number of Employees (ALUs) | Number of Firms | Employment (ALUs) |
|---|---|---|
| 0<5 | .97 | .97 |
| 5<20 | .96 | .96 |
| 20<50 | .92 | .92 |
| 50<100 | .85 | .84 |
| 100+ | .65 | .43 |
| Total | .96 | .65 |

*Source:* Hendricks, Arnot, and Whistler (1997).

*Note:* An ALU is a standardized unit of labor input, measured by payroll divided by the average wage for each industry/province/size class category.

(one hundred or more employees). In the United States, S corporations account for about 40 percent of total receipts for asset size classes up to $25 million; their share then declines sharply with increasing size.

More detailed data are available for CCPCs and other Canadian companies for two broad asset size classes—under $15 million and $15 million and over. Data for nonfinancial corporations are presented in figure 4.7 and table 4.6. The results show that CCPCs dominate the smaller asset size group: CCPCs hold 86 percent of assets, earn 89 percent of revenue, and constitute 95 percent of these corporations. For the larger asset size class, CCPCs are much less important, holding 10 percent of assets and earning 14 percent of revenue. In terms of numbers of firms, CCPCs are more significant—38 percent of the larger firms were CCPCs.

For comparative purposes, we have constructed a table for two broad

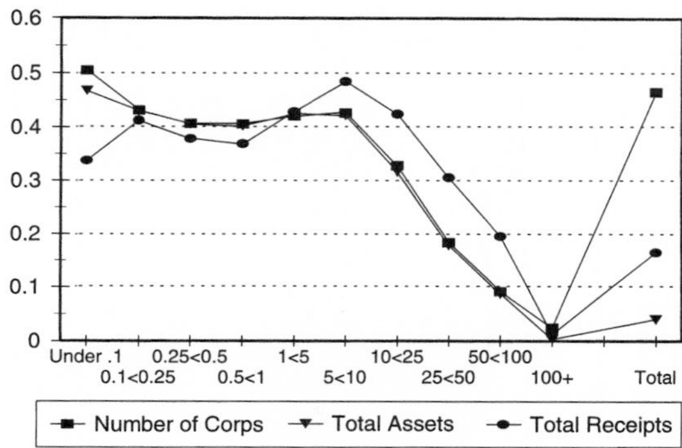


**Fig. 4.6 U.S. S corporations as a share of all corporations, 1994, by asset size ($million)**

**Table 4.5 S Corporations' Shares of All Incorporated Firms by Firm Size (assets), United States, 1994**

| Assets ($million) | Number of Corporations | Total Assets | Total Receipts |
|---|---|---|---|
| Under 0.1 | .505 | .467 | .337 |
| 0.1<0.25 | .431 | .429 | .412 |
| 0.25<0.5 | .407 | .406 | .379 |
| 0.5<1 | .405 | .402 | .369 |
| 1<5 | .421 | .425 | .429 |
| 5<10 | .426 | .422 | .485 |
| 10<25 | .328 | .317 | .424 |
| 25<50 | .184 | .178 | .306 |
| 50<100 | .091 | .087 | .195 |
| 100+ | .025 | .003 | .013 |
| Total | .466 | .040 | .165 |

*Source:* IRS (1994).

size classes for all corporations in the United States divided between those with assets under $10 million and those with assets of $10 million and over (see fig. 4.8 and table 4.7). These may be compared with data for all Canadian corporations presented in figure 4.9 and table 4.8. S corporations accounted for 41 percent of receipts for the smaller size group but only 7 percent for the larger size group. In contrast, CCPCs accounted for 88 percent of revenue for smaller and 12 percent for larger firms (see fig. 4.9 and table 4.8).

## 4.3.2 Summary

It is clear from the data we have reviewed that private companies play a much larger role in the Canadian than in the U.S. economy. The greater

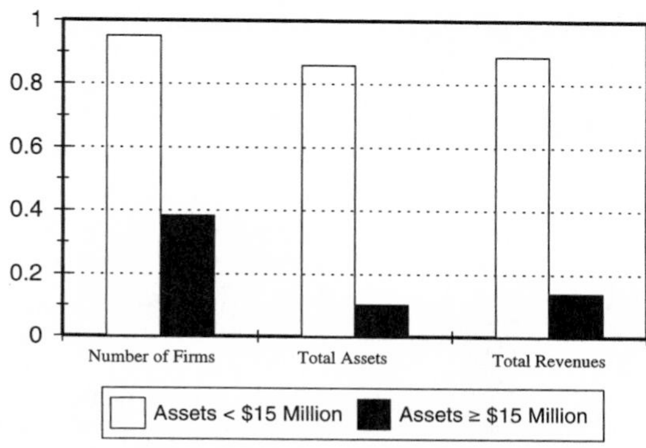


**Fig. 4.7 CCPCs' share of nonfinancial corporations by asset size, Canada, 1994**

**Table 4.6 CCPCs' Shares of Nonfinancial Corporations by Firm Size (assets), Canada, 1994**

| Assets ($million) | Number of Corporations | Total Assets | Total Revenues |
|---|---|---|---|
| Under 15 | .951 | .860 | .887 |
| 15+ | .384 | .104 | .139 |

*Source:* Statistics Canada, special tabulation of Canadian nonfinancial corporations by type, 1992–96.

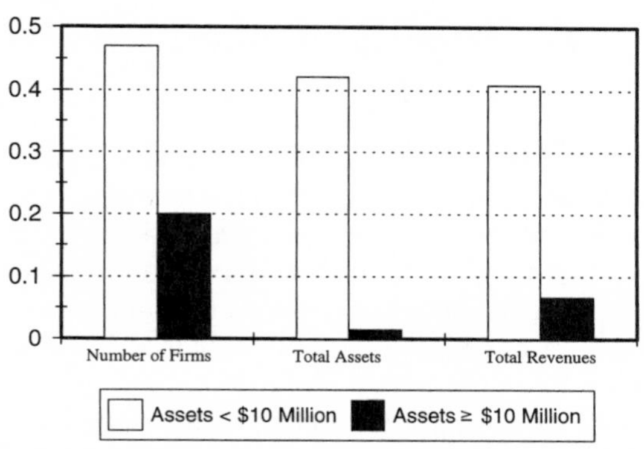


**Fig. 4.8 S corporations' share of all corporations by asset size, United States, 1994**

**Table 4.7 S Corporations' Shares of All Incorporated Firms by Firm Size (assets), United States, 1994**

| Assets ($million) | Number of Corporations | Total Assets | Total Receipts |
|---|---|---|---|
| Under 10 | .470 | .422 | .409 |
| 10+ | .200 | .015 | .067 |

*Source:* IRS (1994).

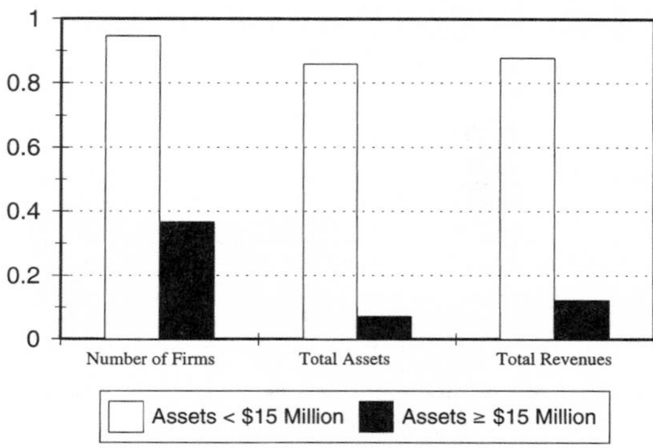


**Fig. 4.9 CCPCs' share of all incorporated firms by asset size, Canada, 1994**

**Table 4.8 CCPCs' Shares of All Corporations by Firm Size (assets), Canada, 1994**

| Assets ($million) | Number of Corporations | Total Assets | Total Revenues |
|---|---|---|---|
| Under 15 | .946 | .859 | .878 |
| 15+ | .367 | .072 | .122 |

*Source:* Statistics Canada, special tabulation of Canadian corporations by type, 1992–96.

importance of subsidiaries of foreign corporations in Canada explains only part of the difference. Domestic private companies are more important in Canada than are their counterparts in the United States.

Whether tax rather than nontax factors provided the greater encouragement for private firms in Canada cannot be resolved here. But it is clear that the combination of full integration for dividend income, substantial deferrals for retained earnings, and a special capital gains tax exemption provide a powerful incentive for attaining and retaining CCPC status. The data provide some confirmation of these results.

# Appendix

## *Simulations of Decisions to Go Public under Representative Tax Regimes*

The purpose of this appendix is to explore how the Canadian and U.S. tax structures may affect the decision to go public. We first determine representative tax systems for the two countries. The basic rates used to construct the effective tax rates shown in table 4.1 above are presented in table 4A.1. The rates shown in table 4A.1 capture the essential features of the two systems of taxation.

The U.S. system consists of a "classic" corporate tax unintegrated with the personal tax, except for S status corporations, which are treated as equivalent to partnerships. The Canadian system has full integration for dividend income from small CCPCs and partial integration, through dividend credits, for other corporations. Canada also has a $500,000 lifetime capital gains exemption for shareholders of large or small CCPCs. Both countries provide favorable tax treatment for capital gains. U.S. tax rates are generally lower than Canadian rates, with the exception of dividend income and corporate income of small corporations, where Canadian rates are lower.

Effective combined tax rates on shareholders of corporations are derived by applying the applicable personal tax rates on dividends and capital gains to corporate distributions and retentions, as follows:

$$T = tc + (1 - tc)P \cdot td + (1 - tc)(1 - P)tg,$$

where $tc$ is the corporate tax rate, $td$ is the tax rate on dividends, $tg$ is the effective accrual tax rate on capital gains, $P$ is the dividend-payout ratio, and $T$ is the total effective tax rate.

The results are presented in table 4A.2. Of course, what matters for the

**Table 4A.1** **Representative Effective Marginal Tax Rates**

| Income Type | Canada | United States |
|---|---|---|
| Corporate income:[a] | | |
| Public corporations | .43 | .39 |
| Private corporations | .21 | Partnership treatment |
| Personal income:[b] | | |
| Dividends | .34 | .44 |
| Interest income | .51 | .44 |
| Capital gains: | | |
| Nominal rate | .38 | .20 |
| Effective accrued rate | .22 | .10 |
| Under lifetime capital gains exemption | 0 | N.A. |

*Note:* N.A. = not applicable.

[a]For Canada and the United States, the corporate tax rates are from Technical Committee on Business Taxation (1998, p. 3.26).

[b]For Canada, these rates are the combined federal and provincial rates for a top-bracket taxpayer in Ontario in 1998. For the United States, these rates are based on federal rates for 1998, with an assumed effective net state personal income tax rate of 4 percent. Relevant personal tax rates are for top bracket taxpayers. (Source: *Tax Facts, 1997–98* 1997.)

**Table 4A.2 Effective Total Tax Rates by Type of Corporation and Payout Ratio, 1998**

| Payout Ratio and Corporate Type | Private | Public[a] |
|---|---|---|
| *100 percent* | | |
| Canada: | | |
| Small CCPC | .48 | .626 |
| Large CCPC | .626 | .626 |
| United States: S corporations | .44 | .658 |
| *50 percent* | | |
| Canada: | | |
| Small CCPC: | | |
| Under CGE | .345 | .592 |
| Above CGE | .433 | .592 |
| Large CCPC: | | |
| Under CGE | .528 | .592 |
| Above CGE | .592 | .592 |
| United States: S corporations | .44 | .555 |
| *0 percent* | | |
| Canada: | | |
| Small CCPC: | | |
| Under CGE | .21 | .558 |
| Above CGE | .386 | .558 |
| Large CCPC: | | |
| Under CGE | .43 | .558 |
| Above CGE | .558 | .558 |
| United States: S corporations | .44 | .451 |

[a]When a CCPC or an S corporation goes public, it loses CCPC or S status.

decision to go public is not so much the average levels of taxation but the differences in tax burdens between public and private corporations. These are presented in table 4A.3.

The tax incentive for private status is actually stronger in the United States for firms with high payout ratios. As partnership status and full integration are equivalent when the payout ratio is 100 percent, the advantages of S status in the United States are greater than those of CCPC status in Canada because there is no dividend credit for public companies in the United States. At medium payout ratios, the situation is reversed, with small CCPCs having a greater tax incentive to remain private than S corporations. Finally, at low payout ratios, both small CCPCs and large CCPCs where shareholders have not exhausted their lifetime capital gains exemption have a greater tax incentive to remain private than do S corporations in the United States. U.S. corporations ineligible for S status and Canadian CCPCs that have exhausted their small business deductions and

**Table 4A.3** **Tax Incentives for Private Status, Canada versus United States, by Payout Ratio**

| Payout | Tax Advantage of Staying Private | | | | | |
|---|---|---|---|---|---|---|
| | Canada | | | | United States | |
| | Small CCPC | | Large CCPC | | | |
| | Under CGE | Above CGE | Under CGE | Above CGE | Eligible for S Status | Ineligible for S Status |
| 100 percent | .15 | .15 | Nil | Nil | .22 | Nil |
| 50 percent | .24 | .16 | .06 | Nil | .11 | Nil |
| 0 percent | .35 | .17 | .13 | Nil | .01 | Nil |

lifetime capital gains exemptions are essentially treated the same as public corporations.[20]

In order to explore the effect of these tax rates on the decision to go public, we have constructed a simulation model with the underlying revenue function represented by a quadratic function. The parameters are selected so that a cash-constrained firm would choose to go public in the absence of taxes. Effective tax rates are then introduced into the model, and the model is solved to determine whether the firm will go public or remain private.

The revenue function $f(y)\varphi(e)$ is represented by the quadratic function

$$ay - \frac{1}{2}by^2 + me - \frac{1}{2}ge^2 + dey.$$

Parameters specified are $a = 3$, $b = 0.5$, $d = 0.25$, $g = 0.5$, and $m = 3$. This function is then used in equation (6). We also set the real return ($r$) at 0.04, and the marginal cost of effort ($c$) is normalized at 1. Tax parameters are from table 4.1 above. For each case shown in table 4.1, we determine the level of initial wealth $W^1(1 - \tau)$ where going public would increase total wealth. If no positive level is found, we determine that the firm will stay private. If there is any range of values for $W^1(1 - \tau)$ where going public would increase total wealth, we determine that the firm will go public.[21]

20. This refers to basic rates of tax. However, there are other features of the tax laws that may favor private status.

21. Total wealth includes the wealth of outside investors as well as the wealth of the entrepreneur. In all cases, a side payment to the entrepreneur is required for the firm to go public.

In three of the Canadian cases shown in table 4.1, the firm would go public for any value of initial wealth below $W^1$. In one of the U.S. cases, the firm would go public if initial wealth is below 78 percent of $W^1(1 - \tau)$.

## References

Amit, R., J. Brander, and C. Zott. 1997. Venture capital financing of entrepreneurship in Canada. In *Financing growth in Canada,* ed. P. Halpern. Calgary: University of Calgary Press.
Berle, A., and G. Means. 1932. *The modern corporation and private property.* New York: World.
Demsetz, H. 1983. The structure of ownership and the theory of the firm. *Journal of Law and Economics* 26:375–93.
Guenther, D., and M. Willenborg. 1998. Capital gains tax rates and the cost of capital for small business: Evidence from the IPO market. University of Connecticut, School of Business Administration. Mimeo.
Hart, O., and J. Moore. 1998. Default and renegotiation: A dynamic model of debt. *Quarterly Journal of Economics* 112, no. 1:1–41.
Hendricks, K., R. Arnot, and D. Whistler. 1997. Business taxation of SMES in Canada. Working Paper no. 97-11. Ottawa: Technical Committee on Business Taxation.
Internal Revenue Service (IRS). 1994. *Statistics of income.* Washington, D.C.: U.S. Government Printing Office.
Jensen, M. C., and W. Meckling. 1976. Theory of the firm: Managerial behavior, agency costs, and capital structure. *Journal of Financial Economics* 3:305–60.
Poterba, J. 1997. The estate tax and after-tax investment returns. NBER Working Paper no. 6337. Cambridge, Mass.: National Bureau of Economic Research.
*Tax facts, 1997–98.* 1997. Toronto: KPMG.
Technical Committee on Business Taxation. 1998. *Report.* Ottawa: Finance Canada.
Williamson, O. E. 1978. *Markets and hierarchies: Analysis and anti-trust implications.* New York: Free Press.

## Comment Daniel Feenberg

The days when Arnold Harberger could model the corporate tax system with a single parameter are but a nostalgic memory for older public finance economists. The change is partly progress made by economists in understanding the nature of corporate taxation and partly backsliding by legislatures with little regard for efficiency or horizontal equity. The results are that tax-induced effects on the cost of capital depend not only on the income of shareholders, the financing method, and the holding period but also the age, number, and nationality of controlling shareholders.

Brown, Mintz, and Wilson build a combined model of all these tax parameters to find the differential between the total tax rate on privately and publicly held corporations in Canada and the United States. In Canada, the tax rates are calculated for Canadian-controlled private corporations, while, in the United States, the somewhat similar S corporations are mod-

Daniel Feenberg is a research associate of the National Bureau of Economic Research.

eled. The perspective is one of a newly formed corporation rather than a preexisting one.

Except for firms expecting very high payout rates, the authors find a noticeably stronger tax incentive to remain private in Canada than exists in the United States. This could well be the reason for the observation documented in this paper that a greater share of business equity is private in Canada than in the United States.

While nearly comprehensive in its treatment of taxes, the paper does not quantify some related tax issues that might affect the decision to remain private. In the United States, the estate tax is a significant levy, typically over 50 percent at moderate levels of wealth. Although the estate tax is often offered in the popular press as a reason for companies to go public (to raise liquidity to pay the tax), it is more likely that the effect goes the other way. Private firms are treated to a valuation discount of 35 percent, the tax on a closely held family firm can be paid in installments over ten years, and the appraised valuation of a private firm is likely to be far lower than stock market valuations of the similar firms in public hands. Gifts of partial interests can often be structured to have little taxable value. While it would be difficult to judge the quantitative significance of these considerations, they all point to the desirability of maintaining private control. The Canadian system of taxing capital gains at death appears to create a smaller incentive (in the same direction).

Another consideration is the far greater latitude that private companies have to press the edges of tax avoidance. The public company is restricted by the desirability of obtaining an audited financial statement from a nationally respected auditor with few reservations. The private company can stand a few reservations about the need for a reserve against future tax assessments.

Other explanations for the prevalence of private companies in Canada are not excluded by the evidence presented. The industrial mix is different in Canada. Mining is a larger share of the economy, and information asymmetries provide an obvious possible explanation for the unsuitability of such firms for public ownership. Some Canadian firms have grown large in a protected home market that is much smaller than the corresponding U.S. market. Smaller firms are better suited for private ownership. Bankruptcy laws differ between the two countries, as do many other institutions and customs. Restrictions on branch banking may have encouraged U.S. firms to be publicly held. This list is hardly exhaustive. Any of these cross-country differences could be the true explanation for the difference. So this paper is not necessarily the last word on the subject, even if it seems convincing to a discussant now. I will not comment on the possibility that training in public finance made me more sympathetic to this view than others might be.

One particularly disquieting note is the observation that private firms are always preferentially taxed relative to publicly held firms. The tax-minimizing strategy is always private in both countries. In reality, as in the authors' model, the desire to deploy more capital without assuming more risk drives the firm to public markets. But, while most capital in both countries is in publicly traded firms, the structure of firms is very different. Canadian firms are often arranged in vertical pyramids with substantial minority equity at lower levels. U.S. firms are either subsidiaries or independent, (La Porta, Lopez-de-Silanes, and Shleifer 1998). In the United States, the limitations on the intercorporate dividend deduction make it expensive for controlled subsidiaries to raise equity of their own. This explains the absence of pyramids in the United States. But what explains their presence elsewhere?

The controlling shareholders in a pyramid may control an empire while supplying only a small fraction of the capital and absorb only a small portion of the risk. That is a benefit for them, but only if they can attract and exploit outside finance. What is the advantage to the minority shareholders providing that capital? Are minority shareholders even a significant source of capital? Do they share fully in company profits? Are they protected through the legal system, through relationships of blood, marriage, or business? If not, are their alternative investments restricted by capital controls or weak property rights?

Shleifer and Vishny (1997) have argued that outsider finance is a feature of common law countries with strong protection for investors. Canada is one of those countries with a strong common law heritage, yet many Canadian corporations are organized in pyramids typical of countries with weak protection for shareholders. What is the motivation for that organization?

A full deduction for intercorporate dividends would appear to be a logical part of correctly valuing corporate income. If the United States joined the rest of the world in providing such a deduction, would the U.S. corporate structure drift toward the Canadian form? Would that be a good thing? There are lots of good questions left.

## References

La Porta, Rafael, Florencio Lopez-de-Silanes, and Andrei Shleifer. 1998. Corporate ownership around the world. NBER Working Paper no. 6625. Cambridge, Mass.: National Bureau of Economic Research.

Shleifer, Andrei, and Robert W. Vishny. 1997. A survey of corporate governance. *Journal of Finance* 52:737–83.

# II

# The Law and Concentrated Corporate Ownership

# 5

# Constraints on Large-Block Shareholders

Clifford G. Holderness and Dennis P. Sheehan

There is a growing belief among both academics and practitioners that firm performance can often be improved by large-block shareholders. These can be either individuals or entities (such as other corporations or partnerships) that own large-percentage blocks of stock and work with or join management to improve firm performance. Concentrated ownership is viewed as ameliorating the separation of ownership from control that has been long seen as a bane of large public corporations.

There is a major potential problem with large investors, however, a problem that is often overlooked. The very thing that gives large investors the ability to improve management, the voting power of block ownership, also gives them the power to consume corporate resources, either through poor management or by outright expropriation. Consider, for example, a chief executive who owns more than 50 percent of his firm's stock. What constrains this individual from maximizing the firm's expected cash flows and then expropriating those cash flows through excess compensation, consuming perquisites, borrowing from the firm at below-market interest rates, paying differential dividends, or the like? This apparently is what Robert Maxwell did at two large public corporations. Likewise, what will stop a block investor's well-intentioned but ill-conceived management? This describes the path of Wang Laboratories into bankruptcy.

Block investors who do not join management pose a similar threat. For instance, management can place a block of "sweetheart" preferred stock

Clifford G. Holderness is professor of finance at Boston College. Dennis P. Sheehan is the Benzak Professor of Finance in the Smeal College of Business at Penn State University.

The authors have benefited from the comments of James Brickley, Linda DeAngelo, Gordon Hanka, Mark Huson, Randall Kroszner, Michele LaPlante, Claudio Loderer, Roberta Romano, Michael Weisbach, conference participants, and an anonymous referee.

with an investor with the understanding that the investor will support management in control contests. The large-block investment made in the Polaroid Corporation by Corporate Partners during an attempted takeover in the late 1980s appears to be such a case. Outside blockholders also have the capability to use their voting power to secure favorable contracts with the firm.

Legal scholars have long held that the law does not effectively constrain block shareholders. Rock (1994, 989), for example, describes Delaware corporate law, federal securities law, and federal antitrust law as "rather toothless [for limiting] corrupt relational investing." Gilson (1986, quoting in part Eisenberg 1976, 309) summarizes, "The academic evaluation of [legal] limitations . . . is unambiguous. . . . The checks on unfair dealing by the parent are few. In theory, of course, the fairness of the parent's behavior is subject to the check of judicial review; but in practice such review is difficult even where the courts have the will to engage in it, and they often lack the will."[1] If such assessments are correct, the potential for block investors to improve firm performance would be more limited than currently acknowledged.

The pessimism over the potential of the law to constrain block investors is based on reading cases and statutes. We know of no empirical evidence on the subject. In this paper, we empirically investigate whether the conventional wisdom on the ineffectiveness of legal constraints on block investors is warranted. We base most of our analyses on firms that presumably offer the most latitude for opportunistic behavior toward minority shareholders: firms in which one shareholder owns more than 50 percent of the common stock. These firms should illustrate most clearly the constraints, if any, on block investors.

We start by documenting that firms with concentrated ownership are surviving and do not appear to trade at substantial discounts to firms with diffuse ownership. This suggests that something constrains block investors—minority shareholders are not totally at the mercy of their larger brethren. We next investigate whether organizational mechanisms are strengthened or modified to counterbalance the power of block investors. If so, the perceived weakness of the law would be relatively unimportant, as minority shareholders would rely on organizational constraints.

Our empirical investigations reveal that boards of directors of majority-owned firms differ little from those of firms with diffuse stock ownership. Another potential organizational constraint on majority shareholders, capital market activity, also appears to differ little between firms with concentrated and firms with diffuse ownership. Likewise, there is little evi-

1. Although some such assessments are made in the context of parent-subsidiary relations, commentators do not seem to distinguish corporate large-block shareholders from individual large-block shareholders.

dence that new organizational mechanisms have widely evolved to constrain block investors.

Finally, we review the much-criticized legal doctrines applicable to large-block shareholders. We attempt to assess the effect of these constraints by examining the frequency of and the wealth effects for minority shareholders associated with mergers, the going private, restructurings, and liquidations of majority-shareholder firms. We find that minority shareholders on average receive premia of 20 percent over preannouncement stock prices when they are bought out by majority shareholders—approximately the same premia that shareholders in diffusely held firms receive when they are bought out. This suggests that the law prevents majority shareholders from using their voting power to freeze out minority shareholders at low prices. Despite these premia, majority shareholders buy out minority shareholders at least as often as do firms with relatively diffuse ownership. These payments appear in part to be the price that majority shareholders must pay to remove the threat of minority-shareholder litigation. Additional evidence of legal constraints comes from the treatment of minority shareholders in reorganizations that follow block trades, from comparing the U.S. experience with the New Zealand experience (New Zealand has few protections for minority shareholders), and from evidence on the treatment of minority shareholders in other countries. The totality of the evidence suggests that, counter to the opinion of many legal scholars, the law protects minority shareholders. Indeed, our findings raise the possibility that the law may be the primary constraint on large-block shareholders in public corporations.

## 5.1 The Survival and Value Effects of Block Investors

Some scholars have suggested that the sole protection for minority shareholders might be price protection. That is to say, the price at which minority shareholders buy their stock simply reflects the discounted value of the expected expropriation or incompetence of the firm's large shareholders.

Although price protection may exist, it can never be the sole protection for minority shareholders. If large-block shareholders are subject to neither organizational nor legal constraints, they could, through poor management or by outright expropriation, consume corporate resources without limit. Once this possibility became known, a "lemons" problem would arise, and individuals would refuse to become minority shareholders at any price. Ultimately, firms with block investors would not survive. This is why Fama and Jensen (1983) conclude that firms in which chief executive officers own a majority of the common stock will not survive.

We start our analysis of the constraints on large shareholders by examining the existing empirical evidence on the extent of concentrated ownership. If large-block shareholders exist only infrequently, one might conclude that they are anomalies that are not destined to last. Next, we examine a variety of evidence on the effect of large shareholders on firm value. This will give us insights into the possible importance of price protection for minority shareholders.

### 5.1.1 The Survival of Firms with Block Investors

The available evidence shows that many firms have concentrated ownership. Mikkelson and Partch (1989) document that, in approximately 30 percent of a random sample of 240 corporations listed on either the New York Stock Exchange (NYSE) or the American Stock Exchange (Amex), the board and top officers control at least 20 percent of the votes. Holderness and Sheehan (1988) identify 663 NYSE- or Amex-listed firms with majority shareholders; they analyze 114 of these firms and document that, in over 90 percent of them, the majority shareholder or a representative of the corporate majority shareholder is a director or a top officer. They report that firms with majority shareholders appear to be surviving. Ritter (1981) documents that insiders retained on average 72 percent of the common stock in the 559 firm-commitment initial public offerings registered with the Securities and Exchange Commission (SEC) between 1965 and 1973.[2]

Block investors have been around since the early days of the modern public corporation. J. P. Morgan, for example, played a key role in reorganizing bankrupt railroads at the turn of the century. To facilitate the sale of securities in the reorganized firm, he typically would serve as chairman of the company for several years, during which time he and his representatives ran the firm. De Long (1991) estimates that one Morgan partner on a board increased the value of the firm's equity by approximately 30 percent. Goldman Sachs played a similar role with retail firms. Finally, Holderness, Kroszner, and Sheehan (1999) find that average inside ownership of the common stock among a large sample of U.S. exchange-listed firms increased from 13 percent in 1935 to 21 percent in 1995.

### 5.1.2 Firm Value and Large Shareholders

*Market-to-Book Studies*

Several studies measure the effect of large-block ownership on a firm's market-to-book ratio (the ratio of the market value of a firm's assets to their replacement cost). In general, these studies offer little support for the proposition that block investors significantly reduce firm value, which they

2. Additional evidence on the extent of large-block ownership among managers is reported in Demsetz (1983), Demsetz and Lehn (1985), and Herman (1981). Denis and Denis (1994) contains further evidence on the history of majority-controlled firms.

would do if there were few constraints on them. Morck, Shleifer, and Vishny (1988b) report that, for 371 Fortune 500 firms, the market-to-book ratio increases when managerial stockholdings go from 0 to 5 percent, decreases between 5 and 25 percent, and increases above 25 percent. McConnell and Servaes (1990) use a larger sample and find that, in one year studied (1986), the market-to-book ratio increases until top management owns 40 or 50 percent of the stock and declines thereafter. Holderness and Sheehan (1988) find no significant difference in the market-to-book ratios for a paired sample of majority-owned and diffusely held firms.

The strongest evidence that blockholders can reduce firm value comes from closed-end funds. Barclay, Holderness, and Pontiff (1993) find that, the greater the managerial stock ownership, the larger are the discounts to net asset value (book value). Even here, discounts seldom exceed 25 percent, suggesting that there are significant constraints on even the largest blockholders in closed-end funds.

*Equity Carve-Outs*

An equity carve-out occurs when a parent corporation sells partial ownership interest in a subsidiary to the public. In most such reorganizations, the parent retains at least half the common stock and therefore controls the carved-out subsidiary (Schipper and Smith 1983; Klein, Rosenfeld, and Beranek 1991).

Klein, Rosenfeld, and Beranek (1991) report that the parent eventually reacquired the subsidiary's publicly held shares in twenty-five of the eighty-three carve-outs between 1966 and 1983. (In fourteen additional cases, the parent sold its block to a third party; nine of these buyers declared that they intended to buy the public's interest.) If block investors are unconstrained, it is unclear why individuals voluntarily invest in carve-outs and why parent corporations so often go to the expense of reacquiring the public's shares.

Klein, Rosenfeld, and Beranek (1991, 457) further report that the announcements of these reacquisitions are associated with insignificant abnormal stock returns for the parent firms. In contrast, public shareholders in the subsidiary earn statistically positive abnormal returns that approximate those earned by target firms in arm's-length mergers and acquisitions. The authors interpret this evidence to suggest "that parents did not generally take advantage of their dominant positions to capture gains accruing to subsidiary shareholders."

*Thermo Electron*

A final observation comes from the Thermo Electron Corporation, a NYSE company that has done twenty-three carve-outs of publicly traded firms and still retains majority control in all. In SEC filings Thermo Electron acknowledges that it controls the carve-outs by appointing directors and officers and by providing a variety of legal, accounting, and financial services.

As of 1998, the value of Thermo Electron's shares in its subsidiaries exceeded the market value of Thermo Electron itself by 16 percent (about $1 billion).[3] This arguably understates the discount of Thermo Electron to its controlled subsidiaries because it places no value on Thermo Electron's own operations. Thermo Electron thus offers no evidence that block investors substantially reduce firm value. Indeed, this evidence suggests that any subsidies go from the dominant parent to the subsidiaries.

### 5.1.3 Summary

Two points emerge from the evidence presented above. First, firms with large shareholders appear to be surviving. Second, the evidence of the effect of large shareholders on firm value is mixed. There is no evidence, however, that block investors have a large negative effect on firm value. In short, the evidence—from a number of studies, over different time periods, representing a cross section of industries—strongly suggests that large-block shareholders in public corporations are constrained and that the primary constraint is not price protection.

## 5.2 Organizational Constraints on Block Investors

In spite of the evidence presented above of the survival and value effects of block investors, the widespread criticisms of the ineffectiveness of the law could still be correct if the binding constraints are organizational, not legal. We therefore investigate whether organizational constraints are altered to counterbalance the additional power that comes with large-block investors. We also search for evidence of innovative organizational constraints in firms with block investors.

Turner Broadcasting Corporation (one of the firms in our sample, described below) illustrates how existing organizational mechanisms can be modified and new ones developed to constrain a large-block shareholder (Holderness and Sheehan 1991). Since taking his firm public in 1980, Ted Turner owned a majority of the common stock and relied primarily on debt and retained earnings to finance an ambitious expansion into cable television and satellite broadcasting. In early 1987, Turner Broadcasting had a debt–to–total asset ratio of 0.72; by May of that year, it was apparent that the company would have difficulty meeting its debt obligations. Accordingly, Turner contracted with a group of cable companies to pur-

3. These figures come from Thermo Electron itself, which values the publicly traded subsidiaries at closing prices as of 22 June 1998 and values the wholly owned subsidiaries at twenty-five times 1998 earnings. These figures also include the value of cash held by Thermo Electron net of debt and intercompany loans.

chase newly issued preferred stock. Among the conditions imposed by the cable companies as a condition of investing were amending the bylaws to enable them to elect seven of fifteen directors, requiring supramajority approval by the board of major management decisions, restricting the alienability of the preferred stock so that its ownership stayed with the cable companies, and acquiring the right of first refusal to buy Ted Turner's stock. This agreement remained in force, despite Ted Turner's subsequent expressions of dissatisfaction, for the remainder of the time that Turner Broadcasting was a stand-alone public corporation.[4] (Turner Broadcasting merged with the Time/Warner Corp. in 1996.) Under these conditions, Ted Turner was effectively constrained by organizational mechanisms, his majority ownership of the common stock notwithstanding.

### 5.2.1 Sample Description

We use a sample of public corporations that have majority shareholders to investigate constraints on large-block shareholders. We choose this sample for several reasons. First, these block investors presumably have the greatest latitude for opportunistic behavior toward minority shareholders. If there are constraints on majority shareholders, it is likely that the same constraints bind blockholders who own less than a majority of the stock. Second, we used this sample in Holderness and Sheehan (1988) to investigate the organizational role of large-block shareholders. A major conclusion of that research was that "the evidence is inconsistent with the proposition that individuals or corporations hold majority blocks of stock in publicly traded corporations primarily to expropriate or consume corporate resources" (p. 344). It thus appears that the blockholders in this sample are constrained. In the current paper, we attempt to identify and analyze these constraints. Finally, we have no reason to believe that the constraints on large shareholders, whatever they are, have changed significantly since the sample was constructed.

To generate a sample of majority shareholder corporations, we search CDA Investment Technology's January 1980 *Spectrum,* which lists major shareholders in several thousand public firms. For inclusion in the sample, we require that a firm have a majority shareholder for at least two consecutive years.[5] In the interests of data availability, we limit our sample to NYSE and Amex firms. This process yields 114 firms that had majority shareholders for approximately 500 firm years between 1978 and 1984.

4. It should be noted that such dissatisfaction was voiced by the block investor, not by minority shareholders. Turner Broadcasting stock significantly outperformed the market while these constraints were in place (Holderness and Sheehan 1991).

5. Majority shareholders are defined as individuals or entities that own more than 50 percent of a firm's common stock. Entities are typically other corporations but occasionally include charitable or voting trusts.

Information about the block investors and their firms is collected from annual proxy statements and Compustat.

To ascertain whether organizational constraints are strengthened or modified in majority-shareholder firms, we attempt to pair each of the 114 majority-shareholder firms with a firm that has the same two-digit SIC industry code, is closest in total assets, and is listed on the NYSE or Amex. To identify differences associated with concentrated ownership, we require that no single shareholder owns more than 20 percent of the comparison firm's stock. Using these criteria, we are able to pair 101 majority-shareholder corporations. These paired comparisons are the basis for many of the tests in this section of the paper.

Two characteristics of majority-shareholder firms are pertinent to our analysis. First, corporations are majority shareholders in 50 percent of the firm years in the sample, individuals own the blocks in 46 percent of the firm years, and the remaining blocks are held by charitable or voting trusts. Many of the empirical regularities reported in Holderness and Sheehan (1988) differ for corporate and individual majority shareholders. Interestingly, some legal scholars have been particularly critical of judicial laxness in regulating the relations between parent corporations and partially owned, publicly traded subsidiaries. Accordingly, throughout this paper, we differentiate between firms controlled by other corporations and those controlled by individuals.

The second regularity is that 90 percent of the individual majority shareholders and representatives of 94 percent of the corporate majority shareholders are either directors or officers. In other words, majority shareholders are active investors. Because most empirical regularities do not depend on whether a majority shareholder or a representative of a corporate majority shareholder is an officer or a director, and because those few majority shareholders who are not managers can become so at their option, our investigations are based on the full sample of majority-shareholder firms.

### 5.2.2 Boards of Directors

Boards of directors are widely viewed as the central internal control mechanism in public corporations. It was the directors, for example, who engineered the replacement of long-standing CEOs at General Motors, Westinghouse, and IBM. Academic research confirms the potential importance of directors. Gilson (1990), for example, finds that board turnover following financial distress is significantly greater than ordinary board turnover. Furthermore, the reconstituted board has more bankers, blockholders, and outsiders. Similarly, Byrd and Hickman (1992) find that announcement-day returns of bidders in tender offers are higher for firms with a majority of independent outside directors.

For the board to exercise control, however, it needs the power to con-

**Table 5.1** **Comparisons of Board Membership of Majority-Shareholder Firms on the NYSE or Amex and a Paired Sample of Firms with Diffuse Ownership in Which No Shareholder Owns More Than 20 Percent of the Common Stock (1980–84)**

| | Mean (Median) Value | | *p*-Value | | |
|---|---|---|---|---|---|
| Variable | Majority-Shareholder Firms | Diffuse-Ownership Firms | Difference in Means | Wilcoxon Signed-Rank Tests | Sample Size |
| Full sample: | | | | | |
| Number of directors | 9.5 (9) | 10.2 (10) | 0.18 | 0.09 | 97 |
| Number of outside directors | 6.2 (6) | 7.1 (7) | 0.03 | 0.04 | 97 |
| Ratio of outside to total directors | 0.62 (0.67) | 0.68 (0.69) | 0.01 | 0.02 | 97 |
| Individual majority shareholders: | | | | | |
| Number of directors | 8.4 (8) | 9.4 (9) | 0.15 | 0.18 | 40 |
| Number of outside directors | 4.8 (4) | 6.3 (6) | 0.03 | 0.03 | 40 |
| Ratio of outside to total directors | 0.54 (0.50) | 0.64 (0.64) | 0.01 | 0.01 | 40 |
| Corporate majority shareholders: | | | | | |
| Number of directors | 10.4 (9) | 10.8 (10) | 0.53 | 0.28 | 54 |
| Number of outside directors | 7.4 (7) | 7.8 (7) | 0.52 | 0.73 | 54 |
| Ratio of outside to total directors | 0.69 (0.72) | 0.71 (0.71) | 0.51 | 0.62 | 54 |

*Sources:* Data are from annual proxy statements.

*Note:* Outside directors are defined as anyone not currently an employee of the firm or (with corporate majority shareholders) the parent firm.

strain management. When managers' stockholdings are small, the board has this power because the managers have relatively few votes in the election of directors. The boards of majority-shareholder firms, by contrast, would seem to lack this power because a majority shareholder has the votes to elect and fire directors unilaterally. Under the conditions described below and summarized in tables 5.1 and 5.2, however, the board has greater power to constrain a block investor.

### *Outside Directors*

Outside directors are usually portrayed as being more independent of management and thus offering more protection for shareholders than inside directors, who, by definition, are employees of the firm. For example,

**Table 5.2** **Comparisons of Methods of Electing Directors and the Frequency of Board Subcommittees for 101 Majority-Shareholder Firms on the NYSE or Amex and a Paired Sample of Firms with Diffuse Ownership in Which No Shareholder Owns More Than 20 Percent of the Stock (1980–84)**

| Variable | Mean (Median) Value (%): Majority-Shareholder Firms | Mean (Median) Value (%): Diffuse-Ownership Firms | *p*-Value of $\chi^2$-Statistic Testing for Homogeneity of Populations |
|---|---|---|---|
| Full sample: | | | |
| Firms having staggered elections for directors | 7 | 40 | < .01 |
| Firms having cumulative voting for directors | 16 | 23 | .24 |
| Firms having: | | | |
| Audit subcommittee | 84 | 91 | .16 |
| Compensation subcommittee | 63 | 72 | .16 |
| Individual majority shareholders: | | | |
| Firms having staggered elections for directors | 3 | 32 | < .01 |
| Firms having cumulative voting for directors | 15 | 22 | .42 |
| Firms having: | | | |
| Audit subcommittee | 85 | 85 | .96 |
| Compensation subcommittee | 51 | 63 | .31 |
| Corporate majority shareholders: | | | |
| Firms having staggered elections for directors | 9 | 48 | < .01 |
| Firms having cumulative voting for directors | 17 | 21 | .59 |
| Firms having: | | | |
| Audit subcommittee | 89 | 96 | .14 |
| Compensation subcommittee | 76 | 77 | .82 |

*Sources:* Data are from annual proxy statements.

press reports suggest that outside directors took the lead in the three prominent replacements of CEOs noted above. Rosenstein and Wyatt (1990) report that the appointment of outside directors on average produces a positive stock-price response. Weisbach (1988) finds that poor stock-price performance is more likely to lead to CEO turnover as the ratio of outside directors to total directors increases. It seems reasonable that the independence of outside directors would be a constraining influence on managers who own large blocks of stock as well.

Table 5.1, however, reports that both the absolute number of outside directors and the ratio of outside to inside directors are lower in majority-shareholder firms than in their paired firms with diffuse ownership. These differences can be attributed largely to firms with individual majority shareholders; little difference emerges in either the total number of directors, the number of outside directors, or the ratio of outside to total directors for firms with corporate majority shareholders and their paired firms.[6] For neither subsample do we find systematic evidence of additional outside directors to counterbalance the power of majority ownership. In a similar vein, the probability of a recalcitrant director who, through his oversight of management and access to confidential firm information, can increase the costs to the block investor of acting against the minority should increase with the absolute number of directors. The fact that majority-shareholder firms tend to have smaller boards than their paired firms is evidence that boards typically do not change to counterbalance the additional power of a majority shareholder.

*Staggered Elections*

Staggered elections of directors are viewed in the agency literature as reducing shareholder wealth because they can delay the election of directors more attentive to shareholders. But staggered elections also delay the firing of directors by a manager with large stockholdings. When a block investor elects directors who then prove to be too attentive to minority shareholders, under staggered elections he must wait before firing them. In the interim, those directors can monitor the investor. As seen in table 5.2, however, staggered elections are used in fewer firms with majority ownership than firms with relatively diffuse ownership: in our sample, 7 versus 40 percent (the *p*-value of the difference is less than 0.01). This pattern holds when the sample is divided into individual and corporate majority shareholders.

*Cumulative Voting*

Cumulative voting increases directors' power to constrain managers who own large blocks of stock by increasing the likelihood that minority shareholders will be able to elect representatives to the board. Gordon (1993) argues that cumulative voting can assist institutional investors in monitoring management. Although directors elected by minority shareholders lack the power to veto a majority shareholder's decisions, they nevertheless gain access to confidential firm information and are included in board deliberations. Moreover, if the manager acts counter to the interests of minority shareholders, the directors elected by the minority shareholders can take the lead in opposition, perhaps by initiating litigation. As reported in table 5.2, however, cumulative voting is found less often in

6. For analysis of percentages in table 5.1 and throughout the paper, we report the probability value of the two-tailed $\chi^2$-statistic used to test whether the paired samples are drawn from a homogeneous population.

majority-shareholder firms than in their paired firms (16 vs. 23 percent), although the *p*-value of the difference is only 0.24.

*Subcommittees*

Other potential board constraints on managers with large-block holdings are subcommittees of the board, in particular, an audit subcommittee composed entirely of outside directors, a similarly composed compensation subcommittee, or a special subcommittee to monitor transactions between the firm and a dominant shareholder. As detailed in table 5.2, both audit and compensation subcommittees are found in fewer majority-shareholder firms than paired firms (84 vs. 91 percent and 63 vs. 72 percent), with the differences being marginally significant (*p*-value of both differences of 0.16).[7] In addition, majority shareholders sit on these subcommittees significantly more often than do the largest shareholders in the paired firms, further reducing the probability that these bodies constrain majority shareholders.[8] Finally, in the several hundred proxy statements and news articles that we examined for our sample, there were no reports of special subcommittees to monitor a majority shareholder.

### 5.2.3 Monitoring by Nonmanager Stockholders and Debtholders

Although the board is typically viewed as the central organizational control mechanism, it is not the only one. Both nonmanager shareholders and debtholders have incentives to monitor top managers, especially when those managers have the additional powers that come with substantial stock ownership. Free-rider problems with small shareholders imply that large-block shareholders are likely to be more effective monitors (Shleifer and Vishny 1986). Our investigations, however, show that, typically, there are few large-block shareholders to monitor majority shareholders. In 75 percent of the approximately five hundred firm years in our sample, no shareholder other than the majority shareholder owns as much as 5 percent of the common stock. Likewise, 89 percent of the majority-owned firms have no directors (other than the majority shareholder) who own 5 percent of the stock. This is revealing in that the legal rights of directors lower monitoring costs.

Debtholders could also play an important role in constraining block investors, either through board membership or through covenants that

7. More of the diffusely held firms are listed on the NYSE, which, in contrast to the Amex, requires audit subcommittees. Because a majority shareholder can presumably choose the exchange listing, however, the difference between the samples remains noteworthy.

8. Majority shareholders (or representatives of corporate majority shareholders) sit on 40 percent of the audit subcommittees and on 72 percent of the compensation subcommittees. In contrast, only 13 percent of the largest shareholders in the paired firms are on the audit subcommittee, and only 25 percent of them are on the compensation subcommittee. The *p*-values of the differences between the paired samples are less than 0.01.

limit the investors' discretion. A necessary (but not sufficient) condition for bondholders to exercise additional control rights would be a substantial debt ratio. Individual majority-shareholder firms, however, have significantly lower total debt-to-asset ratios than their paired firms, and corporate majority-shareholder firms have total debt-to-asset ratios that equal those of their paired firms.[9] The low debt levels further suggest that the need to meet debt obligations typically does not discipline managers with majority ownership any more than it does managers with smaller ownership interests.[10]

### 5.2.4 Monitoring by Auditors

A firm's auditor can constrain block investors by identifying and exposing mismanagement or opportunistic behavior.[11] Because Big Six accounting firms have the most valuable reputations to lose if information about low-quality audits is exposed, they should offer higher-quality audits and thus more protection for minority shareholders than do smaller, less well-known accounting firms (see DeAngelo 1981). In our paired years, 92 percent of the majority-shareholder firms and 87 percent of the comparison firms employ Big Six firms ($p$-value of difference of 0.29). (This comparison changes little when the sample is divided into individual and corporate majority-shareholder firms.) Accordingly, it is difficult to maintain on the basis of these data that block investors trigger additional monitoring by auditors.

### 5.2.5 Reputation as a Constraining Influence

Finally, block investors could be constrained by reputational considerations. Individuals, for example, might restrain themselves for this reason, or they could be restrained by relatives' monitoring to prevent harm to the family's reputation, as might occur with inept management or oppor-

9. Individual majority-shareholder firms have an average debt-to-asset ratio of 0.18 (median 0.16), compared with an average ratio of 0.26 (median 0.26) for their paired firms. The $p$-value of a $t$-test on the difference in means is 0.02 (the $p$-value of the Wilcoxon signed-rank test is 0.01). Corporate majority-shareholder firms have an average debt-to-asset ratio of 0.22 (median 0.20), compared with an average ratio of 0.22 (median 0.22) for their paired firms. Both parametric and nonparametric tests show the samples to be indistinguishable.

10. Jensen (1986) discusses the disciplinary role of debt.

11. Events at Coated Sales Inc. illustrate how auditors can constrain block investors. In 1988, Peat Marwick resigned as the firm's auditor, "saying that it wasn't satisfied with representations" made by the company. At that time, Coated Sales said that the dispute involved a $6 million payment, but Wall Street analysts were "puzzled that an auditing firm would lose an account over a dispute of this nature" (Naj 1988, 12). A special committee of the board was formed to investigate the reasons for Peat Marwick's resignation. Several weeks thereafter, the committee found evidence of a false $6 million transaction, and the board suspended Michael Weinstein, who was the chairman, CEO, and founder and a 12 percent blockholder. The board then retained another Big Six accounting firm to investigate Weinstein and several other top managers further. Shortly thereafter, Weinstein resigned.

tunistic behavior.[12] Similarly, corporate block investors will find it more costly to transact with others if they develop a reputation for acting opportunistically toward minority shareholders in partially owned subsidiaries.

Although it is important to acknowledge these possible constraints, it is difficult to measure their effectiveness. We can, however, test whether majority shareholders are constrained by the expectation of trips to the capital markets.[13] When capital market participants observe opportunistic behavior toward minority shareholders, they will demand a premium for investing (if they invest at all). In contrast, a reputation for acting honestly toward minority shareholders will enable a majority shareholder to raise capital on more favorable terms.

If past trips to the capital markets are a reasonable proxy for future trips, it is noteworthy that in only 9 percent of the firm years in our sample do majority-shareholder firms issue public debt or equity. Their paired firms, on the other hand, go to the capital markets in 15 percent of the years ($p$-value of the difference of 0.24). This difference is more pronounced between firms owned by individuals and their paired firms (8 vs. 15 percent, $p$-value 0.33) than between corporate-owned firms and their paired firms (9 vs. 11 percent, $p$-value 0.88).

A firm's payout policy offers complementary insights into potential monitoring by capital market participants, on the theory that high payouts to shareholders increase the probability of external financing, ceteris paribus. High payouts also signal a block investor's good faith to minority shareholders. As detailed in table 5.3, the dividend yield and the dividend payout ratio are lower in majority-shareholder than in diffusely held firms. Following the pattern of several of the previous tests, the statistical significance (but not the point estimate) is somewhat more pronounced for firms with individual than with corporate majority shareholders. For instance, individual majority-shareholder firms distribute to shareholders an average of only 13 percent of their pretax earnings, whereas their paired firms distribute 25 percent, a difference that produces a $p$-value of 0.02; corporate majority-shareholder firms distribute 37 percent, whereas their paired firms distribute 26 percent, a difference that produces a $p$-value of only 0.61.

### 5.2.6 Time-Series Evidence of Changes in Organizational Constraints

We supplement the preceding cross-sectional evidence with an analysis of organizational changes in our 114 majority-shareholder firms between 1978 and 1984. Large and systematic changes associated with changes in

12. Fama and Jensen (1983) and DeAngelo and DeAngelo (1985) suggest intrafamily monitoring in other corporate settings.

13. Rozeff (1982) and Easterbrook (1984) analyze how frequent trips to the capital markets can result in the monitoring of management.

**Table 5.3** **Comparisons of Payments to Shareholders for Majority-Shareholder Firms on the NYSE or Amex and a Paired Sample of Firms with Diffuse Ownership in Which No Shareholder Owns More Than 20 Percent of the Stock (1980–84)**

| | Mean (Median) Value | | *p*-Value | | |
|---|---|---|---|---|---|
| Variable | Majority-Shareholder Firms | Diffuse-Ownership Firms | Difference in Means | Wilcoxon Signed-Rank Tests | Sample Size |
| Full sample: | | | | | |
| Dividends as a percentage of year-end stock price | 2.3 (1.1) | 3.2 (2.7) | .02 | .05 | 94 |
| Dividends per share divided by earnings per share | 26.5 (9.9) | 25.7 (25.7) | .98 | .03 | 96 |
| Individual majority shareholders: | | | | | |
| Dividends as a percentage of year-end stock price | 1.9 (1.0) | 3.0 (1.4) | .07 | .24 | 41 |
| Dividends per share divided by earnings per share | 13.1 (9.4) | 24.7 (23.1) | .02 | .04 | 41 |
| Corporate majority shareholders: | | | | | |
| Dividends as a percentage of year-end stock price | 2.6 (1.2) | 3.2 (2.7) | .20 | .19 | 50 |
| Dividends per share divided by earnings per share | 36.6 (9.3) | 25.9 (29.5) | .61 | .24 | 51 |

*Source:* Data from Compustat.

ownership concentration would suggest that firms adapt internally to reduce agency problems associated with majority ownership. Using time-series data, we conduct two tests. First, we compare the averages for a variable (say, the ratio of outside to total directors) for the firm years before and after a corporation becomes majority controlled, a "before/after classification." Second, we compare firms on the basis of the year relative to their becoming majority controlled, a "relative-year classification," by defining the year in which a firm becomes majority controlled as year 0 and calculating our statistics by stratifying on years relative to year 0. In

**Table 5.4** **Time-Series Analyses of Changes in Organizational Constraints on Top Management Associated with the Realization of Majority Ownership for 114 NYSE- or Amex-Listed Corporations (1978–84)**

| Variable | Relative-Year *p*-Value | Before/After *p*-Value | Direction of Before/After Change Associated with Majority Ownership |
|---|---|---|---|
| Number of directors | .42 | .63 | No change |
| Number of outside directors | .54 | .48 | Decrease |
| Ratio of outside directors | .61 | .18 | Decrease |
| Audit subcommittee | .99 | .65 | Increase |
| Compensation subcommittee | .54 | .17 | Increase |
| Cumulative voting | .91 | .09 | Increase |
| Staggered voting | .31 | .02 | Decrease |
| Big Six auditor | .99 | .46 | Decrease |
| Change in auditor | .94 | .53 | Increase |
| Debt-asset ratio | .87 | .44 | Decrease |
| Amount of financing | .08 | .16 | No change |
| Dividend yield | .95 | .98 | Increase |
| Dividend payout | .15 | .01 | Increase |

*Sources:* Data from annual proxy statements and Compustat.

*Note:* Before/after test compares the values of the variables by splitting the observations into a period before the firm is controlled by a majority shareholder and the period in which it is controlled. Relative-year test stratifies the sample by the year in relation to when a firm becomes majority owned. The *p*-value is for the $\chi^2$-statistic if the variable is categorical or for the Wilcoxon signed-rank test (or Kruskal-Wallis test) if the variable is continuous. Direction of change denotes the change in the median of the variable using the before/after classification.

contrast to the first time-series test, this test enables us to identify trends in relative time.

Table 5.4 summarizes the time-series tests by reporting the *p*-values of the test statistics and the direction of the difference in the point estimate of a variable using the before/after classification. Most of the relative-year tests lack statistical significance. In addition, we are unable to perceive any economically meaningful trends in the averages or medians of the variables in relative time. The before/after tests, in contrast, reveal some statistically reliable differences. As far as constraining majority shareholders, however, the direction of these changes is inconsistent. For example, more firms use cumulative voting after becoming majority owned, but the use of staggered voting declines. Dividend-payout ratios increase, but the amount of external financing is essentially unchanged. Other variables do not show strong statistical differences. We interpret the evidence in table 5.4 to mean that few dramatic changes occur in an array of potential organizational constraints when firms go in and out of majority ownership.

### 5.2.7 Summary

Four patterns emerge from the empirical investigations in this section. First, the primary organizational mechanisms that the agency literature and the financial press view as constraining management do not appear to be altered to counterbalance the power of managerial majority stock ownership. Indeed, if anything, the data seem to point to fewer organizational constraints on management in majority-controlled firms. Second, this tendency toward fewer organizational constraints is more pronounced when individuals rather than corporations are majority shareholders. Third, time-series analysis reveals little evidence that movement from relatively diffuse to majority ownership is associated with dramatic or systematic changes in organizational constraints. Finally, we find few examples of unusual or innovative organizational constraints on block investors. Turner Broadcasting is the exception.

In the light of these four patterns, and because some prominent control devices—notably, hostile control activities—are inoperable in the face of a large block of stock held by a block investor, we conclude that organizational mechanisms are likely to impose fewer constraints on managers who own large blocks than on managers who have small stockholdings. Nevertheless, individuals are still willing to invest in firms controlled by block investors, and firms with block investors do not appear to trade at significant discounts in comparison to diffusely held firms. This suggests the need to examine the legal constraints on large-block shareholders.

## 5.3 Legal Constraints on Block Investors

### 5.3.1 Overview

*Potential Legal Constraints*

The breadth of potential common law, statutory, and administrative constraints on large shareholders is evident from examples of day-to-day management decisions by large-block shareholders that have violated the law.[14] Among these are looting the firm; furnishing a house, buying expensive cars, and taking sizable cash advances at corporate expense;[15] taking excessive compensation;[16] diverting a business opportunity from the firm;[17] selling property owned by a large shareholder to the firm at above-market

14. For a more extensive review of the legal doctrines applicable to block investors, see Magnuson (1984) and O'Neal (1975).

15. *Corbin v. Corbin*, 429 F. Supp. 276 (M.D. Ga. 1977).

16. *Miller v. Magline, Inc.*, 76 Mich. App. 284, 256 N.W.2d 761 (1977).

17. *Guth v. Loft Inc.*, 23 Del. Ch. 255, 5 A.2d 503 (1939); *Blaustein v. Pan American Petroleum & Transport Co.*, 174 Misc. 601, 21 N.Y.S.2d 651 (1940).

prices;[18] borrowing money from the firm at below-market interest rates or lending to it at above-market rates;[19] paying dividends that leave the firm strapped for cash; preventing dividends from being paid to "force" minority shareholders to sell their shares to the blockholder at "depressed" prices;[20] paying differential dividends; increasing the marketability of the majority's shares by decreasing the marketability of the minority's shares;[21] selling the control block to someone who plans to loot the firm;[22] issuing stock at prices that dilute the value of the minority's stock;[23] and making misrepresentations when issuing securities.[24] In general, these laws prevent non pro rata distributions of corporate assets (Barclay and Holderness 1992a). Remedies include disgorged profits, money damages, and injunctive relief; in extreme cases, large-block shareholders can be ordered to return all compensation to the firm.

Many of the legal doctrines applicable to block investors' management decisions, in particular, common law fiduciary obligations, also apply when the minority's shares are redeemed through mergers, going-private restructurings, and liquidations. In such transactions, additional legal doctrines become relevant, notably, the appraisal remedy, which allows shareholders who dispute an offer price to seek judicial valuation of their shares. When fraud or overreaching is alleged, minority shareholders may also seek equitable relief.[25] Finally, there are potential causes of action under federal and state security laws.

*Assessments of the Law's Effectiveness*

In spite of so many decisions against majority shareholders, legal scholars have widely concluded that the law does not significantly constrain block investors. The cases in which block investors are constrained apparently are viewed as anomalies. Brudney's (1978, 69–70) summary is representative:

> The parent will inevitably exercise discretion—lawfully as well as unlawfully, but substantially undetectable—to divert assets to itself instead of

18. *Efron v. Kalmanovitz,* 226 Cal. App. 2d 546 (1964).
19. See 31 A.L.R.2d 671.
20. Ibid.
21. *Jones v. H. F. Ahmanson & Co.,* 1 Cal. 3d 93 (1969).
22. *Insuranshares Corp. v. Northern Fiscal Corp.,* 35 F. Supp. 22 (D. Pa. 1940); *Gerdes v. Reynolds,* 28 N.Y.S.2d 622 (County Ct. Term 1941).
23. See Annotation, 38 A.L.R.2d 1366 (1954).
24. *Thomas v. Duralite Co., Inc.,* 386 F. Supp. 698 (D.N.J. 1974).
25. In *Weinberger v. UOP, Inc.,* 457 A.2d 701 (Del. 1983), the Delaware Supreme Court held that the appraisal remedy is the primary relief for minority shareholders disputing the price offered for their shares. The court noted, however, that it did "not intend any limitation on the historic powers of the Chancellor to grant such relief as the facts of a particular case may dictate. The appraisal remedy we approve may not be adequate in certain cases, particularly where fraud, misrepresentation, self-dealing, deliberate waste of corporate assets, or gross and palpable overreaching are involved" (p. 714).

> sharing them, all to the disadvantage of the public stockholders of the subsidiary. . . . [T]here is no doubt that the probability of a parent overreaching in self-dealing or appropriating opportunities for itself improperly but without being successfully challengeable is real. No less real than the probability of the parent thus exploiting the subsidiary on a continuing basis is the probability that it will force a merger of the two companies on terms which are disadvantageous to the subsidiary. As the parent's ownership of the subsidiary's stock increases—e.g. from 15 to 20 percent—the likelihood that it will exercise that power increases, not merely because it is more feasible but because of the temptation to eliminate at modest cost the nuisance value represented by so small a minority.

Cary's (1974, 679) critique of Delaware is similar: "The Delaware courts have tended to encourage freedom of action on the part of parent companies incorporated in that state and have indicated little concern over the fairness of dealings with subsidiaries. The consistent philosophy favors controlling shareholders and leaves fiduciary questions to the business judgment of an indentured board. The old concept that each party is 'entitled to what fair arm's length bargaining would probably have yielded' has been enveloped in a new and labyrinthine rationale."[26]

The pessimistic assessment of legal scholars evidently comes from interpreting case and statutory law. To our knowledge, the law's critics have cited no empirical evidence. This approach has a potentially serious flaw. Even if one concedes that there are only a "few anomalous" cases in which block investors have been constrained, it does not follow that the law is ineffective. As Gould (1972) explains, no lawsuit on an issue is consistent both with a law that is totally ineffective and with one that is totally effective. In the latter case, all parties realize that the law is perfectly enforced; they rationally avoid the prohibited act; and no lawsuits are therefore ever filed.[27]

We first assess the effectiveness of legal constraints on block investors by evaluating the frequency of reorganizations in which majority shareholders redeem the minority's shares. If block investors—especially majority shareholders—can do whatever they want, there would appear to be little reason to buy out minority shareholders. Reorganizations of majority shareholder firms would be rare. We next examine the wealth transfers from the majority to the minority shareholders. Small payments would

26. For a similar but more recent critique of Delaware law, see Rock (1994).

27. We could find no reports in the Dow Jones News Retrieval Service or in Standard and Poor's News Reports for the period 1979–September 1986 of any lawsuits contesting management decisions of majority shareholders in our sample of 114 firms. As noted above, this finding is consistent with the proposition that minority shareholders perceive that they have no legal protection as well as with the contrary proposition that all parties perceive the law as perfectly protecting minority shareholders.

indicate relatively minor legal constraints. We then examine trades of large-percentage blocks of stock. We also compare how minority shareholders fare in reorganizations in the United States, which at least has laws on the book to protect minority shareholders, with anecdotal evidence on how minority shareholders fare in New Zealand, which has no such laws. Finally, we cite recent research on the lack of protections for minority shareholders in countries other than the United States.

### 5.3.2 Evidence from Corporate Reorganizations

#### *Frequency of Reorganizations*

Table 5.5 reports how often firms in our paired sample were acquired, taken private, or liquidated between 1980 and 1986. Over the seven years followed, 36 percent of the majority shareholders redeem the minority's shares. By comparison, only 29 percent of the paired firms are reorganized over the same period.[28] This evidence is consistent with Morck, Shleifer, and Vishny (1988a), which found that the probability of a Fortune 500 firm's being acquired between 1981 and 1985 increased with the percentage of common stock owned by its top two managers. Our evidence is also consistent with the frequency with which parent firms reacquire the public's shares in partially owned carve-outs.[29]

#### *Wealth Transfers to Minority Shareholders*

The effect on minority shareholders' wealth associated with reorganizations is measured with a sample of forty-three mergers, going-private restructurings, and liquidations of majority-shareholder firms. Twenty-two of these reorganizations are drawn from the sample of 101; three involve firms from the original sample of 114 that we were unable to pair; ten are identified by searching the annual company index of the *Wall Street Journal* line by line for the period 1978–82; and eight are identified from Austin Associates' database of tender offers between 1981 and 1984. All the reorganizations involve NYSE or Amex firms, announcements reported in the *Wall Street Journal,* and a majority block in place at the time of the offer to minority shareholders.

We use standard event-study methodology to measure stock-price reactions associated with the initial public announcement that a majority-shareholder firm is being acquired, taken private, or liquidated. The

28. Table 5.5 also shows that minority shareholders are bought out significantly more often by corporate majority shareholders (40 percent) than they are in similar firms with diffuse ownership (21 percent) (the difference is significant at the 0.05 level).

29. Klein, Rosenfeld, and Beranek (1991) report that the parent eventually reacquired the subsidiary's publicly held shares in twenty-five of the eighty-three carve-outs between 1966 and 1983. In fourteen additional cases, the parent sold its block to a third party; nine of these buyers declared that they intended to buy the public's interest.

**Table 5.5** **Frequency of Reorganizations between 1980 and 1986 for 101 Majority-Shareholder Firms on the NYSE or Amex and a Paired Sample of 101 Firms with Diffuse Ownership in Which No Shareholder Owns More Than 20 Percent of the Common Stock**

| | Full Sample (%) | | Individual Majority Shareholder (%) | | Corporate Majority Shareholder (%) | |
|---|---|---|---|---|---|---|
| | Majority-Shareholder Firms | Diffuse-Ownership Firms | Majority-Shareholder Firms | Diffuse-Ownership Firms | Majority-Shareholder Firms | Diffuse-Ownership Firms |
| Merger | 25 | 18 | 12 | 19 | 33* | 16* |
| Going private | 6 | 7 | 5 | 5 | 5 | 5 |
| Liquidation | 5 | 4 | 12 | 12 | 2 | 0 |
| None | 64 | 71 | 71 | 64 | 60* | 79* |

*Source:* Data from Compustat and the *Wall Street Journal.*

*$p$-value of $< 0.05$ for a test of equality between proportions of the two samples.

market model is estimated to adjust for general movements in stock prices. The intercept and slope are estimated from a sample of approximately 100 trading days, beginning 351 days before the event day, which is the day the reorganization is announced in the *Wall Street Journal.*[30] Using these estimated parameters, we generate predicted returns for 250 trading days before through 10 trading days after the event day. Abnormal returns are calculated as the difference between the actual and the predicted returns. The abnormal returns are next averaged across events, that is, across initial announcements of the reorganizations, to form a portfolio abnormal return:

$$\mathrm{AR}_t = \sum_{i=1}^{n} \frac{\mathrm{AR}_{it}}{n},$$

where $\mathrm{AR}_{it}$ is the abnormal return for firm $i$ at time $t$, and $n$, which is constant over all days in the event period (250 days before through 10 days after the event day), is the number of firms. Finally, cumulative abnormal returns are formed by summing the daily abnormal returns over the event period.

We use a standard $t$-test to measure the statistical significance of the abnormal returns associated with the announcement that a majority shareholder is buying out minority shareholders. The standard deviation of the average abnormal returns is computed over the comparison period. Under the null hypothesis of zero abnormal returns, the ratio of the event-period abnormal return to the standard deviation is treated as a unit-normal random variable. The variance of the cumulative return is generated by summing the sample variance of the abnormal returns over the number of days contained in the cumulative return; a similar procedure is followed for the event-day returns (days −1, 0, where day 0 is the day of the initial *Wall Street Journal* announcement of the transaction).

Table 5.6 summarizes the cumulative returns and $t$-statistics for various periods surrounding these announcements. Minority shareholders experience substantial wealth gains when their ownership interest is redeemed by majority shareholders. At the announcement itself (days −1, 0), stock prices increase on average by 12 percent. The null hypothesis of a zero abnormal return over these two days can easily be rejected ($t$-statistic 19.6). Stock-price increases immediately preceding the announcements suggest that the event-day returns understate the wealth effects for minority shareholders (possibly because of leakage of information). From twenty days preceding through ten days after announcements of reorganizations, stock

30. The actual number of observations in the estimation period varies because not all securities trade on all days. If a security did not trade on a particular day, that day is passed over for both the firm's and the market return.

**Table 5.6** **Summary of Abnormal Stock-Price Returns for Various Periods Surrounding the Initial *Wall Street Journal* Announcement That a Majority-Shareholder Firm on the NYSE or Amex Is Being Acquired, Taken Private, or Liquidated (1978–84)**

| | 250 Days before through 10 Days after the Initial Announcement of a Reorganization | Initial Public Announcement of a Reorganization | 20 Days before through 10 Days after the Initial Public Announcement of a Reorganization |
|---|---|---|---|
| Average abnormal stock return (%) | 30 | 12 | 23 |
| *t*-statistic | 4.1 | 19.6 | 9 |
| Sample size | 43 | 38 | 43 |

*Source:* Data from the *Wall Street Journal.*

prices increase on average by 23 percent (*t*-statistic 9.0). Ninety-one percent of the abnormal returns over this period are positive.

Payments to minority shareholders in these reorganizations approximate those made in reorganizations in general. For instance, Jensen and Ruback (1983) summarize a number of empirical studies and report that premiums to shareholders in friendly mergers average approximately 20 percent.[31]

### 5.3.3 Evidence from Block Trades

As part of the perceived ineffectiveness of the law, some scholars warn that small shareholders will be taken advantage of by larger shareholders in reorganizations. Although, under federal securities law, all shareholders must receive the same price per share in a tender offer, in other circumstances there is no requirement of equal treatment. Thus, the way is seen as open for someone to purchase a large block, wait a short period, and then purchase the minority's interest at a lower price per share. Robert Clark (1986, 468) sees "the equal treatment problem as . . . the salient problem posed by two-step acquisitions."

Barclay and Holderness (1989, 1992a, 1992b) examine 106 trades of at least 5 percent of the common stock of exchange-listed corporations. After 51 of these trades, the firm is acquired, typically by the block purchaser. Contrary to the fears of legal scholars, Barclay and Holderness

31. Similarly, Slovin and Sushka (1998) find that, when parent corporations merge with partially owned subsidiaries, shareholders in the subsidiaries receive approximately the same premiums as do shareholders in arm's-length mergers. Klein, Rosenfeld, and Beranek (1991) find that, when parent firms reacquire the public's interest in an equity carve-out, the minority shareholders in the acquired firm earn abnormal returns that approximate those earned by target firms in arm's-length mergers and acquisitions.

(1992a) find that, in 86 percent of these reorganizations, minority shareholders receive at least as much per share as did the block seller (unadjusted for market movements or inflation).

This equality of payments to majority and minority shareholders appears to be an example of an implicit legal constraint, as no law explicitly requires equal payment in reorganizations that follow block trades. Implicit constraints will be overlooked if (as the legal critics have apparently done) one interprets only reported case law and fails to examine the empirical evidence.

### 5.3.4 New Zealand Comparison

The treatment of minority shareholders in reorganizations in the United States appears quite different from the experience of minority shareholders in New Zealand, which has few legal protections for minority shareholders. In New Zealand, minority shareholders typically receive substantially less in reorganizations than do large-block shareholders. For example, when the Lion Corporation was taken over by the L. D. Nathan Corporation, minority shareholders received only 60 percent on a per share basis of what was paid to Fay Richwhite, a 35 percent blockholder in Lion. Similarly, when the James Smith Corporation was purchased by Mancorp Holdings, an 81 percent blockholder received twice as much per share as did other shareholders (Easton 1988, 40; see also Nathan 1986). Despite public outcries over such inequality, many defend it. For example, the chairperson of a major New Zealand corporation "said that small shareholders would be naive to expect the same treatment as larger holdings." In 1984, the New Zealand Treasury announced its opposition to a "proposal to give small shareholders more rights in takeovers because it would attenuate property rights to the proceeds of investments in controlling blocks of shares and investments in information" (Easton 1988, 40).

### 5.3.5 Assessment of the Evidence

It is difficult to reconcile the evidence reported above with the widespread belief that the law does not constrain block investors. If minority shareholders cannot constrain block investors, majority shareholders—who should be the least constrained of all block investors—would have little reason to reorganize their firms to eliminate minority shareholders.[32]

32. For example, even if a blockholder has nonpublic, favorable information about the firm's expected cash flows, it would still be irrational for him to buy out minority shareholders if they were powerless to constrain him. In this case, he could simply expropriate the higher than anticipated cash flows through opportunistic behavior. On the other hand, if minority shareholders can constrain the blockholder, then such asymmetry of information could provide the impetus for a buyout of minority shareholders (see Bebchuk and Zingales, chap. 2 in this volume).

These buyouts are neither isolated events nor insignificant wealth transfers from majority to minority shareholders.

The payments to minority shareholders suggest a lower bound on the constraints that minority shareholders can impose on majority shareholders. To be sure, the removal of minority shareholders can result in additional benefits for majority shareholders, notably, elimination of the direct costs of complying with SEC regulations. These costs, however, are estimated to range between only $75,000 and $200,000 annually.[33] If they are capitalized (say, at a real rate of 5 percent), majority shareholders would save between $1.5 and $4 million, far less than the transfers we observe, which average $313.1 million (median $20.5 million).

Although it would be inappropriate to attribute these reorganizations and transfers solely to minority shareholders' legal rights to constrain majority shareholders, our evidence that organizational constraints appear to be less important in majority-owned firms than in diffusely held firms makes the case for the influence of law compelling.

The influence of the law is further suggested by the conceptual differences between offers to acquire diffusely held firms and offers to acquire the minority's stock in a majority-shareholder firm. Although the determinants of offer premiums are not yet well understood, several reasons why acquirers typically offer substantial premiums to acquire publicly held corporations have been advanced: to match alternative bids; to induce the tender of more shares when the supply curve slopes up (perhaps reflecting different tax situations among the firm's shareholders); to reduce managerial resistance; and to overcome free-rider problems that can cause atomistic shareholders not to tender their shares. All these considerations are less relevant with majority-shareholder firms than with diffusely held firms. Theoretically, majority shareholders can unilaterally approve most reorganizations because they control more than 50 percent of the votes.[34] Moreover, through side payments for majority blocks, majority shareholders and acquirers should be able to avoid sharing with minority shareholders the benefits of deploying corporate resources to more productive uses. Yet, in spite of these differences, minority shareholders in majority-owned firms receive approximately the same premium for their shares as shareholders in diffusely held firms.

Finally, one can also discern the constraining influence of the law from casual evidence, such as reports in the financial press and litigation insti-

33. DeAngelo, DeAngelo, and Rice (1984, 372) report the estimates of a number of corporations on the direct costs of SEC compliance to arrive at this range.

34. To be sure, majority shareholders sometimes choose not to vote in reorganizations. But this raises the question why? As courts often look to this factor in appraisal proceedings, it appears that the decision of majority shareholders not to vote in reorganizations is one result of legal constraints.

tuted by minority shareholders, as well as from the difference between the treatment of minority shareholders in the United States and New Zealand. In the absence of alternative explanations or contradictory evidence, the case for the influence of law appears persuasive.

Our finding regarding the importance of the law as a protector of minority shareholders is also largely consistent with the finding of La Porta et al. (1997) that legal protections for small shareholders in public corporations vary substantially across countries, with the greatest protection coming in common law countries, such as the United States. Although we do not make systematic international comparisons, our finding that the law protects minority shareholders from large shareholders in the United States is consistent with their finding that the common law protects small investors. The apparently greater protection for minority shareholders in reorganizations in the United States compared with New Zealand raises the possibility of important differences in the legal protections for minority shareholders among common law countries (a possibility not explored by La Porta et al.).

La Porta et al. (1997) further suggest that concentrated ownership is a partial response to inadequate legal protections for small investors. We have our doubts about this claim because of the possibility of large shareholders exploiting minority shareholders. There are certainly press reports of this happening, for example, in Asian corporations ("Asia's minority shareholders have every reason to worry about how they are treated. . . . Dominant families, byzantine corporate structures and overly cozy political relationships leave minority shareholders at a disadvantage" ["Asia's Stock Nightmare" 1997, 107]). In any event, an international analysis of the legal constraints on large shareholders is a topic worthy of future investigation.

### 5.3.6 Evidence of Additional Concerns about Block Investors

Our evidence also addresses other concerns that have been raised about block investors. Here again, the pessimism of legal scholars is not supported by the evidence.

#### *Management Prior to Acquiring Minority's Interest*

Our evidence is inconsistent with the suggestion that a block investor might manage the firm in a way that drives down eventual payments for minority shareholders in a reorganization.[35] Specifically, the average stock-

35. Bebchuk (1985, 1712–13), e.g., argues, "The acquirer [of a substantial percentage of a firm's common stock] might also manage the target's operations so as to lower further the elements of the appraisal remedy. For example . . . the acquirer might depress the target's market price in that period by using its control over both the target's dividend policy and its release of information. Finally, it is worth noting that the prospect of a future takeout might by itself depress the market price of minority shares."

price increase over the year preceding the reorganization (from day −250 through day −10) is 9.8 percent (*t*-statistic 1.4). Over the entire event period (from day −250 through day 10), abnormal returns average 30 percent (*t*-statistic 4.1).

*Magnitude of Payments to Minority Shareholders*

Although size, of course, is in the eye of the beholder, one must question whether the payments that we document are consistent with the claim that large-block shareholders often choose "to eliminate at modest cost the nuisance value represented by so small a minority" (Brudney 1978, 70). Payments to minority shareholders are in the tens and sometimes hundreds of millions of dollars and approximate those paid in arm's-length mergers.

*Potential Problems with Corporate Blockholders*

The wealth gains for minority shareholders are statistically similar whether individual managers or corporations redeem the shares, despite underlying differences in the nature of the restructurings. From day −20 through day 10, shareholders in corporate-controlled firms experience abnormal gains of 24 percent (median 16 percent), and shareholders in firms controlled by individuals experience wealth gains of 28 percent (median 23 percent). Both parametric and nonparametric tests yield insignificant differences. Similar results are documented at the announcement of the reorganization. This evidence and the evidence that payments to minority shareholders approximate the acquisition payments to shareholders in diffusely held firms are inconsistent with the assertion that premiums in parent-subsidiary mergers will "not [be] as much as in arm's-length mergers or overhead take-overs" (Brudney 1978, 73).

## 5.4 Conclusion

There is a widespread belief that the law does not effectively constrain large-block shareholders. Such a conclusion presents a challenge to those who maintain that large shareholders can improve corporate performance. The empirical evidence presented in this paper—which to our knowledge is the first evidence of constraints on block investors—calls into question the widespread pessimism about the power of the law to constrain block investors. We base this conclusion on three broad empirical regularities.

The first regularity is that firms with block investors are surviving. This is evidenced by the number of firms with blockholders and by data showing that these firms are decreasing in neither size nor numbers. Moreover, concentrated ownership does not appear to decrease firm value significantly. We would not observe these regularities if block investors were unconstrained. Given their voting power, there simply would be too much latitude for opportunistic behavior and inept management.

The second regularity is that managers who own majority blocks of stock appear to be less constrained by organizational mechanisms than are managers with small stockholdings. Most majority-shareholder boards lack features such as cumulative voting and a preponderance of outside directors that would help them constrain majority shareholders effectively. Likewise, because majority-shareholder firms typically have lower debt-to-equity ratios than similar firms with diffuse ownership, it seems unlikely the debtholders monitor majority shareholders to a greater extent than they monitor managers with smaller stockholdings. A pattern of internal financing suggests that trips to the capital markets do little to augment other reputational considerations that may constrain majority shareholders. Finally, we find few examples of innovative organizational constraints counterbalancing the power of large-block ownership.

The final broad empirical regularity that we identify is that the law appears to constrain majority shareholders both in their day-to-day management and when they redeem the ownership interest of minority shareholders. In mergers, going-private restructurings, and liquidations, minority shareholders receive premiums similar to those paid when more diffusely owned corporations are reorganized, suggesting that the law prevents block investors from using their voting power to freeze out minority owners at low prices. Despite these premiums, majority shareholders buy out minority shareholders at least as often as firms with relatively diffuse ownership are similarly reorganized. In addition, although the law does not explicitly require it, small shareholders receive the same amount per share in acquisitions that follow block trades as do block sellers. These payments appear in part to be the price that majority shareholders must pay to eliminate the constraint of minority-shareholder litigation.

We do not conclude that the evidence suggests that the law perfectly constraints block investors. Examples of block investors who have led their firms into financial distress, such as the Wang family, show this not to be the case. Nor do we conclude that the law is a greater constraint on block investors than are organizational factors. Instead, we conclude that the law, especially legal prohibitions on non pro rata distributions of firm assets, is an important constraint on block investors. Our conclusion that the law effectively constrains blockholders, however, conflicts with the prevailing academic view. Logic, however, supports it. The fundamental difference between the law and most internal organizational constraints on managers who own large blocks of stock is that the law is largely beyond the influence of those who are to be constrained. This is the essence of a constraint.

## References


Asia's stock nightmare. 1997. *Economist,* 20 December, 107–8.

Barclay, Michael J., and Clifford G. Holderness. 1989. Private benefits from control of public corporations. *Journal of Financial Economics* 25:371–97.

———. 1992a. The law and large-block trades. *Journal of Law and Economics* 35:265–94.

———. 1992b. Negotiated block trades and corporate control. *Journal of Finance* 46:861–78.

Barclay, Michael J., Clifford G. Holderness, and Jeffrey Pontiff. 1993. Private benefits from block ownership and discounts on closed-end funds. *Journal of Financial Economics* 32:263–91.

Bebchuk, L. 1985. Toward undistorted choice and equal treatment in corporate takeovers. *Harvard Law Review* 98:1693–1808.

Brudney, V. 1978. Efficient markets and fair values in parent-subsidiary mergers. *Journal of Corporation Law* 4:63–86.

Byrd, John W., and Kent A. Hickman. 1992. Do outside directors monitor managers? Evidence from tender offer bids. *Journal of Financial Economics* 32:195–221.

Cary, William L. 1974. Federalism and corporate law: Reflections upon Delaware law. *Yale Law Journal* 83:663–705.

Clark, Robert. 1986. *Corporate law.* Boston: Little, Brown.

DeAngelo, Harry, and Linda E. DeAngelo. 1985. Managerial ownership of voting rights: A study of public corporations with dual classes of common stock. *Journal of Financial Economics* 14:33–71.

DeAngelo, Harry, Linda DeAngelo, and Edward Rice. 1984. Going private: Minority freezeouts and stockholder wealth. *Journal of Law and Economics* 27: 367–401.

DeAngelo, Linda E. 1981. Auditor size and audit quality. *Journal of Accounting and Economics* 3:183–99.

De Long, J. Bradford. 1991. Did J. P. Morgan's men add value? In *Inside the business enterprise,* ed. Peter Temin. Chicago: University of Chicago Press.

Demsetz, Harold. 1983. The structure of ownership and the theory of the firm. *Journal of Law and Economics* 26:375–90.

Demsetz, Harold, and Kenneth Lehn. 1985. The structure of corporate ownership: Causes and consequences. *Journal of Political Economy* 93:1155–77.

Denis, David J., and Diane K. Denis. 1994. Majority owner-managers and organizational efficiency. *Journal of Corporate Finance* 1:91–118.

Easterbrook, Frank H. 1984. Two agency-cost explanations of dividends. *American Economic Review* 74:650–59.

Easton, Brian. 1988. Cheating the small investor. *NZ Listener,* 23 July, 40–41.

Eisenberg, M. 1976. *The structure of the corporation.* Boston: Little, Brown.

Fama, Eugene F., and Michael C. Jensen. 1983. Separation of ownership and control. *Journal of Law and Economics* 26:301–26.

Gilson, Ronald J. 1986. *The law and finance of corporate acquisitions.* Mineola, N.Y.: Foundation Press.

Gilson, Stuart. 1990. Bankruptcy, boards, banks, and blockholders. *Journal of Financial Economics* 27:355–88.

Gordon, Jeffrey N. 1993. What is relational investing and how cumulative voting can play a role. Columbia University Law School. Typescript.

Gould, John P. 1972. The economics of legal conflicts. *Journal of Legal Studies* 2:279–399.

Herman, Edward S. 1981. *Corporate control, corporate power.* New York: Cambridge University Press.

Holderness, Clifford G., Randall S. Kroszner, and Dennis P. Sheehan. 1999. Were the good old days that good? Changes in managerial stock ownership since the Great Depression. *Journal of Finance* 54 (April): 435–69.

Holderness, Clifford G., and Dennis P. Sheehan. 1988. The role of majority shareholders in publicly held corporations: An exploratory analysis. *Journal of Financial Economics* 20:317–46.

———. 1991. Monitoring an owner: The case of Turner Broadcasting. *Journal of Financial Economics* 30:325–46.

Jensen, Michael C. 1986. Agency costs of free cash flow, corporate finance, and takeovers. *American Economic Review* 76:323–50.

Jensen, Michael C., and Richard S. Ruback. 1983. The market for corporate control: The scientific evidence. *Journal of Financial Economics* 11:5–50.

Klein, April, James Rosenfeld, and William Beranek. 1991. The two stages of an equity carve-out and the price response of parent and subsidiary stock. *Managerial and Decision Economics* 12:449–60.

La Porta, Rafael, Florencio Lopez-de-Silanes, Andrei Shleifer, and Robert Vishny. 1997. Legal determinants of external financing. *Journal of Finance* 52:1131–50.

Magnuson, Roger J. 1984. *Shareholder litigation.* Chicago: Challaghan.

McConnell, John, and Henri Servaes. 1990. Additional evidence on equity ownership and corporate value. *Journal of Financial Economics* 27:595–612.

Mikkelson, Wayne H., and M. Megan Partch. 1989. Managers' voting rights and corporate control. *Journal of Financial Economics* 25:263–90.

Morck, Randall, Andrei Shleifer, and Robert W. Vishny. 1988a. Characteristics of targets of hostile and friendly takeover. In *Corporate takeovers: Causes and consequences,* ed. A. J. Auerbach. Chicago: University of Chicago Press.

———. 1988b. Management ownership and market valuation: An empirical analysis. *Journal of Financial Economics* 20:293–316.

Naj, Amal Kumar. 1988. Coated Sales, Inc. directors suspend firm's chairman. *Wall Street Journal,* 1 June, 12.

Nathan, Rabindra S. 1986. Controlling the puppeteers: Reform of parent-subsidiary law in New Zealand. *Canterbury Law Review* 3:1–34.

O'Neal, F., ed. 1975. *Oppression of minority shareholders.* Chicago: Challaghan.

Ritter, Jay R. 1981. Two essays on information in financial markets. Ph.D. diss., University of Chicago.

Rock, Edward B. 1994. Controlling the dark side of relational investing. *Cardozo Law Review* 15:987–1031.

Rosenstein, Stuart, and Jeffrey Wyatt. 1990. Outside directors, board independence, and shareholder wealth. *Journal of Financial Economics* 26:175–92.

Rozeff, Michael S. 1982. Growth, beta, and agency costs as determinants of dividend payout ratios. *Journal of Financial Research* 5:249–59.

Schipper, Katherine, and Abbie Smith. 1983. Effects of recontracting on shareholder wealth: The case of voluntary spinoffs. *Journal of Financial Economics* 12:437–67.

Shleifer, Andrei, and Robert W. Vishny. 1986. Large shareholders and corporate control. *Journal of Political Economy* 94:461–88.

Slovin, Myron, and Marie Sushka. 1998. The economics of parent-subsidiary mergers: An empirical analysis. *Journal of Financial Economics* 49:255–79.

Weisbach, Michael S. 1988. Outside directors and CEO turnover. *Journal of Financial Economics* 20:431–60.

## Comment Mark R. Huson

Large percentage blocks of shares may be accumulated to improve management, to secure benefits that do not accrue to other shareholders, or both. In the first case, the blockholder monitors management in order to promote good decisions and/or prevent bad ones. In these instances, all shareholders share the benefits that arise. Such blockholders will be associated with higher firm values. In the second case, the blockholder uses his superior voting power to secure private benefits. Blockholders who acquire control positions in order to expropriate will be associated with lower firm values to the extent that they can actually consume private benefits. The paper by Clifford Holderness and Dennis Sheehan is concerned with the second case. In particular, it asks what prevents blockholders from diverting value to themselves at the expense of minority shareholders.

Their paper does several things. First, it documents that firms with majority ownership survive and that they do not trade at substantial discounts to firms with diffuse ownership. Next, it looks to organizational mechanisms that might control a majority holder's ability to consume perquisites. Finally, it looks to the law as a constraint on the behavior of blockholders. This last exercise is in a way the central focus of the paper. The authors look at this issue in the light of what they see as a pessimistic view held by legal scholars about the effectiveness of laws designed to control blockholders.

### Blockholders, Survival, and Discounts

While reading the section on the survival of majority-ownership firms, I was reminded of William H. McNeill's *Plagues and Peoples* (1976), which discusses disease vectors and their effects on populations. What made me think of this book was the idea that majority owners who accrue private benefits are a lot like parasites. McNeill's book discusses virulent and nonvirulent parasites. Nonvirulent parasites "realize" that they depend on their hosts for survival and do not consume the host to the point of its demise. If majority owners are of the nonvirulent nature, it is not surprising that the firms they control survive. I discuss this issue more when I deal with the legal constraints on blockholders.

As far as discounts for majority-controlled firms, it is not clear a priori whether they should be expected. Consider a majority owner who both monitors and consumes. In this case, the positive effects of increased monitoring will offset the negative effects of perquisite consumption. The net effect of this on firm value is ambiguous. Even if majority owners either

Mark R. Huson is assistant professor of finance at the University of Alberta.

monitor or consume, this problem affects the examination of average discounts. The positive effects that monitors have on some firms will be offset by the negative effect of self-dealing in other firms.

What might be more informative is an examination of the dispersion in discounts of majority-owned firms relative to the dispersion of discounts in diffusely owned firms. Such an analysis might point to firms where the consumption effects are stronger than the alignment effects. Finally, a stronger test might come from looking at marginal *Q*-ratios. What I have in mind is an analysis of the market reaction to acquisitions made by majority-owned firms and diffusely held firms. If majority-held firms make acquisitions to benefit the majority owner at the expense of the other shareholders, the market should react more negatively to announcements by these firms. Huson (1998) finds differential market responses to announcements of acquisitions and divestitures by firms under different governance regimes.

In their summary of the evidence regarding survival and discounts, Holderness and Sheehan conclude that there is no evidence that block investors pronouncedly decrease firm value. Given the possible offsetting effects of monitoring and consumption and the problem with averages mentioned above, this conclusion is strong. They go on to say that majority owners must be constrained. However, there is evidence consistent with the proposition that majority owners do consume. For example, Barclay and Holderness (1989) document an average control premium of 20.4 percent associated with the exchange of blockholdings.[1] They interpret this premium as representing the anticipated (net) private benefits of the control stake. Additionally, Holderness and Sheehan report various instances of majority owners who have been caught consuming. The nature of the constraint, therefore, must be that of an upper bound on self-dealing.

## Organizational Mechanisms to Counter Self-Dealing

In this section of the paper, we are introduced to a sample of majority-owned firms and their two-digit-SIC- and size-matched control firms. This section looks at differences in organizational constraints on self-dealing between the majority-owned firms and the diffusely held firms. The sample of majority-owned firms consist of firms that have a single holder of at least 50.1 percent of a firm's common stock. I will make two comments about this sample and then discuss the results of the analysis.

First, suppose that the constraints on self-dealing are constant. The benefits of self-dealing are decreasing in ownership. Perhaps a more powerful sample design would include firms with effective control, say, owner-

1. Additional evidence that majority owners consume private benefits comes from Bradley (1980) and Meeker and Joy (1980).

ship stakes between 30 and 40 percent. It would be reasonable to expect more self-dealing in these firms. These firms could be compared with the majority-owned firms. This comment is made with consideration of the arguments put forward in Morck, Shleifer, and Vishny (1988).

The second point deals with the identity of the majority shareholder. Holderness and Sheehan are careful to separate individual blockholders from corporate blockholders. This is an important distinction since people, not corporations, make decisions. If diffusely held corporation X holds a majority stake in corporation Y, the CEO of X would have little incentive to loot Y since the benefits would accrue to the shareholders of X, not to the CEO.[2] Also related to the identity of the majority owner is the issue of founders. Ritter (1981) documents that insiders retain 72 percent of the common stock in the 559 firm-commitment IPOs between 1965 and 1973. This raises the question of how many majority-owned firms in this sample are "young" and founder controlled. It might be worth examining the different types of majority owners in more detail and considering the effect of relative firm age on the relation between firm value and ownership concentration.

## Boards of Directors

The first organizational constraint on self-dealing examined is the board of directors. In particular, the paper looks at differences in board composition between majority-owned and diffusely owned firms. Evidence of an organizational adaptation would be a higher proportion of outside directors in majority-owned firms. The second characteristic is the incidence of staggered boards. Holderness and Sheehan argue that staggered boards would help prevent self-dealing at majority-owned firms.

The evidence reported indicates that majority-owned firms have fewer outside directors and use staggered boards less frequently than do the control firms. In the paper, this is interpreted as evidence that internal mechanisms have not evolved to constrain self-dealing. There are other possible interpretations. First, this could indicate that the majority holding sufficiently aligns incentives. Since holdings are in excess of 50.1 percent, the holdings could be a bonding mechanism. If this were the case, there would be less need for outside directors to monitor. There would also be no need for a staggered board to insulate the manager from wronged shareholders. Another interpretation is that the majority owner is a looter and does not want to be watched. In this case, keeping outsiders off the board and maintaining the ability to fire directors is crucial if self-dealing is to be concealed. Finally, if the sample of majority-owned firms com-

2. Since Holderness and Sheehan do not find large differences between corporate majority-owned firms and diffusely held firms, the remainder of my comments will refer to the results for the individual majority-owned firms.

prises young, founder-run firms, the status of the boards could be a function of the firms' investment opportunity sets. Perhaps expertise is more valuable than monitoring in these firms.

### Capital Markets

Constraints may also come from capital markets. Debtholders could monitor via covenants that limit self-dealing. Additionally, external financing would be prohibitively expensive for a firm with a reputation for self-dealing. In examining the role of debtholders, Holderness and Sheehan consider a substantial debt ratio to be a necessary (but not sufficient) condition for bondholders to exercise additional control rights. I do not think that the magnitude of the debt load is as important as the nature of the debt load. All else equal, a firm that has $10 million in short-term debt is more constrained than a firm that has $10 million in long-term debt. Additionally, for similar levels of similar maturity debt, differences in covenant structures play a role in constraining activity.

Examination of trips to the capital markets shows no significant difference between majority-owned firms and their controls. However, the point estimates show that majority-owned firms go less often. When paired with the statistically lower dividend-payout rates for majority-owned firms, this lends some support for the proposition that capital markets provide some monitoring of majority owners.

Evidence to help us understand the monitoring of capital markets might come from an analysis of the terms that govern new security issues by majority-owned firms. Holderness and Sheehan (1991) point to constraints put on Ted Turner when he went to the capital markets. It would be interesting to see whether other majority-owned firms must agree to similar constraints or whether they have a "high" cost of capital.

The conclusion of this section is that organizational constraints have not evolved to limit the consumption of private benefits. The lack of organizational constraints and the survival of majority-owned firms lead Holderness and Sheehan to the law as the constraint on self-dealing.

## Legal Constraints on Majority Shareholders

Holderness and Sheehan point to numerous cases where majority owners have violated the laws and been called on it. In spite of this evidence that the law constrains blockholders, it is reported that legal scholars generally conclude that the law does not significantly constrain block investors. This section of the paper attempts to supply empirical evidence that, on average, majority owners do not engage in self-dealing. The laboratory for this analysis is a sample of reorganizations where majority owners redeem the minority's shares. The supposition is that, if the law were no constraint, such reorganizations would be infrequent and that, when they did occur, minority shareholders would receive small payments.

The reported evidence indicates that there is little difference in the reorganization frequencies of majority-owned and diffusely held firms.[3] Additionally, it shows that the buyouts involve significant wealth transfers from majority owners to minority shareholders. One possible benefit to taking out the minority shareholders is the savings on direct costs of complying with SEC regulations, which are estimated to be worth between $1.5 and $4 million. This is considered briefly but readily dismissed as being too small. If we choose $2.5 million as the savings, this represents about 7 percent of the median market capitalization of the firms controlled by individuals and over 10 percent of the median wealth transfer to minority shareholders. While not the sole determinant of the premia, these savings are not trivial.

This still leaves the question of why premia are paid at all if the majority owner is unconstrained and whether the treatment of minority holders in mergers is evidence that the law constrains majority owners in their day-to-day management. I think that Holderness and Sheehan are correct in concluding that it is fear of legal action that prevents majority owners from freezing out minority shareholders. Around the time from which their data are taken, there was a great deal of uncertainty as to the legal standing of minority shareholders. Gilson (1986) reports that, although the letter of the law provided minority shareholders with little protection, there was opportunity for interpretation that would benefit minority shareholders. He goes on to discuss the risk aversion of the lawyers structuring the deal relative to that of the majority owner. He suggests that the lawyers might have suggested paying off minority owners rather than face the likelihood of being associated with a failed or stalled deal.

There were also two new weapons added to minority shareholders' arsenal at this time. In *Singer v. Magnavox* (1977), the cost of litigating perceived self-dealing in mergers was reduced.[4] Prior to *Singer,* shareholders had to act individually. *Singer* allowed for class actions. Additionally, in 1979, the SEC passed rule 13e-3, which required officers to state whether they believed the offer to minority shareholders to be fair. Making such statements opens the majority owners to possible legal actions.

Holderness and Sheehan consider the lack of self-dealing in merger transactions to be evidence that majority owners are constrained. If the null hypothesis is that the law is entirely toothless, self-dealing should be

3. An exception is that mergers are more likely for firms with corporate majority owners than for the control firms. A possible explanation for this is that many of the firms in this sample were carved out to facilitate an eventual merger. It would also include the firms that are eventually merged back into the parent company.

4. *Singer v. Magnavox Co.,* 380 A.2d 969 (Del. 1977).

as obvious in merger decisions as anywhere else. However, this is an arena where legal scrutiny is likely to be very great. This increases the likelihood that self-dealing will be detected and at least undone. Majority owners must also consider externalities such as reputation effects. This is not the most powerful experiment for detecting self-dealing.

Evidence that majority owners do not fleece minority owners when they redeem the latter's shares in mergers is not evidence that majority shareholders are constrained in their day-to-day management. Perhaps better evidence comes from the case law anecdotes. In fact, these instances of majority owners being caught with their hands in the till suggest that majority owners are constrained by the law. That is, there are certain activities that are not permitted.

Since the effectiveness of a law can be measured only with respect to instances of its application, the effectiveness of the law may well be a secondary consideration when the self-dealing propensity of majority owners is examined. Suppose that the law is fully effective. That is, in the event of exposed self-dealing, the majority owner is forced to pay damages and banned from ever owning a publicly traded firm again. You might think of Victor Posner, the former chairman of the DWG Corporation. In these cases, becoming a noticeable self-dealer is not necessarily the optimal course. Rather, a majority owner may decide to be less virulent and base consumption decisions on the likelihood of discovery and how much he is taking from minority shareholders. He can consume to the point where it is in no individual shareholder's interest to incur the costs of preventing it.

When we look at discovered self-dealers, we are observing the outcome of a process that equals one if they are caught and zero if they are not. However, self-dealing is not a discrete and dichotomous event. Think of it in the following context:

$$Z = 1 \quad \text{if } z^* \geq L,$$

$$Z = 0 \quad \text{if } z^* < L.$$

The amount of self-dealing is given by $z^*$. The event that a self-dealer is caught and has legal actions directed against him corresponds to $Z = 1$. Whether the self-dealing is enough to trigger legal action depends on $L$, the level of self-dealing high enough to warrant legal action. This level of self-dealing will be a function of the gains that accrue to minority shareholders from ending the self-dealing and the costs of bringing legal action.[5]

Majority owners have a wide latitude of behaviors in which they can engage to their own benefit if $L$ is high. $L$ would be high if, for example,

5. This assumes that the minority shareholders act in concert. If they cannot act in concert, then the relevant gains are those to the largest holder in the minority-shareholder group.

class actions are not allowed or if the self-dealing is difficult to identify. In the latter case, I have in mind hiring your cousin's consulting firm to do some research, which would be difficult to classify as self-dealing, as opposed to buying your cousin a new yacht with corporate funds, which would be easy to classify as self-dealing. The problem with mergers is that *L* is probably low since the price paid to the minority can be compared to the price paid to the majority owner. This makes the law relatively effective in this case. A test of the effectiveness of this through time might be of interest. Examination of the levels and types of self-dealing that are caught would show whether *L* has been changing through time.

Holderness and Sheehan conclude that, while the law is not a perfect constraint, it is an important constraint on majority owners. I think that the law provides an upper bound on expropriation. Majority owners who stay below this bound will survive. The legal scholars' view that the law does not significantly constrain majority owners may just be a comment about their perception of where the upper bound should be. Holderness and Sheehan provide us with some evidence of where it is, which should help move the debate forward.

## References

Barclay, Michael J., and Clifford G. Holderness. 1989. Private benefits from control of public corporations. *Journal of Financial Economics* 25:371–97.

Bradley, Michael. 1980. Interfirm tender offers and the market for corporate control. *Journal of Business* 53:345–76.

Gilson, Ronald J. 1986. *The law and finance of corporate acquisitions.* Mineola, N.Y.: Foundation Press.

Holderness, Clifford G., and Dennis P. Sheehan. 1991. Monitoring an owner: The case of Turner Broadcasting. *Journal of Financial Economics* 30:325–46.

Huson, Mark R. 1998. Does governance matter? Evidence from CalPERS interventions. Working paper. University of Alberta.

McNeill, William H. 1976. *Plagues and peoples.* New York: Anchor.

Meeker, L., and O. Joy. 1980. Price premiums for controlling shares of closely held stock. *Journal of Business* 53:297–314.

Morck, Randall, Andrei Shleifer, and Robert W. Vishny. 1988. Management ownership and market valuation: An empirical analysis. *Journal of Financial Economics* 20:293–316.

Ritter, Jay R. 1981. Two essays on information in financial markets. Ph.D. diss., University of Chicago.

6

# Trust and Opportunism in Close Corporations

Paul G. Mahoney

A central problem for closely held corporations is the possibility of opportunistic behavior by a majority shareholder. Many closely held corporations have a 50 percent–plus shareholder and one or more owners of minority interests. The majority shareholder may use its control of the corporate machinery to appropriate wealth from the minority.

A growing literature examines how close corporation shareholders (through organizational choices) and the legal system (by providing organizational default settings and adjudicating disputes) can reduce the costs associated with majority opportunism. This paper formalizes the analysis by modeling the interaction between majority and minority shareholders as a noncooperative trust game. In the game, the majority is constrained by the possibility of nonlegal sanctions, including family or social disapproval and loss of reputation, and, as a result, a rational minority shareholder will sometimes invest despite the potential for exploitation. The strength of those sanctions is assumed to vary over time, and the minority's ex ante rational investment can therefore result in ex post appropriation.

The paper uses the trust game model to revisit a long-standing debate over the best exit rule for minority shareholders in close corporations. Corporations differ from partnerships in that, absent a contrary agreement, a shareholder can withdraw capital from the firm only pursuant to a majority vote, a rule that I call *exit by consent.* A partner, by contrast,

Paul G. Mahoney is professor of law and the Albert C. BeVier Research Professor at the University of Virginia.

The author thanks Larry Dann, Mike Dooley, Kevin Kordana, Chris Sanchirico, Eric Talley, an anonymous referee, conference participants, and participants in the University of Pennsylvania Roundtable for comments.

can (again absent a contrary agreement) dissolve the firm and withdraw capital at will. The ability to withdraw capital gives the minority leverage over the majority and may deter opportunism.

The limited anecdotal and survey evidence available, however, suggests that minority shareholders infrequently contract for exit rights or other organizational devices that might restrict majority opportunism, particularly in family businesses or other small closely held corporations, with which this paper will be concerned.[1] There are two schools of thought on why this is, or appears to be, so. One holds that transaction costs are to blame. Minority shareholders may be ignorant of the potential for appropriation by the majority, and the costs of becoming informed and negotiating for effective organizational constraints may be greater than the potential benefits. On this view, the default rule for close corporations should be switched to provide for easy exit or other organizational constraints as a matter of right. Thus, Hetherington and Dooley (1977) argue that close corporation shareholders should have the right to withdraw capital at will.

The alternative argument is that such minority entitlements do not merely deter majority opportunism but also create a threat of minority opportunism. The minority may use a strategically timed exit demand to threaten to impose large costs on the majority and thereby gain a larger share of the firm's cash flows. Easterbrook and Fischel (1986, 1991), therefore, argue that the failure of minority shareholders to bargain for exit rights or other organizational constraints does not reflect ignorance or large transaction costs. Instead, it reflects a judgment that, at the margin, the organizational benefits of the traditional corporate form outweigh the benefits of a more partnership-like structure. Rock and Wachter (chap. 7 in this volume) focus on asset specificity and valuation problems as a potential source of minority exploitation. O'Kelley (1992) similarly argues that the choice of exit rule involves a trade-off between majority and minority opportunism.

The present paper notes that a minority shareholder's withdrawal of capital through a buyout or dissolution takes place at a price set by, or negotiated in the shadow of, a judicial proceeding. Unless judicial valuations are systematically biased, expanded exit rights for minority shareholders will not result in minority opportunism because the minority's threat to exit is not credible so long as the majority is cooperating. Contrary to Easterbrook and Fischel's and O'Kelley's analysis, then, minority

1. The universe of closely held corporations includes some very large firms. There are also publicly traded corporations that have majority shareholders, raising analogous risks of majority opportunism. I will confine myself, however, to the problem of majority opportunism in small businesses organized as closely held corporations. As discussed in section 6.3 below, the legal solutions developed for large firms are unlikely to work for small firms without alteration.

opportunism does not explain the failure to adopt partnership-style governance unless judicial valuations are biased or the minority is risk preferring or irrational.

I therefore explore other possible explanations for the survival of exit by consent. Minority shareholders can insure against opportunism through the price they pay for the shares. This is not a complete explanation because the majority could offer a buyout right in order to reduce the variance of the minority's returns and receive a higher price from risk-averse investors. Alternatively, corporate law may do a sufficiently good job of constraining majority shareholders that minority shareholders do not find it necessary to bargain for exit rights.

The latter explanation contrasts with frequent criticisms of the courts' willingness to use dissolution or fiduciary duty actions as a form of ex post settling up when minority shareholders allege that the majority has acted unfairly. Commentators often argue that courts are not competent to determine whether the majority has upheld its bargain and that judicial intervention therefore produces costly uncertainty. Correctly understood, however, judicial intervention to uphold the parties' "reasonable expectations" is a sensible adaptation of the fiduciary principles that courts uncontroversially enforce against the managers of publicly traded companies.

Section 6.1 briefly reviews the debate between proponents of different exit rules. Section 6.2 develops the trust game model. Section 6.3 considers why, despite the predictions of the model, close corporation shareholders do not appear to bargain for exit rules and identifies legal constraints as a likely answer. Section 6.4 describes judicial intervention in close corporations and the debate over its effectiveness.

## 6.1 The Debate over Exit Rules

Organizational constraints may limit the majority's ability to appropriate minority returns. Minority shareholders may bargain for (or a corporate statute may provide as a default setting) supermajority voting provisions for certain transactions, proportional board representation, or similar organizational devices to reduce the majority's power to make decisions unilaterally. The literature on close corporations has focused on a particular organizational choice—exit rules—as a check on the majority. That focus is not surprising because corporate exit rules differ sharply from those of partnership.

It should be emphasized that the debate over statutory exit rules seeks to choose the optimal default rule—that is, the rule that should govern when the parties have not specified a contrary preference. The default rule matters to the extent that the costs of bargaining around the rule are substantial. The higher those costs, the greater the likelihood that some parties will be stuck with an undesired rule, and the greater the potential social payoff from identifying the most efficient rule.

### 6.1.1 The Argument in Favor of Exit at Will as a Default Rule

Under standard corporate law rules, a shareholder has no right to receive a return of his investment from the corporation or other shareholders. He may sell to a third party, of course, but, if his desire to exit stems from opportunistic behavior by the majority, the purchase price will reflect that behavior and therefore provide neither recompense nor deterrence. Corporate assets are distributed to shareholders on a dissolution, but that typically occurs only pursuant to a majority vote unless a shareholder can establish the conditions for a judicial dissolution.

A general partner of a partnership, by contrast, has the right to withdraw from the partnership on demand and receive the value of his pro rata share of the partnership's assets. Like the exit-by-consent rule of corporate law, this "exit-at-will" rule is a default rule that can be altered by agreement.

Hetherington and Dooley (1977) argue that shareholders in a close corporation are in a position that closely resembles partnership and that the partnership rule of exit at will is appropriate. They propose a statutory provision that would give a close corporation shareholder the right to have his shares purchased by the corporation or the other shareholders at an agreed-on price or, failing agreement, at a judicially determined price. Although Hetherington and Dooley identify the key feature of the solution as liquidity, an equally important feature is independent valuation. A buyout rule will deter majority opportunism only if the court can be counted on to set a price that compensates for the effects of majority misbehavior.

The put right proposed by Hetherington and Dooley is not the same as the partnership exit rule because the latter provides for dissolution of the partnership rather than a sale of the partnership interest to the other partners. The effects of the two rules, however, are often the same because dissolutions of profitable partnerships typically result in the remaining partners cashing out the departing partner and continuing the business. So long as the business is worth more as a going concern than in liquidation and more in the hands of the current management than in the hands of alternative managers, we would expect a dissolution decree to result in a buyout of the dissenting shareholder or partner by the remaining shareholders or partners. Bebchuk and Chang's (1992) model of bargaining in bankruptcy (where the alternative to a negotiated solution is a liquidation) could be adapted to this situation to predict the price at which the buyout will take place.

The argument for facilitating exit by minority shareholders has influenced courts and legislatures. Although no corporate code provides for exit at will, modern statutory provisions for judicial dissolution provide increased opportunities for minority shareholders to exit. As noted by Thompson (1993), courts have taken an increasingly broad view of their authority under these involuntary dissolution statutes. They have, for example, entertained petitions for dissolution by shareholders claiming that actions of the majority have frustrated the "reasonable expectations" of the minority. Courts have also used the threat of dissolution to encourage a buyout of the minority or have simply used their equity powers to order a buyout. These developments are not limited to the United States; as noted by Cheffins (1988), Canadian company law now includes statutory provisions that give courts substantial flexibility to define and remedy majority opportunism.

### 6.1.2 The Argument in Favor of Exit by Consent as a Default Rule

Easterbrook and Fischel (1986, 1991) criticize the proponents of exit at will for ignoring the risk of minority opportunism that accompanies a rule (or contract) giving minority shareholders greater exit rights. Raising cash for a buyout (through loans, sales of new shares, or sales of assets) is costly. These costs may vary over time, permitting the minority to time its exit for maximum strategic advantage. Consider, for example, a situation in which the shareholders have private information suggesting that the value of the firm's future cash flows is greater than expected but do not yet have any credible means to signal that information to potential lenders or investors. The majority may lack sufficient assets outside the firm to buy out the minority, the company's assets may be illiquid, and the information asymmetry may preclude obtaining outside financing for a buyout at an acceptable cost.

In those circumstances, the argument goes, the cost of exit at will is high, and the minority can use the threat of exit to extract a greater share of the returns than initially agreed. In general, the buyout or dissolution demand can be used opportunistically whenever the cost of replacement financing is high.

Thus, Easterbrook and Fischel argue, the choice of organizational structure reflects an inevitable trade-off between majority and minority opportunism. Devices such as buyout rights that give the minority leverage over the majority decrease the likelihood that the minority will receive less than the return to which it is entitled, but at the cost of increasing the risk that it will receive too much. The notion that minority opportunism is an inevitable cost of expanded exit rights is widely shared. O'Kelley (1992), for example, argues that the choice between partnership and close corporation organization represents a trade-off between the greater adaptability of partnership and the greater risk of minority opportunism that accompanies exit at will. Rock and Wachter (chap. 7 in this volume) argue that the problem of opportunism is acute because close corporation assets are often project specific and have limited value in their next-best use. Dissolution, therefore, may mean the destruction of considerable potential (although unrealized) value. The "lock-in" feature of exit by consent guards against this value destruction.

Easterbrook and Fischel take the observed tendency of close corporation shareholders to accept the default rule of exit by consent as evidence that there is not enough difference between the expected cost of majority opportunism under exit by consent and minority opportunism under exit at will to justify the cost of bargaining around the default rule. They further argue that the costs of bargaining around the rule are not substantial. Majority and minority shareholders typically negotiate face to face and use lawyers to create the corporation's governing documents, and it should not, therefore, be prohibitively costly to contract around the state-supplied default rule when they prefer a different rule. These observations suggest that parties are generally satisfied with exit by consent and that legislatures and courts should leave well enough alone.

## 6.2 The Trust Game

The interaction between majority and minority shareholders in a close corporation can be modeled as a noncooperative trust game in which an investor (A) gives money to an entrepreneur (B). B combines A's funds with B's specialized skills to undertake a business organized as a corporation. The game begins with B offering A a specified share of the cash flows at a specified price, which A must accept or decline. To simplify the analysis, I will assume that B always offers A 49 percent of the cash-flow rights (represented by a single class of common stock). By retaining 51 percent of the stock, B controls all corporate decisions. The value of the firm under B's management is assumed to be $2r$.

If B's promise is kept, both parties receive (approximately) equal distributions, each with a present value of $r$. Given the price specified by B, A could invest the same amount of money elsewhere to receive a return with a present value of $s$. We can think of $s$ as corresponding to the market rate of return and $2(r - s)$ as the economic rents generated by the new undertaking.

### 6.2.1 Interactions under the Traditional Exit-by-Consent Rule

*A Model without Renegotiation*

Although B promises to split the firm's cash flows equally with A, B's promise is not binding. That is, it is prohibitively expensive to define B's obligations in a way that makes cheating impossible. To do so would, among other things, require a complete specification of the salary and perquisites to be received by B in all possible states and provisions to guard against surreptitious transfers such as payments of salary to or purchases of supplies from family members or friends, corporate reimbursement for personal expenses, and so on. The parties cannot at reasonable cost write a contract that specifies how the equal sharing principle will apply in all possible states. Moreover, I assume that A has not contracted for exit rights and, therefore, cannot withdraw capital from the firm without B's consent.

Having obtained A's money, B may renege on his promise. In the extreme, B may implement a "freezeout"—that is, pay no dividends, terminate A's employment (if any) with the firm, and use all profits to B's advantage. B cannot get rid of A involuntarily except through a merger that would be subject to judicial scrutiny for fairness if challenged by A, but, through the freezeout, B can appropriate A's entire share of the firm's cash flows.

Corporate actions that maximize the wealth transfer from A to B will likely be inconsistent with maximizing firm value. For example, if A is an employee and B fires A, B may have to hire a replacement employee who knows less about the business. By refusing to pay dividends, B may also make the company's common stock an unattractive vehicle for bonuses or other incentive payments to employees. The resulting conflict between the shareholders may deflect some of B's attention from running the business. For this reason, the game is not zero sum; B's opportunism destroys value. To capture this feature, I assume that, in a freezeout, A receives a payoff of zero and B receives a payoff of unity, where $r < 1 < 2r$.

Were B able to freeze out A without constraint, B would always do so. Knowing this, A would not invest. There are, however, extralegal constraints that make opportunism costly to B. Often, the shareholders of a close corporation are relatives or close friends, and the threat of social disapproval will constrain opportunism. B may also wish to raise capital in the future for this or other business ventures and may therefore care about reputation. These informal sanctions impose a cost, $m_B$, on opportunism. A diagram of the game and its payoffs appears in figure 6.1.

As thus described, the game is the familiar trust game (see, e.g., Kreps 1990; Brennan, Güth, and Kliemt 1997). After B makes an offer, A decides whether to invest ($I$) or not to invest ($N$), and B then chooses whether to reward ($R$) or to exploit ($X$). If $r$ and $m_B$ are taken as fixed at the beginning of play and known to both parties, the game has a straightforward equilibrium; when $r > 1 - m_B$, B will choose not to exploit, and A will therefore choose to invest ($I$, $R$); otherwise, A will not invest. Under no circumstances will A invest and B exploit.

This simple, deterministic structure makes the game unrealistic; it cannot account for the observed instances in which majority shareholders exploit minority shareholders. Nevertheless, the model demonstrates that close corporations can exist where shareholders have rational expecta-

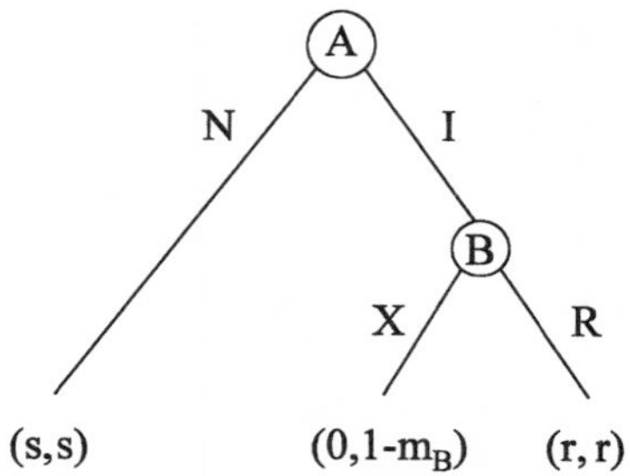


**Fig. 6.1 Trust game model under exit by consent**

tions, majority shareholders are unable to make binding commitments not to exploit, and minority shareholders have no exit rights.

A more realistic structure must treat $r$ and/or $m_B$ as random variables whose realizations are unknown at the outset of play. To introduce uncertainty but keep things reasonably simple, I will make only one of these variables, $m_B$, stochastic. Note that many disputes in close corporations arise precisely because $m_B$ varies over time. Family members become estranged, friendships or marriages erode, and the strength of informal sanctions otherwise changes with time, leading to disputes and exploitative behavior. I assume the following: The density function of $m_B$ is $f(m_B)$ on the closed interval [0, 1] and zero elsewhere, and the associated distribution function and complementary distribution function are $F(m_B)$ and $\Phi(m_B)$, respectively. The distribution is common knowledge to the parties. The firm value, $2r$, is fixed and known throughout to the parties but not verifiable by them to third parties, including the courts.

Under these assumptions, A's expected payoff from investing, $V^A$, is $r\Phi(1 - r)$. If $V^A < s$, A will not invest even though $r > s$. B's inability to make a credible promise to share the cash flows will therefore reduce the number of corporations created compared to an (unrealistic) baseline in which B could make a credible promise. It may also affect the type of business that is incorporated. $V^A$ will tend to be small, all other things equal, when A and B are strangers. There will then be a tendency for closely held corporations to arise most frequently within communities linked by kinship or other bonds.

Even when the expected value of $m_B$ is such that it is rational for A to invest, the variance in $m_B$ and the resulting potential for opportunism reduces the parties' aggregate payoffs. When $V^A > s$, A will invest but will value the shares in the light of the expected payoff. In order to induce investment with variable $m_B$, B must offer a higher rate of return (i.e., sell the shares at a lower price) than he would were it possible to make a binding commitment not to behave opportunistically. Recall that $s$, the present value of A's next-best alternative to investing, is a function of the price specified by B. B can make A's expected payoff from investing greater than the payoff from not investing by offering the shares at a reduced price. B's expected payoff if A invests, $V^B$, is

$$r\Phi(1 - r) + \int_0^{1-r} (1 - m_B) f(m_B) dm_B,$$

and the total expected payoff to the parties where A invests is

$$(1) \qquad V^A + V^B = 2r\Phi(1 - r) + \int_0^{1-r} (1 - m_B) f(m_B) dm_B.$$

It is clear by inspection that the aggregate payoff is less than $2r$. Thus, by dividing up the right to the firm's cash flows and thereby creating the possibility of opportunism, B reduces the aggregate expected value of these entitlements.

Despite its simplicity, then, the model generates two important results. The first is that, in a rational expectations framework, majority opportunism does not "oppress" the minority in the sense of producing an unexpectedly low return; the minority pays less for the shares because of the potential for majority opportunism and on average receives an adequate return on the investment. This is analogous to the familiar result from Jensen and Meckling's (1976) model of agency costs, in which the agent's compensation is reduced by the expected value of his opportunistic behavior. The second result is that the outcome of the game is not Pareto optimal because majority opportunism does not merely transfer wealth from the minority to the majority but produces lower aggregate expected payoffs.

Compare the ex post payoffs when A invests and B rewards to those when A invests and B exploits. In the former case, the aggregate payoff is $2r$. In the latter case, A gets nothing, and B gets $1 - m_B$, for an aggregate payoff of $1 - m_B$. The difference between the two, $2r - 1 + m_B$, consists of two components. The first, $(2r - 1)$, is that part of the firm's value destroyed by B's choice of inefficient corporate policies in order to freeze out A. The second component, $m_B$, represents B's socially wasteful investments in rent seeking (i.e., his willingness to bear the costs of social sanctions or loss of reputation). Ex ante, B receives a lower share price reflecting the expected loss of firm value and wealth transfer in the event of exploitation.

### *A Model with Renegotiation*

Once the value of $m_B$ is realized, both parties know whether it is in B's interest to exploit. Because B's threat to freeze out A is credible given a sufficiently low value of $m_B$, the parties can avoid some of the costs of a freezeout if B buys A's shares after $m_B$ is realized. B may offer A a price of $r - \alpha$ for A's shares, which would leave B with a value of $r + \alpha - m_B$ (I assume that the parties are unable to keep B from incurring the cost $m_B$—

in other words, B's reputation or social interactions will suffer as a result of behaving opportunistically, whether that opportunism operates through a freezeout or a purchase of A's shares for less than their promised value). The bargain would make both parties better off because it would enable B to avoid adopting inefficient corporate policies in order to freeze out A and, as a result, increase the value of the firm by $(2r - 1)$.

A may accept B's offer or reject and make a counteroffer. The situation is a bargaining game as in Rubinstein (1982). The parties will agree on some value of $\alpha$ that divides between them the difference between the value of the firm absent a freezeout ($2r$) and the value of the firm with a freezeout (unity).

With the possibility of renegotiation, there is no loss in firm value because B adopts optimal policies. B nevertheless incurs the cost $m_B$ ex post and bears the expected private cost of opportunism to A (represented by $\alpha$) in the form of a lower ex ante share price. Once again, there is no "oppression" on average so long as A makes unbiased estimates of the relevant parameters at the beginning of the game.

### 6.2.2 Interactions under Hetherington and Dooley's Buyout Rule

#### *A Model without Renegotiation*

Let us now assume that the relevant state's close corporation statute provides an unconditional buyout right along the lines suggested by Hetherington and Dooley (1977). That is, on request by A, B must purchase (or cause the corporation to purchase) A's shares at a negotiated price. If the parties cannot agree on the price, it will be determined by the court. I will represent the price determined by the court as $\rho$ and assume that it is realized only at the end of the litigation, although prior to litigation the parties know its distribution. Because I am for the moment assuming no renegotiation, on a buyout demand by A, both parties receive the judicially determined payoffs.

The buyout right may enable A to behave strategically because a buyout can be costly for B. B may be liquidity constrained and therefore unable to purchase A's shares from personal resources. In order to make the purchase, B will then have to sell assets or securities of the corporation, leaving it with an inefficient mix of assets or an undesired capital structure. A change to a more debt-heavy capital structure may violate covenants with preexisting lenders or raise the cost of future credit.

To emphasize the qualitative similarity of these efficiency costs to those created when B freezes out A, I will again assume that the value of the firm decreases to unity after a strategically timed buyout demand by A. Like B in figure 6.1, A is constrained by informal sanctions that impose a cost, $m_A$, on opportunism. Whether A's buyout demand was prompted by B's exploitation or was opportunistic is assumed to be common knowledge

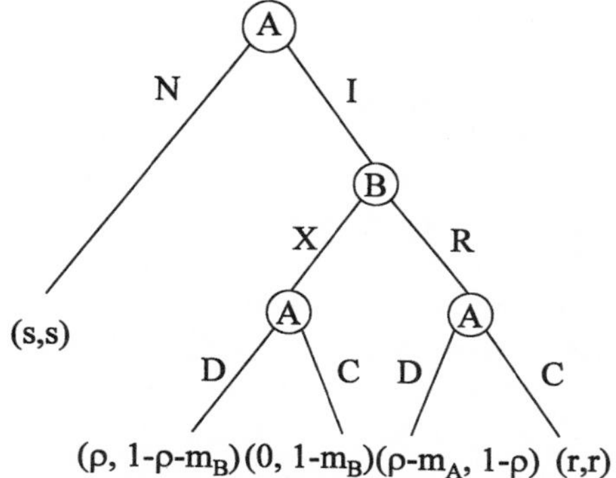


**Fig. 6.2 Trust game model under exit at will**

within the relevant community, with the result that A bears the cost $m_A$ if and only if his buyout demand was opportunistic.

The resulting game is diagrammed in figure 6.2. As in the prior model, A decides whether to invest or not to invest, and B then decides whether to reward or to exploit. If B exploits, A will clearly choose to exercise the buyout right ($X$, $D$), which will reduce A's losses from exploitation. If B rewards, however, A can choose to reward as well ($R$, $C$) or to exploit by making a strategically timed buyout demand ($R$, $D$).

There is an important distinction between the games in figures 6.1 above and 6.2. In the latter, it may never be rational for A to exploit (demand a buyout) when B rewards. If the court's valuation is unbiased (i.e., if $E[\rho] = r$, where $E$ is the expectation operator), then A's expected payoff from rewarding ($r$) always exceeds the expected payoff from a buyout ($E[\rho] - m_A = r - m_A$), given B's decision to reward.

A contrary result requires one of several assumptions. First, A may be risk preferring and therefore willing to gamble on the court's valuation being too high. Second, the court's valuation may be systematically biased in A's favor (i.e., $E[\rho] > r$). Third, A may be motivated by spite or otherwise irrational—that is, willing to impose large costs on B even though the expected outcome is less favorable to A than continued cooperation. I assume for the time being that one of these conditions holds so that A may choose to exploit, but in section 6.2.3, I return to the distinction between the games in figures 6.1 and 6.2.

The losses from A's opportunism are qualitatively similar to those from B's. The reduction in payoffs when B rewards and A exploits, compared to when both reward, is $2r - [(\rho - m_A) + (1 - \rho)]$, or $(2r - 1) + m_A$. Recall that, in the no-renegotiation exit-by-consent model, when A invests and B exploits through a freezeout, the difference in payoffs is $(2r - 1) + m_B$. A will pay a higher price for the shares than he would pay could he make a credible promise never to exploit, and again the deal is "fair" in that sense.

*A Model with Renegotiation*

If A can make a credible threat to exploit, A might offer to avoid the court-supervised buyout and negotiate a buyout that would not significantly reduce the firm's value. For example, A might agree to accept a note rather than cash in payment for the shares in order to alleviate B's liquidity problem. As in the model of majority opportunism, renegotiation could permit A to receive a wealth transfer from B without destroying part of the value of the firm. If $\beta$ is the amount of the wealth transfer, then the payoffs to A and B when B rewards and A exploits are $(r + \beta - m_A)$ and $(r - \beta)$, respectively. The result is analogous to that in section 6.2.1 above.

### 6.2.3 Will A Exploit?

The games diagrammed in figures 6.1 and 6.2 are similar but not identical, and the differences suggest that buyout rights do not necessarily replace majority opportunism with minority opportunism. Under exit by consent, B is constrained only by informal sanctions—B's control of the corporate machinery makes it otherwise possible to appropriate all the firm's cash flows. By contrast, the buyout made possible by an exit-at-will rule takes place in the shadow of a judicial valuation of the firm.[2] Unless that valuation is biased (putting aside the possibility that A is risk preferring or irrational), A's threat to demand a buyout is not credible when B has rewarded. As a consequence, B cannot be induced to bribe A to forgo the buyout.

In order to illustrate the point as simply as possible, I have used a one-shot game in which the strength of the informal sanctions, $m_A$ and $m_B$, is exogenously determined. The sanctions could be endogenized in a repeated-game framework in which B may sell equity and A may invest multiple times, either with one another or with additional players. When either party exploits, he reveals himself to be an exploiting "type" (i.e., one subject to low informal sanctions), as in the repeated-game model of Kreps et al. (1982). Once player B is known as an exploiter, future investors will expect a lower payoff from investing, which will in turn reduce B's expected payoffs.

Depending on his discount rate, B may be willing to give up future gains for the opportunity to exploit today. Player A is once again, however, in a

2. Unlike a statutory right, a contractual buyout right might not incorporate judicial valuation, but it would have to incorporate some valuation procedure if the parties cannot reach agreement. That valuation procedure would play the role of a court's valuation in the analysis that follows.

different position because he does not experience an immediate gain in expected-value terms from exploiting. Moreover, it does not seem plausible that A's decision to exploit today could improve (rather than reduce) his future payoffs. Having been revealed as an exploiter, A will not get additional opportunities to invest, as an entrepreneur would always do better in expected-value terms to pick a new investor who might or might not be an exploiter.

The credible-threat argument on which I have relied requires unbiased judicial valuations. If judges routinely overcompensate minority shareholders, it may be rational for the minority to exploit. Easterbrook and Fischel's (1986, 1991) argument that exit at will creates a risk of minority exploitation appears to reflect an underlying assumption that judicial valuations are systematically too high. Easterbrook and Fischel focus in particular on a wrong turn taken by the courts in Massachusetts and California.[3] These courts have adopted a rigid "equal treatment" rule that entitles the minority to equal pro rata sharing (in amount, timing, and form) of all cash flows. If followed routinely, that approach would systematically overcompensate minority shareholders. In order to maximize firm value, shareholders are often willing to provide specific financial incentives for the majority shareholder-managers. Such incentives are inconsistent with equal treatment. The Massachusetts/California approach would allow minority shareholders to escape from these deals ex post, thereby creating a threat of minority exploitation.

The Massachusetts and California cases, however, may be aberrations. Courts in many states scrutinize managers of close corporations more closely than they do managers of publicly traded corporations, but these courts have generally not applied a rigid equal treatment rule.[4] While we cannot reject the possibility that courts systematically overcompensate minority shareholders and majorities consequently refuse to agree to buyout rights, for most states (including Delaware), the evidence is equally consistent with unbiased valuation.

## 6.3 Why Don't Shareholders Bargain for Buyout Rights?

There is no large-sample evidence on the extent to which shareholders in closely held corporations bargain for buyout rights. It is widely believed by lawyers and commentators, however, that they do so rarely (Dooley 1995). A survey of practicing lawyers found that deviations from the state-

3. See *Donahue v. Rodd Electrotype Co.*, 367 Mass. 578, 328 N.E.2d 505 (1975); *Jones v. H. F. Ahmanson & Co.*, 460 P.2d 464 (Cal. 1969).

4. See, e.g., *Toner v. Baltimore Envelope Co.*, 498 A.2d 642 (Md. 1985); *Delahoussaye v. Newhard,* 785 S.W.2d 609 (Mo. Ct. App. 1990). The Delaware Supreme Court explicitly declined to adopt an equal treatment rule in a case similar to *Donahue* (see *Nixon v. Blackwell,* 626 A.2d 1366 [Del. 1993] [en banc]).

supplied default settings are uncommon (Hochstetler and Svejda 1985). The reported judicial opinions concerning the valuation of close corporations, moreover, arise in the context of statutory dissolution proceedings, not contractual buyout rights, suggesting that the latter may be uncommon.

If buyout rights do not create a significant risk of opportunism, as I have argued, what explains minority shareholders' apparent failure to bargain for them? The most common responses are that minority shareholders fail to appreciate the danger of majority opportunism (O'Neal and Thompson 1985; Bradley 1985) or that the costs of bargaining for a buyout right are prohibitively high. Johnston (1992) demonstrates that, when the parties have private information about their proclivity to exploit, it may be difficult to bargain to the desired rule without revealing more information than the parties wish.

It would also be possible to create a model in which A and B are asymmetrically informed about the value of the firm. Under some values of the parameters representing A's and B's beliefs about firm value, exit by consent could be superior to exit at will. However, the prior literature focuses on the difficulty of verifying firm value to a court, rather than on the parties' differing beliefs about firm value, as the source of A's ability to exploit. Using the trust game model, I have shown that the inability to verify firm value to third parties is not sufficient to enable A to exploit. The following sections explore two alternative explanations for the survival of exit by consent that do not require an assumption of shareholder ignorance, private information about firm value, or high transaction costs.

### 6.3.1 Price Protection

In the trust game model, the minority pays a price that reflects its expected losses from majority opportunism. The exit rule would be a matter of indifference to a well-informed minority shareholder as the shareholder can pay a price that reflects the expected utility loss. When opportunism may destroy part of the firm's value, however, the majority is made worse off by the prospect of its own opportunism. The majority, therefore, has an incentive to select the most efficient rule and, therefore, to offer a buyout right if the buyout right reduces majority opportunism at an acceptable cost.

The destruction of firm value, however, can be substantially reduced by ex post renegotiation, not merely by ex ante contracting. In the model developed in section 6.2.1 above, where renegotiation is possible, the expected decrease in the parties' aggregate payoffs due to B's opportunism is

$$\int_0^{1-r} m_B f(m_B) dm_B .$$

The net loss, in other words, is the cost of social or other sanctions imposed on B multiplied by the probability that they will be incurred. To state the obvious, B exploits only when these costs are small. Investment takes place only when $E(m_B) > 1 - r$, and exploitation occurs only when the realized value of $m_B$ is less than $1 - r$. The expected losses from opportunism are therefore increasing in the variance of $m_B$. Shareholders may choose to negotiate for buyout rights (or form a partnership rather than a corporation) only when that expected variance is large.

Nevertheless, price protection cannot fully explain majority shareholders' failure routinely to offer buyout rights. A risk-averse minority would demand compensation not only for the expected reduction in wealth but also for the greater variance of outcomes produced by majority opportunism. Close corporation shareholders, who often invest a significant portion of their wealth or effort in the business, are likely risk averse with respect to their returns from the corporation. The majority could obtain a higher price by offering greater protection against opportunism and therefore lower variance of returns.

### 6.3.2 Fiduciary Duty Constraints

Holderness and Sheehan (chap. 5 in this volume) argue that the fiduciary duties imposed by corporate law constrain large-block shareholders in publicly traded firms from appropriating wealth from minority shareholders. They reach the conclusion by process of elimination, noting that organizational and capital market constraints do not explain the survival of the controlled public company. A similar point can be made with respect to majority shareholders in closely held corporations. The organizational devices that commentators have suggested to combat majority opportunism, such as buyout rights, do not appear to be used, yet close corporations survive as a common business form. A plausible reason is that corporate law provides sufficient constraints.

It does not follow automatically from the fact that fiduciary constraints are effective in publicly traded corporations with controlling shareholders that they would also be effective in close corporations because there are important differences between the two. Judicial intervention in publicly traded corporations is most common when there is an allegation of management self-dealing. Where there is no such allegation, the business-judgment rule shields management's business decisions from judicial scrutiny. Managers must justify self-interested transactions, by contrast, as "entirely fair" to shareholders.[5]

These constraints are looser where small close corporations are concerned because low levels of self-dealing are ubiquitous, accepted, and probably cost effective in this context. Many closely held corporations are family businesses in which family members of the controlling shareholder may be employees, suppliers, or customers of the business. The board of directors of a family business is unlikely to have an independent compen-

5. See, e.g., *Weinberger v. UOP, Inc.*, 457 A.2d 701, 710 (Del. 1983).

sation committee. Shareholder monitoring is also more difficult in the case of a close corporation compared to a publicly traded corporation, as the latter are subject to the Securities and Exchange Commission's proxy rules, which require disclosure of self-dealing transactions and relationships.[6]

The smaller size of the classic close corporations with which I am concerned, compared to the typical publicly traded corporation, also complicates judges' attempts to police majority behavior by scrutinizing self-dealing. Consider a firm that pays its CEO/controlling shareholder a salary of $100,000 per year and has annual profits (after payment of salaries) of $200,000 per year. If the minority owns 49 percent of the stock, the directors can appropriate about a quarter of the profits that the minority would otherwise receive by raising the CEO's salary by 50 percent. Contrast this to a company that pays its controlling shareholder/CEO $1 million per year and has annual profits of $500 million. Doubling the CEO's pay would appropriate less than 1 percent of the 49 percent minority's share of profits. It is of course possible for a CEO to receive compensation measured in the tens or hundreds of millions of dollars, but amounts that large are typically tied to the performance of the company's stock, which mitigates the wealth-transfer component of the compensation.

The amounts at stake in publicly traded corporations are such that the controlling shareholder can appropriate a large fraction of minority-shareholder wealth primarily through an extraordinary transaction such as a management buyout, a cash-out merger, or a recapitalization. Not surprisingly, courts pay the closest attention to these transactions and apply a stringent fairness test. The controlling shareholder of a small close corporation, by contrast, can appropriate a significant fraction of the minority's stake through everyday transactions that courts cannot scrutinize with the same care.

This suggests that the law constrains the controlling shareholder of a typical close corporation less effectively than it does the controlling shareholder of a typical publicly traded corporation if courts apply identical forms and levels of scrutiny to each. This is not, however, what the courts have done. Instead, they have adapted the inquiries that they make to fit the close corporation context. Courts and commentators have often erred in identifying the problem—they argue that the difference between public and close corporations stems from illiquidity or the "intense relationship" between close corporation shareholders (see O'Neal and Thompson 1985), rather than the fact that large-scale appropriation in the public company context, unlike the close corporation context, usually involves an extraordinary transaction. Nevertheless, courts have developed a set of responses to majority opportunism, described in the next section, that appear to deter such appropriation.

6. See item 404 of regulation S-K, 17 C.F.R. sec. 229.404.

## 6.4 Judicial Scrutiny in Close Corporations

As noted above, a common setting for judicial intervention on behalf of the shareholders of a publicly traded company is a breach-of-fiduciary-duty suit challenging an extraordinary transaction such as a merger or recapitalization. In a close corporation, by contrast, the majority often has no need to rid itself of the minority in order to appropriate a large share of the minority's wealth. Thus, the most common setting for intervention is a minority shareholder's suit for dissolution of the corporation on the grounds of "oppressive" conduct by the majority.[7]

Although statutes are typically silent on what constitutes oppressive conduct and court decisions describe oppression in various ways, Haynsworth (1987) notes that many courts now ask whether conduct of the majority is inconsistent with the "reasonable expectations" of the minority. The majority and minority are assumed to have entered into the relationship with certain understandings of how the firm's cash flows would be shared, which they could not reduce to well-defined obligations for all possible states. The court's objective is to determine the parties' expectations regarding the allocation of cash flows and enforce those expectations.

Courts have also become willing to fashion equitable remedies other than the all-or-nothing remedy of dissolution. These remedies may include money damages, rescission of a transaction found to have violated the majority's fiduciary duties, or an order to pay a special dividend. Thompson (1993) details these remedial choices and notes that they have made the action for dissolution resemble a standard breach-of-fiduciary-duty action. He argues that the two distinct causes of action are gradually evolving into a single cause of action for oppression in which the substantive inquiry is whether the majority's actions are consistent with the parties' reasonable ex ante expectations and the court can apply a wide range of remedies.

The strategy is consistent with courts' behavior faced with long-term contracts in which it is prohibitively costly to specify the parties' required actions in all states. Legal scholars often call these transactions *relational contracts* (see Goetz and Scott 1981). Close corporations fit the paradigm because the parties' failure to build in specific protections against the majority appropriating wealth from the minority is plausibly a result, not of their desire to permit such appropriation, but rather of the prohibitive cost of writing a contract to achieve that result. To the extent that courts can supply implicit contract terms that are consistent with the parties' preferences, they can reduce the cost of forming close corporations.

The trend toward greater judicial intervention in close corporations has

7. See Model Act, sec. 14.30 (court may dissolve a corporation in an action by a shareholder if shareholder establishes that "the directors or those in control of the corporation have acted, are acting, or will act in a manner that is illegal, oppressive, or fraudulent").

been strongly criticized, however. Commentators argue that judicial valuation errors will ensure that these remedies do more harm than good. Ribstein (1994, 955), for example, states that judge-made or statutory "oppression" remedies "create a potential judicial 'wild card' that creates costly uncertainty." Gevurtz (1996, 288) argues in favor of greater organizational protections for minority shareholders but contends that discretionary judicial intervention is an inferior solution because it "is likely to be no more accurate than flipping a coin." Oesterle (1995, 883) argues that legislative experimentation with waivable fiduciary duties in limited-liability statutes has been driven by dissatisfaction with judicial "meddling" in close corporation governance.[8]

What commentators have described as a greater degree of intervention in close corporation governance can be better understood as an adaptation of standard fiduciary principles to the close corporation setting. In publicly traded corporations, courts have relied almost exclusively on process-based standards for evaluating the behavior of corporate directors. So long as directors follow appropriate procedures, their behavior will survive judicial scrutiny, and, absent appropriate procedures, even actions that create significant shareholder wealth can result in liability.[9] By contrast, courts have paid more attention to outcomes when close corporations are concerned. Because the managers of a small close corporation can appropriate a significant share of the minority's cash flows through day-to-day operations, courts have paid attention to the substance of those operations.

## 6.5 Conclusion

Legislatures, courts, and commentators have devoted considerable attention to the problem of majority opportunism in close corporations. Minority exit rights, in the form of easily available judicial dissolution or legislatively granted or contractual buyout provisions, have generated the greatest controversy. Contrary to the views of recent commentators, it is not obvious that minority shareholders could use exit rights to extort a greater share of the cash-flow rights from the majority. More generous exit rights may be unnecessary, however, as a result of the courts' ability to deter majority opportunism through statutory dissolution and "oppression" proceedings.

8. Oesterle's main point—that fiduciary duties, buyout rights, and other protections should be waivable by contract—is correct whether or not courts do a good job of identifying and remedying majority misconduct. Some parties will be able to design effective organizational mechanisms to obtain their desired outcomes, and such parties should be able to rely on self-help in preference to judicial intervention.

9. See *Smith v. Van Gorkom,* 488 A.2d 858 (Del. 1985). In *Van Gorkom,* the board obtained what appeared to be a high price in a sale of the company, but the Delaware Supreme Court concluded that the board's deliberations were too hasty and found the board members liable for a breach of fiduciary duty.

## References


Bebchuk, Lucian A., and Howard Chang. 1992. Bargaining and the division of value in corporate reorganization. *Journal of Law, Economics, and Organization* 8:253–79.

Bradley, Edwin J. 1985. An analysis of the Model Close Corporation Act and a proposed legislative strategy. *Journal of Corporate Law* 10:817–47.

Brennan, Geoffrey, Werner Güth, and Hartmut Kliemt. 1997. Trust in the shadow of the courts. CentER Discussion Paper no. 9789/1997. University of Tilburg.

Cheffins, Brian. 1988. The oppression remedy in corporate law: The Canadian experience. *University of Pennsylvania Journal of International Business Law* 10: 305–39.

Dooley, Michael P. 1995. *Fundamentals of corporation law.* Westbury, N.Y.: Foundation Press.

Easterbrook, Frank H., and Daniel R. Fischel. 1986. Close corporations and agency costs. *Stanford Law Review* 38:271–301.

———. 1991. *The economic structure of corporate law.* Cambridge, Mass.: Harvard University Press.

Gevurtz, Franklin A. 1996. California's new Limited Liability Company Act: A look at the good, the bad, and the ambiguous. *Pacific Law Journal* 27:261–302.

Goetz, Charles J., and Robert E. Scott. 1981. Principles of relational contracts. *Virginia Law Review* 67:1089–1150.

Haynsworth, Harry J. 1987. The effectiveness of involuntary dissolution suits as a remedy for close corporation dissension. *Cleveland State Law Review* 35:25–93.

Hetherington, J. A. C., and Michael P. Dooley. 1977. Illiquidity and exploitation: A proposed statutory solution to the remaining close corporation problem. *Virginia Law Review* 63:1–75.

Hochstetler, William S., and Mark D. Svejda. 1985. Statutory needs of close corporations—an empirical study: Special close corporation legislation or flexible general corporate law? *Journal of Corporation Law* 10:849–1049.

Jensen, Michael C., and William H. Meckling. 1976. Theory of the firm: Managerial behavior, agency costs, and ownership structure. *Journal of Financial Economics* 3:305–60.

Johnston, Jason S. 1992. Opting out and opting in: Bargaining for fiduciary duties in corporate ventures. *Washington University Law Quarterly* 70:291–340.

Kreps, David M. 1990. Corporate culture and economic theory. In *Perspectives on positive political economy,* ed. James E. Alt and Kenneth A. Shepsle. Cambridge: Cambridge University Press.

Kreps, David M., Paul Milgrom, John Roberts, and Robert Wilson. 1982. Rational cooperation in the finitely repeated prisoners' dilemma. *Journal of Economic Theory* 27:245–52.

Oesterle, Dale A. 1995. Subcurrents in LLC statutes: Limiting the discretion of state courts to restructure the internal affairs of small business. *University of Colorado Law Review* 66:881–920.

O'Kelley, Charles R., Jr. 1992. Filling gaps in the close corporation contract: A transaction cost analysis. *Northwestern University Law Review* 87:216–53.

O'Neal, F. Hodge, and Robert B. Thompson. 1985. *O'Neal's oppression of minority shareholders.* 2d ed. Deerfield, Ill.: Clark Boardman Callaghan.

Ribstein, Larry E. 1994. The closely held firm: A view from the United States. *Melbourne University Law Review* 19:950–76.

Rubinstein, Ariel. 1982. Perfect equilibrium in a bargaining model. *Econometrica* 50:97–109.

Thompson, Robert B. 1993. The shareholder's cause of action for oppression. *Business Lawyer* 48:699–745.

## Comment Larry Y. Dann

The study by Paul Mahoney adds to the growing body of literature that examines highly concentrated ownership in corporations. Discussion of mechanisms for resolving disputes between minority and majority shareholders in closely held, private corporations has been a topic of attention in the legal literature for at least twenty years, but, until recently, most of the attention paid in the financial economics literature to highly concentrated ownership has been confined to publicly traded corporations. Increasingly, however, financial economists are analyzing the institutional arrangements of companies in the "prepublic" stage of development. Consequently, this study, which uses a game-theoretic model to shed light on the economic and legal issues of potential opportunistic behavior by shareholders, lies at an interesting and expanding intersection of the legal and financial economics literatures.

The paper focuses specifically on so-called exit rules—arrangements by which shareholders in closely held corporations can cash out their ownership stakes. The absence of a public market for the firm's shares, and the possibility of opportunistic behavior by both minority and majority owners, makes specification of the exit rule potentially important. Debate in the legal literature has centered on the economic efficiency of the default exit rule, that is, identifying the default rule that minimizes the aggregate value loss from shareholders behaving opportunistically. By modeling shareholder opportunism in a simple setting, Mahoney sharpens the focus of the debate. The conclusion that he reaches, that the threat of minority-shareholder opportunism may have been overstated by earlier writers on the subject, and the reasons why we rarely observe contractual buyout rights for minority shareholders are examined in turn.

The model consists of one minority shareholder (A) and one majority shareholder (B). Each may be able to behave opportunistically (capture value belonging to the other) but incurs a reputational cost of doing so. In addition, the model assumes a loss in corporate value from actions taken by B to exploit A and/or from B's adjustments to opportunistic actions taken by A. Under *exit by consent* (the normal corporate rule whereby a shareholder can sell his or her shares back to the corporation only if approved by the majority of shareholders), B will find it advanta-

Larry Y. Dann is the Richard W. Lindholm Professor of Finance and Taxation in the Lundquist College of Business at the University of Oregon.

geous to expropriate value from A (via withholding dividend payments, terminating A's employment, etc.) when B's reputational cost of doing so, $m_B$, is low. Reputational costs will be high for B when (*a*) B's relationship with A consists of more than just co-ownership of shares (e.g., B and A are family members, friends, or members of a small community, etc.) or (*b*) B is likely to be seeking capital market resources in the future and knowledge of B's opportunism will affect his or her future capital market dealings. Under the alternative regime of *exit at will* (akin to the partnership dissolution rule, which permits any owner to demand that the business buy back the owner's claim), A might time the buyout demand to B's disadvantage (e.g., when B does not have the personal resources to buy A's claim and the cost of raising capital is high). Demanding a buyout at such a time would benefit A if either (*a*) renegotiation with B is possible such that B buys out A at a high price or (*b*) A expects a judicially determined buyout price that favors A over B. A's reputational cost of making an opportunistic buyout demand is $m_A$.

Under each exit-rule regime, the game is modeled both with and without the opportunity for renegotiation between B and A. This highlights two aspects of the game. One is that renegotiation between B and A allows for the possibility that the loss in corporate value from adopting non-value-maximizing policies can be avoided (although the reputational costs are still borne). Thus, ex post renegotiation limits the social loss from opportunism. The second is the apparent asymmetry of the consequences of opportunism by B versus by A. Since B controls corporate decision making, B can and will exploit A when $m_B$ is sufficiently low. Judicial intervention does not limit B in the model since B can freeze out A (drive A's payoff to 0). For A credibly to exploit B, however, A needs help. A's threat of opportunistic behavior will be credible only if A can benefit from the behavior. This requires either the possibility of renegotiation such that A can expropriate some of the value of B's claim to the firm or, absent renegotiation, an *expected* judicial determination that favors A over B. Without either renegotiation or judicial bias, the paper correctly argues, it may never be rational for A to behave opportunistically. However, if either judicial bias favoring A over B or even the less stringent assumption of unbiased judicial intervention were an element of the exit-by-consent regime, the conditions under which B would rationally exploit A are also reduced. It appears that the consequence of allowing the existence of a judicial remedy, consistently invoked, for whether the choice of a default exit-rule regime is important depends on the costs of seeking the judicial intervention.

In section 6.3, Mahoney explains why the model treats the element of judicial intervention differently across the two exit-rule regimes. This section offers some of the best insights in the paper, especially for financial economists who (like me) are not extensively informed about the differences in legal treatment of the minority/majority-shareholder situation for closely held versus publicly traded corporations. In essence, one argument is that detection of majority-shareholder exploitation of minority shareholders (e.g., by shareholder monitoring) is more costly in closely held corporations than publicly traded ones because of the more limited reporting requirements regarding self-dealing transactions and relationships. Furthermore, since there are significant fixed costs to policing self-dealing, it is uneconomic to scrutinize judicially the small-scale valuation consequences of majority-shareholder opportunism in many closely held corporations.

Section 6.3 also explains why the model in this paper reaches a different conclusion about the threat of minority-shareholder opportunism than do such earlier writers as Easterbrook and Fischel (1986, 1991) and O'Kelley (1992). Mahoney models behavior by the minority shareholder as occurring in response to observed behavior by the majority shareholder. In contrast, he argues, the analysis underlying Easterbrook and Fischel and O'Kelley does not treat the choices made by B and A as sequential. Mahoney asserts that the natural sequence of play captured by his model is more realistic, and I tend to agree, but the point is that one important thing that we learn from the explicit modeling is the *reason* for the different conclusions being reached. Explicit specification of the form of the game envisioned sharpens the analysis.

One empirical regularity that the game does not explain is why we so infrequently observe minority shareholders obtaining, or apparently even seeking, a contractual buyout right. Mahoney posits that one explanation is that intervention by the courts has worked well as a minority-shareholder safeguard. While this conclusion is not as strong as one reached affirmatively from the analysis (instead of being arrived at by ruling out posited alternative explanations), it is nevertheless at least as plausible as any of the other alternatives mentioned. Further analysis to address this conjecture would be a valuable contribution.

Two additional questions arise from this study that, with further investigation, would advance our understanding of the extent of opportunistic behavior among shareholders in the closely held corporation. One question is how the game would change if the reputational costs of opportunism, $m_B$ and $m_A$, are not known by the other player. Second, as one whose heart ultimately lies with empirical analysis, I would find it interesting (although obtaining data would be challenging) to test the empirical implication of the reputation model that we are more likely to observe exit-at-will rules or exit rights bargained for when minority shareholders do not have a personal relationship with the majority shareholder.

## References

Easterbrook, Frank H., and Daniel R. Fischel. 1986. Close corporations and agency costs. *Stanford Law Review* 38:271–301.

———. 1991. *The economic structure of corporate law.* Cambridge, Mass.: Harvard University Press.

O'Kelley, Charles R., Jr. 1992. Filling gaps in the close corporation contract: A transaction cost analysis. *Northwestern University Law Review* 87:216–53.

7

# Waiting for the Omelette to Set
## Match-Specific Assets and Minority Oppression

Edward B. Rock and Michael L. Wachter

Closely held corporations (or "close corporations") form an important subset of corporations with concentrated ownership.[1] The category includes an interesting variety of enterprises, including the traditional "mom-and-pop" businesses, high-tech start-ups, and mature publicly held corporations post–leveraged buyout. More generally, close corporations are important because of their number and because even the largest publicly held corporations often started out as closely held corporations. As such, close corporations are incubators for tomorrow's publicly held corporations.

Two sets of problems have arisen repeatedly in closely held corporations but only rarely in publicly held firms. The first, now resolved, revolved around the enforceability of attempts by participants to tailor the terms set by the general corporation law. Because states historically have provided one corporation law for all corporations, participants in closely held corporations have often tried to modify the statutory structure by contract to serve their needs. These variations raised the question of the extent to

Edward B. Rock is professor of law at the University of Pennsylvania and codirector of the Institute for Law and Economics. Michael L. Wachter is the William B. Johnson Professor of Law and Economics at the University of Pennsylvania and codirector of the Institute for Law and Economics.

The authors are grateful for comments from Howard Chang, Zohar Goshen, Lawrence Hamermesh, Peter Huang, Michael Klausner, Dale Oesterle, Steven Rosenblum, David Skeel, Lynn Stout, Eric Talley, Robert Thompson, conference participants, and participants in presentations at the University of Colorado, the University of Pennsylvania, Georgetown University, and the American Law and Economics Association.

1. Closely held corporations are typically defined as corporations for which there is no public market for shares and, sometimes, no market at all. An alternative and largely coextensive definition is corporations with few (typically fewer than twenty-five) shareholders (see, e.g., American Law Institute 1994, sec. 1.06).

which parties can contract out of the rules provided by the statute. The evolution toward greater flexibility was long and, at times, difficult, but flexibility is no longer a central issue. Today, participants in the close corporation can largely tailor its terms to their purposes.

The second set of problems, and the focus of this paper, goes under the caption *protection of minority shareholders.* To what extent should the law protect minority shareholders from "oppression" by majority shareholders, beyond what the parties have contracted for? This set of questions, unlike the first set, remains alive and controversial. It has been the subject of an enormous amount of judicial and legislative effort, much of which has been devoted to expanding the rights of minority shareholders. The questions raised, however, go to the very core of what corporations are about.

There are several repeated scenarios that raise the issue of minority oppression. Consider the following:

*Case A.* There is a falling out between the majority shareholder, Major, and the minority shareholder, Minor, both of whom work in the business. Major fires Minor, who then can either hold on to his shares, which pay no dividends (all distributions are through excessive salaries), or sell them back to the firm for whatever the majority shareholder is willing to offer. A variant arises when there are three equal shareholders, A, B, and C. After a falling out, A and B gang up on C and fire him, at which point he is left with shares that pay no dividends and that only the firm is willing to buy.[2]

*Case B.* The majority shareholder or a group of shareholders enters into a transaction with the firm in which, for example, the firm buys back a portion of the majority shareholders' shares, without making the opportunity available to the minority shareholders.[3] Easier variants of this scenario include the full range of transactions between controlling shareholders and the firm, including compensation, selling/buying property, and diversion of corporate opportunities.[4] More difficult variants include the situation in which the majority shareholder takes advantage of opportunities that are not clearly corporate opportunities, such as developing a more liquid market for shares, in which the minority shareholders would like to participate but are not offered the opportunity.[5]

2. See, e.g., *Wilkes v. Springside Nursing Home,* 353 N.E.2d 657 (Mass. 1976); and *In re Topper,* 433 N.Y.S.2d 359 (Sup. Ct. 1980).

3. Classic examples are *Donahue v. Rodd Electrotype Co.,* 328 N.E.2d 505 (Mass. 1975); and *Nixon v. Blackwell,* 626 A.2d 1366 (Del. 1993).

4. See, e.g., *Crosby v. Beam,* 548 N.E.2d 217 (Ohio 1989); and *Alaska Plastics v. Coppock,* 621 P.2d 270 (Alaska 1980).

5. *Jones v. H. F. Ahmanson & Co.,* 460 P.2d 464 (Cal. 1969).

*Case C.* The majority shareholder sells its majority (controlling) stake to a third party without giving the minority shareholder an opportunity to participate.

This paper addresses the question of what, if anything, the courts should do for the minority shareholders in such cases when the parties have not provided for the problem by contract.[6] Our basic answer is that the courts should not do anything except enforce the participants' contracts and vigorously prevent non pro rata distributions to shareholders. This second principle provides a guide to the expansion of minority-shareholder protection against oppression.[7]

We proceed as follows. First, we make a fundamental break with the traditional legal treatment of the problem of minority oppression by rejecting the analogy between close corporations and partnerships and the intuitions and implications that flow from it. We also show that the alternative argument that emphasizes the low agency costs of close corporations needs to be expanded to explain the Silicon Valley start-up-type close corporation. Second, we show that the close corporation form is best suited to companies that require extensive investments in match assets. In such cases, the close corporation acts as an incubator, and the lock-in is a benefit, not a cost. Low agency costs are more likely a result of the choice of form, not the reason that the form is adopted in the first instance. Third, we argue that the problem of minority oppression combines two fundamentally separate problems: the issue that, in the employment context, is raised by the doctrine of "employment at will" and the quite separate problem of controlling shareholder attempts to make non pro rata distributions of firm assets. Building on an earlier analysis of employment at will, we then show that the same norm of judicial nonintervention that governs the employment relationship solves closely similar problems in the close corporation context. This norm, combined with vigorous judicial enforcement of the rule of no non pro rata distributions, including ancillary enforcement of minority-shareholder information rights, and limitations on the ability of control shareholders to sell shares to the firm, allows the close corporation to maximize the value of its match assets. We close by drawing the implications of the analysis for a larger theory of close corporations.

6. For a very interesting and important game-theoretic analysis that arrives at many of the same points as we do, but from a different direction, see Johnston (1992). Other important treatments that overlap with ours are Easterbrook and Fischel (1991) and O'Kelley (1992).

7. There is a third problem that is not normally thought of as a close corporation problem—namely, "piercing the corporate veil." This is the issue of when a creditor can pierce the corporate veil of limited liability in order to reach the assets of the shareholders. Although formally a question that arises in both publicly held and close corporations, in fact, in the United States, at least, the issue arises only in close corporations. It is, however, beyond the scope of this paper.

## 7.1 Defining the Issue

There are two types of structures that fall under the heading *close corporation.* One is the traditional close corporation, often small scale and family owned. The other is what we will call the *Silicon Valley start-up.*[8] Several traits typically characterize the closely held firm: there are few shareholders, no public market for the shares, and a substantial overlap between suppliers of capital and suppliers of labor. Because of the overlap between managers and shareholders and the absence of public markets, the shareholder-managers of the close corporation are in continuous contact with each other. Because of the lack of a public market, the parties are locked in to their investments to a much greater extent than in either the partnership or the publicly traded corporation. Since the majority shareholders elect the directors and control the management of the corporation, minority shareholders are particularly vulnerable if there is a falling out with the majority.

### 7.1.1 Existing Positions

In a famous and influential article, John Hetherington and Michael Dooley (1977, 2) expressed the intuition that lies at the heart of the evolution of minority shareholders' remedies for oppression: that, in all important respects, "the close corporation is the functional equivalent of the partnership."[9] On their view, participants choose the corporate form over the partnership form simply in order to take advantage of limited liability. The problem with close corporation law, they argue, is that, despite this functional equivalence, shareholders cannot exit their investment with anything like the ease of partners, who always have the power to trigger a buyout by dissolving the partnership "by the express will of any partner at any time."[10] To them, the difficulty of exit is a flaw in the legal structure.

8. There is, now, a substantial literature on the structure and governance of venture capital start-ups (see Barry et al. 1990; Sahlman 1990; Gorman and Sahlman 1989; Lerner 1994, 1995; and Gompers 1995). For a more comprehensive description of the "private equity" market, see Fenn, Liang, and Prowse (1995).

9. For a classic judicial expression of the same intuition, see *Donahue v. Rodd Electrotype Co.,* 328 N.E.2d 505, 512 (Mass. 1975).

10. Uniform Partnership Act, sec. 31(2). While the dissolution may be wrongful, it will nonetheless be effective and will immediately trigger a winding up of partnership affairs, with the pro rata distribution of net proceeds. The Revised Uniform Partnership Act (1997), in effect in some states, has tried to limit the potential damage to going concerns caused by this power, but individual partners retain much of their power to dissociate from the partnership and, by doing so, to trigger a buyout regime without triggering dissolution of the partnership itself. Thus, under secs. 601 and 602, a partner may dissociate from the partnership at will, at any time, rightly or wrongly. Under sec. 602(a), partners have the power to withdraw at any time, a power that is immutable under sec. 103(b)(6) (see the comment to sec. 601). Under sec. 701, if a partner is dissociated from the partnership and the partnership continues, the partnership must buy out the dissociated partner's interest for "the amount that would have been distributable to the dissociating partner . . . if, on the date of dissociation, the assets of the partnership were sold at a price equal to the greater of the liquidation value

Their proposed solution is legislation to provide shareholders of the close corporation the same exit option that partners have.

Indeed, it is Hetherington and Dooley's intuition that lies at the heart of the evolution of minority shareholders' remedies for oppression. Although the law has not gone as far as they proposed, it has moved in that direction, driven, at least in significant measure, by an acceptance of their core claim of equivalence. Courts have been more willing to order dissolution and buyouts when convinced that the majority has engaged in oppressive conduct and have been more willing to find oppressive conduct when the minority's reasonable expectations have been violated.

A literature has also developed that explores the conditions under which oppression, that is, opportunistic behavior, is likely to occur. This literature also provides support for buyouts and other remedies for minority oppression (see, e.g., Thompson 1993; and Mahoney, chap. 6 in this volume).

Frank Easterbrook and Daniel Fischel (1991, 228–52) have provided an alternative agency-cost argument. They argue that the limited number of shareholders and the overlap of managers and shareholders naturally align the interests of the two. This occurs for a variety of reasons. First, since managers are the largest residual claimants, actions taken by them will directly affect the value of their investment. The alignment is strengthened when shareholders have a large percentage of their wealth tied up in the venture. And, since they cannot easily alienate their holdings, they will be focused on maximizing the return. Second, participants in close corporations often have familial or other personal relationships. The bond between them constrains conflicts of interest. The result of the close alignment and the familial bond is that a close corporation can have very low agency costs.

In Easterbrook and Fischel's view, companies choose the close corporate form in order to maximize the return on their low agency costs. If they wanted, they could either have adopted the partnership model, have contracted for shareholder agreements, or have adopted specific protections for minority shareholders in the articles of incorporation. Consequently, those who choose the corporate form without modification should be assumed to prize stability of operations. The implications of Easterbrook and Fischel's approach to the minority-oppression debate is clear. Providing ease of dissolution or buyouts would only serve to weaken the bonds that align the parties' interests. Consequently, controlling shareholders in close corporations should be held to the same fiduciary standards as directors in publicly traded corporations, and no additional protections should be accorded minority shareholders.[11]

or the value based on a sale of the entire business as a going concern," less any damages caused by wrongful dissolution.

11. Easterbrook and Fischel, on one side, and Hetherington and Dooley, on the other, have provided for a grand debate that has engaged not only the academic literature but also

But is Hetherington and Dooley's intuition correct? Are close corporations nothing more than "incorporated partnerships"? Do close corporations better serve the interests of the participants when exit is easy? Are Easterbrook and Fischel correct that the primary virtue of the close corporation is that it reduces agency costs and that no additional protection should be accorded minority shareholders? In order to answer these questions, we must place close corporations in a broader context, one that allows us to see that any explanation of the close corporate form must be able to explain the second type of close corporation: the Silicon Valley start-up.

### 7.1.2 Our Position and the Silicon Valley Start-Up

In Silicon Valley, close corporations are started when the entrepreneur has an idea for a new product or service, such as a network switch. In the initial stage, the venture attempts to develop the new product. Whether the product will be successful cannot be known since its precise form and potential revenue streams have not yet taken shape. At this stage, the company will have relatively few shareholder-managers who supply the ideas, the initial capital for the venture, or both.

In the early stages of the development of this new switch, the venture is highly dependent on these individuals either for the critical product ideas or for the financial capital. Vulnerability arises because the parties' investments are match specific. That is, the value of the investments is tied to the success of their unproved product. Were the product to be a success, the payoff to the investment would be huge. But, were the venture to be abandoned, the investment would be lost. At a conceptual level, investments in our hypothetical network switch create match assets. Match assets are those that have a value to the parties to the venture but little value to outsiders. We use the terms *match-specific assets, match assets,* and *match-specific investments* interchangeably.[12] A defining characteristic of the Silicon Valley start-up is that its key assets are specific to the match.

The intensity of match assets creates a second important characteristic of close corporations. Between the time of the initial investments in research, development, and marketing and the time at which the world can

courts faced with allegations of minority oppression. For example, to Easterbrook and Fischel, minority oppression is no more likely in the close than in the public corporation and should not be a cause of action with distinctive standards and remedies.

12. Investments in match are defined to be investments that are more valuable to the contracting parties than to a third party. We use the term *match-specific investment* in this paper in place of the more common *firm-specific training* for several reasons. First, the term *match investment* captures the broader range of activities that create a good partnership, including training and learning by doing but also including adaptations to each other's styles of interaction. In addition, the term is more general and does not restrain the investments to take place inside a firm or an industry. Finally, the term *match specific* leads one to identify the specific asset created or improved by the parties' investments.

see whether the switch will be a commercial success, it will be difficult to convince outsiders to invest in the project. Second-stage venture capitalists can be interested in the venture but, given the still unproved value of the concept, will need to be brought in as insiders. The high cost of learning and staying informed about the switch's potential value makes outside investors unwilling bidders at a price that values the match assets at the insiders' valuation. As a consequence, the company will be capital constrained with no easy access to outside financing at an appropriate valuation of the assets.

If any of the company insiders could trigger dissolution of the enterprise midstream, the forced sale of the match assets would result in substantial losses to the participants. Either the insider with the deepest pocket would buy the assets, or the assets would be sold at a low price equal to the outsiders' bid price. If critical insiders could credibly threaten dissolution, they could use the threat to extract a great share of the value of the enterprise. The resulting potential for opportunism would interfere with inducing optimal investment.[13] The problem is akin to making an omelette: between the time the eggs are broken and the time the omelette sets, the cook knows his grand plan for the omelette, but, to outsiders, the half-cooked omelette is unappetizing. Forced sales of half-developed switches and uncooked omelettes go poorly.

In our approach, low agency costs are a natural result of the choice of form but not the reason for adopting it. The close corporation will always have lower agency costs than an otherwise identical publicly owned company as a consequence of the limited number of shareholders and the overlap of shareholders and managers. But agency costs do not explain why any given firm would adopt the close corporation form. The important exception, noted by Easterbrook and Fischel, is the family business. In a family business, low agency costs already exist in the familial relationship, and the parties can thus capitalize on the relationship by adopting the close corporation form. But the Silicon Valley start-up is different. These shareholder-managers are unlikely to have preexisting family ties and hence are unlikely to bring low agency costs to the formation of the close corporation. For at least the Silicon Valley start-up, the explanation for the choice of form is an operational factor: the need to lock in parties while developing vulnerable match-specific assets. Reduced agency costs are the result rather than the cause.

The problem of match-specific investments in a context with substantial asymmetry of information characterizes many other centrally important

13. *Rent seeking,* or, more generally, *opportunism,* can be defined as the expenditure of resources or effort by one party in order to transfer resources from the other party to itself. This investment by the rent payers wastes the joint profits of the parties because it creates no new wealth. Moreover, rent seeking by one party typically causes the prospective rent payer to expend resources in order to protect its share of the joint investment.

economic relationships. The employment relationship in which an employee with match-specific training is more productive than an employee hired from the external labor market provides a classic example. That employment relationship provides a critical foundation for our analysis precisely because most or all of the shareholders of close corporations are also employees.

Focusing on match assets also shows the fundamental differences between classic partnerships and close corporations. The dissolution-at-will feature of classic partnerships means that the form will best fit enterprises in which there are few, if any, assets that are not easily sold to third parties. In such cases, the benefits of dissolution at will are clear: by providing easy exit, it prevents opportunistic rent seeking. And the costs are minimal: when there are no sunk costs, when the principal assets are easily divided or sold, dissolution at will causes little harm. Thus, for a small law firm in which partners have their own clients but wish to share office space and staff and occasionally to refer business to other lawyers in the office with greater expertise or receive referrals, the partnership form is optimal. If the firm breaks up one day, very little value is trapped. Indeed, as one would predict, small law partnerships dissolve and re-form constantly.

But, if participants can trigger dissolution at will, they will be unwilling, ex ante, to make investments in match for fear that, ex post, they will be held up. Because of this, when there are high investments in match, such as with the Silicon Valley start-up, the costs of a rule of easy dissolution explode. The traditional close corporation manifests the same features, although in a less highly articulated form. As in the Silicon Valley start-up, at the early stage of a new venture, the product or service will have no revenue but high costs. Similarly, once the initial investments of human and physical capital are made, the participants are locked in. In one respect, the traditional family-business close corporation poses an even more difficult problem of protecting match investments. Unlike the Silicon Valley start-up, the traditional close corporation often expects to remain privately held indefinitely: the nature of the products or services is often such that selling to a third party is never a live option. But traditional close corporations come in many forms, and, at least in their formative years, many often hope to develop a product or service that may eventually be successful enough to be sold to a third party.

Easy dissolution would also make it even more difficult to raise equity or debt capital than it already is. Were the firm required to retire the capital of an existing owner who sought to cash out, the cash-constrained close corporation would be forced to raise new capital in a potentially unfavorable climate. Indeed, the shareholder dissension that characterizes a minority-oppression case is likely to be highly correlated with negative events in the firm. A legal rule favoring easy exit threatens to shift the engine for raising new money into reverse, forcing capital to be retired under unfavorable conditions.

Similarly, the lock-in of the corporate form is important to creditors. In a setting of limited liability, creditors cannot be repaid from the individual wealth of the owners of a bankrupt concern. In return, and in distinction to the rules of partnership, they are protected by the existence of an entity that is difficult for the current owners to dissolve. It is only with this protection that the squabbles among those who manage the company will be of limited interest to the creditors. Nowhere is this more important than in the close corporation, whose assets are difficult to value and whose current realizable market value—at forced sale—may be considerably below its future value. In such a setting, easy dissolution or buyout increases the risk of bankruptcy, thereby reducing the credit worthiness of the company. The traditional judicial reluctance to order dissolution or a buyout of minority shareholders lowers the credit risk of close corporations and allows them to borrow at more favorable terms.

Clearly, not all close corporations will be marked by heavy investments in match. Parties can and do choose alternative corporate and noncorporate forms on the basis of very different motivations. In addition, parties sometimes make mistakes in their choice of form. In this regard, the analysis can be interpreted as defining the paradigm close corporation that is best served by the legal rules. Choose the close corporation form when heavy investments in match make restrictions on exit valuable. Choose the partnership form when exit is not costly and the parties can be given free rein to withdraw from the match.

## 7.2 Legal Setting

In this section, we describe the legal and nonlegal features of the close corporation. In so doing, we show how minority oppression arises and how it is constrained. This begins to set the stage for providing an answer to how the three cases noted at the outset should be resolved.

### 7.2.1 Core Solution: The Corporate Form

The standard, off-the-rack, corporate form provides a robust solution to the problem caused by threats of opportunistic exit. The standard form has several relevant terms. Directors are elected by a majority of the shares.[14] Dissolution requires a board resolution and a vote of the majority of the shares.[15] Individual shareholders have no general right to sell their shares back to the firm.

14. See, e.g., Delaware General Corporation Law (Del. GCL), sec. 216.
15. See, e.g., ibid., sec. 275.

The lock-in of the close corporation is created by the interaction of these terms with the absence of a public market for the shares. But the lock-in affects only the minority shareholder (Minor). The majority shareholder (Major) can dissolve the corporation through a board resolution and a vote of a majority of the shares. The individual minority shareholders have no power to trigger dissolution. Minor likewise has no right to be bought out because, under the standard corporation laws, *no* shareholder has a general right to be bought out. But, if Major dissolves the corporation, Minor will receive his pro rata share if and when the firm is dissolved.[16] In the meantime, Minor has a very limited right to be bought out by the firm, namely, the right to judicial appraisal upon a merger and, sometimes, a sale of all or substantially all the assets.[17]

In addition to the lock-in provided by the statutory form, there are additional core properties of the form provided by a combination of statute and case law. The single most important is the prohibition on non pro rata distributions during the life of the firm, combined with close scrutiny of self-dealing transactions that attempt to evade this prohibition. The restrictions on non pro rata distributions are quite clear and derive from several sources. A majority shareholder may not pay itself dividends without also paying the same per share dividend to the minority shareholders.[18] It would be clearly illegal—and easily challenged—if the majority shareholder paid itself $1.00 per share in dividends while paying minority shareholders only $0.10 per share.

Indirect means are also constrained. For example, if the majority shareholder attempts to divert assets by entering into a contract with the firm on preferential terms, the contract is subject to close judicial scrutiny, and the majority shareholder bears the burden of establishing that the transaction is "entirely fair" to the corporation, where *entirely fair* is, when possible, defined by an arm's-length market comparison. Compensation agreements are subject to the same rule.[19] Generally, in order to avoid "entire fairness" scrutiny, compensation arrangements must be authorized in advance by disinterested directors or disinterested shareholders and, even then, are subject to scrutiny by the court under a "waste" standard. Similarly, attempts by the majority shareholder to take opportunities that belong to the corporation, or to use corporate assets for its own benefit, are limited (again imperfectly) by the "corporate opportunity" and related doctrines.[20]

While no one believes that these rules eliminate non pro rata benefits of

16. See, e.g., ibid., sec. 281.

17. See, e.g., ibid., sec. 262; Revised Model Business Corporation Act (RMBCA), sec. 13.02.

18. Del. GCL, sec. 170; RMBCA, sec. 6.40.

19. ALI Principles of Corporate Governance, sec. 5.03.

20. Ibid., secs. 5.10–5.14.

control, most would agree that they do limit the magnitude of such diversion significantly. Indeed, as Clifford Holderness and Dennis Sheehan (chap. 5 in this volume) show, empirical investigation suggests that legal restraints are surprisingly effective and probably the *primary* protection for minority shareholders.

The centrality of these terms is clear: by limiting non pro rata distributions, these provisions go a long way toward making the relationship incentive compatible. So long as the majority shareholders cannot prefer themselves in distributions, minority shareholders can depend on the majority to protect their, the minority's, interests.

A second set of standard protections is equally important in facilitating and protecting the beneficial lock-in. These provisions address endgame scenarios. When, for example, the majority shareholder triggers dissolution in order to take its capital out of the enterprise, the minority shareholders share pro rata in the net proceeds.[21] Similarly, if the firm merges with another firm, shareholders receive equal shares, and minority shareholders have a right to be bought out at "fair value" whether the firm survives or disappears.[22] Under the Revised Model Business Corporation Act (RMBCA), minority shareholders are also entitled to appraisal if the firm sells all or substantially all of its assets.

Attempts by Major to circumvent these rules are constrained. If, for example, Major engineers a "squeeze-out merger" to rid itself of minority shareholders, Minor will be entitled to a judicial valuation of its shares, often with favorable procedural protections. Under Delaware law, Minor will be entitled to appraisal.[23] In addition, Minor may also be entitled to bring a breach-of-fiduciary-duty action.[24] In evaluating such a squeeze-out merger, the Delaware court will place the burden on Major to prove the entire fairness of the price.[25]

### 7.2.2 Majority Opportunism and the Remedy for Minority Oppression

But the very provisions that protect against opportunistic exit create the problem of opportunistic lock-in. Consider case A outlined above. When Major has a falling out with Minor and Minor is left holding a minority interest in a firm controlled by Major, the standard corporation codes do not give Minor any right to be bought out or any right to dissolve the corporation. As a result, Minor may find itself locked into an investment that pays no dividends, in which Major makes all the decisions, and from which the only exit is to sell to Major at Major's bid price.

The core protection against majority oppression is the prohibition on

21. See, e.g., Del. GCL, secs. 275, 281; RMBCA, secs. 14.02–14.05.
22. Del. GCL, secs. 251, 262; RMBCA, secs. 11.01–11.06, 13.01–13.02.
23. Del. GCL, sec. 262.
24. *Weinberger v. UOP, Inc.*, 457 A.2d 701 (Del. 1983).
25. *Kahn v. Tremont Corp.*, 694 A.2d 422 (Del. 1997).

non pro rata distributions and the related prohibitions on self-dealing, discussed above. The doctrine of minority oppression can be understood as a supplemental judicial response to this problem. Over the last twenty-five years, in response to the perceived plight of the locked-in minority shareholder, courts and legislatures have modified the law to provide remedies to minority shareholders not available to shareholders of publicly held corporations.[26] This has been done in a variety of ways. First, legislatures in many states have broadened the circumstances in which minority shareholders may force the judicial dissolution of a corporation. In addition, legislatures have expanded the range of remedies beyond dissolution, namely, to include judicially mandated buybacks at a fair price. In most jurisdictions, shareholders can petition for dissolution on the grounds of illegality, fraud, misapplication of assets, or waste. Oppressive conduct by the majority shareholder is often listed as a basis for dissolution.[27] Similarly, frustration of shareholders' reasonable expectations is often a ground for dissolution (Thompson 1988). In other jurisdictions, shareholders' reasonable expectations are the measure of whether the majority shareholder has oppressed the minority.

Second, judges have become more willing to order dissolution or a buyout, particularly if they are convinced that majority shareholders have engaged in oppressive conduct or that shareholders' reasonable expectations have been violated.

Third, courts have made it easier, substantively and procedurally, for minority shareholders to bring suit against majority shareholders for breach of fiduciary duties. Minority shareholders have benefited from several trends. First, courts have demonstrated a tendency to make stricter the fiduciary duty owed by majority shareholders. Second, courts have shown an increased skepticism toward whether the majority has fulfilled its duties. Finally, courts have broadened the situations in which a minority shareholder can bring a (procedurally simple) direct suit in place of a (procedurally complex) derivative suit. Together, these developments have moved close corporation law toward partnership law, both with regard to the ease of dissolution and with regard to the duties owed by one shareholder to the others.

These various doctrines have proved difficult to contract out of (Oest-

26. In the following, extremely cursory summary, we follow the excellent treatment in Thompson (1993). For further details, see Thompson (1988). For even more details, see O'Neal and Thompson (1985, [1986] 1995).

27. See, e.g., RMBCA, sec. 14.30(2)(ii): "The court may dissolve a corporation . . . in a proceeding by a shareholder if it is established that . . . the directors or those in control of the corporation have acted, are acting, or will act in a manner that is illegal, oppressive, or fraudulent." Under sec. 14.34(a), when shares are closely held, "the corporation may elect, or, if it fails to elect, one or more of the shareholders may elect to purchase all shares owned by the petitioning shareholder at the fair value of the shares."

erle 1995). Because the doctrines find their foundation in either a contractual covenant of good faith or a fiduciary duty, and because contracts waiving such duties are typically void, a straightforward contractual opt-out will not be effective. Similarly, contractual attempts to divest courts of authority to dissolve the corporation are generally void. Ironically, while the overwhelming trend in close corporation law has been to permit tailoring of the standard terms by contract, the area of minority protection has stood out as an exception.

In summary, then, a cause of action has evolved for shareholder oppression or, perhaps more accurately, as Robert Thompson (1993, 708) suggests, for "shareholders' dissension." This cause of action has increased the ability of shareholders of the close corporation to turn to a third-party decision maker for relief from what that shareholder argues is oppression or unfair conduct by the controlling shareholders. Although the cause of action is still evolving and its boundaries remain obscure, these developments have increased the bargaining power of the minority, ex post, vis-à-vis the majority.

The critical question is whether such developments are likely to benefit the participants in close corporations. Our point is that the close corporation is the ideal form for enterprises with a high density of match assets because of, and not despite, its lock-in feature. Accordingly, the development of shareholder-oppression law may interfere with the efficiency of the close corporation form. To reduce this possibility, what principles should guide its evolution?

### 7.2.3 When Is a Legal Solution Appropriate?

The possibility of opportunistic behavior does not, itself, provide a sufficient basis for judicial or legal intervention. While the problem of opportunism is pervasive in relationships characterized by investments in match and asymmetry of information, only sometimes are such problems solved by legal intervention. To put it somewhat differently, the issue is when a non–legally enforceable norm-governed relationship serves the parties' interests better than a third-party law-governed relationship.

From this perspective, one cannot understand the role of legal intervention in the close corporation until one first understands the extent to which the relationship is already self-governed by non–legally enforceable norms enabled by the core legal form. We proceed in several steps. First, because many minority-oppression cases are employment related and the employment relationship is the best example of a relationship with match investments and asymmetric information that is almost entirely norm governed, we start with a brief summary of that analysis. Second, we apply that mode of analysis to the close corporation, examining the analogous non–legally enforceable structures that constrain opportunistic behavior. Third, we examine the fundamental legal protections that make possible that self-government. With that groundwork laid, we then turn to the appropriate judicial role in rooting out residual opportunism.

## 7.3 Constraints on Opportunism

### 7.3.1 The Employment Relationship and Investments in Match

The employment relationship and, particularly, the relationship between managers and the firm is often characterized by large investments in match.[28] These include employee investments in identifying the employer, in understanding and improving job performance, and in learning the organizational and operating structures of the company and its core competencies. The company, in turn, invests in identifying and training the employee in the factors listed above and in monitoring the employee's performance to determine the most profitable future path of joint match investments. Many of these investments are match specific and would be lost if the employee left the company.

Given the magnitude of the sunk investments in match, the threshold question is why the parties enter an ongoing relationship without adopting (legally enforceable) contract terms to protect their interests. The explanation is twofold. First, contracting over the multitude of interactions would be extremely costly in a relationship that is continuous and evolving. Second, self-enforcing but non–legally enforceable norms emerge to constrain opportunistic behavior.

The widespread but puzzling features of the employment relationship can be best understood as a remarkably robust set of self-enforcing employee protections. Consider, for example, why firms choose to discharge an employee for inferior performance rather than adopting a less severe penalty, such as reduction in wages. While this may initially seem to be in conflict with the presumed interest of the parties in maintaining the employment relationship, asymmetric information requires termination rather than a wage reduction. Because of asymmetric information, employees know their work effort, but firms do not. Firms can learn by monitoring, but constant monitoring is very costly. To save on costs, workers are infrequently monitored. The harsh penalty is driven by the low detection rate. If most shirking goes undetected, workers must be penalized an amount greater than the expected loss of any specific incident.

But this optimal deterrence explanation does not explain why the penalty for inferior performance cannot be a large salary reduction. The answer is that, if the firm could simply declare that an employee was under-

28. For a fuller analysis, see Rock and Wachter (1996) and, more generally, Wachter and Wright (1990).

performing and cut his salary, the employer would have an incentive to overstate underperformance, thereby reducing costs and increasing profits. Channeling the employer's response into discharge is thus incentive compatible. In declaring inferior performance, the company must accept the loss of the employee. The company is willing to do this if the employee's performance is indeed inferior, but not otherwise. The practice of laying off workers during a slowdown, rather than reducing wages, can be understood in a similar fashion.

From this perspective, the legal doctrine of employment at will—the doctrine according to which companies can discharge employees for good reasons, bad reasons, or no reason at all—is best understood as a rule of judicial nonintervention, not the incorporation of a substantive norm of the employment relationship.[29] Even the critics of the rule do not claim that companies often discharge workers for bad reasons or no reason. Why, when the substantive norm that governs the employment relationship seems to be no discharge without cause, would the parties prefer a legal rule that says no intervention? The answer follows from the preceding analysis.

An enforceable contract must be specified ex ante in terms that can be verified ex post by the third-party enforcer. In the employment context of continuous and evolving interactions, such a contract would invariably be incomplete. Consequently, the expectations of the parties would be difficult to establish at any given point in time. Since much of the information is asymmetrically available to one party, many of the outcomes cannot be verified by third parties.

In this context, legal enforcement of the norm of no discharge without cause would undermine the norm-based system because of the difficulties of ex post third-party verification. As a starting point, proving just cause would require that the employer engage in additional detection costs, which reduces the value of the match. In addition, the third party would have to learn enough about the internal norms of the firm to determine whether a violation of the norm was meaningful enough to constitute cause. Moreover, the presence of investments in match increases the likelihood of error when third parties enforce the norms because the valuations of those assets depend, not on market prices, but on the parties' own valuations. From the employer's perspective, just cause exists when the continuation of the match with the particular employee has negative net present value, including the reputational cost of taking too tough or too easy a stance in the face of the perceived violation.

Self-enforcing norms better serve the parties' interests. On the one hand, they allow the party with the detailed information to act on his or her knowledge at low cost. At the same time, they protect the uninformed

29. For a fuller analysis, see Rock and Wachter (1996).

party by forcing the informed party's actions into channels that make opportunistic behavior unprofitable.

In cases where norms are insufficient to deter opportunistic behavior, other, nonlegal remedies are available. The parties are involved in repetitive interactions, and the employer is also a repeat player in the competitive external labor markets. Both make it costly for an employer to act opportunistically. In the ongoing employment relationship, bad play by the employer generates retributive bad play by the employees, whether in concert or individually. This can take the form of hard-to-detect work slowdowns, bad-mouthing the employer in the public domain, or even covert vandalism and theft. Such actions cause direct losses to the employer and force an increase in monitoring, which is also costly. In the labor market for new employees, a reputation for bad play is similarly costly in the form of increased difficulty attracting or retaining the best employees. Finally, in the case of nonsupervisory employees, unionization is an effective alternative, forcing the relationship into the domain of explicit contracting with a collective-bargaining agreement.

Given these advantages, the resilience of the employment-at-will doctrine in the employment relationship is not surprising. Whenever courts encroach on the doctrine through a theory of contractual interpretation, one finds that, to the extent permitted, the parties contract around the interpretation by specifying, for example, that the terms of the employment handbook are not to be taken as legally binding. The best explanation for this resilience is that, in a relationship characterized by match investments and asymmetry of information, the parties are best served by self-enforcing rather than third-party enforced agreements. It is not that opportunistic behavior is eliminated entirely, only that the benefits of the flexible norm-governed relationship outweigh the costs of residual opportunism.

We now turn to the analogous problem in the closely held corporation.

### 7.3.2 Close Corporation: Nonlegal Constraints on Opportunism

As in the employment context, many of the persistent features of the close corporation provide substantial, albeit non–legally enforceable, protection against opportunities for abuse that are opened up by the form itself. In this subsection, we explore how these nonlegal constraints operate and show that the seemingly detrimental lock-in of the close corporation, supplemented by the prohibition on direct and indirect non pro rata distributions, renders the form largely incentive compatible. By locking in Major and prohibiting non pro rata payments, Major will maximize Minor's stake in seeking to maximize the value of his own stake in the firm.

This is particularly true in the case in which the close corporation is like an unfinished omelette. Like the shareholders' individual inability to trigger dissolution, the lack of a market prevents exit or opportunistic threats of exit, except under narrowly defined circumstances. Locked in together, the parties can count on each other's dedication to cooking the omelette properly. This issue is also handled, at least in the Silicon Valley start-up, by legally enforceable contracts that protect early investors through particular financing structures (Sahlman 1990; Gompers 1995). In general, then, the close corporation forces the investor into a high degree of illiquidity, an unfavorable state from a traditional investment perspective, but an illiquidity that serves the interests of the parties by locking up participants in the enterprise.

A variety of other features of the close corporation can be understood as supplementing and complementing this structure. The overlap between suppliers of capital and labor reduces information asymmetries and transaction costs. Whether in the traditional or the Silicon Valley variety, the overlap puts all the relevant players into continuing contact, providing both the entrepreneur and the capital suppliers with continuing information on their own and on the company's performance.

The result is that the operations of the close corporation are akin to the stylized employment relationship discussed above. The same types of self-enforcing norms are operational. In both cases, the participants are engaged in repetitive interactions where the parties can sanction each other for bad play and can apply the appropriate sanctions more reliably than third parties who cannot observe and monitor the behavior of the parties. In the close corporation, the ability of the participants to identify improper behavior will be much greater than the ability of any third party. Moreover, the ability of the participants to punish bad behavior will likewise be great. The disenchanted minority shareholder-manager armed with greater access to company-performance information has more leverage to sanction bad play by the employer than does the individual manager in a public corporation.

Indeed, if anything, the results found in the employment relationship are stronger in the case of the close corporation because of Easterbrook and Fischel's point on agency costs. The most difficult problem in the employment relationship is aligning the interests of the employees with those of the company. Pay for performance, particularly, stock options for senior executives, reduces the misalignment in the public company, but the device is costly to the shareholders and imperfect. In the close corporation, pay for performance is a natural result of the fact that employees are also shareholders. More generally, in the public corporation's employment relationship, senior executives and shareholders occupy mostly independent spheres. In the close corporation, the spheres overlap. The wide governance mandate of its board of directors results from the overlap of roles between capital and labor providers. The shareholder-employee is involved in the governance issues normally reserved for shareholders (in the publicly held corporation) and for employees (in the employment relationship).

The robustness of the norm protection is illustrated by the high-tech sector. The occasions for opportunistic renegotiation that arise from sequential performance are a particular problem in high-tech start-ups. Venture capitalists (VCs) worry that, after accepting early financing from the VC, the entrepreneurs will find other financing once the idea proves its worth or will quit and go to work elsewhere after the VC has invested millions of dollars. Entrepreneurs worry that the VCs will find other managers once the idea has been committed to paper and has proved its worth. These concerns, which are simply a special and detailed case of the more general problems of the close corporation, are the subject of intense contracting (and research). We illustrate by considering a few details.

The VCs protect themselves in several ways.[30] First, a surprising stylized fact of the Silicon Valley start-up is that the VCs have the right to replace the entrepreneur with a professional manager (Hellmann 1998). In addition, the terminated entrepreneur can often be forced to sell his stock back to the firm at cost, which will be well below its actual value. Finally, entrepreneurs do not automatically receive generous severance packages.

Thomas Hellmann (1998) explains why the VCs would demand such terms as a response to a holdup problem. Entrepreneurs gain private benefits of control, which lead them to stay on longer than they should. By contrast, the VCs' incentives are much better aligned with maximizing firm value, and, moreover, they are better situated to identify better professional managers. In Hellmann's model, unless the VC receives the right to displace the entrepreneur, it will not invest optimally in searching for replacement managers.

How the entrepreneurs protect themselves is equally interesting. After all, if the VC has the right to terminate the entrepreneur, which triggers a stock buyback at cost, there would seem to be an incentive to do so. The entrepreneur's protections here are entirely nonlegal, but they are substantial. Most important, VCs are repeat players in the start-up business and are likely to be constrained on a number of fronts. First, they compete to provide financing for the most promising start-ups and are thus likely to be constrained by reputational effects in their aim to maintain their position in relation to other start-up companies. In addition, the VC has to replace the entrepreneur with another person. Wrongful discharge of the CEO, even if protected from judicial second-guessing by the employment-at-will doctrine, is not a strong starting point in any recruitment process.

30. For further discussion of the provisions in this paragraph, see Fenn, Liang, and Prowse (1995, 32–33), Barry et al. (1990), Gorman and Sahlman (1989), Gompers (1995), and Lerner (1995).

Finally, the discharge will raise questions with other capital suppliers. It is a negative signal under the best of circumstances and is likely to raise the company's cost of capital. This, of course, is precisely the story we told about employment at will more generally, and the fact that employment at will governs even in a domain of such intensive contracting as the Silicon Valley high-tech sector is further support for our analysis.

That still leaves open the question of why the entrepreneur's stock position can be bought out at cost. The likely answer here, as stressed throughout the paper, is the difficulty of determining market value for a start-up company that does not trade in a public market. The contract term that sets the buyback price at cost, however, is a default setting. Here again, the VC will have a strong reputational incentive to deal fairly with the discharged entrepreneur, including paying a higher price if that can be reliably determined.

Another feature that is particularly striking is the absence of any general right to trigger dissolution or to be bought out at a pro rata share of firm value. The choice made in the high-tech sector, where contracting is most explicit, is to leave the lock-in in place and to avoid judicial valuation of hard-to-value assets, even at the cost of some residual opportunism. This is consistent with the more general reactions to the special close corporation chapters of corporation codes, promulgated by some jurisdictions in response to developments in the law and academic commentary: few firms avail themselves of the opportunity to organize under such statutes. On the contrary, close corporations seem stubbornly to adhere to organizing under the general corporation codes.

## 7.4 The Proper Judicial Role in the Three Cases

We have argued that the lock-in effect of the corporate form is what makes it so attractive for firms that benefit from extensive investments in match. We have argued further that there are a variety of structural features that limit the incentives and constrain the ability of the participants to act opportunistically, the principal threat to optimal match investment. In addition, the law limits significantly the non pro rata distribution of assets from the corporation and provides for pro rata treatment on dissolution and merger. Moreover, the law provides for a judicial valuation of minority shares in a sharply limited number of situations. Finally, participants are free to contract for additional or different terms, an opportunity that participants liberally use.

The remaining question is what room, if any, is there for further judicial intervention on behalf of minority shareholders? The worry is that judicial attempts to protect minority shareholders against opportunistic behavior will jeopardize the web of features and protections that makes the close corporation form so attractive and popular for firms with substantial match-specific assets.[31] In guarding further against the potential for minority oppression, do we end up increasing the potential for opportunism in the relationship by providing Minor with more chances to act opportunistically against Major?

### 7.4.1 Case A: Employment at Will as Minority Oppression?

Consider case A, in which Major fires Minor. Minor, the terminated minority shareholder who invested in match-specific assets related to a new network switch, had the expectation that he would share in the returns generated from the venture. We worry that Minor will not be able to share the fruit of his efforts now that he has had a falling out with fellow shareholder Major. Moreover, we worry that, having lost his job, Minor will be forced by economic necessity, and the absence of a liquid market for shares, to sell his shares at a fraction of the pro rata value of the firm. The Minors of the world, we worry, never being sure whether they will end up on the wrong end of a disagreement, will not invest optimally in match-specific assets unless their employment and investment expectations are protected.

There are two variants of case A that must be considered. First, assume that Major is the entrepreneur who supplies the ideas and has 60 percent of the stock and that Minor supplies the money and has 40 percent. What possibilities for opportunism arise in the absence of any special protection for minority shareholders? Suppose that, after Minor has invested his money and the idea is developing well, Major says, "I want an additional 10 percent of the equity, or else you will never see a dime of profit," or any number of variants that amount to the same thing. Is this a credible threat? Clearly, the answer is no. First, because of the restrictions on non pro rata distributions, if Minor does not get any dividends, neither does Major. Second, if Minor is providing more than money (management advice, industry contacts, etc.), Major may still need him. Third, the market and the need for a stream of additional capital will constrain Major's ability to threaten Minor. In these circumstances, Minor will be unwilling to put more capital into the business. Other potential investors are likely to refuse as well as soon as they learn of the incident. As long as Minor remains a material owner of the company or is known in the financial community, those in the financial community who are considering investments will undoubtedly learn of Major's opportunism. Empirical research on the

31. A weaker proposal would be to make the minority protection a default setting, from which firms could opt out. The experience of states that have special optional close corporation provisions suggests that there would be boilerplate opt-out of default settings. The widespread contracting around departures from the employment-at-will doctrine through the interpretation of employee handbooks likewise suggests that any variation would have to be mandatory to be effective.

high-tech sector confirms that the financial people are quite good at contracting for particular sorts of devices to protect against this sort of opportunism.

Consider, now, the reverse scenario: Major supplies the financial resources and holds 60 percent, while Minor is the entrepreneur who supplies the ideas and has 40 percent. Once Minor commits his idea to patentable paper, Major fires Minor. Minor has neither an employment agreement nor any shareholders' agreement that provides for a buyout right. Does Minor have a claim on our sympathies?

In this case, a threshold question is whether Minor's contribution is "one off." If it is, then Minor opens himself to opportunistic renegotiation if Minor commits the contribution before Major finishes performing. But, when the contribution really is one off, without the necessity for ongoing involvement (the scenario that gives rise to the threat of opportunism), there is an easy transactional solution: a license or sale. The person (or persons) who discovers something important but has nothing further to contribute should license or sell the idea to Major, who will then develop it. Similarly, when the capital provider has only a single investment to make and has nothing else to contribute, he should buy limited partnership shares with a VC who can then control the opportunistic Majors because of his superior knowledge and network. Of course, the onetime, would-be financier may purchase the patent or license it, only to go broke owing to his own lack of good follow-up ideas. The critical fact, however, is the following: when the contribution is, indeed, one off, there is no business reason to use the corporate form at all.

Focus, then, on the difficult cases that will involve plaintiffs who believe that they are still making contributions to the firm. If brought before a third party for resolution, Major will explain that Minor was fired because Minor has been shirking or is not suited to the current demands of his job or needs of the firm. That is, Minor is no longer making a valuable contribution. Minor will maintain that he was fired because Major wanted to take Minor's ideas for himself and capture all the gains.

This is precisely the same problem that is addressed in employment law by the employment-at-will doctrine. Sorting out the truth, here, raises precisely the difficulties of relying on a third party to resolve employment disputes. It is very difficult for the court to determine ex post what the parties' reasonable expectations were ex ante. Even if the court could determine the parties' expectations, performance is largely unobservable, so the court will be unable to determine whether the expectations have been satisfied. As in the employment context, Major and Minor know much more about who is telling the truth than a judge can ever discover. In addition, valuing the relationship-specific assets to determine whether opportunism has occurred and, if so, to set damages is, in theory and in practice, necessarily speculative. Finally, permitting Minor to sue for oppression or breach of reasonable expectations will, as in the employment context, undermine the web of self-enforcing relationships that provides the principal protection for investments in match.

Against this background, consider the classic case A case, *Wilkes v. Springside Nursing Home.*[32] Wilkes, along with three others, established a nursing home, with the work and profits apportioned more or less equally. After a falling out, the others forced Wilkes out of active participation in the management of the enterprise and cut off all corporate payments. Wilkes alleged that his termination constituted a breach of the fiduciary duties owed him by the majority shareholders. According to the court, "The severance of Wilkes from the payroll resulted not from misconduct or neglect of duties, but because of the personal desire of [the other shareholders] to prevent him from continuing to receive money from the corporation."

In holding for Wilkes, the court stated:

> A guaranty of employment with the corporation may have been one of the "basic reason[s] why a minority owner has invested capital in the firm." . . . The minority stockholder typically depends on his salary as the principal return on his investment, since the "earnings of a close corporation . . . are distributed in major part in salaries, bonuses and retirement benefits." . . . Other noneconomic interests of the minority stockholder are likewise injuriously affected by barring him from corporate office. . . . Such action severely restricts his participation in the management of the enterprise and he is relegated to enjoying those benefits incident to his status as a stockholder. . . . In sum, by terminating a minority shareholder's employment or by severing him from a position as an officer or director, the majority effectively frustrate the minority stockholder's purposes in entering on the corporate venture and also deny him an equal return on his investment.

That said, the court recognized the extent to which the controlling group needed "room to maneuver in establishing the business policy of the corporation." As a compromise, the court established a "legitimate business purpose" test: "When an asserted business purpose for their action is advanced by the majority, . . . we think it is open to minority stockholders to demonstrate that the same legitimate objective could have been achieved though an alternative course of action less harmful to the minority's interest." Because the majority had not shown a legitimate business purpose in terminating Wilkes's involvement in the firm, the court held for Wilkes.

There is, in addition, a second argument suggested that raises some additional issues. The court notes, "Other noneconomic interests of the minority stockholder are likewise injuriously affected by barring him from corporate office. . . . Such action severely restricts his participation in the

32. *Wilkes v. Springside Nursing Home,* 353 N.E.2d 657 (Mass. 1976).

management of the enterprise and he is relegated to enjoying those benefits incident to his status as a stockholder." The exact thrust of the court's argument here is somewhat unclear. One reading of this claim is that there are valuable, noneconomic benefits that come with participation in the firm. To the extent that this is the argument, it simply amplifies the no-just-cause claim.

But there is a much more relevant alternative reading, namely, that terminating Wilkes's participation in the firm made it impossible for him to continue to monitor his coshareholders and that, because of the asymmetry of information that characterizes the close corporation form, this renders his continued participation as a shareholder untenable. This is an argument that differs both from the faulty employment-at-will concerns and from the non pro rata distribution concerns discussed below.

Could the other shareholders in *Wilkes* have been behaving opportunistically? Could they have terminated Wilkes's relationship with the firm in order to expropriate his investment now that he had already committed whatever special skills and knowledge he had? Absolutely. Opportunistic behavior is clearly possible in such circumstances. But that, alone, is not sufficient to justify the court's response, namely, a case-by-case analysis of termination to see whether the firm acted with "legitimate business purpose" and with no "less harmful alternative." That is the same as saying that, because opportunistic behavior is possible in the employment relationship, a court should scrutinize each termination to see if it was for just cause.[33]

Case A and *Wilkes* both present situations in which the majority shareholder or shareholders could be behaving opportunistically. But, in both cases, there are numerous nonlegal constraints on such behavior. If Major treats Minor badly, Major will have greater difficulty convincing current shareholder-employees to continue investing time, money, and effort in the enterprise and convincing prospective investors or prospective employees to join the firm on the same terms as Minor did. These are the reputation and self-help stories described earlier.

But suppose that Minor's idea or Wilkes's stake is so valuable that Major is willing to suffer whatever reputational cost it will incur by acting badly? Minor and Wilkes are still not unprotected. If Major successfully markets or develops Minor's patent or sells it, or if Springside Nursing Homes sells the nursing home to a national chain, Minor and Wilkes are still protected by the rule of no non pro rata distributions. If Major ultimately decides to liquidate or sell the firm in order to take its profits on Minor's invention, Minor will likewise receive his share. In the meantime, Minor will be in a position to make Major's life difficult with requests

33. This, of course, is precisely the argument that opponents of the employment-at-will doctrine make.

for information and threats of litigation. Finally, if these protections are insufficient and the problem is significant, future Minors always have the option of specifying additional protections by contract.

On the other side of the equation, to permit judicial scrutiny of Minor's or Wilkes's termination is to undermine the very advantages of the informal, non–legally enforceable set of protections that constitute relational "contracts." As we have argued elsewhere (Rock and Wachter 1996) in connection with the employment-at-will doctrine, the attempt to root out residual opportunism—opportunism that slips through the network of legal and nonlegal constraints—threatens to undermine the self-enforcing character of the overall relationship. Moreover, as we discuss in more detail below, the court's difficulties determining whether a discharge was for a "legitimate business purpose" are aggravated by the difficulties of valuing match assets in awarding Minor the "fair value" of his shares in a judicially mandated buyout.

The *Wilkes* case is a good example of the difficulties that courts have with the employment issues that frequently overlay close corporation cases.[34] For example, was the court correct in saying that there was no legitimate business purpose in terminating Wilkes's employment? On the one hand, we are told that there was no misconduct and that Wilkes "had always accomplished his assigned share of the duties competently." The court, however, made no attempt to determine whether Wilkes's services were still needed. Apparently, he was not replaced, suggesting overstaffing. By not appreciating the norms of the employment relationship, the court stumbled badly, inferring a right to continued employment subject only to proof of misconduct. Such a right is so at variance with employment practice anywhere that its insertion in the case undermines the logical application of the legitimate-business-purpose standard.

### 7.4.2 Case B: Stock Buybacks as Minority Oppression?

Consider, now, case B: Major forces the firm to buy back a portion of Major's shares (but leaving Major in control) at an entirely fair price, without giving Minor a proportionally equal opportunity to cash out. The principal variant of case B is where Major Group, the controlling shareholder group, buys back the shares of one of the control group without giving Minor a proportionally equal opportunity to cash out. In either case, does Minor have a claim on our sympathies? Here, we worry that, even if his transaction with the firm meets the entire fairness valuation standard, Major gets a benefit that Minor does not: the ability to cash out a portion of his holdings when doing so is profitable. We worry that Major's ability to "have his cake and eat it too" will undermine Minor's incen-

34. The importance of employment disputes and the employment-at-will doctrine in the close corporation setting is stressed in Johnston (1992).

tive to invest optimally in the firm by breaking the beneficial lock-in feature of the corporate form.

This is the issue in *Donahue v. Rodd Electrotype.*[35] In *Donahue,* the controlling shareholder, Dad, distributed most of his shares to his children who worked in the business. Subsequently, his sons wished that Dad would retire, and he was agreeable, but he would do so only if he could sell some of his remaining shares back to the firm (with the remainder distributed later to his sons). The firm bought back Dad's shares without offering an equal opportunity to the minority shareholders, who challenged this as a breach of fiduciary duty. After a lengthy discussion of the extent to which close corporations are really little more than incorporated partnerships, a discussion that is not only wrong but unnecessary to the decision of the case, the Supreme Judicial Court of Massachusetts held: "If the stockholder whose shares were purchased was a member of the controlling group, the controlling stockholders must cause the corporation to offer each stockholder an equal opportunity to sell a ratable number of his shares to the corporation at an identical price."

*Nixon v. Blackwell* likewise involved a stock-repurchase plan.[36] In *Nixon,* the firm established an ESOP (employee stock-option plan) that held company stock and provided departing shareholder-employees with the right to receive cash for their interest in the ESOP when they retired. In addition, the company established key-man insurance policies that allowed proceeds from the plan to be used to purchase stock in executives' estates. The nonemployee minority shareholders objected on the grounds that they were not provided an equal opportunity to sell their shares. The Chancery Court held that it was "inherently unfair" for the controlling shareholders to provide liquidity for themselves without providing comparable liquidity for the nonemployee shareholders.[37] The Delaware Supreme Court reversed, holding that the stock-repurchase plans served a legitimate corporate interest by maintaining an overlap between employment and ownership and that the defendants met the entire fairness standard.

Plaintiffs claimed that the preferential repurchase of shares was a breach of fiduciary duty. The claim raises the question of the extent to which preferential repurchase schemes are problematic not solely because the price is too high (a version of pure self-dealing) but because they undermine the alignment of interests between the majority and the minority shareholders that makes the form work. There are two aspects to the claim here. First, as we describe in more detail below, to the extent that a high density of match assets characterizes close corporations, it becomes very difficult for the court to determine whether the repurchase price was en-

35. *Donahue v. Rodd Electrotype Co.,* 328 N.E.2d 505 (Mass. 1975).
36. *Nixon v. Blackwell,* 626 A.2d 1366 (Del. 1993).
37. *Blackwell v. Nixon,* 1991 WL 194725 (Del. Ch. 1991).

tirely fair because there is no market benchmark. Second, even if one could value the shares, the preferential repurchase can be objectionable because it undermines the incentive-compatible lock-in that is the great attraction of the legal form. It is these aspects of the problem that lie at the heart of both *Nixon* and *Donahue* and that are not explicitly discussed in either decision. These are very different situations than those that occurred in case A: they do not raise the intrafirm employment questions that made the prior case so difficult.

But, at the same time, these cases also differ from the classic non pro rata distribution of firm assets. Here, the firm receives something of value in return for cash: shares of the firm. Normally, under the duty of loyalty, transactions between a fiduciary and the firm are not per se void or voidable. Rather, they are judged under the entire fairness standard and, if entirely fair, are valid.

The question is whether regulating such transactions is necessary to supplement the prohibition on non pro rata distributions and, if so, how to do so. The dimensions of the problems and the trade-offs among different approaches are complex. First, one needs to maintain the beneficial lock-in of participants that harnesses the self-interested efforts of the controlling shareholders in the interests of all participants. Second, one must prevent non pro rata distributions, distributions that can be made by the advantageous purchase or sale of shares. Third, one needs to maintain flexibility in the management of the firm's capital structure and compensation practices. Finally, one needs to provide for the orderly exit of participants.

There are three types of cases that must be accounted for. First, the control group may decide to buy out a minority shareholder. In such cases, there is little potential for opportunism. Second, the control group may decide to buy out a shareholder-employee who is exiting, or has exited, the firm, as in both *Donahue v. Rodd* and *Nixon v. Blackwell.* Here, the potential for opportunism is greater as the control shareholders may prefer one of their own over outside nonemployee shareholders and there may be disguised self-dealing. On the other hand, as continuing shareholder-employees, they will also bear a pro rata share of the cost. Finally, the controlling shareholder sells shares to the firm without giving up control. This is the most dangerous circumstance: the controlling shareholder has a clear incentive to receive an excessively high price while not giving up any of the private benefits of control.[38]

38. A related issue is presented by *Kahn v. Tremont Corp.,* 694 A.2d 422 (Del. 1997). In that case, Harold Simmons, the controlling shareholder of Valhi Corp. and, through Valhi, of NL Industries, was alleged to have used his control over a third corporation, Tremont, to cause Tremont to buy Valhi-owned shares of NL Industries at an excessively high price. Simmons was able to reduce his holdings in NL, without giving up control, at an allegedly excessive price, without other shareholders having an equal opportunity to cash out.

How does the law handle this range of cases? One reading of the law is to generalize *Donahue v. Rodd* into a general prohibition on the selective buyback of shares in close corporations, that is, an equal opportunity rule. This largely eliminates the opportunistic use of buybacks, but at the cost of impairing the firm's flexibility in adjusting its capital structure and compensation policies and providing exit to shareholders.

A second possibility is to generalize *Nixon v. Blackwell* into a general standard permitting selective stock repurchases whenever they are entirely fair. This preserves the firm's flexibility in compensation and in providing exit, but at the cost of diluting the beneficial lock-in.

A final possibility—which is plausible—is that *both Donahue v. Rodd* and *Nixon v. Blackwell* are correctly decided within their individual domains. *Nixon* addresses one aspect of the more complicated middle cases. Note that the Supreme Court's ruling in *Nixon* emphasized that the buyback was pursuant to a long-standing corporate policy to which the minority apparently did not object when first instituted and that the policy was adopted to benefit the corporation. Indeed, the Court viewed the policy as a form of deferred compensation that provided the firm with flexibility to adopt standard deferred-compensation packages used in other firms to encourage superior employee performance. Moreover, the court emphasized how the policy was applied in an entirely nondiscriminatory fashion among retiring employees. By contrast, the Chancery Court viewed the policy, not as a deferred-compensation practice, but as a straight financial structure issue in which members of the control group were given preference over nonemployee shareholders in cashing out.

As in case A, courts must be careful not to confuse employment-relationship issues with straightforward capital structure questions. If courts prevent firms from adopting deferred-compensation plans because of an equal opportunity rule on the exit end, close corporations will not be able to develop optimal incentive-based compensation mechanisms. In evaluating such cases, courts must look to both the compensation and the financial capital aspects of the situation, with particular attention to indicia of self-dealing.

Because of the potential for self-dealing when a control group buys out one of its own, the entire fairness rule applies. Under entire fairness, the Delaware courts look at both fair dealing and fair price. For the Delaware Supreme Court, the fact that the stock-purchase plans were adopted for legitimate corporate purposes (maintaining the overlap between ownership and control) and were provided to the shareholder-employees on a nondiscriminatory basis established fair dealing. Interestingly, the issue of whether the price paid for the shares was excessive did not come up.

In the close corporation context, both fair price and fair dealing can be problematic. Whether a repurchase plan is discriminatory depends on how the relevant group is defined. In *Nixon,* the Chancery Court found the plan discriminatory because it did not treat employee and nonemployee shareholders equally.[39] By contrast, the Delaware Supreme Court could have found it nondiscriminatory because it treated all employee shareholders equally, although, ultimately, it held that the discrimination against nonemployee shareholders was justifiable.[40] Similarly, relying on fair price is problematic when, as we discuss in more detail in the next section, the valuation problem is often intractable.

How, then, can one understand *Donahue v. Rodd* and its relation to *Nixon?* The primary difference between the two cases is that the control group in *Donahue* was a family group. One worries that the payment to Dad is disguised self-dealing, that the more Dad gets for his shares, the less the children who work in the business will have to contribute to buy him an apartment in Miami. The very family relations that Easterbrook and Fischel emphasize as important in reducing agency costs within the close corporation increase significantly the potential for self-dealing when the family group is dealing with nonfamily shareholders.

If the existence of a family relationship significantly increases the risks of self-dealing, then one can understand *Donahue v. Rodd* as consistent with *Nixon.* Reading them together, the standard in both is entire fairness, a standard not met in *Donahue* because of a (conclusive) presumption that the repurchase was not entirely fair. One can also understand the role of equal opportunity here. If adopted by the control group, it is powerful evidence that the transaction is entirely fair. In *Donahue*-type cases, offering minority shareholders an equal opportunity to exit reverses the presumption that buying back Dad's shares redounds to the sons' individual benefit by relieving them of some other financial obligation.

Appreciate, for a moment, the subtlety of the structure. While the firm is developing or producing omelettes and therefore has a reputational stake in not breaching its agreements, there are a variety of structural features that align interests, and the principal legal restriction is no non pro rata distributions. This means that the majority shareholder can refuse to pay dividends, but only at the cost of all shareholders' capital remaining trapped in the firm. This lock-in, plus the other features outlined above, provides a strong incentive for the majority shareholder to maximize firm value, thereby protecting the minority shareholders' investments as well.

But the lock-in is not absolute. As reconstructed above, the law has evolved to permit sufficient flexibility to allow the firm selectively to offer some shareholders the opportunity to cash out without offering the same opportunity to all shareholders when doing so benefits the firm. In doing so, the law distinguishes according to the potential for opportunistic be-

39. *Blackwell v. Nixon,* 1991 WL 194725 (Del. Ch. 1991), at *6.
40. *Nixon v. Blackwell,* 626 A.2d 1366, 1379 (Del. 1993).

havior by controlling shareholders. Thus, when the firm buys shares from noncontrolling shareholders, the business-judgment rule applies. When it buys shares from members of the control group who are exiting, the entire fairness standard applies, with equal opportunity being powerful evidence of entire fairness. Finally, when the firm buys back shares from a controlling shareholder or shareholding family who is remaining in the firm, the potential for self-dealing is so great that entire fairness is not satisfied absent equal opportunity.[41]

Once, however, the company enters the last period, defined by the distribution of a firm's equity capital, the norm against non pro rata distributions again protects locked-in minority shareholders. The rule of no non pro rata distribution now means that minority shareholders are able to cash out at the pro rata valuation. As the majority owner, Major gets to define when the omelette is finished and signals that fact by voiding the lock-in, either by dissolution, by merger, or by an initial public offering of stock. But, now, Minor gets to exit, either through a pro rata share of the firm equity in dissolution, or through an appraisal proceeding if the firm is merged into another firm, or by selling out to the market after a public offering of shares.

The rule against non pro rata distributions is the linchpin: it is the rule that prevents the participants from jumping out of these channels. So long as non pro rata distributions are controlled, remaining problems that arise between shareholders can be handled by analogy to employment at will: courts should not intervene in the absence of an explicit contract.

The analysis, then, largely parallels the employment-at-will account. In both cases, locking participants in to a relationship in which there are substantial investments in match is valuable because it avoids the holdup problem (threatening to leave before the omelette is done). It also forces the parties to resolve the problems themselves, avoiding defections; provides high-powered incentives to succeed; and prevents the parties from threatening to impose heavy costs (by threatening expensive litigation) as a way of renegotiating the division of the joint surplus.

In this sense, the principles applied in cases A and B are the same. In case A, Minor wants to be cashed out, at least if he cannot continue as an employee. In case B, Major wants to be cashed out, at least if he can continue in control. On our analysis, the answer is the same in both cases: neither can cash out without the other shareholders cashing out to the same degree. And, in both cases, the reason is the same: the omelette may

41. Paul Mahoney (chap. 6 in this volume) argues for minority exit at will as a default setting, using a game-theoretic model. In arriving at his conclusion, Mahoney assumes full information and, further, that, on average, courts will be correct in their valuation of closely held firms. But, when there is a high density of match assets, neither assumption will likely be correct.

not be finished yet. Major gets to decide when the omelette is finished, but, once Major declares the omelette finished, Minor shares pro rata. Meanwhile, neither gets to pull out equity.

### 7.4.3 Courts' Comparative Advantage: Do Cases A and B Differ?

Our analysis distinguishes sharply between case A and case B. But, say some, our distinction misses the point of what the courts are doing in these cases and, in particular, why it is important for courts to intervene in case A situations.[42] The problem, they say, is that courts cannot distinguish between market rates of compensation and excessive compensation and therefore should and do protect minority shareholders' employment in the firm as a second-best technique for protecting their investment expectations. On this view, unless you protect the expectation of employment, including the expected salary, the financial investment in the firm becomes worthless. That is, if pro rata distributions are to be defended, case A must be treated like case B in the sense of judicial intervention to protect the minority shareholder.

But this argument misses the fundamental reason that courts should not and generally do not intervene in employment cases. The argument incorrectly assumes that a court is better at distinguishing discharge for cause from minority oppression, and, when the remedy is a buyout, calculating fair value, than it is at figuring out whether payments by the firm to the majority shareholder constitute a non pro rata distribution to a shareholder. In fact, because of the presence of significant investments in match, exactly the opposite is the case, and the court is likely to be far better at policing non pro rata distributions than employment issues.

Compare the two inquiries. In case A, the court must first determine whether a termination was for cause or, more or less equivalently, for a legitimate business purpose. Having determined that a termination was unjustified, the court must then either order reinstatement or, more likely, given the bad blood between participants, order either dissolution of the corporation or a buyout of the minority shareholder at fair value. In either case, the court will have to calculate the value of the firm because, given the presence of substantial investments in match, the highest-valuing buyer in a dissolution will likely be the majority shareholder.

The first inquiry faces all the problems that have been discussed with regard to the employment-at-will doctrine. Not only is the for-cause/fair-value standard a much harder standard to apply, but it does not even eliminate the need to police non pro rata distributions. Even if an employee shareholder has been discharged for cause, so long as he is a shareholder, his financial investment in the firm must still be protected against such distributions by the majority.

42. We owe the acute articulation of this point to Robert Thompson.

The second inquiry is even worse. If we are correct that the close corporation form is most appropriate for firms with substantial investments in match, the valuation problem will be intractable: a market valuation will be unavailable (because the assets are worth much less to third parties than to the participants in the enterprise), and a cash-flow analysis will face all the information problems that make it impossible to sell the assets to third parties.

Generally, a company's assets are valued by first estimating the future discounted stream of the free cash flow that they generate and then attaching a multiple that reflects the discount rate and the risk associated with the cash flow. The estimate of free cash flow is based on several factors, including the past performance of the company in generating revenue, the performance of comparable assets in other companies, and the market outlook for the products produced by the assets. While this standard valuation methodology is adequate for established firms, it does not work well in most close corporations because the required data are not available. The company may have very limited past performance, the management may be too untested to allow reliable future predictions, and the company's products or services may be too novel to allow easy comparisons with seasoned firms. It requires time to determine whether the product ideas will work out and produce free cash flow of any given size.

Indeed, the difficulties of valuing the assets of the close corporation are, at least in the Silicon Valley context, an important explanation for why the company continues to be privately held. By the time enough information is available on likely performance to value the match assets of the close corporation, it is time for the close corporation to go public. Similarly, for firms furthest from access to a public market, the valuation problems are the greatest. Take, for example, the classic mom and pop. Where mom and pop are the enterprise, it is difficult to distinguish any ongoing market value from the value provided by the principals. The enterprise's match assets may be so tied to mom and pop that no independent valuation can be attributed to the firm's other assets. Moreover, in this case, generating additional years of performance data will not bring the firm closer to a reliable market valuation. Valuing the firm by looking at the sale value of comparable firms would also be stymied by the distinctiveness of the enterprise and the difficulty identifying comparables. Finally, when comparable companies can be found, one's confidence in the resulting valuations would be challenged by the thinness of the market.

By contrast, consider the judicial inquiry under the norm of no non pro rata distributions in case B. First, insofar as the claim is one of a failure to pay dividends, the inquiry is straightforward: as long as no one is receiving dividends, so long as the earnings are retained in the corporation, the court can defer to the discretion of the board, knowing that everyone's earnings are equally locked in.

Second, consider the manifold varieties of basic self-dealing, ranging from excessive salaries, to non pro rata dividends, to diversion of corporate opportunities, to sales to or purchases from the corporation. This is the classic domain of the duty of loyalty. The basic principle, here, is that the majority shareholder will bear the burden of establishing entire fairness, where *entire fairness* is defined with reference to an unconflicted arm's-length transaction.

Consider salaries as an example, although the analysis applies equally to other transactions with the corporation. The standard is a market standard: Are the controlling shareholders receiving more than the market wage? When, as is often the case, the controlling shareholders set their own salary, standard corporate law analysis imposes the burden of establishing entire fairness on the controlling shareholders, that is, showing that the wage is at or below the comparable market level. While plaintiffs typically fail in challenges to dividend policy or employment policy, they apparently fare substantially better in challenges to excessive compensation.[43]

Moreover, courts have already had experience in determining, in the tax context, whether close corporation salaries are excessive.[44] When there were tax advantages to paying dividends as above-market salary, the IRS scrutinized such payments on precisely this basis. As the tax preference for distributions in salary disappears, determining whether a salary meets the market test is likely to be easier because relevant benchmarks will be less distorted.

In addition, the courts have at their disposal their traditional methods of shaping the decision process by allocating burdens of proof. Thus, the courts will be more deferential to salaries that are set by independent outside directors than by the majority shareholders themselves. Interestingly, for example, the problem of diversion of profits to majority shareholders through excessive salaries seems nonexistent in the Silicon Valley high-tech context, in part at least because managers' salaries are set by, or at least in consultation with, the venture capitalists.

While judicial intervention in case A forces courts to value the firm, with the associated problems created by the high density of match-specific assets, no such difficulties bedevil case B. In the salary context, the question is whether a salary is excessive relative to market equivalents. In the context of other transactions with the firm, the issue is likewise whether

43. *Donahue* at n. 15: "Attacks on allegedly excessive salaries voted for officers and directors fare better in the courts. . . . What is 'reasonable compensation' is a question of fact. . . . The proof which establishes an excess over such 'reasonable compensation' appears easier than the proof which would establish bad faith or plain abuse of discretion." See also *Alaska Plastics v. Coppock,* 621 P.2d 270 (Alaska 1980); and *Crosby v. Beam,* 548 N.E.2d 217 (Ohio 1989).

44. See, e.g., *Alaska Plastics v. Coppock,* 621 P.2d 270 (Alaska 1980).

the terms of the transaction between the majority shareholder and the firm meet the market test. In the case of dividends, the question is only whether all shareholders receive the same amount.

Indeed, the only times the court must enter the thicket of valuing the firm are when the firm is being sold (by a merger or a sale of assets, in some jurisdictions) and the minority shareholders request appraisal or when there is a selective stock repurchase. In the case of an arm's-length merger, the shareholders have the opportunity to receive the same consideration as the majority shareholder but believe that their shares are worth more. But, in those circumstances, precisely because the firm is being sold, there is at least one measure of valuation available. Moreover, because all shareholders share equally in the proceeds of a sale or dissolution, the majority shareholder is likely to represent the interests of the minority shareholders. Major is unlikely to sell the firm unless it has reached the stage where its third-party value is beginning to approach the value to the participants.[45] As discussed earlier, selective stock repurchases present genuinely difficult issues.

The focus on preventing non pro rata distributions points the way toward incremental modifications within the existing framework to increase the level of enforcement without entering the for-cause thickets, without disturbing the employment-at-will standard, and without judicial valuation. For example, once it is clear that the issue is preventing non pro rata distributions, the courts should make it easier to challenge contracts between the controlling shareholder and the firm. Consider *Crosby v. Beam,* in which the majority shareholders entered into self-dealing contracts with the firm, including unreasonable salaries, use of corporate property, life insurance, low-interest loans, and so forth.[46] The legal issue was whether the minority shareholders must challenge the agreements through a derivative suit, which is subject to the demand requirement and in which any recovery is paid into the corporate treasury, or whether the minority shareholders could bring a direct suit. After a long discussion of how, in a close corporation, the majority shareholders owe fiduciary duties to the minority shareholders, the court held that the suit could be brought as a direct suit, with recovery going directly to the plaintiffs: "Given the foregoing, if we require a minority shareholder in a close corporation, who alleges that the majority shareholders breached their fiduciary duty to him, to institute an action pursuant to Civ. R. 23.1, then any recovery would accrue to the corporation and remain under the control of the very parties who are defendants in the litigation. Thus, a derivative remedy is not

45. A more difficult problem arises when it is the majority shareholder who is buying out the minority shares. Under these circumstances, the court has no choice but to enter the difficult problem of valuation, and, although it can and does seek to avoid the difficult valuation questions by encouraging the use of independent negotiating structures to mimic an arm's-length sale, its success in doing so is only limited.

46. *Crosby v. Beam,* 548 N.E.2d 217 (Ohio 1989).

an effective remedy because the wrongdoers would be the principal beneficiaries of the recovery. See, generally, 2 O'Neal's Close Corporations, at 120–123 section 8.11."

According to our analysis, the court got it half right. The fact that the majority is accused of engaging in a self-interested transaction with the firm is, of course, central and, in a derivative suit, would fully justify excusing demand as obviously futile and allowing the plaintiff to proceed directly to the merits of the action. But, if the guiding principle is preserving the beneficial lock-in effect of corporate form against attempts at non pro rata distributions, then the right result is that any excessive payments go back into the corporation, where they remain locked up until the majority chooses to make some sort of pro rata distribution. This is an adjustment to the procedural requirement for derivative suits in the light of the special nature of close corporations (or, perhaps, simply an application), but it is a quite different sort of adjustment than that adopted by the Ohio Supreme Court.

Along the same lines, an appreciation of the central issue will lead courts to give less deference to the board of directors in setting its own compensation or in approving asset distributions of other sorts. Finally, it makes it clear that, in the absence of some independent decision maker, the burden of proof falls on the majority shareholder to justify salaries and other payments as entirely fair.

### 7.4.4 Case C: Is the Sale of Control for a Premium a Non Pro Rata Distribution?

In the close corporation, we take the rule of no non pro rata distributions to have the status of a commandment. It is the principle that makes the whole thing work, that allows minority shareholders to rely on majority shareholders to manage the firm in the general shareholder interest. It is this principle that allows for optimal investment in match-specific assets. Finally, enforcing this principle frees the courts from having to enter on the impossible (and destructive) tasks of sorting out, on the one hand, whether a discharge of a minority shareholder-employee was for cause and, on the other, how much the firm is worth.

What, then, does one make of case C, in which Major sells its majority block to a third party who is unwilling to buy the minority shares on equal terms? Under U.S. corporate law, the general common law rule is that the majority shareholder may sell its holdings, and a buyer may buy its holdings, without offering the minority shareholders an opportunity to participate.[47] The principal exception is when the majority or controlling shareholder has reason to believe that the buyer will loot the corporation.[48]

47. See, e.g., *Zetlin v. Hanson Holdings,* 397 N.E.2d 387 (N.Y. 1979).
48. See, e.g., *Gerdes v. Reynolds,* 28 N.Y.S.2d 622 (Sup. Ct., Spec. Term 1941).

There are a few cases to the contrary, but this is the general rule (see, generally, Elhauge 1992). Much has been written on the efficiency of competing rules governing sales of control. We cannot enter that thicket here but must address the relation between sales of control and non pro rata distributions and, more generally, the connection between sales of control and firms with heavy match investments.

Case C seems to be an interesting and difficult mix of cases A and B: when the majority shareholder sells control, he thereby terminates his relationship with the firm while taking a larger than pro rata share of firm value. On its face, the majority shareholder's sale might seem to violate the no non pro rata distribution norm or, at the very least, the related norm governing endgames. When a majority shareholder sells its block, it gets cash at a time when the other shareholders do not. Moreover, the minority shareholders cannot even check the effect of the sale on their share of the presale equity of the firm. Finally, unlike an arm's-length merger or dissolution, in which the shareholders share on an equal basis, often with a right of appraisal, here the minority shareholders not only do not share but also have no right to appraisal. In short, we worry that the majority shareholders will sell out the minority shareholders in the process of selling control. As before, we worry about this prospect to the extent that it undermines the minority shareholders' willingness to invest in match-specific assets, thereby reducing the parties' joint surplus.

Yet the situations also seem quite different. The sale of a majority block differs from the non pro rata payment of dividends, for example, in several important respects. First, the sale of the blocks results in a change of control, while the various non pro rata distributions leave the incumbent controller in place. Second, the new controller steps into the shoes of the old controller, with all the same restrictions on non pro rata distributions, restrictions that, suggests the work of Holderness and Sheehan (chap. 5 in this volume), may be surprisingly effective. Third, to sell a majority block, one needs to find a buyer, which imposes a barrier that is not present in non pro rata distributions.

Indeed, in form at least, there is no difference between Major selling his shares to a new Major and any Minor selling its shares to a new Minor, except perhaps the amount received for the shares. There is, indeed, an active market for shares of closely held Silicon Valley start-ups, in which (sophisticated) minority shareholders sell their shares to other (sophisticated) investors pursuant to rule 144A.[49]

Why might minority shareholders, ex ante, agree to permit the majority shareholder to sell its block without an equal opportunity rule, despite the extent to which it may be in tension with the beneficial lock-in and the principle of no non pro rata distributions? This old chestnut of corporate

49. Securities Act of 1933, rule 144A ("Private Resales of Securities to Institutions"), 17 CFR, sec. 230.144A (1997).

law looks somewhat different against the backdrop of our emphasis on match investments. Take again, as given, that the close corporation is characterized by a large percentage of match assets. Moreover, assume that the lock-in of the corporate form, with exit at the close of play, is part of what renders the form incentive compatible.

The principal concern with permitting sales of a majority block is that the buyer and seller may collude to impose additional costs on third parties, here, the minority shareholders. Absent third-party effects, one can trust the buyer and seller to figure out what is best for them.[50] So long as the constraints on private benefits of control are reasonably binding, the likelihood of third-party effects is small, and one can leave it to the buyer and seller of control to negotiate terms.[51] In such cases, the seller will sell only if the buyer is better at managing the corporation than the seller, which will benefit the minority. Indeed, because of the difficulties in valuation, the buyer will likely have to be substantially better than the seller.

The key point in the close corporation context is that private benefits of control are restrained by a set of formal and informal sanctions. For example, suppose that the trapped minority believes that, through one mechanism or another, the planned sale will itself diminish the value of its investment. One remedy is to sue for a breach of the duty of loyalty. Whether or not the minority wins, such suits raise a red flag for any diligent new person thinking of becoming a controller. The reaction of the potential buyer is now threefold. First, he doubles the due diligence concerning the information provided by the majority. Presumably, the disgruntled frozen-in person might even be helpful here in supplying information. Second, the potential entrant may think twice about buying into a close corporation where the minority is disgruntled. In some circumstances, this may lead the buyer to insist on buying 100 percent. Third, the buyer may react by a standard "curse on both their houses" and choose to pull his bid entirely or to bargain hard to buy the controller's share at a cheap price. In brief, because of limited numbers, the parties can hurl mud at each other with great accuracy.

Another consideration figures in as well: the orderly exit of controllers. Sometimes, the majority shareholder gets tired of being the majority shareholder or knows that he has lost his effectiveness. Sometimes, also,

50. One might also worry that the exiting controller is selling a lemon and that the entering controller does not know that. But, even if this occurs, the minority is no worse off, just as badly off as before. Moreover, this should not be a likely event. Those who buy into an existing close corporation are, in general, likely to be highly diligent. Indeed, they are likely to be more careful than the controller who entered at the outset.

51. This is the core of Elhauge's (1992) channeling explanation for existing doctrine: the looting cases (highly liquid assets, big premium) identify those cases in which the likelihood of collusion between buyer and seller is highest; the free sale cases, by contrast, are situations in which it is difficult for buyer and seller to collude successfully, either because of the nature of the assets (illiquid) or for other reasons.

the firm is not yet ready to be sold to a third party because the omelette is not yet cooked. How do you make sure that there is someone around to play the role of majority shareholder, with all its burdens and risks? The common law answer may be the legal equivalent to the informal rule in voluntary organizations that you cannot stop chairing a committee until you find a replacement. Because the omelette is not finished, it will be very difficult to convince a third party to take over the omelette business, and it may be that the majority shareholder may have to take a substantial *discount* in order to induce a third party to take over. In such cases, the minority shareholders are beneficiaries, not because the buyer will have bribed the controller to leave, but because the controller has bribed the new controller to enter.[52]

If this is more or less right, then, so long as the prohibition on non pro rata distributions is reasonably well enforced, the incentive-compatible rule in the close corporation context is the same as in the public corporation context, namely, that, absent a shareholders' agreement to the contrary, any shareholder, majority or minority, is free to sell to whomever is willing to buy (except a looter). The buyer, majority or minority, steps into the shoes of the seller and is locked in to the same extent.

This means that, in the articulation of the pro rata principle, one must emphasize that it applies to *distributions.* On this view, the control on diversions of the cash flow does most of the work. Indeed, this may support Elhauge's (1992) argument that the laissez-faire rule is most appropriate for those situations or, more generally, those systems in which non pro rata distributions are sharply limited, while the equal opportunity rule may better fit those situations in which such distributions are badly controlled.

### 7.4.5 Minority Shareholders' Information Rights

In the earlier discussion, we discourage judicial intervention in cases A and C. In both cases, however, there are potential problems with respect to the minority's access to company information that, if addressed, strengthen our case. Recall the argument suggested in *Wilkes:* once Minor is terminated, the underlying asymmetry of information will make it untenable to continue as a minority shareholder. This is an important argument as we have argued that the asymmetry of information associated

52. The difficulty of valuation may enter in another way. Because the omelette is only partly cooked, it would be extremely difficult for a court to determine whether the selling majority shareholder got too much, whether he was paid a "premium" for control. This may be the reason that courts focus on preventing non pro rata distributions rather than on measuring the extent to which the majority shareholder was overpaid. But, of course, a rule preventing a majority shareholder from selling control for a premium need not involve judicial valuation: an equal opportunity rule would be as easily implemented here as it was in the *Wilkes* case.

with a high density of match-specific investments is part of what makes the close corporation form appropriate and that the overlap between shareholders and managers helps manage that asymmetry of information.

On the one hand, it may be that this untenability is optimal for the parties, under the circumstances. Both the high-tech sector and the traditional close corporation sector show that mandatory provisions that provide for the buyback of employee shares on termination of employment at either cost or book value (easily measured amounts that are often far below actual, pro rata value) are quite common.

But, as the case B cases indicate, it is not always the case that it is untenable to be a minority nonemployee shareholder. Whether, and the extent to which, such a position may be tenable depends, in part, on the extent to which the courts police the norm of non pro rata distributions. This, in turn, depends on the extent to which courts provide for and enforce minority rights to information. Like the enforcement of the norm against non pro rata distributions, enforcing minority information rights protects the beneficial characteristics of the close corporate form without dragging the courts into either adjudicating employment-at-will issues or firm valuation.

To operate effectively, however, Minor must know when Major is acting opportunistically. Minor, as either a shareholder-employee or a shareholder, has the ability to impose or threaten Major with informal sanctions. When Minor is employed, he has all the normal methods of sanction that apply to an employee. In his role as a shareholder in a closely held company, Minor also holds considerable power to impose sanctions. But, if Minor is either discharged from the company or left employed but in a nonmanagerial capacity, he is unlikely to obtain the requisite information needed to know when and how to act.

Minority shareholder information rights come from two sources: state law and federal law. Under state law, shareholders are entitled to substantial information. Delaware corporate law provides that "any stockholder, in person or by attorney or other agent, shall, upon written demand under oath stating the purpose thereof, have the right during the usual hours for business to inspect for any proper purpose the corporation's stock ledger, a list of its stockholders, and its other books and records, and to make copies or extracts therefrom. A proper purpose shall mean a purpose reasonably related to such person's interest as a stockholder."[53] As interpreted, Delaware section 220 provides minority shareholders of the close corporation substantial rights to information. First, "in the case of a close corporation, inspection rights will be liberally construed in favor of a minority stockholder" (Welch and Turezyn 1993, sec. 220.6.3, p. 466).

53. Del. GCL, sec. 220. Minority shareholders have similar information rights under the RMBCA (secs. 16.01–16.04).

Second, finding out the facts necessary to determine whether Major is engaging in self-dealing, or mismanagement, or both, is clearly a "proper purpose" under section 220 (Welch and Turezyn 1993, sec. 220.6.3, p. 466).[54]

The federal securities laws provide the second principal source of information rights for minority shareholders. Although close corporations are not subject to the periodic-disclosure obligations, section 10(b) of the Securities Exchange Act and rule 10b-5 apply fully.[55] Rule 10b-5 has proved most important in endgame scenarios. Minor, who is terminating his relationship with the firm, negotiates to sell his shares back to the firm or to the majority shareholder. At the same time, unbeknownst to Minor, Major is engaged in serious discussions with a potential acquirer of the firm or with an investment banker who wishes to take the firm public. Sometime after Minor sells his shares, the acquisition is announced, placing a value on the firm far in excess of what Minor received. Minor sues, alleging that, had he known of the merger discussions, he would not have sold his shares. In such circumstances, the courts have held that, when Major is buying out Minor, Major has a duty to disclose all material nonpublic information, including negotiations to sell the firm or take it public.[56]

This structure fits well with our previous analysis. Like the vigorous enforcement of the norm against non pro rata distributions, so, too, the enforcement of these information rights protects the incentive compatibility of the close corporation form. The state law rights to information help alleviate (although clearly not eliminate) the underlying asymmetry of information while Minor is a shareholder. Major's duty under 10b-5 to disclose material facts or abstain from buying Minor's shares protects and reinforces the endgame norm: on liquidation or merger, shareholders share equally.[57]

54. In addition, minority shareholders who are in litigation with the corporation have substantial rights to information under the civil discovery rules, whether in federal or in state court.

55. Under rule 10b-5, "It shall be unlawful for any person . . . (a) to employ any device, scheme, or artifice to defraud, (b) to make any untrue statement of a material fact or to omit to state a material fact necessary in order to make the statements made, in the light of the circumstances under which they were made, not misleading, or (c) to engage in any act, practice, or course of business which operates or would operate as a fraud or deceit upon any person, in connection with the purchase or sale of any security" (17 C.F.R., sec. 240.10b-5). On the applicability of 10b-5 to close corporations, even in the sale of the entire business, see *Landreth Timber Co. v. Landreth,* 471 U.S. 681 (1985).

56. See, e.g., *Rochez v. Rhoades,* 527 F.2d 880 (3d Cir. 1975), cert. denied, 425 U.S. 993 (1976); *Thomas v. Duralite Co.,* 524 F.2d 577 (3d Cir. 1975); *Michaels v. Michaels, Michaels and Hyman-Michaels,* 767 F.2d 1185, 1194–97 (7th Cir. 1985); and *Homes v. Bateson,* 583 F.2d 542, 558 (1st Cir. 1978).

57. An additional set of issues arises when Minor is subject to a mandatory buyback provision on termination of his relationship with the corporation. The issue arises whether and when Major has a duty to disclose news that may be of significance to Minor in deciding

## 7.5 Conclusion

The close corporation form is ideally suited to enterprises in which there is a high density of match-specific assets. The limitations on exit, combined with the rule against non pro rata distributions, largely prevent opportunistic behavior by the majority shareholder toward the minority. By locking both into the enterprise, the majority shareholders, in maximizing their own wealth, will, to a large extent, also maximize the wealth of the minority. Indeed, many of the persistent features of close corporations can best be understood as self-enforcing mechanisms to protect the participants from misbehavior by fellow participants.

This is not to say that all enterprises that use the close corporation form make use of these attributes. An important result of this paper is that, by isolating the distinctive features of close corporations, we identify those enterprises that are best suited for the close corporation form. The enterprises that most value the lock-in are precisely those Silicon Valley startups with new products that need time to set. In its best use, the close corporation thus serves as an incubator for tomorrow's publicly owned corporations.

For close corporations without intensive match investments, the costs of the lock-in may well exceed the benefits. For such corporations, there are two obvious alternatives. First, they can retain the close corporation form and allow minority exit in the articles of incorporation. Alternatively, they can choose other organizational forms, such as partnership, that allow exit at will as a default. We argue against a third alternative—case-by-case adjudication based on a finding that the minority's reasonable expectations have been defeated. Gap filling in this context suffers badly because of the great likelihood of judicial error given the difficulties of first evaluating claims of defeated expectations and then, when necessary, valuing match investments.

whether to terminate his relationship with the firm (*Jordan v. Duff & Phelps,* 815 F.2d 429 [7th Cir. 1987]; *Smith v. Duff and Phelps,* 891 F.2d 1567 [11th Cir. 1990]). A related issue is whether such a mandatory buyback provision should be read to displace the employment-at-will presumption in the employment relationship. The answer has been negative (see, e.g., *Ingle v. Glamore Motor Sales, Inc.,* 73 N.Y.2d 183 [N.Y. Ct. App. 1989] [mandatory buyback provision does not get shareholder-employee any protection against at-will discharge]). Indeed, in some cases, the buyback provisions explicitly provide that "nothing herein contained shall confer on the Employee any right to be continued in the employment of the Corporation" (*Jordan v. Duff & Phelps,* 815 F.2d at 446). Finally, the question also arises whether the firm can fire an employee simply in order to trigger the mandatory buyback provision (*Gallagher v. Lambert,* 549 N.E.2d 136 [N.Y. 1989] [no breach of fiduciary duty to terminate minority shareholder triggering mandatory buyback even if firing is motivated by desire to take advantage of lower valuation]; *Knudsen v. Northwest Airlines,* 450 N.W.2d 131 [Minn. 1990] [stock-option agreement that expires when employee ceases to work for employer does not imply any covenant of good-faith termination for cause]; cf. *Jordan v. Duff & Phelps,* 815 F.2d at 439 [Easterbrook] with 815 F.2d at 446 [Posner, dissenting]). While these issues are fascinating, they are beyond the scope of this paper.

After examining the extent to which the enterprise form itself constrains opportunistic behavior by participants, we analyzed the classic problem(s) of minority oppression in the close corporation. As we understand it, minority oppression can best be understood as a combination of two separate and separable problems. The first aspect, captured in case A, is a version of precisely the same problem that, in employment law, arises under the heading *employment at will:* the situation in which Major terminates Minor's employment. Here, we showed that, by adopting the same passive stance as it does in the employment context, the law avoids threatening and undermining the self-enforcing structure in place.

The second aspect of the problem, captured in case B, is fundamentally different from employment at will and involves attempts by Major to make non pro rata distributions of company assets. Here, we showed that vigorous judicial enforcement of a prohibition on such distributions, including the vigorous protection of ancillary rights to information, is necessary to enforce norms of nonopportunism. We further showed that courts are much better at sorting out issues of this sort than they are at sorting out employment-at-will type issues because doing so does not require either relying on unverifiable factors or valuing assets that the courts cannot value.

Out of our appreciation of the beauty of the close corporation come several conclusions. First, our analysis implies that the parties themselves, rather than the courts, are best able to resolve the nasty employment issues that animate many bitter close corporation cases. Second, the analysis indicates that vigorous judicial enforcement of the sacred norm against non pro rata distributions is necessary to block the attempts of majority shareholders to profit from self-dealing transactions with the corporation. Finally, with an expanded menu of enterprise forms, there is little cost in allowing the close corporation to maintain its distinctive qualities. Firms that are not waiting for omelettes to set can choose another form that allows easy exit of capital suppliers.

## References

American Law Institute. 1994. *Principles of corporate governance: Analysis and recommendations.* Philadelphia.

Barry, Christopher B., et al. 1990. The role of venture capital in the creation of public companies: Evidence from the going-public process. *Journal of Financial Economics* 27:447–71.

Easterbrook, Frank H., and Daniel R. Fischel. 1991. *The economic structure of corporate law.* Cambridge, Mass.: Harvard University Press.

Elhauge, Einer R. 1992. The triggering function of sale of control doctrine. *University of Chicago Law Review* 59:1465–1532.

Fenn, George W., Nellie Liang, and Stephen Prowse. 1995. The economics of the private equity market. Staff Study no. 168. Board of Governors of the Federal Reserve, December.
Gompers, Paul A. 1995. Optimal investment, monitoring, and the staging of venture capital. *Journal of Finance* 50:1461–89.
Gorman, Michael, and William A. Sahlman. 1989. What do venture capitalists do? *Journal of Business Venturing* 4:231–48.
Hellmann, Thomas. 1998. The allocation of control rights in venture capital contracts. *Rand Journal of Economics* 29:57–76.
Hetherington, John A. C., and Michael P. Dooley. 1977. Illiquidity and exploitation: A proposed statutory solution to the remaining close corporation problem. *Virginia Law Review* 63:1–75.
Johnston, Jason. 1992. Opting in and opting out: Bargaining for fiduciary duties in cooperative ventures. *Washington University Law Quarterly* 70:291–340.
Lerner, Joshua. 1994. Venture capitalists and the decision to go public. *Journal of Financial Economics* 35:293–316.
———. 1995. Venture capitalists and the oversight of private firms. *Journal of Finance* 50:301–18.
Oesterle, Dale A. 1995. Limiting the discretion of state courts to restructure the internal affairs of small business. *University of Colorado Law Review* 66:881–920.
O'Kelley, Charles R. 1992. Filling the gaps in the close corporation contract: A transaction cost analysis. *Northwestern University Law Review* 87:216–53.
O'Neal, F. Hodge, and Robert B. Thompson. 1985. *O'Neal's oppression of minority shareholders.* 2d ed. Wilmette, Ill.: Callaghan.
———. [1986] 1995. *Close corporations: Law and practice.* 3d ed. Mundelein, Ill.: Callaghan.
Rock, Edward B., and Michael L. Wachter. 1996. The enforceability of norms and the employment relationship. *University of Pennsylvania Law Review* 144: 1913–52.
Sahlman, William A. 1990. The structure and governance of venture-capital organizations. *Journal of Financial Economics* 27:473–521.
Thompson, Robert B. 1988. Corporate dissolution and shareholders' reasonable expectations. *Washington University Law Quarterly* 66:193–238.
———. 1993. The shareholder's cause of action for oppression. *Business Lawyer* 48:699–745.
Wachter, Michael L., and Randall D. Wright. 1990. The economics of internal labor markets. In *The economics of human resource management,* ed. Daniel J. B. Mitchell and Mahmoud A. Zaidi. Oxford: Blackwell.
Welch, Edward P., and Andrew J. Turezyn. 1993. *Folk on Delaware corporation law.* Boston: Little, Brown.

## Comment Vikas Mehrotra

The organization of economic enterprises has its own rainbow coalition of followers: legal scholars, economists and historians of all hues, organization theorists, even sociologists and behaviorists, all with their own pe-

Vikas Mehrotra is associate professor of finance at the University of Alberta.

culiar slants on the issue. The central question, however, remains common: Why do we observe the prevalence of certain forms of business organization in certain activities? In their paper, Edward Rock and Michael Wachter focus on the close corporation and its peculiarities vis-à-vis other, possibly competitive, forms of organization. What advantages are conferred by the close corporation on its main protagonists? What features of the close corporation deserve scrutiny?

The answer to the first question is made obvious by the authors' choice of title. There is an omelette in the making. The eggs and hardware have been financed by a venture capitalist (VC), and the chef is exercising her skills to prepare the omelette. There are strong incentives for both parties to remain locked in until the omelette is done since there appears to be no market for partially done omelettes. Both the VC and the chef have considerable match-specific investments in the omelette, and, therefore, an abiding interest in seeing it through to completion. This is the essence of the argument favoring the close corporate form over other alternative forms.

For example, the limited partnership, with its ease of exit and dissolution, would not suit the locked-in nature of this relationship. On sensing a particularly well-done omelette, the controlling partner can force the noncontrolling partner to relinquish a large portion of the gains from the enterprise. It does not matter, ex post, that the product of the enterprise required joint input. Ease of exit provides grounds for a credible holdup threat.

What about the open corporation? The open corporate form is characterized by diffuse ownership and easy transferability of equity shares and would require enormous resources to provide periodic updates as to the status of the omelette. These costs render the open corporate form unsuitable for ventures characterized by a high degree of information asymmetry between capital providers and managers. Moreover, it is not clear whether the open corporation, with diffuse ownership, can overcome the free-rider problem of monitoring the omelette-making process. The close corporate form overcomes both these limitations: it discourages easy dissolution and maintains the identities of the ex ante contracting parties at least until the omelette is done.

So far, this is familiar territory. Studies by Telser (1980), Klein and Leffler (1981), and Williamson (1983) have made important contributions to the literature on corporate form and self-enforcing contracts. The main, and perhaps unsurprising, message in these studies is that contracts remain self-enforcing until one of the parties finds it in its interest to quit, with the only penalty being the voiding of the contract and, naturally, all attendant future benefits. In fact, form is dictated primarily by the cost of contracting. Whereas market transactions are suitable for exchanging general purpose assets, more internalized governance is required as asset specificity and frequency of exchange increase. However, there are other determinants of self-enforcing contracts as well. In particular, as pointed out by Barzel (1982), the measurement cost of information plays a role in determining the extent of the holdup problem created when two parties lock in to a contract. This simple observation brings us to the two features related to minority protection of the close corporation—employment at will and restrictions on non pro rata distributions—highlighted by Rock and Wachter.

Obviously, providing ex ante minority protection benefits the majority (the controlling party) since, absent such protection, the minority party would either demand higher compensation or not enter into the contract at all. Rock and Wachter argue that the employment-at-will feature in the close corporation should be treated with the same passivity as is the norm in regular employee-employer relationships. They correctly point to the onerous measurement costs of untangling employee dismissal cases. The argument that malicious or arbitrary dismissals inhibit formation of VC-financed start-ups suffers from two main problems.

First, it ignores the role of reputation in curbing opportunistic behavior by the VC. Most VCs intend to hang around only until the start-up is taken public (allowing them to cash out); thus, VC wealth is the discounted value of the VC's association with all future start-ups. To wit, capturing an *unfair* share of one omelette must therefore be judged against the expected present worth of the *fair* share of all future omelettes. Second, even if such an equation is violated (owing to malice, which must be economically irrational to make the point), the courts will find it extremely costly to untangle the mess of allegations and counterallegations that frequently characterize such malice-inspired dismissals. Judicial services have their bottom lines, too.

Breach of another kind is treated differently in the view of Rock and Wachter. Non pro rata distributions transfer wealth from the minority to majority and, if left unchecked, will increase the contracting cost of start-ups. In what sense is this manner of oppression different from employment at will? After all, employment at will also confers the opportunity to transfer wealth in a way that violates ex ante rules of sharing. The arbitrary dismissal is a way to precipitate non pro rata distribution of corporate resources, insofar as the dismissed party is denied its share of the discounted worth of corporate profits. So, obviously, non pro rata distributions must refer to specific forms of denials and distributions. And herein lies the rub: how to discriminate among the various forms of non pro rata distributions?

The big contribution of this paper is that the proscription on non pro rata distributions is an outcome of the ease of documentation and presentation of evidence. To be sure, the honesty equation that cements self-enforcing contracts applies to non pro rata distributions as well. However, breaches can now be examined by the courts in a cost-efficient manner. Furthermore, whereas firing an entrepreneur-manager also relieves the VC of the entrepreneur's skills, non pro rata distributions, within limits and excluding malicious cases, need not bring the venture to a stop. Indeed, a rational VC will engage in non pro rata distributions to extract only the quasi rents from the venture, leaving just enough on the plate for the minority party to offset her external opportunities, as opposed to grabbing the entire omelette. Clearly, court intervention in these cases would raise the cost of such opportunistic behavior and lower the ex ante cost of contracting between the VC and the minority party. But, returning to the question posed in the last paragraph, what particular forms of non pro rata distributions qualify for judicial intervention?

Self-dealing transactions by the majority party with the firm are an obvious candidate that merit court-ordered protection for the simple reason that these cases are relatively simple to document. For example, cash dividends that accrue only to the majority shareholder are typically forbidden. So are interfirm transactions that are carried out at nonmarket prices. But what if the VC owns preferred shares with deferred coupons whereas the minority party owns common shares with no contractual dividends? As long as the coupon rate on the preferred shares is well specified in advance, this poses no problems. Examination of non pro rata distributions must therefore be restricted to *unanticipated* events. This point is implied throughout by the authors, but not explicitly stated.

What about transactions where the majority sells its shares to another party, without involving the minority in the sale? In my view, such transactions can easily be contracted out of at the start of the relationship. The absence of such protection does not create an unanticipated event. If, in its assessment, the minority party feels that the risk of such control changes is large, it could either ask for a negative covenant prohibiting such sales or receive a larger ex ante compensation package. The courts should not interfere with control changes for the same reasons that it *should* intervene in self-dealing transactions: the former are easy to restrict in ex ante contracts, while the set of self-dealing transactions is so large and varied that a comprehensive ex ante contract prohibiting such actions would be costly to write.

Overall, the paper makes an important contribution to our understanding of the close corporation, beginning with a clear rationale for the existence of this form of organization in certain sectors of the economy, such as the Silicon Valley start-up, and highlighting two features of minority oppression in the close corporation. The authors rightly argue that the courts maintain their passivity in employment-at-will cases and vigorously enforce non pro rata distributions of corporate resources. The arguments are built mainly on the cost of using judicial intervention to correct violations of ex ante sharing rules.

## References

Barzel, Y. 1982. Measurement cost and the organization of markets. *Journal of Law and Economics* 25, no. 1:27–48.

Klein, B., and K. Leffler. 1981. The role of market forces in assuring contractual performance. *Journal of Political Economy* 89, no. 4:615–41.

Telser, L. 1980. A theory of self-enforcing agreements. *Journal of Business* 53, no. 1:27–44.

Williamson, O. 1983. Credible commitments: Using hostages to support exchange. *American Economic Review* 83, no. 4:519–40.

8

# Adverse Selection and Gains to Controllers in Corporate Freezeouts

Lucian Arye Bebchuk and Marcel Kahan

An important element in the governance scheme of a corporation is its ownership structure. Most publicly traded companies in the United States have a dispersed ownership structure: no single shareholder owns sufficient shares to control the company. A substantial minority of companies, however, have a controlling shareholder.[1] A controlling shareholder exercises powers that are available neither to the dispersed shareholders in a company without a controlling shareholder nor to the minority shareholders in a company with a controlling shareholder. As the Delaware Supreme Court recently summarized, a controlling shareholder can "(a) elect directors; (b) cause a break-up of the corporation; (c) merge it with another company; (d) cash-out the public stockholders; (e) amend the certificate of incorporation; (f) sell all or substantially all of the corporate assets; or (g) otherwise alter materially the nature of the corporation and the public stockholders' interests."[2]

Lucian Arye Bebchuk is the William J. Friedman and Alicia Townsend Friedman Professor of Law, Economics, and Finance at Harvard Law School and a research associate of the National Bureau of Economic Research. Marcel Kahan is professor of law at the New York University School of Law.

An earlier version of this paper was circulated as "The 'Lemons Effect' in Corporate Freezeouts," Discussion Paper no. 248, John M. Olin Center for Law, Economics, and Business, Harvard Law School. For helpful comments and conversations, the authors are grateful to Barry Adler, Bill Allen, J. P. Benoit, Bernie Black, John Coates, Jeff Gordon, Zohar Goshen, Ehud Kamar, Lewis Kornhauser, Bo Li, Brandon Vergas, workshop participants at the American Law and Economics Association meeting, Hebrew University, Interdisciplinary Center (Herzliah), Tel-Aviv University, and the NBER conference. For financial support, Lucian Bebchuk thanks the National Science Foundation and the John M. Olin Center for Law, Economics, and Business, and Marcel Kahan thanks the Filomen D'Agostino and Max E. Greenberg Research Fund at the New York University School of Law.

1. For example, Barclay and Holderness (1989) report that, in a randomly chosen sample of 394 publicly traded companies in 1986, 20 percent of the companies had a shareholder with a block exceeding 35 percent of equity.

2. *Paramount Communications Inc. v. QVC Network Inc.*, 637 A.2d 34 (Del. 1994).

This paper focuses on one of these enumerated powers—the power to cash out, or "freeze out," the minority shareholders. Such freezeouts are accomplished by a merger with a corporation wholly owned by the controlling shareholder. After the freezeout, the controlling shareholder emerges as the sole equityholder of the company. In most states, mergers require the approval of the company's board of directors as well as of holders of a majority of outstanding shares.[3] A shareholder who holds a majority of shares can effectively control both approval prongs and thus unilaterally set the price at which minority shareholders are frozen out (the "freezeout price"). The power to freeze out the minority shareholders on potentially unfavorable terms is one of several ways through which a controlling shareholder can derive benefits from control to the exclusion of, and at the expense of, the minority shareholders.[4]

While the power of the controlling shareholder to freeze out the minority shareholders and to set the freezeout price is unfettered, minority shareholders have some remedies if they feel that the freezeout price has been set too low. First, they can seek a judicial appraisal of their shares, in which case they will receive the value of their shares as assessed by the court (rather than the freezeout price).[5] Second, in some circumstances, minority shareholders can seek judicial review of the freezeout merger under the "entire fairness" standard, in which case the court will award them damages if the value of the minority shares, as assessed by the court, exceeds the freezeout price.[6] While these two types of proceedings differ in certain respects, they both rely on a judicial assessment of the value of minority shares.[7] Both types of proceedings can, in principle—if the

3. See, e.g., Delaware General Corporation Law (Del. GCL), sec. 251; Revised Model Business Corporation Act (RMBCA), sec. 11.03.

4. In addition to freezeouts, a controlling shareholder can engage in self-dealing transactions with the controlled company, usurp corporate opportunities, structure the company's dividend policy to fit her tax situation or cash-flow needs, or sell "control" to another shareholder. For formal models of sales of corporate control, see Bebchuk (1994) and Kahan (1993).

5. See, e.g., Del. GCL, sec. 262(b); RMBCA, sec. 13.02.

6. See *Weinberger v. UOP, Inc.*, 457 A.2d 701, 714–15 (Del. 1983) (discussing the entire fairness standard in freezeouts and its relations to appraisal rights); RMBCA, sec. 13.02(b) (remedies beyond appraisal rights are available if transaction is fraudulent or unlawful). At least in Delaware, a freezeout merger where the price is unilaterally set by the controlling shareholder appears to allow minority shareholders to bring an entire fairness action. See *Cede & Co. v. Technicolor, Inc.*, C.A. Nos. 7129 and 8358, slip op. at 15, 16 (Del. Ch. Jan. 13, 1987), rev'd on other grounds, 542 A.2d 1182 (Del. 1988) (appraisal is not an exclusive remedy where a breach of fiduciary duty is involved); *Jedwab v. MGM Grand Hotels, Inc.*, 509 A.2d 584, 594 (Del. Ch. 1986) (courts apply entire fairness standard when a controlling shareholder "effectuate[s] a transaction in which [it has] an interest that diverges from that of the corporation or the minority shareholders").

7. In general, the methodology for determining the value of minority shares is the same in entire fairness and appraisal proceedings. See *Rosenblatt v. Getty Oil Co.*, 493 A.2d 929, 940 (Del. 1985); but see *Cede & Co. v. Technicolor, Inc.*, 634 A.2d 345, 371 (Del. 1993) (noting that measure of loss under the entire fairness standard is "not necessarily" limited to the

assessment is accurate—protect minority shareholders from being denied the "no-freezeout value"—the value that their shares would have in the absence of the considered freezeout.[8]

This paper identifies and analyzes a fundamental problem involved in the regulation of corporate freezeouts. When deciding whether to effect a freezeout, a controlling shareholder might take advantage of its private information. When freezeouts take place under conditions of asymmetric information, we demonstrate, allowing controlling shareholders to effect a freezeout at a price equal or close to the pretransaction price of minority shares would enable controlling shareholders to effect such transactions on favorable terms and to extract in this way substantial private benefits of control.

As this paper shows, courts face some difficult, inherent problems in trying to reach an accurate assessment of the no-freezeout value. These problems arise from the fact that controllers, who decide whether to effect a freezeout, are also likely to have private information concerning the firm's value. As a result, the prefreezeout market price of minority shares, which is often used by courts in the assessment of the minority shares' no-freezeout value, is likely to underestimate the no-freezeout value.

Our analysis is organized as follows. Section 8.1 contains a short discussion of the use of market prices to assess the value of minority shares in freezeouts and a numerical example illustrating the adverse selection effect that results from such use. Section 8.2 contains a game-theoretic model demonstrating that, if a controlling shareholder can freeze out the minority shareholders at the prefreezeout market price, that market price will reflect the per share value of the company *assuming that the controlling shareholder has the worst possible private information about the value of the company.* A right to freeze out the minority shareholders at such a market price would therefore confer substantial profits on the controlling shareholder. The model uses several simplifying assumptions, but our work in progress (Bebchuk and Kahan 1999) suggests that its main result—that the presence of private information enables a controlling shareholder to gain systematically at the expense of minority shareholders—holds in a more general setting. Section 8.3 provides a concluding discussion that

difference between the appraised value and the price offered in the merger since the chancellor has discretion to award rescissory damages if appropriate).

8. There is a large literature on whether providing minority shareholders in a freezeout with the no-freezeout value is enough or whether the standard to which they are entitled should be higher. For example, in two classic articles, Brudney and Chirelstein (1974, 1978) argued that minority shareholders should be given the no-freezeout value plus a fraction of the gains created by the freezeout. And Coates (1999) recently argued that minority shareholders in a freezeout should get their pro rata fraction of the company's value—including their pro rata fraction of the controller's existing private benefits of control. Our focus in this paper is on problems with the protection of minority shareholders that arise from problems of estimation, even if one assumes, as many courts do, that minority shareholders are entitled only to the no-freezeout value of their shares.

reports on some of the findings of our work in progress and considers the implications of our model for the controlling shareholder's incentive to pursue investment projects and to reveal information.

## 8.1 The Use of Market Prices in Freezeouts

For an economist, a natural approach in determining the value of the minority shares is to rely on the market price of those shares prior to the freezeout. Economists generally believe that market prices provide the best estimate of the value of a share that can be formed on the basis of publicly available information—or at least a much better estimate than the one that a judge may arrive at after listening to conflicting, and undoubtedly self-serving, testimony of experts hired by the controlling and the minority shareholders. Indeed, several scholars have proposed that courts use the market price as the measure of the value of the minority shares in a freezeout.[9] And courts presently look at the market price as an important, although not the exclusive, factor in appraising minority shares.[10]

As we show below, however, there is a fundamental flaw in using market prices to measure the value of minority shares in a freezeout. The very power of a controlling shareholder to freeze out the minority shares—and to set the freezeout price equal to the prefreezeout market price—will depress the prefreezeout market price of the minority shares. As a result, the prefreezeout market price of minority shares will be substantially below the expected "intrinsic" value of the minority shares absent a freezeout.[11] This is the case even if—in fact, especially if—capital markets are informationally efficient and fully process all publicly available information. Thus, the prefreezeout market price is an unreliable guide for courts in appraising minority shares.

The reason for the discrepancy between the market price and the expected "intrinsic" value of the minority shares is that the controlling

9. See Hermalin and Schwartz (1996), which presents a model not including asymmetric information and argues that awarding the prefreezeout market price in an appraisal proceeding creates efficient incentives to invest.

10. For examples in which market value plays a significant role in valuation, see *Genesco, Inc. v. Scolaro,* 871 S.W.2d 487 (Tenn. Ct. App. 1993); *McCauley v. Tom McCauley & Son, Inc.,* 724 P.2d 232 (N.M. Ct. App. 1986); *Friedman v. Beway Realty Corp.,* 638 N.Y.S.2d 399 (Ct. App. 1995); *In re Glosser Brothers,* 555 A.2d 129 (Pa. Super. Ct. 1989); *In re Valuation of Common Stock of Libby, McNeill & Libby,* 406 A.2d 54 (Me. 1979); *Chokel v. First National Supermarkets, Inc.,* 660 N.E.2d 644 (Mass. 1986); and *Hernando Bank v. Huff,* 609 F. Supp. 1124 (N.D. Miss. 1985). Indeed, market value is sometimes the most significant factor in determining fair value in appraising minority shares; see, e.g., *Armstrong v. Marathon Oil,* 513 N.E.2d 776 (Ohio 1987). Since U.S. courts consider the prefreezeout market price as only one of several possible factors determining the fair price, freezeout prices in the United States can and commonly do exceed the prefreezeout market price. Our model shows why it is sensible for courts not to give conclusive weight to the prefreezeout market price.

11. We use the term *expected "intrinsic" value* to refer to the expected value of minority share if a freezeout is not possible.

shareholder's power to effect a freezeout creates an adverse selection effect that depresses the market price.[12] A controlling shareholder will generally have private information about the value of the company that is not available to the public. Absent the possibility of forcing a freezeout, such private information would cause the market price to be inaccurate but would not cause it to be systematically biased:[13] the market price may sometimes be too high or too low but would still constitute the best estimate of the value of the minority shares that can be formed on the basis of all public information. But, if the controlling shareholder has the power to freeze out the minority shareholders by paying them the prefreezeout market price, she will use that power strategically to effect a freezeout only if her private information indicates that the value of the minority shares is above their market price. This strategic use of the power to effect a freezeout results in an adverse selection effect that causes the market price of minority shares to spiral downward.

Assume, for example, that the per share value of XYZ Corporation can range from $100 to $200. On the basis of public information, any value in this range is equally likely. The expected "intrinsic" value of a share of XYZ Corporation is thus $150. The controlling shareholder, however, knows the exact value of the company. The controlling shareholder can freeze out the minority shareholders at the market price. If she does not effect a freezeout, XYZ will be liquidated, and minority shareholders will receive their proportional interest.

If a freezeout were not possible, the market price of an XYZ share would be $150—the value that the minority shareholders expect to receive on XYZ's liquidation. Now, however, consider the effect of the power to effect a freezeout at the market price. To be in equilibrium, the market price must be equal to the average amount that the minority shareholders receive in a freezeout or on XYZ's liquidation. Let us consider first whether $150 can remain the equilibrium market price. At that price, the controlling shareholder will effect a freezeout if she knows that XYZ's value is above $150 per share and will not effect a freezeout if she knows that the value of an XYZ share is below $150. Each possibility is equally

12. See Akerlof (1970). Other commentators have also suggested that the market price for minority shares will be depressed. These commentators, however, intimate that the depressed price is due to information inefficiencies or to expectations of self-dealing (Brudney and Chirelstein 1974, 1978). By contrast, we show that the market price is depressed even if the market price is set in a rational expectations equilibrium and the controlling shareholder does not derive private control benefits from self-dealing or, for that matter, from *any* source other than the power to freeze out the minority shares.

13. Even absent a freezeout, the controlling shareholder can buy shares at the market price in a regular market transaction. Freezeouts, however, create greater possibility for insider trading. First, in a regular market transaction, the minority shareholders can protect themselves by not selling, at least not at times when they suspect that the controlling shareholder has a lot of private information. Second, the controlling shareholder can buy only a limited number of shares before her purchases are noticed and the market price increases.

likely, and, in the latter case, the minority shareholders would expect to receive $125 on XYZ's liquidation.[14] The expected value of the minority shares (given the possibility of a freezeout) is $137.50 per share—and $150 is therefore not an equilibrium market price.

Alas, for similar reasons, $137.50 is not an equilibrium market price either. The controlling shareholder will effect a freezeout if XYZ's value is above $137.50 per share (62.5 percent probability), and, if there is no freezeout, the minority shareholders expect to receive $118.75 on XYZ's liquidation. The expected value of the minority shares is then $130.47 per share—and $137.50 is not an equilibrium price. But, at a market price of $130.47, a freezeout will occur if XYZ's value exceeds $130.47, and, absent a freezeout, minority shareholders expect to receive $115.24. The expected value of the minority shares is, thus, $125.83 per share ($130.47 × 69.53 percent + $115.24 × 30.47 percent), and so on.

Following this spiral downward, it turns out that the highest equilibrium price is $100—the lowest possible value of an XYZ share. For any market price above $100, minority shareholders will sometimes receive the market price (if the controlling shareholder knows that XYZ's value exceeds the market value) and sometimes less (if she knows that XYZ's value is less than the market value)—meaning that they receive, on average, less than the market price per share. As a consequence, no market price above $100 is an equilibrium. If the market price is $100, however, the controlling shareholder will always effect a freezeout (or be indifferent if XYZ's value is exactly $100 per share), and minority shareholders always receive $100.

As the example suggests, the power to freeze out the minority shares can be an important source of private benefits that a controlling shareholder gains at the expense of minority shareholders. The ability to use private information to gain in a freezeout—and, importantly, the market's expectation that a controlling shareholder will use private information in this fashion—generates benefits in addition to, and independent of, any private benefits that a controlling shareholder gains from self-dealing, salaries, etc.

## 8.2 A Model of Freezeouts under Asymmetric Information

### 8.2.1 The Framework of Analysis

Shares of the company are held by one controlling shareholder and a large number of minority shareholders. Let $Y$ be the value of the company's equity and $\alpha < .5$ be the fraction of shares held by the minority shareholders. Let $n$ be the number of outstanding shares of the company.

14. Since any per share value between $100 and $200 is equally likely, the expected value conditional on the value being below a certain level $\$X$ (with $\$X$ being between $100 and $200) is halfway between $\$X$ and $100. The expected value conditional on the value being below $150 is thus $125.

At $t = 1$, a minority shareholder has to sell one share for liquidity reasons. The sale (market) price is established by an English auction among $m$ bidders with $m \geq 2$, and $P$ is the market price times the number of outstanding shares. Bidders do not own any other shares of the company. Bidders do not know the exact value of $Y$ but do know that $Y$ is distributed in $[Y_L, Y_H]$ with an expected value of $\overline{Y}$. At $t = 1$, the controlling shareholder derives private control benefits $B \geq 0$ from her control. The aggregate expected value of the company to the controlling shareholder and the minority shareholders is thus $\overline{V} = \overline{Y} + B$.

At $t = 2$, the controlling shareholder receives a signal $s$ regarding the value of $Y$ on the basis of which the controlling shareholder forms $\overline{Y}_s$ as an unbiased estimate of $Y$. Without loss of generality, assume that $s$ is distributed in [0, 1] with $\overline{Y}_i \geq \overline{Y}_j$ for $i > j$. In the "no possibility of a freezeout" case, no further action occurs at $t = 2$. In the "possibility of a freezeout" case, the controlling shareholder has the right to freeze out the minority shares by paying a freezeout price per share equal to the market value per share.

At $t = 3$, $Y$ becomes known, the company is liquidated, and $Y$ is distributed pro rata to its (then) shareholders.

For simplicity, assume that the discount rate is zero, that all shareholders are risk neutral, that there are no transaction costs in trading shares or effecting a freezeout, and that the value of $B$ is known. Further assume that a freezeout has no effect on the values of $Y$ and $B$.

### 8.2.2 The Value of Minority Shares in a Regime without Freezeouts

PROPOSITION 1. *If the controlling shareholder does not have the power to effect a freezeout, the equilibrium market price of the minority shares is $\overline{Y}/n$; that is, $P = \overline{Y}$.*

PROOF. The market price is set by bidders' bidding strategies at $t = 1$. In an English auction with symmetric information, a bidder $k$'s strategy is defined by $x_k$, the highest amount the bidder is willing to bid up to (if necessary) for one share. It is a dominant strategy for each bidder to set $x$ to $\overline{Y}/n$.

Let $\hat{x}$ be the highest $x$ chosen by all bidders other than bidder $k$. Bidder $k$'s payoff will depend on the values of $x_k$ and $\hat{x}$. For any $x_k < \hat{x}$, bidder $k$ will lose the auction, and its payoff is zero. For $x_k > \hat{x}$, bidder $k$ will win and purchase the share at $\hat{x} + \varepsilon$, with $\varepsilon$ having an infinitesimal positive value. For $x_k = \hat{x}$, the winning bidder is randomly determined; that is, bidder $k$ will either lose or purchase the share for $\hat{x}$.

For $\hat{x} < \overline{Y}/n$, bidder $k$'s expected profits are maximized by purchasing the share at $\hat{x} + \varepsilon$, that is, by setting $x_k > \hat{x}$. For $\hat{x} > \overline{Y}/n$, bidder $k$'s expected profits are maximized by not purchasing the share, that is, by setting $x_k < \hat{x}$. For $\hat{x} = \overline{Y}/n$, bidder $k$ is indifferent between not purchasing the share and purchasing the share for $\overline{Y}/n$ and maximizes its profits by setting $x_k \leq \hat{x}$.

The only value of $x_k$ that maximizes bidder $k$'s profits in all three cases is $x_k = \overline{Y}/n$. Any value $x_k < \overline{Y}/n$ fails to maximize bidder $k$'s profits for some $\hat{x} < \overline{Y}/n$; any value $x_k > \overline{Y}/n$ fails to maximize bidder $k$'s profits for some $\hat{x} > \overline{Y}/n$. Setting $x_k = \overline{Y}/n$ is, thus, the weakly dominant strategy for bidder $k$. By the same rationale, setting $x = \overline{Y}/n$ is the dominant strategy for any other bidder.

### 8.2.3 The Value of Minority Shares in a Regime with Freezeouts

If a freezeout is possible, the equilibrium market price is determined by the strategic interactions among the bidders and between the bidders and the controlling shareholder:

PROPOSITION 2. *The only set of Nash equilibria in undominated strategies results in* $P = \overline{Y}_0$.

PROOF. The proof of proposition 2 follows from the following lemmas.

LEMMA 1. *The controlling shareholder has two dominant strategies (with* $P$ *determined by the bidders' strategies): (1) effect a freezeout if and only if* $\overline{Y}_s \geq P$*; and (2) effect a freezeout if and only if* $\overline{Y}_s > P$.

The controlling shareholder's expected profit from effecting a freezeout is $\overline{Y}_s - P$, and the controlling shareholder's expected profit from not effecting a freezeout is zero. For $\overline{Y}_s > P$, the controlling shareholder maximizes its expected profit by effecting a freezeout; for $\overline{Y}_s < P$, the controlling shareholder maximizes its expected profit by not effecting a freezeout; for $\overline{Y}_s = P$, the controlling shareholder is indifferent between effecting and not effecting a freezeout. Any other strategy is dominated by these two strategies as they would entail either the possibility of effecting a freezeout when not effecting a freezeout maximizes expected profits or not effecting a freezeout when effecting a freezeout maximizes expected profits.

LEMMA 2. *For any bidder, setting* $x < \overline{Y}_0/n$ *is weakly dominated by setting* $x = \overline{Y}_0/n$.

Bidder $k$'s bid matters to bidder $k$ only if the controlling shareholder does not effect a freezeout and if $x_k \geq \hat{x}$. (Otherwise, bidder $k$ makes profits of zero regardless of its bid.) Assume, therefore, that $\hat{x} \leq \overline{Y}_0/n$ and that the controlling shareholder does not effect a freezeout.

If $\hat{x} = \overline{Y}_0/n$, setting $x_k = \overline{Y}_0/n$ means that bidder $k$ will sometimes buy a share for $\overline{Y}_0/n$. The payoff from buying a share for $\overline{Y}_0/n$ is $Y/n - \overline{Y}_0/n \geq 0$ and thus dominates the payoff from setting $x_k < \overline{Y}_0/n$ and not buying a share (which is always zero). (Recall that, in assessing the dominance of strategies, one does not assume that the controlling shareholder plays its dominant strategy.)

If $\hat{x} < \overline{Y}_0/n$, setting $x_k > \hat{x}$ means that bidder $k$ will buy a share for $\hat{x} + \varepsilon$, with a payoff of $Y/n - (\hat{x} + \varepsilon) > 0$. This payoff dominates the payoff from setting $x_k \leq \hat{x}$. Setting $x = \overline{Y}_0/n$ thus weakly dominates setting $x < \overline{Y}_0/n$.

LEMMA 3. *If the controlling shareholder plays one of its dominant strategies, no strategy of bidders that results in $P > \overline{Y}_0$ is a Nash equilibrium.*

If the controlling shareholder plays one of its dominant strategies, the payoff to the winning bidder is

$$\{\text{prob}(\overline{Y}_s \geq P) \times P + \text{prob}(\overline{Y}_s < P) \times E[Y \mid \overline{Y}_s < P] - P\}/n.$$

This payoff is negative since $E[Y| Y_s < P] < P$. The winning bidder would thus prefer to lower its bid to below $\hat{x}$ (with a payoff of zero). The strategies are therefore not in Nash equilibrium.

LEMMA 4. *The following strategy profiles are Nash equilibria: (1) each bidder sets $x = \overline{Y}_0/n$, and the controlling shareholder effects a freezeout if and only if $\overline{Y}_s \geq P$; and (2) each bidder sets $x = \overline{Y}_0/n$, and the controlling shareholder effects a freezeout if and only if $\overline{Y}_s > P$.*

Both of these Nash equilibria result in $P = \overline{Y}_0$.

The controlling shareholder cannot profit from changing her strategy since she plays a dominant strategy. Since either a freezeout is effected or $s = 0$, all bidders make zero expected profits. No bidder can thus profit from reducing his bid. No bidder can profit from raising his bid since raising one's bid results in $P > \overline{Y}_0$, with a negative expected payoff to the winning bidder (lemma 3).

Lemmas 1–3 show that the strategies of the bidders and of the controlling shareholder are undominated.

It should be noted that there are an infinite number of Nash equilibrium strategies with the features of (i) $P < \overline{Y}_0$ and (ii) the controlling shareholder always effecting a freezeout. (In fact, any combination of strategies with these features is in Nash equilibrium.) The strategies resulting in such Nash equilibria, however, are not undominated.

*Remark.* The intuition behind the result that the equilibrium market price will be equal to the worst possible expected value of the company given the controlling shareholder's set of potential signals lies in the adverse selection effect of the freezeout power. The minority shareholders receive the market price if a freezeout takes place at $t = 2$. If no freezeout takes place at $t = 2$, the minority shareholders can deduce that, given the information available to the controlling shareholder, the value of the minority shares is below their market price; therefore, they would expect to receive less than the market price. (They never *expect* to receive more than the market price.) Thus, if the market price is sufficiently high that the controlling shareholder will sometimes not pursue a freezeout, the amount that the minority shareholders expect to receive is below the market price. No such price can be in equilibrium at $t = 1$. On the other hand, no price below the expected value of the company if the controlling shareholder were to receive the worst possible signal can be in equilibrium since the minority shareholders expect to receive *at least* this amount whether or not a freezeout takes place.

The degree to which $\overline{Y}_0$—the expected value of the company assuming that the private information of the controlling shareholder is the worst possible—differs from $\overline{Y}$—the expected value of the company absent private information—depends on the strength of the signal received. In one extreme case, where the signal reveals the actual value of the company ($\overline{Y}_s = Y$), the equilibrium price drops to $Y_L$. In another extreme case, where the signal conveys no information ($Y_0 = Y_1 = \overline{Y}$), the equilibrium price is equal to $\overline{Y}$.

Rather than by the absolute level of private information, however, the market price is determined by the extent to which the controlling shareholder has private information regarding elements that have an *adverse* effect on the company's value—that is, elements that drive down the value of $\overline{Y}_0$ (even if they do not affect any other $\overline{Y}_s$). In other words, the market price falls with (and the controlling shareholder benefits from) a more accurate signal only if the signal is negative, not if the signal is positive. In the extreme, it is sufficient to have the market price drop to $Y_L$ (the lowest possible value of the company) if the controlling shareholder receives a binary signal: a perfectly accurate signal indicating that the company's value is $Y_L$ and a highly imprecise signal indicating only that the company's value is not $Y_L$.

### 8.2.4 The Effect of Freezeouts on Private Control Benefits

On the basis of propositions 1 and 2, we can calculate the respective equilibrium values of the minority shares and the control block in the absence and the presence of the possibility of a freezeout.

In a regime without freezeouts, the aggregate expected value of the minority shares is

$$\alpha\overline{Y},$$

and the expected value of the control block (at $t = 1$) will be

$$(1 - \alpha)\overline{Y} + B.$$

Relative to the respective pro rata fraction of $\overline{V}$, the value of the minority shares is

$$\alpha\overline{V} - \alpha B,$$

and the value of the control block is

$$(1 - \alpha)\overline{V} + \alpha B.$$

With the possibility of a freezeout, the value of the minority shares is

$$\alpha\overline{Y}_0,$$

and the expected value of the control block (at $t = 1$) is

$$(1 - \alpha)\overline{Y} + \alpha(\overline{Y} - \overline{Y}_0) + B.$$

Relative to the respective pro rata fraction of $\overline{V}$, the value of the minority shares is

$$\alpha\overline{V} - \alpha(\overline{Y} - \overline{Y}_0) - \alpha B,$$

and the value of the control block is

$$(1 - \alpha)\overline{V} + \alpha(\overline{Y} - \overline{Y}_0) + \alpha B.$$

Thus, as a result of the possibility of a freezeout, the value of the minority shares decreases by

$$\alpha(\overline{Y} - \overline{Y}_0),$$

and the value of the control block increases by the same corresponding amount.

The expression $\alpha(\overline{Y} - \overline{Y}_0)$ represents the expected value (at $t = 1$) of the amount that the controlling shareholder can divert from the minority shareholders by the strategic exercise of the freezeout option. This adds to other sources of private control benefits ($B$).

## 8.3 Concluding Discussion

In this paper, we presented a simple model of corporate freezeouts where the controlling shareholder has the option to pay the prefreezeout market price to the minority shareholders. We have shown that this option has substantial value to the controlling shareholder when she has private information about the value of the company. Our work in progress preliminarily indicates that the results of the simple model discussed here are robust to several variations of the model that render the model more complex and more general. In particular, we analyze freezeout pricing rules where the freezeout price is not, or not exclusively, determined by the prefreezeout market price, we examine the case where the freezeout produces efficiency gains and losses (i.e., increases or decreases the company's value), and we extend the analysis to multiple periods where, in each period, new private information becomes available to the controlling shareholder and prior private information becomes available to the market. Although the specific results derived for the value of the minority shares and the control block vary with each of these extensions, the general result of the model—that the freezeout option can be highly valuable to the controlling shareholder—continues to hold.

The fact that the freezeout option is valuable, and that the per share value of the minority shares is below the per share value of the control block, has important policy implications. First, since the value of the freezeout option depends on the extent of the controlling shareholder's private information, a controlling shareholder has excessive incentives (from the social perspective) to obtain private information or, equivalently, to obtain information earlier than the market. Since obtaining private information is costly, a controlling shareholder will expend excessive resources on acquiring information.

Second, once private information is obtained, the controlling shareholder has excessive incentives to withhold such information from the market. These incentives result in social losses to the extent that it is socially desirable to have a more informed market and to the extent that the controlling shareholder expends resources in actively hiding information.

Third, the desire to obtain private information skews the investments that the controlling shareholder would have the company undertake. Different investment projects provide the controlling shareholder with different levels of private information, and the controlling shareholder has an incentive to choose investment projects that yield greater private information even if the projects have a negative net present value. Moreover, as explained before, private information related to adverse developments is particularly valuable. Thus, a controlling shareholder has an incentive to have the company invest in projects that potentially (*a*) have a substantial downside and (*b*) supply the controlling shareholder with private information regarding whether that downside is realized.

Finally, the presence of private control benefits (of any sort) means that a party has a socially excessive incentive to become (or remain) a controlling shareholder. This excessive incentive results in social losses of two types: the transaction costs incurred in assembling a control block of shares and the reduction in diversification benefits due to the fact that one may have to hold an undiversified portfolio in order to hold a control block in a company. Additionally, any source of private control benefits is of concern if a goal of the legal system is to ensure that all shareholders participate proportionally in the value of the company.

## References

Akerlof, George. 1970. The market for "lemons": Quality uncertainty and the market mechanism. *Quarterly Journal of Economics* 84:488–500.

Barclay, Michael, and Clifford Holderness. 1989. Private benefits from control of public corporations. *Journal of Financial Economics* 25:371–95.

Bebchuk, Lucian. 1994. Efficient and inefficient sales of corporate control. *Quarterly Journal of Economics* 91:957–93.

Bebchuk, Lucian, and Marcel Kahan. 1999. Freezeouts under asymmetric information. Harvard Law School. Manuscript.
Brudney, Victor, and Marvin Chirelstein. 1974. Fair shares in corporate mergers and takeovers. *Harvard Law Review* 88:297–346.
———. 1978. A restatement of corporate freezeouts. *Yale Law Journal* 87: 1354–76.
Coates, John C., IV. 1999. "Fair value" as an avoidable rule of corporate law: Minority discounts in conflict transactions. *University of Pennsylvania Law Review* 147:1251–1359.
Hermalin, Benjamin, and Alan Schwartz. 1996. Buyouts in large companies. *Journal of Legal Studies* 25:351–70.
Kahan, Marcel. 1993. Sales of corporate control. *Journal of Law, Economics, and Organization* 9:368–79.

## Comment Paul G. Mahoney

A fundamental problem in corporate law is how to constrain a controlling shareholder from using control to appropriate the full value of the firm. One simple method of appropriation is to "freeze out" the minority shareholders by merging the firm into one wholly owned by the controlling shareholder. Because the controlling shareholder has sufficient votes to approve the merger over the minority's objections, it can cause the merger to occur at any price it wishes. Various features of corporate law try to assure that this price is "fair" to the minority.

It is tempting to say that the best measure of the fair price is the market price of the shares prior to the merger. As Bebchuk and Kahan note, however, this does not account for the information content of the majority's desire to freeze out the minority. The majority can gain from implementing a freezeout whenever it has private information indicating that the current market value of the firm is too low. Therefore, Bebchuk and Kahan argue, the majority's failure to freeze out demonstrates that the value indicated by the private signal is less than or equal to the market price. Rational shareholders will draw an adverse inference and revalue the shares downward until either the majority effects a freezeout or the shares' value reaches the bottom of the possible range of the majority's privately known valuation.

Bebchuk and Kahan argue that this adverse selection problem has implications for legal policy. For example, it might justify judges' longstanding reluctance to recognize market prices as the best measure of the fair price in a freezeout context. More important, however, the paper implicitly challenges lawyers and economists to identify the institutional features of real-world corporations that lead to results contrary to those of the model. Freezeouts cannot have the consequences for real firms that

Paul G. Mahoney is professor of law and the Albert C. BeVier Research Professor at the University of Virginia.

they have in Bebchuk and Kahan's model. If they did, equity markets could not exist where freezeouts are permissible.

In Bebchuk and Kahan's model, shareholders know that the entrepreneur/majority shareholder will receive a private signal regarding the firm's value, that there is a determinate lower bound to that value, and that the majority has only one opportunity to implement a freezeout (which assures that the majority's failure to freeze out at that time is a reflection of private information rather than a strategic delay meant to mislead the minority). Under those circumstances, rational shareholders will not pay more than the lower bound ($Y_0$) if freezeouts are permissible. As a result, the claim held by a "shareholder" is really a bond with a face value of $Y_0$ and a perpetual maturity. If we make the lower bound stochastic rather than determinate, then shareholders will not pay more than the lowest possible value of the relevant distribution, and, recursively, we end up with either a debt claim or a claim worth nothing at all. In short, firms with a shareholder who owns more than 50 percent but less than 100 percent of the equity could not exist.

This is not what we observe. Some features of the institutional landscape—legal rules, extralegal norms, contractual innovations, or all of the above—have made concentrated ownership possible. Although Bebchuk and Kahan do not ask what these institutional features are, their identification is a critical issue for those studying corporate governance. Holderness and Sheehan (chap. 5 in this volume) argue by process of elimination that legal constraints (particularly the fiduciary duties required of majority shareholders) are important, noting shareholders' disinclination to insist on explicit contractual protections.

We might also gain some insight by noting that the freezeout puzzle is a mirror image of the new-issue puzzle. A new issue of stock creates an adverse selection problem because the majority's desire to sell is evidence that the offering price is too high, just as the majority's desire to buy in a freezeout is evidence that the freezeout price is too low. By analogy to Bebchuk and Kahan's model, new issues should not sell at any price greater than the lowest possible valuation of the firm—presumably zero for real-world firms.

Loughran and Ritter (1995) present evidence that new issues (both initial public offerings and seasoned equity offerings) earn unexpectedly low long-term returns. Behavioral finance theorists might see this as evidence that purchasers are overly optimistic. Similarly, one might try to explain the *failure* of firms with concentrated ownership to trade at a discount to firms with diffuse ownership as evidence of overoptimism. If we accept these views, the existence of large public equity markets is a consequence of cognitive error.

An alternative perspective on new issues is that investment bankers act as information intermediaries, putting their reputation on the line to signal investors that the price is not too high. This provides still another avenue to explore in the case of freezeouts. Investment bankers act as information intermediaries, thereby giving fairness opinions. Although lawyers tend to view fairness opinions as a formality that protects directors against fiduciary liability, they also put the banker's reputation behind the claim that the price is not too low.

I would have preferred that Bebchuk and Kahan address explicitly the divergence between observed behavior and the predictions of the model. The paper does, however, provide an excellent starting point for future discussion of the problem of freezeouts and the legal and contractual responses.

## Reference

Loughran, Tim, and Jay R. Ritter. 1995. The new issues puzzle. *Journal of Finance* 50:23–51.

# III

# Economic Effects of Concentrated Corporate Ownership

9

# Emerging Market Business Groups, Foreign Intermediaries, and Corporate Governance

Tarun Khanna and Krishna Palepu

Much has been written about the tendency toward insider control in transitional economies (Aoki and Kim 1995). Indeed, this phenomenon poses a serious challenge for the governance of enterprises in which the usual institutions for external monitoring are missing or underdeveloped.

We investigate the monitoring of enterprises subject to a form of insider control, business groups, in which a family typically has control over multiple enterprises. Our research setting is India, an economy in the process of significant deregulation beginning in 1991. We investigate the interaction between three different kinds of concentrated ownership in India: the insider ownership held by the families that manage the firms that constitute the business groups; the ownership held by domestic financial institutions, typically acting in concert; and the ownership held by foreign financial institutions, recent arrivals on the Indian economic landscape.

A review of the literature suggests that the external monitoring of group affiliates poses more challenges than that of unaffiliated firms. Groups are reputed to be less transparent than nongroups and to have more opportunities, given their more complicated structures, to engage in questionable practices to the detriment of minority shareholders. Their generally better links to the political apparatus in the country also insulate them from external interference and monitoring. Domestic financial institutions, the

Tarun Khanna is associate professor of business administration at the Harvard Business School. Krishna Palepu is the Ross Graham Walker Professor of Business Administration at the Harvard Business School.

The authors are grateful to conference and preconference participants and especially to Randall Morck and Bernard Yeung for helpful comments. James Schorr provided excellent research assistance. The authors are also grateful to the Division of Research at the Harvard Business School for financial support. The usual disclaimer applies.

primary source of institutional investment in India until economic liberalization in 1991, are generally insufficiently oriented, if at all, toward the task of monitoring managers and are thus unlikely to exercise effective governance. Foreign institutional investors, who were allowed to participate in Indian stock markets in recent years, bring with them from advanced capital markets not only fresh capital but also monitoring skills.

Our evidence suggests that domestic financial institutions in India are ineffective monitors, whereas foreign institutional investment is associated with significant monitoring benefits: firm performance is positively correlated with the presence of foreign institutional ownership and negatively correlated with the presence of domestic institutional ownership. Surprisingly, however, we find that there is no evidence of a difference in this relationship between group affiliates and unaffiliated firms, suggesting that monitoring is no less effective for group affiliates than it is for unaffiliated firms. At first glance, the lack of transparency of groups does not appear to pose a differential impediment to monitoring by foreign institutional investors.

We probe this further by investigating factors correlated with the presence of greater foreign institutional ownership (and compare those factors to factors correlated with the presence of greater domestic institutional ownership). After controlling for industry fixed effects, firm size, and the past performance of firms, we find that foreign owners are indeed less likely to invest in group affiliates than in unaffiliated firms, perhaps because of the problems associated with monitoring groups. However, when they do invest in groups, they appear to seek out those groups where the transparency problem, as proxied by the greater incidence of intragroup financial transactions, is lowest.

We interpret this collective evidence as suggesting that foreign institutional investors are a source of not only financing but also scarce monitoring skills in emerging markets like India. Given the rapidly accumulating evidence of the failure of domestic intermediaries in a number of emerging markets and the recent opening up to foreign investment of dozens of countries (Sachs and Warner 1995), these results regarding the nature of investments sought by foreign institutional investors and the effects of such investments are worthy of note. Our evidence is also consistent with the idea that groups are difficult for external agencies to monitor.

The rest of the paper is organized as follows. Section 9.1 provides a literature review and some background on the state of monitoring intermediaries in the Indian context. Section 9.2 describes our data, section 9.3 our results. Section 9.4 concludes.

## 9.1 Institutional Background

### 9.1.1 Monitoring in Emerging Markets

Shleifer and Vishny (1986) point out that, by partially internalizing the externality inherent in providing monitoring services, large shareholders can reduce the incidence of agency problems that arise from the divergence of interests between managers and shareholders. According to Aoki (1995), however, this is a "necessary" rather than a "sufficient" condition for the provision of monitoring services. Indeed, in emerging markets, there are several reasons why existing monitoring is inadequate.

Perhaps the most important of these has to do with the absence of specialized intermediaries that perform monitoring services[1] or with the lack of skills in or incentives offered to such intermediaries as do exist. As Holderness and Sheehan (1991, 326) point out, while it is true that larger shareholders have a greater incentive to monitor, "firm value will not increase if the blockholder lacks the pertinent managerial skills." Examples from emerging markets regarding the paucity of such skills abound. Qian (1995) discusses the creation of a monitoring vacuum in China following the cessation of state monitoring of its enterprises. Frydman et al. (1993) point out that, in Russia, commercial banks have no experience with market accounting and governance and are therefore in no position to hold management's feet to the fire. Rapaczynski (1996, 99), describing the situation in Eastern Europe, reports that the "various supervisory bodies are generally rudderless, incapable of genuine monitoring."

Litwack (1995) adds that it is unclear whether such financial institutions as do exist have the incentives to invest in monitoring skills. Financial institutions may have conflicts of interest that discourage them from developing such skills. Such conflicts of interest appear to exist in Israel (Blass, Yafeh, and Yosha 1997).[2] Indeed, the emergence of concentrated blocks of shareholders does not appear to be synonymous with the provision of monitoring services.[3] Berglof (1995) points out that, despite investment privatization funds holding concentrated blocks of equity, there are few

1. This begs the question of why competent intermediaries have not emerged. There is ongoing theoretical discussion about the circumstances under which intermediaries will find it profitable to collect and disseminate information about firms. Under an assumption of fixed costs of gathering information, there are good reasons to expect intermediaries to emerge (Diamond 1984), but perhaps markets are not large enough (Grossman and Stiglitz 1980) or liquid enough (Kyle 1984; Holmström and Tirole 1993) to foster this process.

2. For example, a fund manager might buy shares so as to boost the value of shares held by a bank with which the fund manager is affiliated. In advanced economies, such potential conflicts of interest are often mitigated through "fire-wall" structures (see Kroszner and Rajan 1997).

3. The theoretical literature on financial market intermediation (Diamond 1984; Krasa and Villamil 1992) posits that diversification of the financial institution's investments ensures that the investors in the financial institution are likely to receive a return on their investment

signs in the Czech Republic of such "control blocks" translating into active corporate governance. It goes without saying that further specialization in the monitoring process, depending on the type of monitoring, is completely absent.[4]

A second reason for the lack of monitoring has to do with the poor availability of information. There are usually no strict disclosure norms, and enforcement of existing disclosure rules is lax. Akamatsu (1995) points out that, of five thousand enterprises privatized in Russia, only one hundred publish financial statements; among these, balance sheets typically consist of three lines on the assets side and two lines on the liabilities side, with no explanatory notes. Intermediaries that specialize in the gathering of information (such as analysts) are generally absent or not as skilled as those in advanced economies. In Chile, managers report that, even after two decades of financial market reform, domestic analysts are not nearly as skilled as foreign analysts (Khanna and Wu 1998).

Finally, even if monitors with the appropriate skill levels exist and have the appropriate incentives to perform their function, there are impediments to their doing so. First, numerous firms in most emerging markets have a large insider shareholding that makes it difficult for intermediaries to monitor and impose discipline.[5] The high level of insider shareholding may imply that insufficient shares trade (as in China [Xu and Wang 1997]), making a disciplinary takeover difficult. The absence of minority-shareholder rights further complicates this situation (La Porta et al. 1998). Second, numerous firms have political connections that make the imposition of discipline impractical.[6]

### 9.1.2 The Indian Institutional Context

All these barriers to monitoring activity exist in India.[7] In fact, in December 1991, a landmark committee set up to review the state of the financial sector, the Narasimhan Committee, admitted that loans had not

and so need not exert undue effort in monitoring the monitor. As an empirical matter, we do not know the extent to which failure of financial institutions in emerging markets to provide monitoring services is due to a failure to monitor the financial institutions themselves.

4. For example, Roe (1990, 36) refers to "specialized monitoring that financial institutions can do well" and distinguishes between different types of monitoring. Aoki (1995) distinguishes between ex ante, interim, and ex post monitoring; different kinds of monitoring are performed by different kinds of financial intermediaries in advanced economies.

5. Stulz (1990) argues that the probability of takeover is inversely related to the level of insider shareholding.

6. Fisman (1998) provides evidence of the effect of such connections in Indonesia. Kroszner (1998) suggests that foreign banks will be less subject to such local political pressure and that monitoring by financial intermediaries is therefore likely to be better in economies where foreign banks are allowed to enter freely.

7. Since our data span the period 1990–94, we confine ourselves to commenting on the Indian institutional context during this period. This part of the discussion draws from multiple sources, prominent among which are SEBI (1994), Goswami and Mohan (1996), and Joshi and Little (1997).

been monitored for decades. The first reason for the poor monitoring of Indian firms is that monitoring is not the primary objective of the dominant financial institutions (almost exclusively state-run banks). Indeed, until 1991, the objective of government policy was to maximize loans to the industrial sector in the belief that this would lead to industrial development. The major financial institutions were often instructed not to disturb management and to side with management in the event of any dispute; they virtually never divested their ownership stake in any firm.

Second, financial institutions were never provided with any incentives to monitor. Pouring more money after a bad loan in the hope that the distressed firm would find its way out of trouble was consistent with the objective of maximizing loans. Further, this was often a preferable course of action given the difficulty of shutting down failing firms under the Sick Industrial Firms Act. Of course, this implicit soft budget constraint led to moral hazard problems on the part of firms.

Third, competition among financial intermediaries was nonexistent for several reasons: (*a*) Government restrictions on lending terms, interest rates, and conditions governing equity ownership eliminated the primary bases on which competition might have occurred. (*b*) There was a great deal of consortium lending. (*c*) All public banks were members of the Indian Banks Association (IBA), which functioned as a de facto cartel and played a major role in fixing wages, prices, and service conditions. (*d*) Finally, under the pre-1991 "license raj," once an entrepreneur received a permit from the government to engage in some form of economic activity, support from the state-run financial institutions was more or less guaranteed. This had the indirect implication that lobbying and political interference in the real sector translated into similar rent-seeking behavior in the financial sector. Indeed, there were accusations of "financial preemption" directed against certain entrepreneurs who sought to restrict finances from becoming available to others by exercising their political muscle. "Industrial embassies" were maintained in the capital by prominent businesses toward this end (Encarnation 1989).

Finally, intermediaries were never monitored themselves. As late as 1992, banks illegally lent stockbrokers money that the latter used to engage in speculation, leading ultimately to a drastic market crash and the exposure of much fraudulent behavior.

In addition to the absence of potential monitoring by banks, there were also constraints on monitoring by external capital markets. The Companies Act placed restrictions on the acquisition and transfer of shares and so prevented the development of a market for corporate control. With half to two-thirds of the equity in any firm being illiquid (since the entrepreneurs and the financial institutions never sold their shares), takeovers were difficult to implement.

Several positive developments have occurred on the corporate-governance front, however, since India's 1991 balance-of-payments crisis: (*a*) The Securities and Exchange Board of India (SEBI) Act of 1992 created a regulatory body with the explicit mandate to improve the functioning of Indian financial markets. (*b*) The incentives given state-run financial institutions to monitor were improved. They began to be weaned off their historically privileged access to funds. The resulting need to access public capital markets made them more conscious of the bad loans on their balance sheets. The deregulation of interest rates and the gradual elimination of consortium requirements increased competition among the financial institutions. Private-sector mutual funds were allowed to compete with the state monopoly. (*c*) A takeover code was introduced in late 1994, after a public outcry over legally sanctioned price rigging.[8] (*d*) Restrictions on the entry of foreign investors were eliminated, and regulations on their investments were substantially clarified. Salient features included no limitations on minimum and maximum investments, no lock-in period for such investments, reduction in long- and short-term capital gains taxes, free repatriation of capital subject to payment of taxes, and a ceiling under which the maximum investment by a foreign institutional investor in a single firm could be up to 5 percent of voting rights (with an aggregate investment limit of 24 percent for all foreign institutional investors in a single firm).

However, as of 1994, Indian corporate governance was still deficient for many reasons, including the following: (*a*) SEBI had found that it had insufficient power to police violations of regulations.[9] It continued to adapt and modify regulations as it learned more about how to regulate financial markets. (*b*) Takeovers continued to be difficult given the paucity of timely information and high transactions costs in both the primary and the secondary equity markets.[10] (*c*) There was still little competition among financial intermediaries. The state-run intermediaries were still saddled with bad loans, which affected their ability to act as monitors. (*d*) Disclosure problems continued to abound. Financial results were published only at half-yearly intervals, and the absence of consolidated accounts reduced the transparency of business-group performance.

8. In 1993–94, many firms issued preferential equity allotments to the controlling shareholders at steeply discounted prices.

9. In a celebrated 1995 case, the stock price of the firm MS Shoes was driven up sharply prior to a new issue by misinformation in its prospectus combined with price rigging. This triggered a series of events that closed down the country's primary stock exchange, the Bombay Stock Exchange, for three days and exposed inadequacies in the regulation of merchant bankers and underwriters, too many poor-quality stock issues, information-disclosure problems, etc.

10. A detailed account can be found in SEBI (1994). The need to transact physically imposes limits on trading volumes and on the speed at which orders can be handled. With the open outcry system (as opposed to screen-based trading), it is difficult to establish audit trails. There were no depositories, making settlement difficult (and no legislative means to establish depositories). Trades were often consummated outside the exchange. This left much room for manipulation, with cases of fraud becoming legion.

### 9.1.3 Relative Monitoring Costs for Groups and Nongroups

Failure to monitor in India, as in several other emerging economies, leads to severe costs. But policy prescriptions require a better understanding of the factors that exacerbate, and those that mitigate, such costs. This, in turn, is likely to be based on a richer understanding of the form that insider control takes and of the nature of the interaction between the insiders and the outside monitors. Very few studies, however, have paid attention to the form that insider control takes. In particular, many large corporations in most emerging markets are members of business groups, often family controlled.[11] While these groups may serve some useful functions,[12] they have a handful of features that make them likely to be less well monitored than nongroup affiliates in the country in question. All these features are commonly believed to be true about many Indian groups.

First, groups are generally alleged to suffer from a greater lack of transparency than stand-alone unaffiliated firms and thereby to be less susceptible to pressure from external monitors. This lack of transparency generally has to do with the ability of the controlling shareholders to move funds across firms within the group, often without adequate disclosure. Such lending to related parties, and the associated lack of accountability, has been viewed as the source of some celebrated financial market failures in recent times in emerging markets.[13] The lack of transparency also arises, especially in many economies in Asia and Latin America, because groups are controlled by extended families that strive to protect their privacy by revealing very little of the group's internal activities.

Second, a common characteristic of groups in many countries is the presence of equity interlocks among the member firms.[14] These exacerbate the transparency problem, particularly when the interlocks involve firms that are not publicly traded. The financial interlocks are also commonly

11. For broad discussions of the phenomenon of business groups in different countries, see Leff (1976, 1978), Amsden and Hikino (1994), Granovetter (1994), and Khanna and Palepu (1997). For Central America, see Strachan (1976). For Belgium, see Daems (1977). For France, see Encaoua and Jacquemin (1982). For Indonesia, see Robison (1986) and Schwartz (1992). For India, see Ghemawat and Khanna (1998), Herdeck and Piramal (1985), Piramal (1996), and Ghemawat and Khanna (1998). For Japan, see Caves and Uekusa (1976), Goto (1982), Aoki (1990), Hoshi, Kashyap, and Scharfstein (1991), and Berglof and Perotti (1994). For Korea, see Chang and Choi (1988) and Amsden (1989). For Mexico, see Camp (1989). For Pakistan, see White (1974).

12. Khanna and Palepu (1997, 1999, 2000, in press), and Fisman and Khanna (1998) have documented some of the useful roles that groups play in India and Chile.

13. A prominent and much-studied example is that of Chile's financial collapse in the early 1980s (see, e.g., the overview in Bosworth, Dornbusch, and Laban [1994]). Unaccounted-for lending and inadequate supervision among business groups are also among the cited causes of the governance problems in the recent financial crisis in Asia.

14. See, e.g., Daems (1977) on interlocks in Belgium, Nyberg (1995) on Sweden and Japan, and Berglof (1995) on the nontransparent web of cross-holdings in Hungary that protects insiders.

believed to be an antitakeover defense mechanism, again insulating firms from control by outsiders.

Third, groups are generally able to reap economies of scale by lobbying the political apparatus and securing favors from bureaucrats and politicians. This is the root of much of the asserted rent-seeking behavior in which groups are often believed to indulge. One form of such rent seeking is to use political connections to prevent outside intervention and to erect barriers to competition in those areas in which groups are disproportionately active.

## 9.2 Data

### 9.2.1 Data Sources and Sample Selection

The data for our research are obtained primarily from a publicly available database maintained by the Centre for Monitoring the Indian Economy (CMIE). CMIE is a privately run, twenty-year-old, Bombay-based firm that maintains databases on private- and public-sector economic activity in India. The database from which we draw our information is analogous to an abridged version of the Compustat database in the United States.[15] The database has computerized information drawn from the annual reports, other regulatory filings, and press releases of several thousand firms operating in India as well as daily stock prices for firms on the Bombay Stock Exchange (BSE). Of all the firms in the database, approximately half are traded on the BSE, with the remainder traded on the several other stock exchanges in the country. In the version of the database to which we have access, the most information is available for 1993. Coverage for subsequent years is sparser owing to delayed release of information by the firms and delays in updating the database.

The data set that we use in our analysis consists of all non-group- and group-affiliated Indian private-sector firms listed on the BSE with the required data. We confine our analysis in this paper to the BSE firms because these are the only firms for which ownership data are available and because we use stock-price data in our tests. For those estimations for which a year of data suffices, we choose 1993 because it is the year for which the coverage of BSE firms is complete. For those estimations for which we need data at two points in time, we identify a subset of BSE firms for which we have data for both 1990 and 1994 and examine the changes between these two time periods.

15. CMIE sells this database under the name *CIMM* (Computerized Information on Magnetic Medium). CIMM has become a standard database used by researchers and management professionals to analyze Indian corporations. As a recent example, Ahuja and Majumdar (1995) use these data to examine the performance of Indian state-owned enterprises.

### 9.2.2 Identifying Business-Group Affiliation

The identification of a firm's business-group affiliation is of particular importance for our empirical tests. For this purpose, we adopt the database's classification of firms into groups.[16] The identification of group membership is more reliable in India than in several other countries for at least two reasons. First, unlike in a variety of countries (Strachan 1976; Goto 1982), firms in India are members of only one group. Further, there is virtually no movement of firms across groups because of little merger activity in India.[17]

As a check on the quality of group construction, we verify data from the CMIE database against detailed case studies that identify firms of three prominent groups, Tata (Khanna, Palepu, and Wu 1998), Thapar (Ghemawat 1996), and RPG Enterprises (Khanna 1996). We also perform similar tests for a random sample of smaller groups largely to our satisfaction. Finally, we also verify that the names of groups that appear within the top one hundred (by sales or assets) appear on lists published by prominent business magazines[18] and that large groups mentioned in historical accounts (Herdeck and Piramal 1985) are present in our database if the groups survive to this day.[19]

The largest groups are very diversified, employ hundreds of thousands

16. While a group is not a legal construct, CMIE uses a variety of sources to classify firms into groups. Prior to the repeal of the Monopolies and Restrictive Trade Practices Act in 1991, a comprehensive list of firms belonging to "large industrial houses" was published by the government. This forms a starting point for the CMIE classification for a number of the groups. Beyond this, those promoting a firm when it was first started are identified and whether the original owners remained affiliated with the firm traced; the interest that a group has in a particular firm as revealed by its presence on the board of directors is identified; also consulted are announcements by individual firms of the groups with which they are affiliated and lists of affiliated firms that are made public by the groups (such information appears periodically in annual reports and advertisements and, at the time of public offerings, in news releases about the groups' and the firms' plans for the future). CMIE also regularly monitors changes in group structure. Shifts in group affiliation are extremely rare, but, when they do occur, they are reflected in the database. Note that the database does not contain a historical record of each firm's affiliation with different groups; rather, the group-membership variable reflects the most current affiliation. There is no ambiguity between CMIE's classification of firms into groups and classifications attempted by other sources against which we cross-checked the data.

17. In the case of family-controlled groups, succession from one generation to another often results in the group being split into multiple parts. We identified several prominent groups that had gone through such periods of succession in the past twenty years and checked to see that CMIE had indeed classified each subgroup separately. Thus, the Birla group is classified in several different parts, as is the group originally run by the Goenkas.

18. The *Economic Times,* a daily financial newspaper analogous to the *Wall Street Journal; Business India* and *Business World,* analogous to *Fortune* or *Forbes.*

19. Note that there are a small number of groups for which information on only one firm is available for a particular year. Such firms are nonetheless classified as group affiliated. The classification as group or nongroup is not inferred solely from the number of entries appearing in the database.

of people, and are very complex to manage.[20] Firms in Indian groups are tied by a common ownership of a significant block of shares in group firms, often by a family. This family ownership cements formal and informal relationships among group firms. The large groups also appear to have the best relationships with the bureaucracy, a fact that confers ongoing advantages in an economy enmeshed in a "kafkaesque maze of controls" (Bhagwati 1993).

Our analysis primarily focuses on the performance of individual firms rather than on group performance. We think that it is sensible to run our estimations using firm-level performance measures rather than group-level measures for several reasons. First, each firm is a publicly traded entity responsible to its own shareholders. Indeed, the group itself, the clarity of its identification notwithstanding, is not a legal construct. The separate legal standing of each firm implies that there are ownership-structure differences across firms in a group. Second, a great deal of variation in performance would be lost if we aggregated firm performance measures into group measures. Indeed, industry-adjusted performance varies substantially across the members of a group. Third, groups differ in the extent to which firms are bound together by social and economic ties. Using group-level performance measures implicitly assumes that the extent of interlock is similar across groups. Instead, we use an estimation approach in order explicitly to recognize that there are group-level unobservables that cause the error term in our specifications to be correlated across members of a particular group.

Because Indian business groups are a collection of public firms, the group's ability to use "internal capital markets" to fund the ongoing activities of one group firm from the cash flows of the other group firms is limited. Therefore, the most important role of the group's internal capital market is to launch new ventures, in which both the family and the other group affiliates might acquire ownership stakes. In this respect, Indian business groups are closer to the leveraged-buyout (LBO) associations than to the diversified public corporations in the United States.

A comparison to Japanese *keiretsu* is also instructive. The main bank in the *keiretsu* has been likened to a central office in a large firm, "providing capital and managerial support, in exchange for . . . an ownership stake in the firm and some say in how it is run" (Hoshi, Kashyap, and Scharfstein 1991, 40), although the *keiretsu* firms have weaker links than do divisions of a U.S. firm. Like the *keiretsu* firms, firms in an Indian group are legally separate entities, have their own shareholders, and publish their own statements. By regulatory fiat, however, there is no group-specific

20. For an analysis that shows that the performance effects of affiliation with a diversified business group are quite different in a country such as India than they are in an advanced economy such as the United States, see Khanna and Palepu (1997).

bank in India. Nonetheless, there is some coordination of actions among group members, partially orchestrated through common board members and through the involvement of the family in each group.

### 9.2.3 Definitions of Dependent and Independent Variables

We use as our primary dependent variable a proxy for Tobin's $q$, which we define as (market value of equity + book value of preferred stock + book value of debt)/(book value of assets), where the market value of equity is calculated using closing stock prices on the last trading day of the year.[21] Data limitations preclude us from computing as close an approximation to Tobin's $q$ as some prior studies have done.[22] However, the data we use is superior in an important way. Prior U.S. studies do not have line-of-business Tobin's $q$'s as the data needed to compute these are not available; they have accordingly had to compare the Tobin's $q$'s of diversified firms to comparable portfolios of Tobin's $q$'s of single-line-of-business firms. Since firms in Indian groups are separately traded, we can compute the equivalent of line-of-business Tobin's $q$'s and can therefore perform a more direct comparison than has been feasible using U.S. data.

The analysis rests on various categories of ownership measures. Foreign institutional ownership aggregates ownership of foreign corporations as well as that of foreign financial intermediaries. Domestic institutional ownership aggregates ownership in the hands of all state-run financial intermediaries, including banks supervised by both the central and the state governments, state-run insurance firms, and state-run mutual funds. Insider ownership includes the stakes held by the group family members and by other group firms, and, for nongroup firms, it measures the stakes held by insiders. This measure is a little difficult to interpret since it stands for somewhat different things for group affiliates and for nongroup firms. Directors' ownership captures the ownership of nonfamily directors. Finally, top fifty ownership captures the largest shareholders not captured in the categories listed above.

Finally, we need to define certain terms used in our analyses of the determinants of the levels of foreign and domestic institutional ownership. In particular, for the group affiliates, we use three measures of intragroup financial transactions: *investments in group firms* is the firm's total investment in shares and debentures of other group affiliates; *receivables from group firms* includes short-term deposits and loans (those with a maturity

21. None of the results are sensitive to the use of prices at different times, or an average market price over the year, for the construction of our approximation to Tobin's $q$.

22. Other studies that have computed $q$ in some detail include Lindenberg and Ross (1981), Montgomery and Wernerfelt (1988), Wernerfelt and Montgomery (1988), and Lang and Stulz (1994). Lang and Stulz (1994), e.g., use several years of data to compute the replacement value of assets under some assumptions, a step that we are unable to replicate as we have only one year of good data.

of less than one year) given by the firm to others in the group; *loans from group firms* is the loans received by the firm from others in the group. Past performance is defined as the simple average of as many annual measures of Tobin's $q$ (computed as above) as are available for the firm in question. Variability in past performance is defined as the variance of daily stock returns over the prior year.

## 9.3 Results

### 9.3.1 Summary Statistics

Table 9.1 reports some summary statistics for our sample of firms, using 1993 data. The sample consists of 567 group affiliates and 437 unaffiliated firms, all publicly traded on the BSE. The group affiliates are members of 252 different groups, with 95 percent of the groups having five or fewer

**Table 9.1** **Summary Statistics**

| | Group Firms | | Nongroup Firms | |
|---|---|---|---|---|
| Variable | Mean | Median | Mean | Median |
| Sales (million rupees) | 1,411 | 666 | 366 | 217 |
| Age (years) | 28.3 | 22 | 19.8 | 14 |
| Tobin's $q$ | 1.39 | 1.14 | 1.37 | 1.06 |
| Change in Tobin's $q$ | 0.62 | 0.31 | 0.48 | 0.24 |
| Ownership by foreign institutional investors (%) | 10.1 | 2.3 | 7.4 | 0.9 |
| Ownership by Indian institutional investors (%) | 15.6 | 13.3 | 11.3 | 6.5 |
| Ownership by insiders (%) | 31.9 | 31.3 | 20.8 | 17.1 |
| Directors' ownership (%) | 5.7 | 1.1 | 14.2 | 10.7 |
| Top fifty owners excluding the above categories (%) | 4.9 | 3.2 | 7.6 | 5 |
| Number of firms | 567 | 567 | 437 | 437 |

*Source:* Data obtained from CMIE for 567 affiliates of 252 different groups and for 437 unaffiliated firms traded on the BSE.

*Note:* The summary statistics in this table are based on 1993 values. Tobin's $q$ is defined as (market value of equity + book value of preferred stock + book value of debt)/(book value of assets). Sales are measured in millions of rupees, with an approximate exchange rate at this time of U.S.$1.00 = Rs 30.00. Age measures number of years since incorporation. Foreign institutional ownership aggregates ownership of foreign corporations as well as that of foreign financial intermediaries. Domestic institutional ownership aggregates ownership in the hands of all state-run financial intermediaries. Insider ownership includes the stakes held by group family members and by other group firms and measures stakes held by insiders for nongroup firms. Directors' ownership captures the ownership of nonfamily directors. Top fifty ownership captures the largest shareholders not included in aforementioned categories. Group membership is based on definitions of groups from CMIE and is described in the text. The mean and median values for all the variables except for the mean value of Tobin's $q$ and change in Tobin's $q$ are significantly different between the group and nongroup firms at the 5 percent significance level.

affiliates traded on the BSE and the largest group having twenty one affiliates traded on the BSE. The mean (median) sales of the firms in the sample are Rs 962 million (Rs 384 million), the mean (median) age is twenty five years (seventeen years), and the mean (median) $q$ is 1.39 (1.10). The table shows that, relative to unaffiliated firms, group affiliates are statistically significantly larger and older (using either means or medians as the basis for comparison). Mean Tobin's $q$ is no different across group affiliates and unaffiliated firms, although the median Tobin's $q$ of group affiliates is statistically significantly greater (at the 5 percent level) than that of unaffiliated firms.

The mean (median) ownership structure of the firms in our sample is as follows: foreign institutional ownership, 8.9 percent (1.6 percent); domestic institutional ownership, 13.9 percent (10.2 percent); insider ownership, 27.1 percent (26.5 percent); directors' ownership, 9.4 percent (3.4 percent); top fifty owners, 6.1 percent (4.0 percent). The remainder are held by dispersed shareholders. As shown in table 9.1, relative to unaffiliated firms, group affiliates have higher percentages of foreign and domestic institutional ownership, higher percentages of insider ownership, and lower percentages of directors' ownership and top fifty ownership. All these differences in categories of ownership are statistically significant at conventional levels (using either means or medians as the basis for comparison).

Table 9.1 also reports changes in Tobin's $q$ between 1990 and 1994 (for the subsample of firms for which we have data for both 1990 and 1994). The mean change in Tobin's $q$ across the entire sample is 0.58, statistically significantly different from zero at the 1 percent level. The median change in Tobin's $q$ is 0.28, with 374 firms reporting positive changes in Tobin's $q$ and 114 reporting negative changes in Tobin's $q$ (the probability of this relative pattern of positive and negative changes in Tobin's $q$ being generated by a binomial [$n = 488$, $p = 0.5$] process is close to zero). The mean (median) change in Tobin's $q$ for group affiliates is 0.62 (0.31), with the mean being significantly different from zero, with 264 of 332 group affiliates reporting positive changes in Tobin's $q$. The mean (median) change in Tobin's $q$ for unaffiliated firms is 0.48 (0.24), with the mean being significantly different from zero, with 110 of 156 unaffiliated firms reporting positive changes in Tobin's $q$. The mean change in Tobin's $q$ for group affiliates is not statistically significantly different from that for unaffiliated firms. However, the median change in Tobin's $q$ for group affiliates is statistically significantly greater, at the 5 percent level, than that for unaffiliated firms.

### 9.3.2 Univariate Analysis

Panel A of table 9.2 displays mean and median Tobin's $q$ values for group affiliates and unaffiliated firms, broken down by "high"- and "low"-foreign-ownership categories. The sample median value of foreign ownership, 1.61 percent, is used to divide the sample into high- and low-foreign-

**Table 9.2 Univariate Tests of Relation between Foreign and Domestic Institutional Ownership and Tobin's *q***

| | Number of Firms | Mean Tobin's *q* | Median Tobin's *q* |
|---|---|---|---|
| | A. Relation between Tobin's *q* and Foreign Institutional Ownership | | |
| Firms with high foreign institutional ownership: | | | |
| Group firms | 306 | 1.58 | 1.26 |
| Nongroup firms | 196 | 1.54 | 1.22 |
| Firms with low foreign institutional ownership: | | | |
| Group firms | 261 | 1.18*** | 1.01*** |
| Nongroup firms | 241 | 1.23 | 0.98 |
| | B. Relation between Tobin's *q* and Domestic Institutional Ownership | | |
| Firms with high domestic institutional ownership: | | | |
| Group firms | 326 | 1.35 | 1.12 |
| Nongroup firms | 176 | 1.43 | 1.09 |
| Firms with low domestic institutional ownership: | | | |
| Group firms | 241 | 1.45 | 1.18 |
| Nongroup firms | 261 | 1.33 | 1.04 |

*Source:* Data obtained from CMIE for 1,004 firms (group affiliated and unaffiliated) traded on the BSE.

*Note:* Tobin's $q$ is defined as (market value of equity + book value of preferred stock + book value of debt)/(book value of assets). Foreign institutional ownership aggregates ownership of foreign corporations as well as that of foreign financial intermediaries. Domestic institutional ownership aggregates ownership in the hands of all state-run financial intermediaries. Group membership is based on definitions of groups from CMIE and is described in the text.

In panel A, firms with high (low) foreign institutional ownership are defined as those for which foreign institutional ownership exceeds (is less than) the sample median value for foreign institutional ownership, 1.61 percent. In panel B, firms with high (low) domestic institutional ownership are defined as those for which domestic institutional ownership exceeds (is less than) the sample median value for domestic institutional ownership, 10.16 percent. Significance levels refer to difference of means or median tests between the high- and low-ownership categories. Mean differences are tested using a $t$-test with unequal variances; median differences are tested using the Wilcoxon signed-rank test.

In panel B, the mean (median) value for the high-domestic-ownership firms is not statistically significantly different from the mean (median) value for low-domestic-ownership firms. Group and nongroup firms' mean (median) values of Tobin's $q$ are not significantly different for the high-domestic-ownership subsample; for the low-domestic-ownership subsample, the means are not different between group and nongroup firms, but the medians are different at the 5 percent level.

***Significantly different from the mean (median) value for the high-foreign-ownership firms at the 1 percent level. Group and nongroup firms' mean (median) values of Tobin's $q$ are not significantly different for either the high- or the low-foreign-ownership subsample.

ownership categories. Mean Tobin's *q* is higher for the high-foreign-ownership category, for each of the group and nongroup samples, with the difference in means being significant at the 1 percent level. This is supportive of the notion that foreign institutional ownership is correlated with higher performance, both for group firms and for nongroup firms. The univariate tests do not support the notion that any beneficial effects of foreign institutional ownership are less likely to be felt in groups than in nongroups. For each of the high- and low-foreign-ownership categories, there is no statistically significant difference in mean Tobin's *q* between group and nongroup firms.

The median results in the same panel yield identical results. Median Tobin's *q* is higher for the high-foreign-ownership category than it is for the low-foreign-ownership category, for both groups and nongroups. The difference of medians is significant at the 1 percent level (Wilcoxon signed-rank test) in both instances. However, within each of the high- and low-foreign-ownership categories, there is no statistically significant difference in medians across groups and nongroups, although median Tobin's *q* is higher for group firms than for nongroup firms.

Similar univariate tests are performed for "high" and "low" categories of domestic institutional ownership and reported in panel B of table 9.2. The sample median value of domestic institutional ownership, 10.16 percent, is used to divide the sample into high- and low-domestic-ownership categories. There is no significant difference in the mean (and median) Tobin's *q* between high- and low-domestic-ownership firms for either the group-firm subsample or the nongroup-firm subsample. These univariate statistics do not suggest a positive relation between domestic institutional ownership and firm performance. There is also no evidence of a significant difference between the mean and the median Tobin's *q* between group and nongroup firms, in the subsample with high domestic institutional ownership; in the low-domestic-ownership subsample, the mean *q* is not significantly different, but the median *q* is significantly higher for the group firms than for the nongroup firms.

We also perform similar univariate tests of the relation between changes in Tobin's *q* and foreign and domestic institutional ownership, reported in table 9.3. Here high and low foreign and domestic institutional ownership are defined on the basis of the medians of the sample on which the changes in Tobin's *q* analyses are carried out (the medians are 3.1 percent for foreign ownership and 14.3 percent for domestic ownership). As reported in panel A of table 9.3, we find that the mean and median changes in Tobin's *q* for group affiliates are significantly higher for the high-foreign-ownership sample than for the low-foreign-ownership sample. In contrast, the changes in Tobin's *q* are not statistically significantly different across high- and low-foreign-ownership samples for unaffiliated firms.

As reported in panel B of table 9.3, we also find that mean change in

**Table 9.3** **Univariate Tests of Relation between Foreign and Domestic Institutional Ownership and Change in Tobin's $q$ between 1990 and 1994**

| | Number of Firms | Mean Change in Tobin's $q$ |
|---|---|---|
| | A. Relation between Change in Tobin's $q$ and Foreign Institutional Ownership | |
| Firms with high foreign institutional ownership: | | |
| Group firms | 176 | .81 |
| Nongroup firms | 68 | .62 |
| Firms with low foreign institutional ownership: | | |
| Group firms | 156 | .42*** |
| Nongroup firms | 88 | .38 |
| | B. Relation between Change in Tobin's $q$ and Domestic Institutional Ownership | |
| Firms with high domestic institutional ownership: | | |
| Group firms | 185 | .50 |
| Nongroup firms | 59 | .44 |
| Firms with low domestic institutional ownership: | | |
| Group firms | 147 | .78** |
| Nongroup firms | 97 | .50 |

*Source:* Data obtained from CMIE, for 488 firms (group affiliated and unaffiliated) traded on the BSE for which data exist for both 1990 and 1994.

*Note:* Tobin's $q$ is defined as (market value of equity + book value of preferred stock + book value of debt)/(book value of assets). Foreign institutional ownership aggregates ownership of foreign corporations as well as that of foreign financial intermediaries. Domestic institutional ownership aggregates ownership in the hands of all state-run financial intermediaries. Group membership is based on definitions of groups from CMIE and is described in the text.

In panel A, firms with high (low) foreign institutional ownership are defined as those for which foreign institutional ownership exceeds (is less than) the sample median value for foreign institutional ownership, 3.07 percent. In panel B, firms with high (low) domestic institutional ownership are defined as those for which domestic institutional ownership exceeds (is less than) the sample median value for domestic institutional ownership, 14.30 percent. Significance levels refer to difference of means or median tests between the high- and low-ownership categories. Mean differences are tested using a $t$-test with unequal variances; median differences are tested using the Wilcoxon signed-rank test.

**Significantly different from the relevant value for the high-domestic-ownership firms at the 5 percent level. The mean value for the high-domestic-ownership firms is not statistically significantly different from the mean (median) value for low-domestic-ownership firms. Group and nongroup firms' mean (median) values of Tobin's $q$ are not significantly different for the high-domestic-ownership subsample; for the low-domestic-ownership subsample, the means and medians are different between group and nongroup firms at the 10 percent level.

***Significantly different from the relevant value for the high-foreign-ownership firms at the 1 percent level. The mean value is not different between high- and low-foreign-ownership samples for the nongroup firms.

Tobin's $q$ is statistically significantly lower for group affiliates with higher domestic institutional ownership than for those with lower domestic institutional ownership, although the difference in the median change in Tobin's $q$ is not statistically significant. Neither the mean nor the median changes in Tobin's $q$ are statistically significantly different across the high- and low-domestic-ownership categories for the unaffiliated firms.

These univariate results suggest that changes in Tobin's $q$ are generally positively correlated with the presence of foreign institutional ownership and negatively correlated with the presence of domestic institutional ownership, with the effects being stronger for group affiliates than for unaffiliated firms.

### 9.3.3 The Effect of Ownership Structure on Performance

Regression results reported in table 9.4 examine the effects of different categories of owners on performance. Using OLS for these estimations implicitly assumes that the error term is uncorrelated across the firms in a group. However, this assumption may be unwarranted, especially across firms affiliated with a group. Following Moulton (1990), we note that observations sharing an observable characteristic like group membership may also share unobservable characteristics that may cause the error terms to be correlated. This would cause the standard errors obtained using OLS to be understated, leading to potentially spurious claims of statistical significance, with the problem being more acute the greater the extent of within-group unobservable correlations (Moulton 1986). Accordingly, we use an estimation approach that assumes that observations are independent across groups but relaxes the independence assumption within groups. Additionally, the standard errors reported are also heteroskedastic-consistent White standard errors. All estimations control for industry fixed effects.

Model 1 regresses Tobin's $q$ on the levels of different categories of ownership for the 983 firms for which the required data exist in 1993. The specification includes variables to control for size (log of sales) and age. The results show that the presence of foreign institutional investors is correlated with higher values of Tobin's $q$ (significant at the 1 percent level). The presence of domestic institutional investors has no discernible effect. The only other ownership category with a statistically significant effect is that of insider ownership, which is positively correlated with Tobin's $q$ (significant at the 1 percent level). We note that the effects of foreign institutional ownership and insider ownership are roughly equal in magnitude (the mean foreign institutional ownership is one-third the mean insider ownership, but the point estimate of the former is roughly three times larger than that of the latter).

Model 2 repeats the previous specification but allows for different effects of foreign and domestic institutional ownership across group affiliates

**Table 9.4 Multivariate Regression Analysis of the Relation between Tobin's $q$ and Ownership Structure**

| Dependent Variable | Model 1, 1993 Tobin's $q$ | Model 2, 1993 Tobin's $q$ | Model 3, Panel Data 1990–94, Tobin's $q$ | Model 4, Change in Tobin's $q$, 1990–94 |
|---|---|---|---|---|
| Constant | 0.582** | 0.608** | 1.746*** | −0.666* |
| | (2.286) | (2.325) | (3.686) | (−1.903) |
| Log sales | 0.030 | 0.028 | 0.202*** | 0.158*** |
| | (1.176) | (1.097) | (7.624) | (2.893) |
| Age | −0.005*** | −0.005*** | −0.004** | −0.003 |
| | (−2.821) | (−3.004) | (−2.384) | (−0.701) |
| Foreign institutional ownership | 0.019*** | 0.020*** | 0.013*** | 0.014*** |
| | (6.064) | (3.727) | (4.544) | (2.871) |
| Domestic institutional ownership | 0.001 | −0.002 | −0.007** | −0.008* |
| | (0.258) | (−0.756) | (−2.324) | (−1.925) |
| Insider ownership | 0.008*** | 0.008*** | 0.006** | 0.005 |
| | (3.324) | (3.385) | (2.058) | (1.259) |
| Directors' ownership | 0.003 | 0.003 | 0.001 | 0.003 |
| | (0.993) | (1.035) | (0.193) | (0.516) |
| Other top fifty owners | 0.006 | 0.006 | −0.001 | 0.011 |
| | (1.476) | (1.447) | (−0.217) | (1.148) |
| Group dummy | −0.053 | −0.114 | −0.076 | −0.036 |
| | (−0.734) | (−0.976) | (−0.924) | (−0.317) |
| Foreign institutional ownership × group dummy | Not included | −0.001 (−0.104) | Not included | Not included |
| Domestic institutional ownership × group dummy | Not included | 0.005 (1.235) | Not included | Not included |
| Industry fixed effects | Estimates suppressed | Estimates suppressed | Estimates suppressed | Estimates suppressed |
| Number of observations | 983 | 983 | 2,435 | 487 |
| $R^2$ | 0.094 | 0.096 | 0.094 | 0.116 |
| | $F = 5.17$*** | $F = 4.86$*** | $\chi^2 = 143.42$*** | $F = 2.45$*** |

*Source:* Data obtained from CMIE for group-affiliated and unaffiliated firms traded on the BSE.

*Note:* Tobin's $q$ is defined as (market value of equity + book value of preferred stock + book value of debt)/(book value of assets). Sales are measured in millions of rupees, with an approximate exchange rate at this time of U.S.$1.00 = Rs 30.00. Age measures number of years since incorporation. Foreign institutional ownership aggregates ownership of foreign corporations as well as that of foreign financial intermediaries. Domestic institutional ownership aggregates ownership in the hands of all state-run financial intermediaries. Insider ownership includes the stakes held by group family members and by other group firms and measures stakes held by insiders for nongroup firms. Directors' ownership captures the ownership of nonfamily directors. Top 50 ownership captures the largest shareholders not included in aforementioned categories. Group membership is based on definitions of groups from CMIE and is described in the text. OLS estimation is used for models 1, 2, and 4, but we relax the assumption of independence of the error term within groups, following Moulton (1986, 1990). Model 3 reports results of a random-effects generalized-least-squares panel estimation. The $t$-statistics reported in parentheses are based on standard errors that correct for heteroskedasticity.

*Significant at the 10 percent level.

**Significant at the 5 percent level.

***Significant at the 1 percent level.

and unaffiliated firms. The results show no support for the hypothesis that there is a significant difference in the relation between performance and institutional ownership (either foreign or domestic) between group and nongroup firms.[23] This is inconsistent with the notion that institutional investors find it more difficult to monitor business groups relative to non-group firms.

It is important to exercise caution in interpreting the observed positive relation between performance and the level of foreign institutional ownership. Our analysis cannot distinguish between the possibility that foreign institutional investors are buying better-managed firms, on the one hand, and the possibility that foreign institutional investors are bringing to bear improved governance on firms, on the other. However, if we knew that foreign ownership existed prior to 1993, then a correlation of foreign institutional ownership with the Tobin's $q$ in 1993 would be less likely to support the former hypothesis.[24] Accordingly, we reestimate both regression 1 and regression 2 for the sample of firms for which our ownership data is pre-1993 and find no difference in the results.[25] We interpret this as suggestive of a governance role played by foreign institutional investors.

We also have access to some data for other years surrounding 1993. We estimate similar year-by-year specifications for each of these years; again, in all cases, foreign institutional shareholding is positively significantly correlated with Tobin's $q$, while domestic institutional shareholding is sometimes significantly negatively correlated with Tobin's $q$.

We also report the results of a random-effects generalized-least-squares panel estimation (model 3) for the 488 firms for which we had data for the five-year period 1990–94.[26] This sample is half the size of the sample used for the earlier specifications, although the proportion of group affiliates is higher in this sample: 68 percent versus 57 percent for the earlier, 1993 sample. The mean Tobin's $q$ for the panel of firms is not different from that for the earlier 1993 sample.

The panel estimation confirms the earlier results, but we also find that domestic institutional ownership is negatively correlated with Tobin's $q$.

23. We also include an interaction term between insider ownership and group membership. The point estimate on this term is positive, with a $p$-value of 0.14; the magnitude and significance of the other point estimates do not change appreciably.

24. This reasoning would be suspect the greater is the positive correlation between the 1993 Tobin's $q$ and the Tobin's $q$ of years immediately prior to 1993.

25. We know only when the ownership data were reported. It is possible, e.g., that ownership data reported in 1994 were accurate descriptors of the ownership structure in prior years as well.

26. The equation estimated is of the form $q_{it} = a + x_{it}\beta + v_i + \varepsilon_{it}$. The estimator is a weighted average of the estimates produced by the "between" estimator (which exploits the variation between the means of the firms and is based on the equation $q_i = a + \overline{x}_i\beta + v_i + \overline{\varepsilon}_i$) and the "within" estimator (or the fixed-effects estimator, which exploits the variation across the various observations within each firm and is based on an estimation of $[q_{it} - \overline{q}_i] = [x_{it} - \overline{x}_i]\beta + [\varepsilon_{it} - \overline{\varepsilon}_i]$).

We note that the magnitude of the effect of foreign institutional ownership (evaluated at the sample mean) is roughly the same as the magnitude of the effect of domestic institutional ownership. It is important to note the sources of variation underlying the panel estimation. Ownership values do not vary from year to year; however, firm sales, Tobin's *q*, and age do vary from year to year.[27] A $\chi^2$-test reveals the joint significance, at the 1 percent level, of all coefficients.[28]

In model 4, we look at the effects of ownership on changes in Tobin's *q*, using data from the firms in the 1990–94 balanced panel. The dependent variable is the change in Tobin's *q* between 1990 and 1994. OLS, with correlated errors permitted for firms belonging to a particular group, is employed again, with heteroskedastic-consistent standard errors reported. We find that foreign institutional ownership is positively correlated with changes in Tobin's *q* while domestic institutional ownership is negatively correlated with changes in Tobin's *q*; the other kinds of ownership do not display any correlation with the dependent variable. There is also no evidence of any differential effect across group affiliates and unaffiliated firms.[29]

A caveat about causality is in order with these estimations as well. We cannot reliably distinguish between the following two possibilities: (*a*) foreign institutional owners have improved corporate governance in the firms in which they invest and have thus caused increases in Tobin's *q*, and (*b*) foreign institutional investors have invested in those firms that ex ante showed the greatest likelihood of improving performance in the deregulating post-1991 environment.

To summarize thus far, there are significant differences in the relation between ownership and performance for domestic and foreign institutional investors in the early 1990s in India. The role of the foreign institutional investors is consistent with their provision of superior monitoring services. We are left, however, with a puzzle. In India, as in other countries, the rhetoric associated with the lack of transparency and opacity of business groups seems difficult to reconcile with there being no difference in the relation between performance and foreign ownership for group and nongroup firms. We investigate this issue further in the next section.

27. Given this, it is not surprising that the $R^2$ "between" is much higher than the $R^2$ "within." Note that these $R^2$'s do not have the property of OLS $R^2$'s, in the sense that they are not tantamount to the fraction of the variance explained. However, they are squared correlations of the prediction implied in the corresponding equation.

28. Since small-sample properties of the random-effects generalized least squares panel estimator are unknown, we do not report an *F*-statistic.

29. The reported estimations use 1993 values for log (sales) and age, although the results are not sensitive to using averages of these values over the period 1990–94. We also investigate an interaction term between insider ownership and group membership; the point estimate is not significant at conventional levels.

### 9.3.4 Determinants of Institutional Ownership

Table 9.5 reports the results of some estimations of the determinants of institutional ownership in India. In model 1, we estimate the extent of foreign ownership in a firm as a function of a set of firm and group characteristics. The estimation method is a tobit that allows for correlated errors across all firms in a particular group (i.e., the estimation assumes independence of the error term across all pairs of observations that are not members of the same group and allows for correlation in the error terms for all pairs of observations that are within a group). Firm characteristics include a measure of firm size (logarithm of sales), its past performance (measured as a simple average of the Tobin's $q$ values of past years), and its past variability in performance. One of the group characteristics of interest is the extent to which institutional investors invest in a group as opposed to in individual firms within the same group.[30] This would manifest itself as ownership stakes in multiple group firms. To address this, we compute the mean level of foreign ownership for all other firms in the same group as the firm in question and use this as one of our regressors. Since our interest is in understanding why the alleged opacity of groups does not appear to have any effect on monitoring, we also focus on the extent to which internal capital markets operate within groups. Discussions of lack of transparency of groups typically suggest that the major concern is the relatively fluid mobility of funds across group firms. To capture this construct empirically, for each firm we use as regressors measures of the extent to which it invests money in, lends money to, or is the recipient of receivables from other group affiliates (all these variables are set to zero for unaffiliated firms).

Model 1 demonstrates that foreign ownership is an increasing function of firm size and of past performance and a negative function of past variability in performance. Results also suggest that foreign institutional investors are less likely to invest in group firms relative to nongroup firms (the point estimate on the group dummy is negative and significant). However, if they do invest in group firms, foreign institutional owners appear to do so in those groups with minimal internal capital market transactions. All three of the measures that proxy for the use of internal capital markets have negative point estimates, with one being significant at the conven-

30. Why might institutional investors be swayed by group-level considerations rather than only by firm-level considerations? Amsden and Hikino (1994) have argued that the group served as an efficient organizational intermediary in the market for cross-border technology investments. Similarly, one might expect that the group could also serve as an efficient financial intermediary in the market for cross-border allocation of capital. To the extent that domestic institutional investment was at least partly a result of a noneconomic calculus, the group-level "industrial embassies" in the capital city designed to foster relations with the government (Encarnation 1989) should translate into the importance of group attributes in the determination of ownership stakes of domestic institutional investors.

**Table 9.5 Tobit Analysis of Relation between Foreign and Domestic Institutional Ownership and Firm and Group Characteristics**

| | Coefficient Estimate | |
|---|---|---|
| Variable | Model 1 (dependent variable is foreign institutional ownership) | Model 2 (dependent variable is domestic institutional ownership) |
| Constant | 5.310** | −4.190* |
| | (1.635) | (−1.625) |
| Group dummy | −3.750*** | −1.940 |
| | (−2.930) | (−1.492) |
| Log sales | 2.217*** | 4.190*** |
| | (4.280) | (8.560) |
| Past average Tobin's $q$ | 3.680*** | −0.959 |
| | (3.880) | (−1.540) |
| Past return variability | −0.003** | 0.000 |
| | (−2.166) | (0.173) |
| Average foreign (domestic) institutional investment in the other firms in the same group | 0.416*** | 0.117** |
| | (5.276) | (2.020) |
| Investment in other group firms (set to zero for nongroup firms) | −0.025 | 0.321*** |
| | (−0.255) | (2.836) |
| Receivables from other group firms (set to zero for nongroup firms) | −0.009 | 0.114* |
| | (−0.075) | (1.615) |
| Loans to other group firms (set to zero for nongroup firms) | −2.810* | 2.211 |
| | (−1.731) | (1.166) |
| Number of observations | 800 | 800 |
| Model $\chi^2$ | 195.4*** | 207.4*** |

*Source:* Data obtained from CMIE for group-affiliated and unaffiliated firms traded on the BSE.

*Note:* Tobin's $q$ is defined as (market value of equity + book value of preferred stock + book value of debt)/(book value of assets). Past performance is defined as the simple average of as many annual measures of Tobin's $q$ (computed as above) as available for the firm in question. Variability in past performance is defined as the variance of daily stock returns over the prior year. Sales are measured in millions of rupees, with an approximate exchange rate at this time of U.S.$1.00 = Rs 30.00. Group membership is based on definitions of groups from CMIE and is described in the text. Investment in other group firms is the firm's total investment in shares and debentures of other group affiliates and is set to zero for unaffiliated firms. Receivables from group firms includes short-term deposits and loans (maturity of less than one year) given by the firm to others in the group and is set to zero for unaffiliated firms. Loans from group firms is the loans received by the firm from others in the group and is set to zero for unaffiliated firms. The estimation method used is a tobit that allows for correlated errors across all firms in a group and assumes that errors are independent otherwise. $Z$-statistics are reported in parentheses.

*Significant at the 10 percent level.

**Significant at the 5 percent level.

***Significant at the 1 percent level.

tional level. We interpret this as evidence that foreign institutional investors seek out those groups where the lack of transparency is least likely to be a problem or invest in those groups where they are able to curtail the operation of internal capital markets and the loss of transparency that might result. The results also provide support for the idea that foreign institutional investors invest in groups rather than in individual firms. The variable that measures the average level of foreign ownership in other group affiliates has a positive coefficient (significant at the 1 percent level). We repeated these estimations for the subsample of group affiliates only, with qualitatively similar results.

As a point of comparison, model 2 estimates the relation between the level of domestic institutional ownership and firm characteristics. We find that the ownership stake is a positive function of size. However, in contrast to foreign ownership, there is no significant correlation between past performance and domestic institutional ownership. In fact, there is weak evidence that the correlation is negative. This result is consistent with Indian institutional investors having insufficient incentives to monitor performance and also with their perverse incentives to bail out troubled firms by investing in them further. Results also show that there is no significant difference in domestic institutional ownership between group affiliates and unaffiliated firms. However, as with foreign institutional investors, there appears to be some evidence that domestic institutional investors invest in groups as a whole rather than in individual firms in a group. The point estimate on the variable measuring investments in affiliates of the same group is positive and significant at the 5 percent level. Finally, in sharp contrast to the case of foreign institutional investors, domestic institutional investors appear to invest in groups where there is a high level of internal capital market activity. Each of the three indicators of internal capital market activity displays a positive sign, and two of them are significant at conventional levels.

In summary, we find that foreign institutional investors have substantially different effects on firm performance, as measured by Tobin's $q$, than do domestic institutional investors. The positive effects of the former, and the negative effects of the latter, however, are no different for group affiliates than they are for unaffiliated firms. This is inconsistent with the general perception that group affiliates are less transparent than are unaffiliated firms. A partial resolution of this puzzle appears to be that foreign institutional investors seek out those groups where transparency is less of a problem, in marked contrast to domestic institutional investors.

## 9.4 Summary

We investigate the relation between performance and ownership in India, an economy in the process of significant deregulation beginning in

1991. We investigate the interaction between three different kinds of concentrated owners in India: the insider ownership held by the families that manage the firms that constitute business groups; the ownership held by domestic financial institutions, typically acting in concert; and the ownership held by foreign financial institutions, recent arrivals on the Indian economic landscape.

Our study is motivated by several observations. A review of the literature suggests that the external monitoring of group affiliates poses more challenges than that of unaffiliated firms. Groups are reputed to be less transparent than nongroups and to have more opportunities, given their more complicated structures, to engage in questionable practices to the detriment of minority shareholders. Their generally better links to the political apparatus in the country also insulate them from external interference and monitoring. Domestic financial institutions in India are generally insufficiently oriented, if at all, toward the task of monitoring managers and are thus unlikely to exercise effective governance. Foreign institutional investors, only recently allowed to own shares in Indian companies, are a potential source not only of capital but also of monitoring technology from advanced capital markets.

Our evidence suggests that domestic financial institutions in India are ineffective monitors, whereas foreign institutional investment is associated with significant monitoring benefits: firm performance is positively correlated with the presence of foreign institutional ownership and negatively correlated with the presence of domestic institutional ownership. Surprisingly, however, we find that there is no evidence of a difference in this relation between group affiliates and unaffiliated firms, suggesting that monitoring is no less effective for group affiliates than it is for unaffiliated firms. At first glance, the lack of transparency of groups does not appear to pose a differential impediment to monitoring by foreign institutional investors.

We probe this further by investigating factors correlated with the presence of greater foreign institutional ownership (and compare those factors to factors correlated with the presence of greater domestic institutional ownership). After controlling for industry fixed effects, firm size, and the past performance of firms, we find that foreign owners are indeed less likely to invest in group affiliates than in unaffiliated firms, perhaps because of the problems associated with monitoring groups. However, when they do invest in groups, they appear to seek out those groups where the transparency problem, as proxied by the greater incidence of intragroup financial transactions, is lowest.

We interpret this collective evidence as suggesting that foreign institutional investors are a source not only of financing but also of scarce monitoring skills in emerging markets such as India. Given the rapidly accumulating evidence of the failure of domestic intermediaries in a number of emerging markets and the recent opening up to foreign investment of dozens of countries (Sachs and Warner 1995), these results regarding the nature of investments sought by foreign institutional investors and the effects of such investments on the governance of business groups that are traditionally viewed as difficult to monitor are worthy of note.

## References


Ahuja, Gautam, and Sumit Majumdar. 1995. An assessment of the performance of Indian state-owned enterprises. Working Paper no. 9550-10, Revision 1. University of Michigan, School of Business Administration.

Akamatsu, Noritaka. 1995. Enterprise governance and investment funds in Russian privatization. In *Corporate governance in transitional economies: Insider control and the role of banks,* ed. M. Aoki and H. Kim. Washington, D.C.: World Bank.

Amsden, Alice. 1989. *Asia's next giant: South Korea and late industrialization.* New York: Oxford University Press.

Amsden, Alice, and Takashi Hikino. 1994. Project execution capability, organizational know-how, and conglomerate corporate growth in late industrialization. *Industrial and Corporate Change* 3, no. 1:111–48.

Aoki, M. 1990. Toward an economic model of the Japanese firm. *Journal of Economic Literature* 28:1–27.

———. 1995. Controlling insider control: Issues of corporate governance in transition economies. In *Corporate governance in transitional economies: Insider control and the role of banks,* ed. M. Aoki and H. Kim. Washington, D.C.: World Bank.

Aoki, M., and H. Kim, eds. 1995. *Corporate governance in transitional economies: Insider control and the role of banks.* Washington, D.C.: World Bank.

Berglof, Eric. 1995. Corporate governance in transition economies: The theory and its policy implications. In *Corporate governance in transitional economies: Insider control and the role of banks,* ed. M. Aoki and H. Kim. Washington, D.C.: World Bank.

Berglof, Erik, and Enrico Perotti. 1994. The governance structure of the Japanese financial *keiretsu. Journal of Financial Economics* 36:259–84.

Bhagwati, Jagdish. 1993. *India in transition: Freeing the economy.* Oxford: Clarendon.

Blass, Asher, Yishay Yafeh, and Oved Yosha. 1997. Corporate governance in an emerging market: The case of Israel. *Journal of Applied Corporate Finance* 10, no. 4 (winter): 79–89.

Bosworth, Barry, Rudiger Dornbusch, and Raul Laban. 1994. *The Chilean economy: Policy lessons and challenges.* Washington, D.C.: Brookings.

Camp, Roderic A. 1989. *Entrepreneurs and politics in twentieth-century Mexico.* New York: Oxford University Press.

Caves, Richard, and M. Uekusa. 1976. *Industrial organization in Japan.* Washington, D.C.: Brookings.

Chang, Sea Jin, and Unghwan Choi. 1988. Strategy, structure, and performance of Korean business groups: A transactions cost approach. *Journal of Industrial Economics* 37, no. 2 (December): 141–58.

Daems, Herman. 1977. *The holding firm and corporate control.* Nijenrode Studies in Economics, vol. 3. Leiden: Nijhoff Social Sciences.

Diamond, Douglas. 1984. Financial intermediation and delegated monitoring. *Review of Economic Studies* 51:393–414.

Encaoua, David, and Alexis Jacquemin. 1982. Organizational efficiency and monopoly power: The case of French industrial groups. *European Economic Review* 19:25–51.

Encarnation, Dennis. 1989. *Dislodging multinationals: India's comparative perspective.* Ithaca, N.Y.: Cornell University Press.

Fisman, Raymond. 1998. The incentives to rent-seeking: Estimating the value of political connections. Columbia Business School. Mimeo.

Fisman, Raymond, and Tarun Khanna. 1998. Facilitating development: The role of business groups. Working paper. Harvard Business School.

Frydman, R., E. Phelps, A. Rapaczynski, and A. Shleifer. 1993. Needed mechanisms of corporate governance and finance in Eastern Europe. *Economics of Transition* 1, no. 2:171–207.

Ghemawat, Pankaj. 1996. Ballarpur industries. Case no. N9-798-067. Harvard Business School.

Ghemawat, Pankaj, and Tarun Khanna. 1998. The nature of diversified business groups: A research design and two case studies. *Journal of Industrial Economics* 46, no. 1 (March): 35–62.

Goswami, O., and R. Mohan. 1996. Industry: An unfinished agenda. In *India: Development policy imperatives,* ed. Vijay Kelkar and V. V. Bhanoji Rao. New Delhi: Tata McGraw-Hill.

Goto, Akira. 1982. Business groups in a market economy. *European Economic Review* 19:53–70.

Granovetter, Mark. 1994. Business groups. In *Handbook of economic sociology,* ed. Neil J. Smelser and Richard Swedberg. Princeton, N.J.: Princeton University Press.

Grossman, Sanford, and Joseph Stiglitz. 1980. On the impossibility of informationally efficient markets. *American Economic Review* 70, no. 3:393–408.

Herdeck, Margaret, and Gita Piramal. 1985. *India's industrialists.* Vol. 1. Washington, D.C.: Three Continents.

Holderness, C. G., and D. P. Sheehan. 1991. Monitoring an owner: The case of Turner Broadcasting. *Journal of Financial Economics* 30, no. 2 (December): 325–46.

Holmström, Bengt, and Jean Tirole. 1993. Market liquidity and performance monitoring. *Journal of Political Economy* 101, no. 4:679–707.

Hoshi, Takeo, Anil Kashyap, and David Scharfstein. 1991. Corporate structure, liquidity, and investment: Evidence from Japanese industrial groups. *Quarterly Journal of Economics* 106, no. 1:33–60.

Joshi, Vijay, and I. M. D. Little. 1997. *India's economic reforms, 1991–2001.* Delhi: Oxford University Press.

Khanna, Tarun. 1996. RPG Enterprises. Case 9-796-111. Harvard Business School.

Khanna, Tarun, and Krishna Palepu. 1997. Why focused strategies may be wrong for emerging markets. *Harvard Business Review* 75, no. 4 (July–August): 41–51.

———. 1999. Policy shocks, market intermediaries, and corporate strategy: The evolution of business groups in Chile and India. *Journal of Economics and Management Strategy* 8, no. 2:271–310.

———. 2000. Is group affiliation profitable in emerging markets? An analysis of diversified Indian business groups. *Journal of Finance* 55, no. 2:867–91.

———. In press. The future of business groups in emerging markets: Long-run evidence from Chile. *Academy of Management Journal.*

Khanna, Tarun, Krishna Palepu, and Danielle Melito Wu. 1998. House of Tata: The new generation. Case no. 9-798-037. Harvard Business School.

Khanna, Tarun, and Danielle Melito Wu. 1998. Empresas CAP. Case no. 9-798-053. Harvard Business School.

Krasa, Stefan, and Anne Villamil. 1992. Monitoring the monitor: An incentive structure for a financial intermediary. *Journal of Economic Theory* 57:197–221.

Kroszner, Randall. 1998. The political economy of banking and financial regulatory reform in emerging markets. *Research in Financial Services* 10:33–51.

Kroszner, Randall, and Raghu Rajan. 1997. Organizational structure and credibility: Evidence from commercial bank securities activities before the Glass-Steagall Act. *Journal of Monetary Economics* 39, no. 3:475–516.

Kyle, Albert. 1984. Market structure, information, futures markets, and price formation. In *International agricultural trade: Advanced readings in price formation, market structure, and price instability,* ed. Gary Storey, Andrew Schmitz, and Alexander Sarris. Boulder, Colo.: Westview.

Lang, Larry, and René Stulz. 1994. Tobin's *q*, corporate diversification, and firm performance. *Journal of Political Economy* 102:142–74.

La Porta, Rafael, Florencio Lopez-de-Silanes, Andrei Shleifer, and Robert Vishny. 1998. Law and finance. *Journal of Political Economy* 106, no. 6 (December): 1113–55.

Leff, Nathaniel. 1976. Capital markets in the less developed countries: The group principle. In *Money and finance in economic growth and development,* ed. Ronald McKinnon. New York: Marcel Dekker.

———. 1978. Industrial organization and entrepreneurship in the developing countries: The economic groups. *Economic Development and Cultural Change* 26 (July): 661–75.

Lindenberg, E. B., and S. A. Ross. 1981. Tobin's *q* ratio and industrial organization. *Journal of Business* 54, no. 1:1–32.

Litwack, John. 1995. Corporate governance, banks, and fiscal reform in Russia. In *Corporate governance in transitional economies: Insider control and the role of banks,* ed. M. Aoki and H. Kim. Washington, D.C.: World Bank.

Montgomery, Cynthia, and Birger Wernerfelt. 1988. Diversification, Ricardian rents, and Tobin's *q*. *Rand Journal of Economics* 19:623–32.

Moulton, B. R. 1986. Random group effects and the precision of regression estimates. *Journal of Econometrics* 32, no. 3:385–97.

———. 1990. An illustration of a pitfall in estimating the effects of aggregate variables on micro units. *Review of Economics and Statistics* 72:334–38.

Nyberg, S. 1995. Reciprocal shareholding and takeover deterrence. *International Journal of Industrial Organization* 12:355–72.

Piramal, Gita. 1996. *Business maharajahs.* Bombay: Viking.

Qian, Yingyi. 1995. Reforming corporate governance and finance in China. In *Corporate governance in transitional economies: Insider control and the role of banks,* ed. M. Aoki and H. Kim. Washington, D.C.: World Bank.

Rapaczynski, Andrzej. 1996. The roles of the state and the market in establishing property rights. *Journal of Economic Perspectives* 10, no. 2 (spring): 87–103.

Robison, Richard. 1986. *Indonesia: The rise of capital.* Sydney: Allen & Unwin.

Roe, Mark J. 1990. Political and legal restraints on ownership and control of public companies. *Journal of Financial Economics* 27, no. 1 (September): 7–41.

Sachs, J., and A. Warner. 1995. Economic reform and the process of global integration. *Brookings Papers on Economic Activity,* no. 1:1–95.

Schwartz, Adam. 1992. *A nation in waiting: Indonesia in the 1990s.* St. Leonards, Australia: Allen & Unwin.

Securities and Exchange Board of India (SEBI). 1994. Indian securities markets: Agenda for development and reform. Discussion paper. Bombay.

Shleifer, Andrei, and Robert Vishny. 1986. Large shareholders and corporate control. *Journal of Political Economy* 94:461–88.
———. 1995. A survey of corporate governance. Paper presented at the Nobel Symposium on Law and Governance, Stockholm, August.
Strachan, Harry. 1976. *Family and other business groups in economic development: The case of Nicaragua.* New York: Praeger.
Stulz, René M. 1990. Managerial discretion and optimal financing policies. *Journal of Financial Economics* 26:3–27.
Wernerfelt, B., and C. Montgomery. 1988. Tobin's *q* and the importance of focus in firm performance. *American Economic Review* 78, no. 1 (March): 246–50.
White, Lawrence J. 1974. *Industrial concentration and economic power in Pakistan.* Princeton, N.J.: Princeton University Press.
Xu, Xiaonian, and Yan Wang. 1997. Ownership structure, corporate governance, and corporate performance: The case of Chinese stock firms. Amherst College/World Bank. Mimeo.

## Comment Bernard Yeung

This is a timely paper reporting important results, one that deserves a round of applause. The paper shows that foreign investors provide important monitoring functions in an emerging economy as it integrates with the rest of the world. This is an important contribution that will receive the attention of policy makers and students of emerging economies and financial economics.

The authors describe well a suboptimal situation in some emerging economies such as India. First, "firm groups" are common, and they are hard to monitor. Second, the incentives to monitor may be absent. Government muddling may leave financial intermediaries no incentive to monitor. Monitoring may not even be profitable. Insiders' control and cross-holdings allow entrenched corporate control (see, e.g., Morck, Stangeland, and Yeung, chap. 11 in this volume). The lack of protection for outsiders' rights and the presence of corrupted government may make the holding of mispriced firms unprofitable because share prices often do not reflect firm-specific information (see, e.g., Morck, Yeung, and Yu 2000). It follows that emerging economies may have a severe lack of local monitoring skills. These features induce managerial agency costs, allow bad management to escape from being disciplined, and ultimately impede the reallocation of asset controls from non-value-creating firms to value-creating firms. Moreover, the situation is difficult to change because the entrenched have the resources and the political connections to preserve the status quo.

Foreign influence can break the logjam,[1] and I believe that that is the

Bernard Yeung is the Krasnoff Professor of International Business and professor of economics at New York University.

1. See also sec. 11.8.5 of Morck, Stangeland, and Yeung (chap. 11 in this volume).

most important contribution of the paper. As the authors point out, several positive developments in corporate governance occurred in India since its balance-of-payments crisis in 1991. An important change is that restrictions on the entry of foreign investors were eliminated and regulations on their investments substantially clarified. Essentially, foreign institutional players can now become active investors. Similar changes have been experienced in many other emerging markets.[2] Do foreign institutional investors play a positive role? Experiencing economic problems, many politicians in emerging markets, particularly those in Asia, consider foreign institutional investors to be speculative devils causing market turmoil. Khanna and Palepu show that foreign institutional investors provide a highly valuable monitoring function.

Their work relies on the statistical relation between Tobin's $q$ and foreign institutional investors' share ownership using data between 1990 and 1994 from the Bombay Stock Exchange. They find that foreign investors' ownership is positively correlated with a firm's market value and is also related to the firm's postreform improvement in market value between 1990 and 1994. Their results clearly suggest that foreign institutional investors invest in good firms and that their monitoring may contribute directly to improved firm performance.

Furthermore, they find that domestic institutional ownership is sometimes negatively correlated with $q$ and change in $q$ between 1990 and 1994. Domestic institutional investors tend to invest in groups where there is a high level of internal capital market activity; presumably, firms in these groups are not more difficult to monitor. The result confirms that domestic institutional investors in India do not carry out their monitoring function.

The relations outlined above hold among both unaffiliated firms and group firms. This suggests, perhaps, that stand-alone firms and group firms are not different. The authors further find that foreign institutional investors tend to avoid group firms that are more difficult to monitor. As a consequence, foreign institutional investors' monitoring contribution is similar between independent firms and group firms. In my opinion, the message is very positive: although group firms are difficult to monitor, foreign investors manage to find some that they can monitor. The implication is that there is pressure on group firms with only murky information to improve their transparency.

To some, the results may raise the question, Does foreign institutional investors' ownership raise firm value because of their monitoring or because they are able to pick up better firms that make good postreform improvements? The authors attempt to shed light on the question by relating 1993 $q$ and pre-1993 foreign institutional ownership data. If foreign ownership is merely a positive signal, then a positive relation between 1993

2. For a comprehensive listing, see the appendix to Kim and Singal (2000).

$q$ and pre-1993 foreign ownership is unlikely. However, if foreign ownership contributes via active monitoring, a positive relation will exist. The authors find a positive relationship.

While the additional result helps, it does not totally eliminate a "tracking" story, which the authors raise at the end of section 9.3.3. Suppose that foreign institutional investors track firms that have a high probability of improving their corporate behavior. When a tracked firm indeed implements improvements, its market value rises because the improvements have been realized. Thus, even if the foreign investors' contribution is merely tracking better firms, 1993 $q$ and pre-1993 foreign ownership are positively correlated.

The differentiation of the tracking story and the monitoring story may not be as important as it appears. The undeniable result is that foreign institutional investors are linked with better local companies, no matter whether they do so by cherry picking or by active monitoring. Foreign investors, at the very least, improve the information content of the emerging economy's stock market. Khanna and Palepu provide the empirical evidence to support the belief that foreign investors help capital markets in emerging markets better carry out their capital allocation function. The results also indicate that we cannot assume that foreign investors have an information disadvantage.

This thinking begs the question of how foreign investors change the equilibrium allocation of capital. Clearly, companies self-select to post only murky information, or companies not able to improve as much as other firms are now more readily identifiable. They should have reduced access to capital, and they must either change or shrink. The results presented in the paper hint that, following the entrance of foreign investors, a transition from one equilibrium to another has to take place, just as those presented in Morck, Stangeland, and Yeung (chap. 11 in this volume) do.

## References

Kim, E. Han, and Vijay Singal. 2000. Stock market openings: Experience of emerging economies. *Journal of Business* 73, no. 1:25–66.

Morck, Randall K., Bernard Yeung, and Wayne Yu. 2000. The information content of stock markets: Why do emerging markets have synchronous stock price movements? *Journal of Financial Economics* 58, nos. 1/2.

10

# Stock Pyramids, Cross-Ownership, and Dual Class Equity
## The Mechanisms and Agency Costs of Separating Control from Cash-Flow Rights

Lucian Arye Bebchuk, Reinier Kraakman, and George G. Triantis

Most literature addressing the structure of corporate ownership compares dispersed ownership (DO) with a controlled structure (CS) in which a large blockholder owns a majority or large plurality of a company's shares. This paper, by contrast, examines an ownership structure in which a shareholder exercises control while retaining only a small fraction of the equity claims on a company's cash flows. Such a radical separation of control and cash-flow rights can occur in three principal ways: through dual class share structures, stock pyramids, and cross-ownership ties. Regardless of how it arises, we term this pattern of ownership a *controlling-minority structure* (CMS) because it permits a shareholder to control a firm while holding only a fraction of its equity. The CMS structure resembles CS insofar as it insulates controllers from the market for corporate control, but it resembles DO insofar as it places corporate control in the hands of an insider who holds a small fraction of the firm's cash-flow rights. Thus, CMS threatens to combine the incentive problems associated with both the CS and the DO ownership in a single ownership structure.

Lucian Arye Bebchuk is the William J. Friedman and Alicia Townsend Friedman Professor of Law, Economics, and Finance at Harvard Law School and a research associate of the National Bureau of Economic Research. Reinier Kraakman is the Ezra Ripley Thayer Professor of Law at Harvard Law School and specializes in corporate law and finance. George G. Triantis is professor of law at the University of Chicago.

The authors thank conference and preconference participants for helpful comments on earlier drafts of this paper. In particular, they thank their discussant, Dennis Sheehan. They also thank Kris Bess and Melissa Sawyer for valuable research assistance. Lucian Bebchuk received support from the National Science Foundation and the John M. Olin Center for Law, Economics, and Business at Harvard Law School. Reinier Kraakman received support from the John M. Olin Center for Law, Economics, and Business at Harvard Law School and the Harvard Law School Faculty Research Fund. George Triantis received support from the Nicholas E. Chimicles Research Chair at the University of Virginia Law School.

CMS structures are common outside the United States, particularly in countries whose economies are dominated by family-controlled conglomerates.[1] Because these structures can radically distort their controllers' incentives, however, they put great pressure on nonelectoral mechanisms of corporate governance, ranging from legal protections for minority shareholders to reputational constraints on controlling families. For the same reason, CMS structures have recently come under close political and market scrutiny in many countries. The time is ripe, therefore, for an analysis of the governance and incentive features of these structures.

We start in section 10.1 by analyzing the ways in which the three arrangements under consideration—stock pyramids, cross-ownership structures, and dual class equity structures—produce a separation of control from cash-flow rights. Indeed, we show how corporate planners can use such arrangements to produce any degree of separation that is desired. We illustrate our analysis with examples of CMS structures drawn from companies around the world.

Section 10.2 analyzes the agency costs of CMS structures. In this section, we show how CMS structures distort the decisions that controllers make with respect to firm size, choice of projects, and transfers of control. Our central contribution here is to highlight the potentially large agency costs that such structures involve. We demonstrate that the agency costs imposed by controlling shareholders who have a small minority of the cash-flow rights in their companies can be an order of magnitude larger than those imposed by controlling shareholders who hold a majority of the cash-flow rights. This is because, as the size of cash-flow rights held decreases, the size of agency costs increases, not linearly, but rather at a sharply increasing rate.

Section 10.3 compares the agency costs of CMS structures with those of debt under circumstances of extreme leverage. Although leverage also separates cash flow from control rights, we argue that the agency costs of debt may well be less troublesome than those of CMS structures. The status of CMS noncontrolling shareholders compares poorly to that of debtholders, who are protected by priority rights and protective covenants. The contrast is so marked that a CMS controller might plausibly incur debt just to signal her willingness to limit the agency costs that she is prepared to impose.

Our analysis of the agency costs of CMS structures raises many issues that call for further empirical and theoretical study. In section 10.4, we put forward the agenda of research that is warranted by our findings concerning the agency costs of CMS structures.

1. La Porta, Lopez-de-Silanes, and Shleifer (1999), who conduct a comprehensive survey of ownership structures around the world, demonstrate that CMS structures, and particularly stock pyramids, are widespread.

## 10.1 Mechanisms of Separating Cash Flow and Control

In this section, we describe the three basic mechanisms that permit a company's controller to retain only a minority of the cash-flow rights attached to the firm's equity: differential voting rights structures, pyramid structures, and cross-ownership structures. Although a minority shareholder often exercises a form of working control when a firm's remaining shares are dispersed, we are not concerned with such contingent forms of control here. Instead, we consider structures in which a minority shareholder possesses entrenched control that is wholly insulated from any takeover threat. Each of the three basic CMS forms firmly entrenches minority control, as do hybrids of these forms that are best analyzed in terms of the basic structures. In each case, the CMS form can be used in principle to separate cash-flow rights from control rights to any extent desired. We denote the degree of separation induced by a CMS structure between control and cash-flow rights by $\alpha$, which represents the fraction of the firm's equity cash-flow rights held by the controlling-minority shareholder.

### 10.1.1 Differential Voting Rights

The most straightforward CMS form is a single firm that has issued two or more classes of stock with differential voting rights. Indeed, such a multiclass equity structure is the only CMS form that does not depend on the creation of multiple firms.

#### *The Separation of Cash-Flow and Control Rights*

Calibrating the separation of cash-flow and control rights in a dual class equity structure is child's play. A planner can simply attach all voting rights to the fraction $\alpha$ of shares that are assigned to the controller while attaching no voting rights to the remaining shares that are distributed to the public or other shareholders.[2]

#### *The Incidence of Differential Voting Rights*

Despite its simplicity, however, dual class equity is not the most common CMS structure. One reason may be that the corporate law of some jurisdictions restricts both the voting ratio between high- and low-vote shares and the numerical ratio between high- and low-vote shares that a firm is permitted to issue. These restrictions implicitly mandate a lower bound on the size of $\alpha$. Yet such legal restrictions cannot wholly explain the lagging popularity of differential voting rights. As La Porta, Lopez-de-Silanes, and Shleifer (1999) observe, even in jurisdictions where firms

2. In their sample of dual class firms, DeAngelo and DeAngelo (1985) found that insiders held a median of 56.9 percent of the voting rights but only 24 percent of the common stock claims to cash flow.

often have stock with differential voting rights, CMS companies typically do not reduce the fraction of controller ownership $\alpha$ to the legal minimum.

Dual class voting structures are particularly common in Sweden and South Africa. The most prominent Swedish example is the Wallenberg group, which controls companies whose stock constitutes about 40 percent of the listed shares on the Stockholm Stock Exchange. Family trusts hold 40 percent of the voting rights but only about 20 percent of the equity in the group's principal holding company, Investor (if allied investors are included, these percentages increase to 65 percent of the votes and 43 percent of the equity, respectively). In turn, Investor controls a large number of operating companies. For example, it holds about 95 percent of the votes but less than 7 percent of the equity in Electrolux, the large manufacturer of household appliances, and it holds 40 percent of the votes but less than 4 percent of the equity in Ericsson Telefon, a large telecom ("Storming the Citadel" 1990). In South Africa, dual class equity is also becoming widely accepted (although it remains less popular than CMS pyramids). Companies have been permitted to list low-vote "N shares" on the Johannesburg Stock Exchange since 1995.

### 10.1.2 Pyramids

A CMS firm can be established with a single class of stock by pyramiding corporate structures. In a pyramid of two companies, a controlling-minority shareholder holds a controlling stake in a holding company that, in turn, holds a controlling stake in an operating company. In a three-tier pyramid, the primary holding company controls a second-tier holding company that in turn controls the operating company.

#### *The Separation of Cash-Flow and Control Rights*

To see the extent of separation of cash-flow and voting rights in a pyramid structure, consider the simple case of a sequence of $n \geq 2$ companies, in which the controller holds a fraction $s_1$ of the shares in company 1, company 1 holds a fraction $s_2$ of the shares in company 2, and so on. In this example, the nonpaper assets will be placed in company $n$.

As long as $s_i \geq 1/2$, $i = 1, \ldots, n$, the controller exercises formal control over the assets. As to cash-flow rights, the controller holds a fraction

$$\alpha = \left(\prod_{i=1}^{n}\right) s_i .$$

PROPOSITION 1. *For any fraction $\alpha$, however small, there is a pyramid that permits a controller to control a company's assets completely without holding more than $\alpha$ of the company's cash-flow rights. This follows from the fact that, by setting n large enough, the product*

$$\left(\prod_{i=1}^{n}\right)s_i$$

*can become as low as desired.*

In the boundary case in which the controller holds 50 percent of voting rights at each level of a pyramid (the minimum necessary for formal control), $\alpha = (0.5)^n$. To take a concrete example of how rapidly pyramiding separates equity from control, consider a three-level pyramid with $s_i$ = 0.50 at each level. Here, the minority investor controls the firm with only 12.5 percent of its cash-flow rights.

*The Incidence of Pyramid Structures*

La Porta, Lopez-de-Silanes, and Shleifer (1999) find that pyramids are the most commonly used mechanism for concentrating control in a CMS structure. Pyramiding is quite common in Asian countries (see Claessens et al. 1999) as well as in some European countries (see, e.g., Bianchi, Bianco, and Enriques 1997; and Holmen and Hogfeldt 1999). One example of a well-known pyramid is the Li Ka-shing group, operating out of Hong Kong. The Li Ka-shing family operates through the Cheung Kong public company, in which it has a 35 percent interest (La Porta, Lopez-de-Silanes, and Shleifer 1999). Cheung Kong, in turn, has a 44 percent interest in its main operating company, Hutcheson Wampoa. Hutcheson Wampoa owns Cavendish International, which is the holding company for Hong Kong Electric (Weidenbaum 1996). A second, Indian example is the Gondrej family, which holds, through the privately held Gondrej and Boyce Manufacturing Company, 67 percent of the publicly traded Godrej Soaps (which is listed on the Bombay Stock Exchange). In turn, Godrej Soaps owns 65 percent of Godrej Agrovet (agriculture) and, together with the Godrej group, 65 percent of Godrej Foods (food processing) (Morais 1998).

### 10.1.3 Cross-Ownership

In contrast to pyramids, companies in cross-ownership structures are linked by horizontal cross-holdings of shares that reinforce and entrench the power of central controllers. Thus, cross-holding structures differ from pyramids chiefly in that the voting rights used to control a group remain distributed over the entire group rather than concentrated in the hands of a single company or shareholder.

*The Separation of Cash-Flow and Control Rights*

To clarify the relation between cross-holdings and control, consider a group of $n$ companies in a cross-holding structure. Let us denote by $s_{ij}$ the fraction of company $i$'s shares that are held by company $j$. And suppose that the controller also holds directly a fraction $s_i$ of the shares of company $i$.

Assuming that, for each $i$, the controller maintains

$$s_i + \left(\sum_{j=1}^{n}\right) s_{ij} > \frac{1}{2},$$

the controller completely controls the assets of all $n$ companies. However, the controller might hold only a small fraction of the cash-flow rights in these companies. The simplest example of a symmetrical case is a controller who holds identical stakes $s$ in two companies with identical cross-holdings $h$ in the other, such that $s + h \geq 1/2$ (i.e., the controller's control in both companies is entrenched). In this case, the controller's fraction of the cash-flow rights is the ratio of its direct holding $s$ over the total fraction of shares that is not cross-held $(1 - h)$:

$$\alpha = \left(\frac{s}{1 - h}\right).$$

PROPOSITION 2. *For any α, however small, it is possible to construct a cross-ownership structure such that the controller will have complete control over the assets but no more than a fraction α of the cash flow from the assets.*

PROOF. In the symmetrical two-company structure considered above, this can be accomplished by choosing $s$ and $h$ such that $s + h \geq 1/2$ and $s/(1 - h)$ gives the desired $\alpha$. These conditions can be satisfied by setting $s$ equal to $1/2\alpha(1 - \alpha)$ and by setting $h$ equal to $1/2[1 - \alpha(1 - \alpha)]$. Although we demonstrate this proposition only for the case of a symmetrical two-company structure, cross-ownership ties yielding a desired $\alpha$ can be constructed for nonsymmetrical or multicompany structures as well.

### *The Incidence of Cross-Holding Structures*

Ethnic Chinese families employ cross-holdings as well as pyramids to secure control of their business groups. Cross-holdings are popular in Asia, it is said, because they make the locus of control over company groups less transparent (Weidenbaum 1996). A prominent example is the vast Chareon Pokphand group (CP), based in Thailand, which owns directly 33 percent of CP Feedmill (agribusiness and some real estate, retailing, manufacturing, and telecom), 2 percent of CP Northeastern (agribusiness), and 9 percent of Bangkok Agro-Industrial (agribusiness). But CP Feedmill owns 57 percent of Northeastern. CP Feedmill also owns 60 percent of Bangkok Agro-Industrial, and CP Northeastern owns 3 percent of Bangkok Agro-Industrial. Bangkok Agro-Industrial owns 5 percent of CP Feedmill (Weidenbaum 1996). CP Feedmill, CP Northeastern, and Bangkok Agro-Industrial are all listed on the Bangkok Stock Exchange.

A second example is the Lippo group, controlled by the Riady family. Lippo controls a financial conglomerate comprising three principal companies that are linked by cross-holdings: Lippo Bank, Lippo Life, and

Lippo Securities. Although the Riady family divested most of its equity stake in Lippo Bank and Lippo Life in 1996, it continues to control those companies through its majority stake in Lippo Securities, which holds 27 percent of the shares in Lippo Life, which in turn holds 40 percent of Lippo Bank (Solomon 1996). When the restructuring was proposed, many observers suspected that it was merely a means for the Riady family to extract assets from Lippo Life and Lippo Bank, and, as a result, there was some doubt as to whether it would be blocked by the shareholders or by the Indonesian stock market regulatory body (Solomon 1996). However, Lippo's restructuring plans succeeded nonetheless, partly on the basis of a pledge by the Riady family to reduce the group's cross-holdings over time ("Nothing Can Hold Back Lippo" 1997).

## 10.2 Agency Costs

In this section, we examine the agency costs associated with the CMS structure in three important contexts: choosing investment projects, selecting investment policy and the scope of the firm, and choosing to transfer control.

The CMS structure lacks the principal mechanisms that limit agency costs in other ownership structures. Unlike in DO structures, where controlling management may have little equity but can be displaced, the controllers of CMS companies face neither proxy contests nor hostile takeovers. Moreover, unlike in CS structures, where controlling shareholders are entrenched but internalize most of the value effects of their decisions through their shareholdings, CMS controllers may hold a very small fraction $\alpha$ of the cash-flow rights in their firms. In this section, we demonstrate that, as $\alpha$ declines, the controllers of CMS firms can externalize progressively more of the costs of their moral hazard and that the agency costs of CMS firms can increase at a sharply increasing rate as a result. Whether agency costs do in fact increase at a sharply increasing rate thus depends on whether there are additional constraints on the decisions of CMS controllers besides the tug of ownership structure and private benefits of control.

### 10.2.1 Project Choice

Consider first a controller's choice of investment projects. Suppose that a firm has a choice of investing in one of two projects. Project X will produce a total value $V_X$, which includes cash flow $S_X$, available to all shareholders, and private benefits of control $B_X$, available only to the firm's controller. ($B_X$ may come from self-dealing or appropriating opportunities.) Similarly, suppose that project Y will produce a total value of $V_Y$, which includes the analogous terms $S_Y$ and $B_Y$. Suppose further that project Y does not give rise to the same private opportunities to the controller, that is, that $B_X > B_Y$. The controller will choose project X if and only if

$$\alpha(V_X - B_X) + B_X > \alpha(V_Y - B_Y) + B_Y.$$

Thus, depending on $\alpha$, the controller might choose the project with the lower value $V$ but the larger private benefits of control $B$. Moreover, as $\alpha$ declines, the difference in value between Y and X will pale in importance in the controller's eyes relative to the difference in the private benefits of control. This relation can be restated as follows:

PROPOSITION 3. *Given a less valuable project* X *and a more valuable project* Y, *a controller of a CSM firm will make the inefficient decision to choose project* X *if and only if*

$$V_Y - V_X < \left(\frac{1 - \alpha}{\alpha}\right)\Delta B,$$

*where* $\Delta B = B_X - B_Y > 0$.

Differentiating the term on the right with respect to $\alpha$ yields $-(\alpha^{-2})\Delta B$. This suggests that, for a given distribution of possible project Y's, the likelihood that the controller will inefficiently choose project X rises and the efficiency loss from such a selection rises at a sharply increasing rate, as $\alpha$ decreases.

To take a concrete example, suppose that $\Delta B$ has the modest value of $0.03V_X$. If $\alpha = 0.5$, the distortion in project selection will be marginal: a controller will forgo the efficient project Y only if its excess value over X is less than 3 percent of $V_X$. However, if $\alpha = 0.1$, the distortion will be large—a controller will reject the efficient project Y unless it exceeds $V_X$ by more than 27 percent.

### 10.2.2 Decisions on Scope

Next, consider the agency costs associated with the controller's decision to distribute cash flows or expand the firm under a CMS regime. Conglomerates operating under a DO structure are frequently criticized for inefficiently retaining free cash flows even when they lack profitable investment opportunities. CMS structures are subject to a similar agency problem when their controllers can extract private benefits from unprofitable projects.

Agency costs can arise whenever a CMS controller is called on to decide whether to contract or expand the firm. To see this, suppose that there is an asset that produces value $V$, which is the sum of cash flows $S$ and private benefits $B$. If this asset belongs to a CMS firm, the firm's controller may refuse to sell it and distribute the proceeds, $P$, to all shareholders because doing so would sacrifice a private benefit. Alternatively, if the asset is held by a third party, the CMS controller may cause his company to pay $P$ for the asset, rather than distribute this sum as a dividend, in order to acquire the private benefit $B$ that the asset confers. In terms of the controller's decision, these two situations are equivalent: in both, the controller's incentives are distorted in favor of increasing the private benefits of control by expanding the firm.

More formally, a controller will prefer to expand (or not to contract) a firm if

$$\alpha(V - B) + B > \alpha P,$$

where $\alpha$ is again the fraction of cash-flow rights held by the firm's controller. This point can be restated:

PROPOSITION 4. *A controller will prefer to expand the firm if and only if*

$$V > P - \left(\frac{1 - \alpha}{\alpha}\right)B.$$

Thus, if $P$ is in the range

$$\left[V,\ V + \left(\frac{1 - \alpha}{\alpha}\right)B\right],$$

a controller will decide to make the enterprise inefficiently large. The magnitude of the inefficiency $(P - V)$ is equal to $(1 - \alpha/\alpha)B$, and the differential with respect to $\alpha$ is equal to $-(\alpha^{-2})B$. Given any distribution of opportunities to expand and contract, the likelihood that a CMS firm will make an inefficient decision (and thus the size of expected agency costs) grows larger as the controller's equity stake $\alpha$ grows smaller. As in the case of project choice, moreover, the potential agency costs increase at a sharply increasing rate as $\alpha$ declines.

Consider, for example, a decrease in $\alpha$ from $\alpha = 0.5$ to $\alpha = 0.1$. For $\alpha = 0.5$, the range over which a controller will make inefficient decisions is $(V, V + B)$; for $\alpha = 0.1$, the range is $(V, V + 9B)$. This is a very large difference. Suppose that $B$ is a modest 5 percent of $V$. In this case, if $\alpha = 0.5$, the controller will make mildly distorted decisions but will agree to sell the asset for a price that exceeds its value by 5 percent. However, for $\alpha = 0.1$, the controller will refuse to sell the asset unless the firm receives a price 45 percent higher than the value of the asset to the firm. A reduction in $\alpha$ deteriorates incentives in two ways: (*a*) it increases the number of inefficient decisions, and (*b*) the inefficient decisions added are especially bad.

Thus, we predict that CMS firms have a very strong tendency, all else equal, to expand rather than contract, to retain free cash flows, and to hold back distributions. It follows that CMS structures are more likely to evolve into conglomerates than are either DO or CS structures, unless their tendency to expand is contained by governance mechanisms other than the immediate incentives of their controllers.

### 10.2.3 Control Transfers

A third set of decisions that can impose significant agency costs on CMS firms is represented by transfers of control. Suppose that the initial controller, I, has a fraction $\alpha$ of the cash-flow rights. Under I, the firm's value is $V_I$, which consists of cash flow $S_I$ and private control benefits $B_I$. Under a potential new controller, N, the corresponding values would be $V_N$, $S_N$, and $B_N$. A transfer of control to N will be efficient if and only if $V_I = S_I + B_I < V_N = S_N + B_N$. However, if $\alpha$ is small, the decision of controller I to sell the firm will depend much less on $V_I$ and $V_N$, the values of the firm in the hands of I and N, than on the relative sizes of $B_I$ and $B_N$, the private benefits of I and N. To demonstrate this point clearly, we must first specify the nature of the legal regime governing control transfers.

*CMS Control Transfers under the Market Rule*

Bebchuk (1994) has previously identified two paradigmatic legal regimes governing control transactions: the "market rule," under which the transferor of control (in our case, I) may retain a control premium, and the "equal opportunity rule," under which noncontrolling shareholders are entitled to participate in a transfer of control on the same terms as the controller. Consider first how transfers of control over CMS firms are likely to be affected by the size of $\alpha$ under the market rule.

Under the market rule, it can be shown (see Bebchuk 1994) that control will be transferred if and only if

$$\alpha S_N + B_N > \alpha S_I + B_I.$$

The intuition is that the value of a control block of shares in a company is $\alpha S + B$, which is the controller's fractional claim on the company's cash flows plus the private benefit of control. It follows that, when the above condition holds, the control block will be worth more to N than to I. Since $V_I = S_I + B_I$ and $V_N = S_N + V_N$, we can rearrange the above relation to establish that, even if $V_I > V_N$, control *will be* transferred as long as

$$B_N - B_I > \left(\frac{\alpha}{1 - \alpha}\right)(V_I - V_N).$$

Conversely, even if $V_N > V_I$, control *will not be* transferred as long as

$$B_I - B_N < \frac{1 - \alpha}{\alpha}(V_N - V_I).$$

In the first case, transfer of control is inefficient; in the second, failure to transfer control is inefficient. In both cases, moreover, it is clear that the magnitude of the inefficiency costs as well as the range of inefficient outcomes increase exponentially as $\alpha$ declines.

*CMS Control Transfers under the Equal Opportunity Rule*

Under the equal opportunity rule, an initial controller will sell her control stake if and only if

$$\alpha S_I + B_I < \alpha V_N,$$

that is, when the sum of her cash-flow rights and private benefits is less than the proportionate share of the firm's total value acquired by the new controller. Rearranging terms, a sale will not take place if and only if

$$B_I < \frac{\alpha}{1 - \alpha}(V_N - V_I),$$

even if $V_N > V_I$. Thus, as $\alpha/(1 - \alpha)$ declines (and it declines much faster than $\alpha$), the equal opportunity rule blocks a wider range of efficient transactions. Indeed, when the initial controller enjoys significant private benefits, even transfers with large potential efficiency gains are unlikely to occur. Consider the example of a pyramid in which $B_I = 0.501\,V_I$ and $\alpha = 0.2$. In this case, a transfer will not occur even if $V_N$ is twice the size of $V_I$.

### 10.2.4 Factors Limiting the Agency Costs of CMS Structures

The discussion of agency costs thus far has implicitly assumed that a CMS controller has no significant constraints on her ability to extract private benefits. In fact, however, there are at least two potential constraints that may limit CMS agency costs and protect the interests of noncontrolling shareholders.

*Reputation as a Constraint on Agency Costs*

The first potential constraint on agency costs is reputation. The fact that CMS structures can impose significant agency costs is well known, even if the magnitude of these costs is not. It follows that CMS controllers who return to the equity market must pay a price for the expected agency cost of CMS structures unless they can establish a reputation for sound management.

There is some evidence that reputational concerns constrain CMS controllers. On one hand, a good reputation appears to facilitate CMS structures. For example, Barr, Gerson, and Kantor (1997) find that South African controlling shareholders with better reputations tend to maintain smaller stakes in CMS firms. Conversely, a reputation for exploiting minority shareholders sharply increases the cost of capital for a CMS firm. Thus, after the Russian firm Menatep was accused of stripping profits from the subsidiaries of AO Yukos, a closely held oil company that it controls, its acquisition of another oil company (Eastern Oil) raised new fears of asset stripping and sharply decreased the share price of Eastern's subsidiary Tomskneft (Cullison 1998).

A further clue about the role of reputation in controlling agency costs is that families—frequently regarded as repositories for reputation—are the most common controlling shareholders in CMS structures (La Porta, Lopez-de-Silanes, and Shleifer 1999). Since family pyramids and cross-holding structures tend to grow gradually through the generation of internal capital and the issuance of minority stock, one might expect family controllers to limit their appropriation of private benefits in order to assure continued growth for the benefit of their offspring. Moreover, the pressure on CMS controllers to maintain a good reputation appears to have increased in countries such as Sweden and South Africa that have recently reduced barriers to the inflow of foreign investment capital ("Storming the Citadel" 1990; Barr, Gerson, and Kantor 1997).

*Legal Constraints on Agency Costs*

A second potential constraint on CMS agency costs is the legal protections accorded minority shareholders. The analysis of this part has suggested that the agency costs of CMS structures tend to grow as the private benefits of control increase. Thus, the agency costs of CMS structures will tend to be comparatively larger in countries in which legal rules are lax and private benefits of control are consequently large.

Note that this point presents a puzzle. It might suggest that CMS structures will tend to be *less* common in countries with a lax corporate law system. Yet the opposite seems to be the case: CMS structures are in fact *more* common in countries with a lax corporate law system. We will remark on how this puzzle might be explained in section 10.4 below.

## 10.3 Comparison with a Leveraged CS Structure

In the broader capital structure decision, cash flows are divided not only among shareholders but also between shareholders and debtholders. Thus, control may be separated from cash-flow rights, not only by allocating control rights to minority shareholders, but also by taking on substantial debt. In what we term a *leveraged controlling-shareholder* (LCS) structure, the controller holds most or all of the equity tickets with their attached control rights, but most of the firm's cash flow must be paid out to debtholders. Debt investors are typically nonvoting stakeholders, and, in this limited sense, they resemble minority shareholders. The comparison is reflected in the contrast between the means by which two of the most prominent business families in Canada secured control over large empires. The Reichmanns financed their Olympia and York through private and public debt; the Bronfmans drew more on equity investment to build the Hees-Edper-Brascan web of interlocking companies.

Despite the superficial similarity between CMS and LSC structures, however, two important differences suggest that these structures have a qualitatively different range of agency costs. These distinctions turn on the priority rights and the covenant protections enjoyed by debtholders.

### 10.3.1 The Priority Rights of Debt

The fact that debtholders generally enjoy a fixed entitlement with priority over the claims of shareholders alters the nature of the agency problem. Take as an example the effect of leveraging on project choice—the problem analyzed in the CMS context in section 10.2.1 above. Suppose that a firm's controller owns all its equity and issues debt with face value $D$. In the simple case in which there is no probability of insolvency, no agency costs arise under this LCS structure because the controlling shareholder, as residual claimant, internalizes all the costs and benefits of her decisions.

But, if there is a significant probability of insolvency, the problem is more complex. Assume for the moment that the probability of insolvency is a function of the amount of debt, $D$, but not of the choice between the projects: that is, $P(V_X < D) = P(V_Y < D) = \pi$ for projects X and Y. Assume also that the controller can extract private benefits before the firm becomes insolvent. The controller would choose project X if and only if

$$(1 - \pi)(V_X - D - B_X) + B_X > (1 - \pi)(V_Y - D - B_Y) + B_Y.$$

If we let $\Delta B = B_X - B_Y$, the controller will make an inefficient decision to choose project X over project Y if and only if

$$0 < V_Y - V_X < [\pi/(1 - \pi)]\Delta B.$$

Differentiating the right side with respect to $\pi$ gives us $(1 - \pi)^{-2}\Delta B$.

This result suggests that agency costs are as sensitive to the probability of insolvency in LCS firms (which increases with leverage) as they are to $\alpha$ in the CMS case. Like $\alpha$, $1 - \pi$ represents the degree to which the controller can externalize the costs of appropriating private benefits through the selection of projects—or, by extension, through distribution policy. And, just as it appears to be in the interest of a CMS controller to reduce $\alpha$ as much as possible, it may seem to be in the interest of a LCS controller to minimize $1 - \pi$ by issuing as much debt as possible.

Yet the LCS controller's preference for project X is more complex if we relax one or both of the assumptions of (*a*) the independence of insolvency risk from project choice and (*b*) the priority of private benefits over debt claims. After relaxing these assumptions, we must reexamine the effect of insolvency risk on a controller's variable interest (her residual claim as a shareholder) and her fixed interest (her "claim" on private benefits of control).

If we relax the assumption that $\pi$ is independent of the project selected, project choice is tilted in a manner that is well known as the agency problem of risk alteration or overinvestment: equityholders, including the controller, will come to prefer more to less risky projects. This may compound or offset the distortion described above. In particular, if the inefficient project X is also the riskier project, the controller will be even more favorably inclined toward it. If, conversely, the efficient project Y is the riskier project, the controller's incentive to choose project X may be tempered somewhat by the attractiveness of the riskiness of project Y to the controller qua shareholder.

However, to the extent that we also relax the second assumption that the controller appropriates private benefits prior to insolvency, benefits effectively become subordinate in priority to the claims of the debtholders. If project X is the riskier choice, its expected private benefits must be discounted by the probability of insolvency and may turn out to be lower than the expected benefits of project Y. If, however, project Y is the riskier choice, the controller's expected private benefits are even more favorable to project X than in the simple case demonstrated above, and this offsets the benefit to the controller (qua shareholder) from risk taking. In sum, the most severe agency problem arises when project X is the riskier alternative and the controller can take her private benefits before insolvency occurs. If either project X is the less risky alternative or the controller's private benefits are threatened by insolvency, then the inefficiency of the controller's incentives (in favor of projects that are either risky or yield large private benefits) may be modest and is almost certainly less than the controller's counterpart in the CMS firm.

Indeed, an LCS controller's incentive qua shareholder to prefer risky projects and high leverage is easily overstated. The interest of equityholders in a leveraged firm is often summarized in corporate finance by observing that they effectively hold a call option: they have the right, but not the obligation, to buy the firm's assets by paying off the firm's indebtedness. Since the value of a call option is an increasing function of the riskiness of the underlying asset, it follows that raising the riskiness of a firm's assets can increase its share value. This conventional account, however, neglects the fact that option values are a function of the time to maturity as well as volatility. In the case of traded financial options, an increase in the risk of the underlying asset does not change the maturity of the option. But, in the case of the leveraged firm, the maturity of the shareholder's option is the firm's default on its debt obligations, which in turn may be accelerated by an increase in the riskiness of the firm's projects. Therefore, an LCS controller's incentive to enhance her option value by increasing the riskiness of the firm is at least partially offset by the resulting abbreviation of the expected life of the option.

The incentive to make distributions to shareholders (e.g., dividends, share repurchases) is more straightforward. The CMS controller receives only a fraction of the corporate distributions but extracts the full private benefit from assets left in the firm. In contrast, the LCS controller receives all the distributions to shareholders, and its claim on private benefits is subject to the risk of losing them in the event of insolvency. Therefore, the incentive to distribute is much higher in the LCS case. While CMS firms may grow inefficiently large, LCS firms may shrink inefficiently small, at least if distributions to shareholders are unconstrained.

Finally, controllers of CMS and LCS firms also differ with respect to sales of their controlling stakes. Where a CMS controller may refuse an efficient sale or accept an inefficient one, depending on the legal regime, a LCS controller will always deal with a higher-valuing purchaser. The reason is that all potential purchasers of the equity in an LCS firm can extract the same value from creditors by leveraging. Moreover, all returns to LCS shareholders with 100 percent of the equity in their firms are shareholder returns, whether they are paid out as dividends or as perks. Thus, there is no danger that differences in private returns will deter the sale of LCS equity. Any purchaser who values the equity of a leveraged firm more than the incumbent controlling shareholder should be able to buy it.

### 10.3.2 The Contractual Protection of Creditors

The second important distinction between the governance of CMS and LCS structures is that creditors typically enjoy far-reaching contractual safeguards in addition to their priority rights. The shareholder's control of a LCS firm is contingent on satisfying the conditions and promises contained in the contract between the firm and its debtholders. For example, where the controllers of firms might otherwise reinvest free cash flows to increase their private control benefits, they are legally bound to make interest payments to their debtholders. This constrains their ability to take private-control benefits (see Jensen 1986). Moreover, given their enforcement rights, debtholders generally contract for a much richer set of protections than minority shareholders do. That is, a leveraged firm must promise to observe numerous constraints and forgo specific forms of misbehavior, and, all else equal, these restrictions become more severe as the firm becomes more leveraged. The sanction for breach, moreover, is the acceleration of the debt and the exercise of creditor rights against firm assets, which exposes the controller of an LCS firm to the risk of removal.

One indication of the importance of contractual protections in reducing the agency costs of debt is the paucity in the United States of preferred stock without conversion or redemption rights (see Houston and Houston 1990, 45). Such stock resembles debt with particularly weak contractual protection.

### 10.3.3 Combining CMS and LCS Structures

Given that corporate debtholders generally impose detailed contractual restrictions on controlling shareholders—and given that debt creates incentives different from, and sometimes opposed to, those that arise under CMS structures—leverage might serve as a commitment device for CMS controllers who wish to refrain from exploiting their opportunities to take private benefits. Thus, debt financing can limit controller latitude to invest in negative net-present-value projects by forcing firms to distribute free cash to investors (Jensen 1986). Moreover, a skilled creditor-monitor, such as a bank, enhances the discipline of debt: to some extent, such a monitor can confer a public good on all corporate stakeholders by deterring the inefficient appropriation of private-control benefits by a firm's controller. Therefore, we might predict that sophisticated shareholders would prefer to invest in leveraged CMS firms, especially if a significant debt were concentrated in the hands of a skilled monitor, such as a bank.

Yet whether CMS controllers actually use the LCS structure as a commitment device is an open question. As we have discussed in this section, the incentives of lenders also diverge from those of noncontrolling shareholders, and the latter group cannot count on the former to protect its interests. Moreover, the discipline of monitoring by lenders is easily frustrated by the managerial, investment, and political links between firms and institutional lenders that are common in countries with CMS structures. Commentators have noted the inadequate supervision of lending relationships among connected parties within family or business groups in many of the troubled Asian economies (e.g., South Korea). Even in the more developed economies, conglomerate borrowers may attract less than rigorous screening and monitoring from their institutional lenders than smaller, stand-alone firms.[3]

## 10.4 Concluding Remarks: An Agenda for Research

We have sought to attract attention in this paper to the incentive problems of CMS structures. CMS firms deserve close scrutiny because they are pervasive outside the handful of developed countries with highly developed equity markets and a tradition of dispersed-share ownership. Our principal contribution here has been to analyze their agency costs. In particular, CMS structures can distort the incentives of corporate controllers to make efficient decisions with respect to project selection, firm size, and roles of control. We have demonstrated that, all else equal, the agency costs associated with CMS firms increase very rapidly as the fraction of equity cash-flow rights held by CMS controllers declines. Moreover, although the agency costs of CMS structures resemble in some respects those of debt, they are not limited by the contractual protections and incentive characteristics that constrain the opportunism of controlling equity-

3. Daniels and MacIntosh (1991, 885) suggest that, in Canada, "institutional shareholders, like banks, insurance and trust companies, may justifiably fear loss of business or loss of access to preferential information flows should they oppose wealth-reducing management initiatives." Sweden's biggest commercial bank has been viewed as the Wallenberg bank even though the family owns only 8 percent of it ("Storming the Citadel" 1990).

holders in leveraged firms. Thus, CMS agency costs can bulk even larger than those of highly leveraged LCS firms.

Our analytic conclusions in this paper, however, are only a first step in the investigation of CMS firms. Our discussion suggests a number of additional questions that together constitute an agenda for research on these structures.

### 10.4.1 Understanding the Choice among Alternative CMS Structures

We have shown that CMS structures can assume the three principal forms of dual class share issues, pyramids, and cross-shareholding structures. Of these, La Porta, Lopez-de-Silanes, and Shleifer (1999) find that pyramid structures are the most common. An obvious but important question is, What factors determine the choice by controllers among CMS forms? Contributing factors are likely to include transaction costs, legal restrictions (e.g., on the use of multiclass equity), and political and reputational constraints (encourage more opaque structures of cross-ownership). Although we have shown that any of the mechanisms alone or in combination can reduce $\alpha$ to almost zero, the evidence suggests that controllers refrain from exploiting fully this potential. This question may also be addressed by examining the economic, legal, and political factors limiting the use of the various mechanisms.

### 10.4.2 Empirically Investigating the Agency Costs of CMS Structures

Given the magnitude of the *potential* agency costs associated with CMS structures, a second important question concerns the *actual* costs associated with these firms. These costs turn on how far legal protections and reputational considerations limit the opportunism of CMS controllers: for example, the extent to which agency costs are reduced by borrowing heavily from sophisticated monitors such as banks. The magnitude of CMS agency costs bears importantly on understanding the incidence and consequences of CMS structures. Some important empirical work in this direction is already under way. Holmen and Hogfeldt (1999) put forward findings on agency costs in Swedish pyramids, and Bianco (1998) presents findings on such costs in Italian pyramids. Claessens et al. (1999) document that firms in a pyramid structure have lower *Q*-values than similar stand-alone firms.

### 10.4.3 Explaining How CMS Structures Arise

Our results indicating the large size of potential agency costs under CMS structures suggest a puzzle that calls for an explanation. What explains the common existence of these structures notwithstanding their large agency costs?

One line of research in search of an answer to this puzzle might be to search for countervailing efficiency benefits associated with CMS structures that offset their agency costs (see Khanna and Palepu 1999, 2000, in press). Such factors, if they could be identified, might naturally explain the existence of CMS structures. One thing that makes this approach difficult is that CMS structures are common in countries with lax corporate rules, even though the agency costs of such structures tend to be larger in such countries. This implies that, to be able to explain the observed patterns of ownership, the considered line of research would have to identify some countervailing efficiency benefits that are likely to be large in countries with lax rules.

Bebchuk (1999a, 1999b) develops an alternative approach to explaining why CMS structures arise. These papers suggest that, even when CMS structures do not have redeeming efficiency benefits, they might nonetheless arise when private benefits of control are large.

Bebchuk (1999b) analyzes how the initial owner of a company who takes it public decides whether to create a structure in which he will maintain a lock on corporate control. This decision is shown to depend heavily on the size of the private benefits of control. When these benefits are large—and when control is thus valuable enough—leaving control up for grabs invites attempts to seize control. In such circumstances, an initial owner might elect to maintain a lock on control to prevent rivals from attempting to grab it merely to gain the private benefits of control. Furthermore, when private benefits of control are large, choosing a controlling-shareholder structure would enable the company's initial shareholders to capture a larger fraction of the surplus from value-producing transfers of control. Both results suggest that, in countries in which lax legal rules allow large private benefits of control, corporate founders will elect to retain a lock on control when taking their companies public. And, if these founders prefer to hold just a limited fraction of the cash-flow rights to avoid risk or conserve funds, they will look to CMS structures to lock in their control.

Bebchuk (1999a) adds an additional element to the explanation by modeling choices of ownership structure made after the initial public offering stage. Following an initial public offering, companies will often have a controlling shareholder who must decide whether to retain its initial lock on control when the company must raise new outside capital. This decision, which shapes the ultimate structure of publicly traded companies in the economy, is again shown to be very much influenced by the levels of private benefits of control. When the corporate law system is lax and private benefits of control are consequently large, controlling shareholders will be more reluctant to relinquish their grip on control. Consequently, they will be more likely to raise additional capital by selling cash-flow rights without voting rights—that is, by creating an CMS structure—even if this structure would impose larger tax and agency costs. The reason is that, while the controller will fully bear the reduction of private benefits from forgoing his lock on control, the efficiency gains from eschewing a CMS structure would be partly shared by the existing public investors. Consequently, in countries in which private benefits of control are large, controllers seeking extra capital for their publicly traded companies will have a strong incentive to sell cash-flow rights with no or disproportionately small voting rights.[4]

Note that the two explanations described above are complementary in that they both suggest that CMS structures will arise when the level of private benefits of control is large. These explanations sit well with the observed patterns of ownership around the world. Many of the examples of well-known CMS structures that we have noted are from countries that seem to be characterized by relatively large private benefits of control. These explanations are also consistent with the findings of La Porta, Lopez-de-Silanes, and Shleifer (1999), who observe that CMS structures are more common in countries where the legal protection of investors, as measured by their index, is low. Finally, these explanations are consistent with the results of Claessens et al. (1999), who find that pyramids are common in Asian countries with little investor protection and, within any given country, in lines of business in which private benefits are large.

### 10.4.4 Public Policy toward CMS Structures

Finally, there is a question of how—and whether—CMS structures should be regulated. CMS structures have come under increasing political and market pressure in recent years. For example, in May 1997, Taiwan's legislature passed a law on connected enterprises that mandates disclosures of cross-holding or pyramid linkages. Last year, a new companies bill was introduced in India that contains a provision stipulating that holding companies cannot be subsidiaries: parents of existing subsidiary holding companies would either have to dilute their stake or have to dissolve them. In South Africa, there has been unbundling of conglomerates, partly under economic and political pressure to foster the emergence of black-controlled business. At the same time, pyramid structures are viewed as the means by which black business groups can control businesses. In Sweden, the Wallenberg family is selectively increasing its stakes in some firms and divesting itself of its stake in others, apparently in order to attract foreign capital ("Whither the Wallenbergs?" 1993). In Canada, the privatizing and consolidation of entities in the Hees-Edper-Brascan group since 1993 have significantly simplified its corporate structure. These transactions have collapsed cross-holdings and eliminated public

4. Wolfenzon (1999) develops an explanation of why pyramids arise that is also based on post–initial public offering decisions. In his model, controllers resort to a pyramid in order to make an additional investment that would increase their private benefits but would have a negative effect on cash flows. Note that, unlike the model in Bebchuk (1999a), this model is limited to circumstances in which firms make poor investments.

companies, apparently in response to investor demands in the early 1990s ("Bronfman Companies" 1993).

A continuing investigation of the agency costs and efficiency characteristics of CSM structures clearly bears on how we evaluate the incipient pressures worldwide to dismantle these structures. On one hand, the case for regulation is made if the agency costs of these structures are large and there is strong evidence of a divergence between private and social benefits in their creation. In this case, the only issue is how to regulate: for example, by explicit prohibitions such as a one-share one-vote rule and a ban on pyramiding or by tax policies such as intercorporate income taxation to discourage pyramids. On the other hand, if further research shows significant constraints on the agency costs of CMS firms and important offsetting efficiencies, then it is the pressures to unravel these structures that deserve closer scrutiny.

## References

Barr, Graham, Jos Gerson, and Brian Kantor. 1997. Shareholders as agents and principals: The case of South Africa's corporate governance system. In *A comparison of the U.S., Japan, and Europe,* ed. Donald H. Chew. New York: Oxford University Press.

Bebchuk, Lucian A. 1994. Efficient and inefficient sides of corporate control. *Quarterly Journal of Economics* 109:957–93.

———. 1999a. Rent protection and the evolution of ownership structure in publicly traded companies. Working paper. Harvard Law School.

———. 1999b. A rent-protection theory of corporate ownership and control. NBER Working Paper no. 7203. Cambridge, Mass.: National Bureau of Economic Research.

Bianchi, Marcelo, Magda Bianco, and Luca Enriques. 1997. Pyramidal groups and the separation between ownership and control in Italy. Working paper. European Corporate Governance Project.

Bianco, Magda. 1998. Pyramidal groups and internal capital markets: Efficiency vs. expropriation. Working paper. Bank of Italy.

Bronfman companies: Feeling the strain. 1993. *Economist,* 20 February, 77.

Claessens, Stijn, Simeon Djankov, Joseph P. H. Fan, and Larry H. P. Lang. 1999. The rationale for groups: Evidence from East Asia. Working paper. Washington, D.C.: World Bank.

Cullison, Alan. 1998. Russia market regulator -3: Tomshneft resolution defeated. *Dow Jones International News Service,* 6 February, 13:54.

Daniels, Ronald J., and Jeffrey G. MacIntosh. 1991. Toward a distinctive Canadian corporate regime. *Osgoode Hall Law Review* 29:863–933.

DeAngelo, Harry, and Linda DeAngelo. 1985. Managerial ownership of voting rights: A study of public corporations with dual classes of common stock. *Journal of Financial Economics* 14:33–69.

Holmen, Martin, and Peter Hogfeldt. 1999. Corporate control and security design in initial public offerings. Working draft. Stockholm School of Economics.

Houston, Arthur L., Jr., and Carol Olson Houston. 1990. Financing with preferred stock. *Financial Management* 3:42–54.
Jensen, Michael C. 1986. Agency costs of free cash flows, corporate finances, and takeovers. *American Economic Review* 26:323–29.
Khanna, Tarun, and Krishna Palepu. 1999. Emerging market business groups, foreign investors, and corporate governance. NBER Working Paper no. 6955. Cambridge, Mass.: National Bureau of Economic Research.
———. 2000. Is group affiliation profitable in emerging markets? An analysis of diversified Indian business groups. *Journal of Finance* 55, no. 2:867–91.
———. In press. The future of business groups in emerging markets: Long-run evidence from Chile. *Academy of Management Journal.*
La Porta, Rafael, Florencio Lopez-de-Silanes, and Andrei Shleifer. 1999. Corporate ownership around the world. *Journal of Finance* 54:471–517.
La Porta, Rafael, Florencio Lopez-de-Silanes, Andrei Shleifer, and Robert Vishny. 1998. Law and finance. *Journal of Political Economy* 106:1113–55.
Morais, Richard C. 1998. Who needs P&G? *Forbes,* 23 March, 130–32.
Nothing can hold back Lippo. 1997. *Euromoney,* April, 182–85.
Solomon, J. 1996. Indonesia's Lippo restructuring approved. *Dow Jones International News Service,* 29 September, 11:33.
Storming the citadel: The Peter Wallenberg business empire. 1990. *Economist,* 23 June, 73.
Weidenbaum, Murray. 1996. The Chinese family business enterprise. *California Management Review* 38:141–56.
Whither the Wallenbergs? Swedish financier Peter Wallenberg. 1993. *Economist,* 25 December, 89.
Wolfenzon, Daniel. 1999. A theory of pyramidal ownership. Harvard University, Department of Economics. Mimeo.

## Comment Dennis P. Sheehan

The paper by Bebchuk, Kraakman, and Triantis focuses our attention on a known issue but one that has been little considered. They discuss the many ways in which a shareholder can separate cash-flow rights from control rights. The object of such separation of course is to control the firm while bearing little of the wealth consequences of decisions made as the controller.

The three devices that are commonly employed are dual class shares, pyramids, and cross-ownership. The authors analyze each of these and demonstrate how a controlling-minority shareholder (CMS) can use them to extract private benefits. More specifically, the authors show that project choice, firm size and scope, and control transfers are all likely to be affected by the separation of control rights from wealth consequences.

One of the important points that the authors make is that the agency

Dennis P. Sheehan is the Benzak Professor of Finance in the Smeal College of Business at Penn State University.

costs imposed by CMS structures can be highly nonlinear in ownership. Controlling-minority shareholders always get the full value of any private benefits that they extract from the firm. But, when they own a significant fraction of the firm, they also bear the consequences of any loss in firm value. As the proportion of cash-flow rights decreases to an arbitrarily small amount, the wealth consequences of extracting private benefits tilt dramatically in their favor even if much firm value is destroyed in the process.

In sum, CMS structures represent an extreme case where it appears that there are no disciplining forces either inside or outside the firm. What, then, prevents these shareholders from looting the firm? The authors identify two constraints on the behavior of controlling-minority shareholders. First, reputation may limit the behavior of controlling shareholders. Controlling shareholders who need to take any of their firms back to the capital markets must take some care to develop a reputation for treating minority claimholders fairly. Second, the legal system may accord rights to minority shareholders that a controlling shareholder cannot ignore. Countries clearly differ dramatically in the extent of this protection, as La Porta et al. (1999) document.

Having absorbed the mechanics of the paper, it is immediately apparent that it presents us with several conundrums. If CMS structures are potentially so costly, why do they appear to be so common? Why are they most common in precisely those countries that seem to afford minority shareholders the least protection? And, perhaps the most interesting one of all, given how abusive CMS structures can be, why would anyone voluntarily be a minority shareholder?

The authors are certainly aware of these issues and, in fact, conclude their paper with a suggested research agenda that would answer them. One of the privileges of a discussant is "to boldly go where no man has gone before." That privilege allows me to speculate about answers without having to worry about the prospect of doing the actual work.

One possibility is that, although agency costs of CMS structures can be large in principle, they are small in practice. A hint of that is contained in the puzzle that controlling shareholders usually do not "go all the way." In the work that Cliff Holderness and I have done on majority shareholders (see Holderness and Sheehan 1988), one of the results that surprised us is that majority shareholders often hold significantly more than is necessary to maintain control. Instead of holding their stakes at exactly 50.1 percent, they will often hold 60, 70, or 80 percent of the common stock. Although the reasons for doing so remain unclear, it is apparent that majority shareholders cannot be motivated solely or even mostly by a desire to expropriate the minority shareholders.

Indeed, one of the surprising things about majority shareholders (at least in the United States) is that it is difficult to find very much evidence that they do exploit their position to the detriment of minority shareholders. This is not to say that it never occurs, as it is easy to find specific examples of abuse (see Barclay, Holderness, and Pontiff 1993). But systematic evidence of widespread abuse is difficult to find in the data.

Similarly, there is not much evidence that dual class share firms are bad for minority shareholders. Results in DeAngelo and DeAngelo (1985) and Partch (1987) support efficiency explanations for dual class firms. Jarrell and Poulsen (1988) do find negative wealth effects when firm adopt dual class shares, but they are small in magnitude. Lehn, Netter, and Poulsen (1990) investigate why firms would choose a dual class recapitalization as opposed to a leveraged buyout (LBO). Both concentrate ownership, but they differ in their wealth effects, with LBOs increasing the wealth effect on owners and dual class recaps decreasing it. The authors, however, find that firms using the two approaches differ in their characteristics, thus favoring an efficiency explanation. Finally, Field and Karpoff (1999) investigate firms going public with antitakeover provisions, among which is dual class shares. Although the dual class arrangement could be viewed as a device for retaining the flow of private benefits, the fact remains that new shareholders willingly buy into firms in which wealth consequences are not proportional to voting rights. It seems likely that these new shareholders buy into these firms at prices that protect them from being exploited.

Here is one more (small) piece of evidence on CMS structures. A firm that regularly gets touted as the prototype for a new form of corporate structure is Thermo Electron, which has turned pyramiding into an art. Thermo has spun off some twenty five "children" or "grandchildren" and generally retains an ownership stake that is sufficient to control its offspring. Despite the potential for the parent corporation to abuse the offspring, the data suggest exactly the opposite. Thermo Electron sells at a significant discount to the value of its holdings in the carve-outs, suggesting that the subsidy flows from the controlling shareholder to the minority shareholders.

One explanation for some of these results is the protection afforded minority shareholders by the legal system in the United States, chiefly the common law tradition. Perhaps this explains why we observe relatively few CMS firms in the United States. That is, in the United States, minority shareholders can prevent controlling shareholders from extracting too many private benefits, so structures that are conducive to the extraction of private benefits are not worth the trouble.

Still, the legal system in the United States cannot explain why controlling shareholders are not as aggressive as they might be with their ownership structures or why Thermo Electron's discount has the wrong sign. And, certainly, the features of the U.S. legal system cannot explain what happens in other countries, which is where CMS structures seem so prevalent. Like most economists, I am partial to efficiency explanations. Looking at the frequency of CMS structures in other parts of the world, it is hard not to be struck by the fact that they seem to flourish in countries where capital markets and legal systems are not as developed as they are in the United States.

Several explanations spring to mind. If it is difficult for entrepreneurs to raise funds, the only way to extend a business may be to leverage a small stake using devices such as pyramids or dual class shares. Or, if markets tend not to be liquid, holding a large stake in any firm is not advisable, so, again, leveraging a small stake is the best strategy. If the legal system is not hospitable to claimholders' rights, perhaps one way to protect yourself is to be the controlling shareholder, assuming that you have the financial wherewithal. Indeed, in an interesting twist, Gomes (1999) shows that controlling shareholder structures might even beneficial! If the controlling shareholder cares about his reputation because of possible future sales of stock, dual class and pyramidal structures allow more of those future sales without losing control of the firm.

With speculation piled on speculation here, it is clear that the only answer is empirical work that will answer the puzzles posed by the authors. I am sure that the authors and I agree on this point. I will also bet that we could agree on another point: we hope that someone else will do the grubby work of data collection necessary to answer all these questions!

## References

Barclay, Michael, Clifford Holderness, and Jeffrey Pontiff. 1993. Private benefits from block ownership and discounts on closed-end funds. *Journal of Financial Economics* 33:263–91.

DeAngelo, Harry, and Linda DeAngelo. 1985. Managerial ownership of voting rights: A study of public corporations with dual classes of common stock. *Journal of Financial Economics* 14:33–70.

Field, Laura, and Jonathan Karpoff. 1999. Takeover defenses at IPO firms. Working paper. Pennsylvania State University.

Gomes, Armando. 1999. Going public without governance: Managerial reputations effects. Working paper. University of Pennsylvania.

Holderness, Clifford, and Dennis Sheehan. 1988. The role of majority shareholders in public corporations. *Journal of Financial Economics* 20:317–46.

Jarrell, Gregg, and Annette Poulsen. 1988. Dual class recapitalizations as antitakeover mechanisms. *Journal of Financial Economics* 20:129–52.

LaPorta, Rafael, Florencio Lopez-de-Silanes, Andrei Shleifer, and Robert Vishny. 1999. Corporate ownership around the world. *Journal of Finance* 54:471–518.

Lehn, Kenneth, Jeffry Netter, and Annette Poulsen. 1990. Consolidating corporate control: Dual class recapitalizations versus leveraged buyouts. *Journal of Financial Economics* 27:557–80.

Partch, Megan. 1987. The creation of a class of limited voting common stock and shareholders' wealth. *Journal of Financial Economics* 18:313–39.

# 11

# Inherited Wealth, Corporate Control, and Economic Growth
## The Canadian Disease?

Randall K. Morck, David A. Stangeland, and Bernard Yeung

Economic value is created by the efficient allocation of an economy's capital. Much of many countries' capital is proffered to corporations controlled by a small number of very wealthy families. This could be desirable if these families provide optimal corporate management. This paper raises the possibility that the currently observed allocation of corporate control may in fact be suboptimal in such countries.

The basic finding of this paper is that countries in which billionaire heirs' wealth is large relative to GDP grow more slowly than other countries at similar levels of development while countries in which self-made entrepreneur billionaire wealth is large relative to GDP grow more rapidly than other countries at similar levels of development. We consider several explanations for this finding. First, old wealth may entrench poor management, and control pyramids may distort their incentives. Second, a sharply skewed wealth distribution may create market power in capital markets, causing inefficiency. Third, entrenched billionaires have a vested interest in preserving the value of old capital and thus in slowing creative destruction. Fourth, old money becomes entrenched through control of the political system and, most especially, by rearing barriers to capital mobility. In contrast, substantial self-made billionaires' wealth is observed where such forces are ineffectual and creative destruction occurs.

Randall K. Morck is the Stephen A. Jarislowsky Distinguished Professor of Finance at the University of Alberta, Edmonton. David A. Stangeland is associate professor of finance at the University of Manitoba, Winnipeg. Bernard Yeung is the Krasnoff Professor of International Business and professor of economics at New York University.

The authors are grateful for helpful suggestions from Juan Alcacer, Mark Casson, Daniel Feenberg, E. Han Kim, David Levy, Krishna Palepu, Michael Weisbach, and Luigi Zingales.

We use micro-level evidence to support or refute these macro-level explanations. Canadian data are useful for this purpose because the large firms in that country exhibit a large range of ownership structures, with billionaire-controlled and widely held firms both abundant enough for statistical analyses. Also, the Canada-U.S. free trade agreement causes a useful regime change that generates testable predictions of our proposed explanations.

Our evidence is consistent with corporate control by heirs leading to slow growth because of inefficiency due to entrenched corporate control, capital market power, high barriers against outside investment, and perhaps also low investment in innovation. We hypothesize that this "Canadian disease" may be a generalizable explanation of our basic cross-country finding. Obviously, further investigation into micro-level data for other countries is called for.

## 11.1 The Ownership Structure of Countries

Table 11.1 displays the 1993 wealth of Forbes 1,000 billionaire residents by country of residence and scaled by 1993 GDP.[1] Our sample was constructed as follows. We began with all countries having 1997 GDP greater than U.S.$1 billion. We drop all postsocialist countries, such as China, the Czech Republic, Hungary, Poland, and Russia; all countries currently subject to economic sanctions, such as Cuba, Iran, and Iraq; the oil sheikdoms Bahrein and Brunei; the tax havens Liechtenstein and Luxembourg; Ethiopia, Kuwait, and Lebanon, which are undergoing postwar reconstruction; Sri Lanka and the Democratic Republic of the Congo, which are currently experiencing civil war; and Bangladesh, Egypt, El Salvador, Ghana, Jordan, Kenya, New Zealand, Nigeria, Saudi Arabia, Syria, Tanzania, and the United Arab Emirates because of missing data.

The final sample contains Argentina, Australia, Austria, Belgium, Brazil, Canada, Chile, Colombia, Denmark, Ecuador, Finland, France, Germany, Greece, Hong Kong, Iceland, India, Indonesia, Ireland, Israel, Italy, Japan, Korea, Malaysia, Mexico, the Netherlands, Norway, Peru, the Philippines, Portugal, Singapore, South Africa, Spain, Sweden, Switzerland, Taiwan, Thailand, Turkey, the United Kingdom, the United States, and Venezuela.

In subsequent econometric work, we drop the United States and the

1. Unfortunately, most studies of economic inequality focus on income distribution rather than wealth distribution. The typical finding is that economic growth is slower in countries with more uneven income distribution (Fishlow 1996; Birdsall, Ross, and Sabot 1995). Wealth-based Gini coefficients appear to be unavailable. We therefore take a practical approach and construct our own proxy for wealth, or capital ownership, concentration. As an innovation in 1997, Forbes included political dynasties ranging from the Suhartos to the Windsors in its billionaire list. For the few countries in which these families are present, we use 1997 family wealth. Our results are robust to dropping or including these families.

**Table 11.1** **Billionaires and Billionaire Wealth by Country and by Source of Wealth**

| | | Millions in Wealth over Billions of GDP | | | | | |
|---|---|---|---|---|---|---|---|
| Country | Billionaires per Million People | Total Billionaire Wealth | Entrepreneur Billionaire Wealth | Heir Billionaire Wealth | Probable Heir Billionaire Wealth | Entrepreneur and Heir Control | Political Family Billionaire Wealth |
| Argentina | 0.118 | 26.378 | 0 | 26.378 | 0 | 0 | 0 |
| Australia | 0.056 | 7.718 | 7.718 | 0 | 0 | 0 | 0 |
| Austria | 0 | 0 | 0 | 0 | 0 | 0 | 0 |
| Belgium | 0 | 0 | 0 | 0 | 0 | 0 | 0 |
| Brazil | 0.038 | 22.852 | 12.431 | 4.936 | 0 | 5.4845 | 0 |
| Canada | 0.173 | 40.204 | 0 | 24.898 | 15.3061 | 0 | 0 |
| Chile | 0.218 | 102.174 | 36.957 | 34.783 | 0 | 30.4348 | 0 |
| Colombia | 0.086 | 39.286 | 0 | 0 | 39.2857 | 0 | 0 |
| Denmark | 0.193 | 17.293 | 0 | 0 | 0 | 17.2932 | 0 |
| Ecuador | 0 | 0 | 0 | 0 | 0 | 0 | 0 |
| Finland | 0 | 0 | 0 | 0 | 0 | 0 | 0 |
| France | 0.191 | 16.799 | 2.07 | 11.863 | 2.8662 | 0 | 0 |
| Germany | 0.504 | 54.648 | 6.523 | 39.856 | 8.2691 | 0 | 0 |
| Greece | 0.48 | 133.333 | 0 | 66.667 | 66.6667 | 0 | 0 |
| Hong Kong | 2.188 | 361.307 | 193.157 | 157.802 | 10.3477 | 0 | 0 |
| Iceland | 0 | 0 | 0 | 0 | 0 | 0 | 0 |
| India | 0.002 | 11.985 | 0 | 8.24 | 3.7453 | 0 | 0 |
| Indonesia | 0.02 | 160.598 | 35.948 | 11.765 | 17.6471 | 0 | 95.238 |
| Ireland | 0 | 0 | 0 | 0 | 0 | 0 | 0 |
| Israel | 0.395 | 41.429 | 41.429 | 0 | 0 | 0 | 0 |

*(continued)*

**Table 11.1** (continued)

| Country | Billionaires per Million People | Millions in Wealth over Billions of GDP | | | | | |
|---|---|---|---|---|---|---|---|
| | | Total Billionaire Wealth | Entrepreneur Billionaire Wealth | Heir Billionaire Wealth | Probable Heir Billionaire Wealth | Entrepreneur and Heir Control | Political Family Billionaire Wealth |
| Italy | 0.088 | 10.352 | 4.658 | 5.694 | 0 | 0 | 0 |
| Japan | 0.289 | 18.252 | 5.5 | 7.895 | 4.857 | 0 | 0 |
| Korea | 0.068 | 31.988 | 12.422 | 19.565 | 0 | 0 | 0 |
| Malaysia | 0.213 | 125 | 70 | 0 | 55 | 0 | 0 |
| Mexico | 0.267 | 128.198 | 15.988 | 2.349 | 60.4651 | 31.3953 | 0 |
| Netherlands | 0.196 | 36.739 | 0 | 18.73 | 0 | 3.8095 | 14.199 |
| Norway | 0 | 0 | 0 | 0 | 0 | 0 | 0 |
| Peru | 0 | 0 | 0 | 0 | 0 | 0 | 0 |
| Philippines | 0.072 | 100 | 17.742 | 37.097 | 27.4194 | 17.7419 | 0 |
| Portugal | 0 | 0 | 0 | 0 | 0 | 0 | 0 |
| Singapore | 0.935 | 85.957 | 28.068 | 22.805 | 35.0846 | 0 | 0 |
| South Africa | 0.025 | 13.158 | 13.158 | 0 | 0 | 0 | 0 |
| Spain | 0.077 | 8.932 | 0 | 5.664 | 3.268 | 0 | 0 |
| Sweden | 0.229 | 56.354 | 0 | 0 | 6.6298 | 49.7238 | 0 |
| Switzerland | 1.133 | 76.953 | 9.375 | 47.656 | 7.4219 | 12.5 | 0 |
| Taiwan | 0.287 | 72.603 | 48.858 | 0 | 9.589 | 14.1553 | 0 |
| Thailand | 0.105 | 122.832 | 12.5 | 26.563 | 41.4063 | 29.6875 | 12.676 |
| Turkey | 0.034 | 28.358 | 0 | 0 | 0 | 28.3582 | 0 |
| United Kingdom | 0.086 | 11.166 | 1.134 | 7.423 | 0 | 2.268 | 0.341 |
| United States | 0.465 | 39.52 | 9.34 | 14.7 | 12.51 | 2.98 | 0 |
| Venezuela | 0.097 | 43.103 | 0 | 43.103 | 0 | 0 | 0 |

*Source:* Forbes 1,000 list of the world's richest people, 1993.

United Kingdom from our sample on the grounds that their corporate ownership structures are highly atypical, in that their large listed companies are predominantly directly held by small shareholders (La Porta et al. 1997). We leave them in table 11.1 since they provide useful benchmarks for wealth-concentration comparisons.

There is a remarkable degree of variation. The average billionaire wealth is 13.3 percent of GDP for the East Asian economies: Korea, Hong Kong, Indonesia, Malaysia, the Philippines, Singapore, Thailand, and Taiwan. Hong Kong is the least egalitarian of these, with billionaires holding wealth equal to 36 percent of its GDP. The average for Latin American countries in our sample is 4.5 percent, with Mexican billionaires' wealth the highest, at 12.8 percent of GDP. Billionaires are less important in rich countries, where the average is 2.4 percent. The least egalitarian rich countries are Greece, Switzerland, and Sweden, with billionaire wealth of 13.3, 7.7, and 5.6 percent of GDP, respectively. This contrasts with 1.1 percent for the United Kingdom, 4 percent for Canada, and just under 4 percent for the United States.

Large as they are, these numbers greatly understate the importance of wealthy families in most economies. La Porta, Lopez-de-Silanes, and Shleifer (1999) show that pyramid ownership structures are ubiquitous outside the United States and the United Kingdom. In a pyramid ownership structure, a wealthy family controls assets worth vastly more than its own wealth by holding controlling interests in companies, which hold controlling interests in other companies, which in turn hold controlling interests in still more companies. A control pyramid ten layers high, with 51 percent ownership at each level, magnifies a billion dollars of wealth into control over $840 billion ($1 billion/$0.51^{10}$) worth of corporate assets. Intercorporate cross-holdings and the use of supervoting shares for insiders and nonvoting shares for outsiders in many countries further extend and strengthen billionaires' control. An example of a fortune extended in this way is that of the Wallenberg family of Sweden. Although their actual wealth fails to get them onto Forbes' billionaire list, the firms that they control through a mixture of pyramids, cross-holdings, and multiple-voting shares constitute 40 percent of the market value of the Swedish stock exchange (Strom 1996). Similarly, firms in the estate of "Lucho" Naboa provide the incomes of about 3 million of Ecuador's 11 million people. The family's banana operations alone, which account for 40 percent of Ecuador's banana exports, generate about 5 percent of the country's GDP (De Cordoba 1995). Yet billionaire wealth for Ecuador is zero in table 11.1 since the family's actual wealth is less than $1 billion. If we conservatively take pyramids as multiplying a billionaire family's wealth into control over assets worth ten times as much, billionaire control averages 133 percent of GDP in East Asia, 45 percent of GDP in Latin America, and 24 percent of GDP in the OECD countries (although this calculation is not applicable in the United Kingdom and, especially, the United States, where control pyramids are seldom used).

## 11.2 Entrepreneurs, Inherited Wealth, and Economic Growth

Should the *ownership structure of a nation's capital,* in this context, the capital controlled by different types of billionaires, matter? There are numerous reasons to think that it might.

Building a fortune and passing it down to one's descendants might be a powerful motivation for prospective entrepreneurs to build great businesses. Wealthy heirs have the resources and incentives to monitor corporate managers carefully and so might improve corporate governance. Powerful families, whose fortunes are tied to their nation's economies, might lobby politicians to enact economically rational policies and might be more successful at this than small atomistic businessmen. Wealthy families might act to safeguard competitive and efficient capital markets and institutions. Wealthy families also have the security and the resources to bankroll innovation. Any or all of these factors could lead to a positive relation between economic growth and billionaire wealth.

However, a negative relation is also plausible a priori. Since intelligence is thought to be, at best, only partly inherited, an entrepreneur's descendants should regress steadily toward average talent with each new generation. If they value the control that pyramids and the like bestow on them, they become entrenched, mediocre managers. Their magnified control of capital may also let wealthy families shape prices in capital markets to further their own welfare at the expense of their countries. Also, with their wealth tied up in existing capital, wealthy families may be loath to finance innovations for fear that the ensuing creative destruction might get out of their control. Finally, their corporate control may give billionaire families economies of scale in political rent seeking and thereby divert public resources to their private goals, again to the detriment of their countries.

### 11.2.1 Observation

The actual relation between a country's capital ownership structure and economic growth is therefore an important but unexplored empirical question. To address this question, we run standard economic-growth regressions of the sort described by Mankiw (1995), with an extra term at the end:

$$\frac{\Delta Y}{Y} = \beta_0 + \beta_1 \ln\left(\frac{Y}{L}\right) + \beta_2 \frac{I}{K} + \beta_3 \ln(E) + \mathbf{b} \cdot \mathbf{C} + \varepsilon. \tag{1}$$

Our dependent variable is economic growth, defined as the average growth rate in real GDP, $Y$, averaged over 1994, 1995, and 1996. The independent variables in such regressions generally include the logarithm of each country's *1994 per capita GDP,* $\ln(Y/L)$; a physical capital accumulation rate, $I/K$, where $I$ is capital investment and $K$ is the existing capital stock; and a measure of human capital, the logarithm of the average years of education, $\ln(E)$. Our data on investment rates and education levels are for 1990 and 1985, respectively, and come from the World Bank Growth Data used by, for example, Barro and Lee (1996).

To these we add **C**, a variable or set of variables describing the capital controlled by different types of billionaires in each country. We use the wealth and the sources of wealth of each country's billionaires to construct these variables. An alternative approach would be to use wealth Gini coefficients. However, our research question is more about the type of wealthy people in a country than about the degree of wealth concentration per se. Another alternative approach would be based on the fractional ownership in each country's largest corporations. But this approach focuses on the billionaire's equity stakes as a fraction of firm value, rather than on their wealth as a fraction of the country's wealth, and so is less useful for our purposes.

We consider two basic types of billionaires, based on *Forbes* magazine's description of each billionaire and on additional information from *Who's Who.* The first is *self-made business entrepreneurs.* These are people who built huge fortunes from nothing or virtually nothing. We define $B$ to be the total wealth of a country's self-made business entrepreneurs and scale this by GDP, denoted $Y$. We thus add $B/Y$ to the regression described in (1) as the first component of **C**.

The second sort of billionaire we call *heirs.* We define their total wealth in each country to be $H$ and again scale by GDP, thus adding $H/Y$ as the second component of **C** in the regression described in (1). We have several alternative measures of this variable. We divide billionaires who are not self-made into different categories. Some are clearly not billionaires because of their entrepreneurial talents. These include heirs to great business fortunes and political dynasties. These we call *heirs.* Other billionaires have inherited substantial fortunes but greatly increased them. We call them *heir-entrepreneurs.* The remaining we classify as *probably heirs.* This category includes fortunes that appear to be controlled jointly by self-made billionaires and their heirs. This wealth is presumably in the process of being transferred across generations. It also includes some fortunes that we are simply unable to classify clearly because of inadequate documentation.

In table 11.2, we consider alternative measures of heir fortunes that include different subsets of the categories given above. Our first measure, $H_1$, is the wealth of heirs to business fortunes and political dynasties. The second, $H_2$, is $H_1$ plus the wealth of probably heirs. The third measure, $H_3$, is $H_1$ plus heir-entrepreneurs. Finally, $H_4$ is $H_1$ plus probably heirs and heir-entrepreneurs. The measures $H_5$–$H_8$ replicate $H_1$–$H_4$, respectively, but

**Table 11.2** **The Cross-Country Relation between Economic Growth and Capital Ownership Structure Controlling for Current per Capita Income, Capital Investment Rate, and Level of Education**

| | (1) | (2) | (3) | (4) | (5) | (6) | (7) | (8) |
|---|---|---|---|---|---|---|---|---|
| Intercept | 1.43 | 1.58 | 1.59 | 1.65 | 1.75 | 1.73 | 1.86 | 1.78 |
| | (.32) | (.30) | (.27) | (.28) | (.22) | (.26) | (.20) | (.25) |
| Log of per capita GDP: $\ln(Y/L)$ | **−1.76** | **−1.77** | **−1.80** | **−1.79** | **−1.54** | **−1.66** | **−1.62** | **−1.69** |
| | (.00) | (.00) | (.00) | (.00) | (.00) | (.00) | (.00) | (.00) |
| Capital accumulation rate: $I/K$ | **0.210** | **0.216** | **0.208** | **0.214** | **0.173** | **0.199** | **0.178** | **0.199** |
| | (.00) | (.00) | (.00) | (.00) | (.00) | (.00) | (.00) | (.00) |
| Average total years of education: $\ln(E)$ | 0.238 | 0.203 | 0.253 | 0.214 | 0.242 | 0.200 | 0.259 | 0.213 |
| | (.27) | (.35) | (.23) | (.32) | (.24) | (.35) | (.21) | (.32) |
| Business-entrepreneur billionaire wealth over GDP: $B/Y$ | **0.440** | **0.37** | **0.42** | **0.37** | **0.495** | **0.382** | **0.45** | **0.37** |
| | (.00) | (.00) | (.00) | (.00) | (.00) | (.00) | (.00) | (.00) |
| Billionaire-heir wealth over GDP: $H/Y$ | **−0.292** | **−0.168** | **−0.268** | **−0.157** | **−0.407** | **−0.191** | **−0.33** | **−0.17** |
| | (.03) | (.10) | (.03) | (.09) | (.01) | (.09) | (.01) | (.08) |
| | Definition of *Heir*[a] | | | | | | | |
| | $H_1$ | $H_2$ | $H_3$ | $H_4$ | $H_5$ | $H_6$ | $H_7$ | $H_8$ |
| $R^2$ | .519 | .488 | .531 | .489 | .545 | .491 | .536 | .491 |

*Note:* Numbers in parentheses are two-tailed $t$-test probability levels for rejecting a zero coefficient. Coefficients in boldface are statistically significant at 90 percent confidence or more. Sample of 39 countries consists of the countries listed in table 11.1 above minus the United Kingdom and the United States.

[a] $H_1$ includes only the wealth of billionaires known positively to be heirs, politicians, or politicians' relations. $H_2$ also includes the wealth of billionaires who are probably heirs. $H_3$ includes $H_1$ plus fortunes jointly controlled by a founder and his heirs. $H_4$ includes all the above. $H_5$–$H_8$ are analogous to $H_1$, $H_2$, $H_3$, and $H_4$ but do not include politician billionaires and their relations.

exclude political dynasties. All eight measures give remarkably similar results.[2] In subsequent tables, we measure *heir billionaire wealth* by $H_1$, fortunes clearly due to either inheritances or political dynasties. We use this measure to minimize the likelihood of contaminating our heir wealth variable with any fortunes that might be controlled by business entrepreneurs. However, this choice turns out to be unimportant: all the analyses in subsequent tables are qualitatively similar if other definitions of *heir* are used.

Table 11.2 confirms previous findings that countries tend to have higher rates of economic growth if their initial per capita GDP is low, if their capital accumulation rates are high, and (more tenuously) if their general level of education is high. Our added variables reveal a clear pattern. Economic growth is positively associated with self-made billionaire wealth but negatively associated with billionaire heir wealth. We emphasize that this is after controlling for per capita GDP, the rate of capital accumulation, and education.

The effect is economically, as well as statistically, significant. The average rate of GDP growth in our sample is 4.16 percent per year. Since the coefficient on heir billionaire wealth over GDP in the first regression is −.292, going from zero billionaire heir wealth to the seventy-fifth percentile, 3.293 percent of GDP, is associated with a slowdown of 0.962 percent per year, and heir wealth at the ninetieth percentile, 6.667 percent, corresponds to a growth slowdown of 1.95 percent per year.

### 11.2.2 Further Exploration

In the following sections, we consider different possible mechanisms by which heir wealth might affect economic growth and consider whether each, in turn, might be empirically rejected. To explore their empirical validity, we utilize firm-level data for Canada. That country is ideal for our purposes because large Canadian firms exhibit a wide range of ownership structures, with enough firms in each category to allow statistical analyses. Firm-level accounting data in Canada are also readily available and reliable. Finally, the United States and Canada are, in most aspects, very similar countries. Although natural resources account for a larger share of Canada's GDP, its resources industries and those of the United States are not dissimilar. The two economies have broadly similar factor endowments and employ virtually identical technology and human capital in similar institutional frameworks. Their corporate sectors differ markedly only in that the ownership structures of their largest firms are radically different. Thus, the U.S. economy provides a useful benchmark.

Table 11.3 displays the ownership structure of the 246 publicly traded firms in the list of the top 500 Canadian firms by sales in 1988, as reported

2. Heir-entrepreneur wealth, probably heir wealth, and political dynasty wealth, treated as separate right-hand-side variables, resemble heir wealth.

**Table 11.3 Publicly Traded Firms among the Largest 500 Canadian Firms by Sales, by Type of Controlling Shareholder**

| Type of Controlling Shareholder[a] | Firms[b] | Average Sales[c] | Fraction of Total Sales |
|---|---|---|---|
| Heir, direct or via pyramid | 44 | 1.15 | 0.20 |
| Business entrepreneur, direct or via pyramid | 27 | 0.42 | 0.05 |
| No controlling shareholder | 53 | 1.37 | 0.29 |
| Controlled by widely held Canadian parent, direct or via pyramid | 14 | 1.03 | 0.06 |
| Other individual or family, type unclear | 29 | 0.32 | 0.04 |
| Financial institution or investment fund | 6 | 0.46 | 0.01 |
| Foreign parent firm, direct or via pyramid | 49 | 1.34 | 0.26 |
| Government | 23 | 1.02 | 0.09 |
| Worker ownership | 1 | 0.16 | 0.00 |
| Total | 246[d] | 1.02 | 1.00 |

*Note:* Sample is firms in the 1988 *Financial Post* 500 for which accounting and ownership data are available.

[a]A controlling shareholder, under Canadian law, is anyone who controls more than 20 percent voting powers. Where there is more than one controlling shareholder, the firm is classified according to the type of the largest shareholder.

[b]Canadian reporting requirements allow consolidated financial reports for corporate groups. Consequently, the number of firms is understated.

[c]The number of firms and average sales are for those firms with reported sales in 1988 and accounting data for the variables used in tables 11.4 and 11.5. (Firms not reporting firm age are included.) Sales are for 1988 and are in billions of U.S. dollars.

[d]Of the 500 largest firms, 254 are privately held, so no details of the ownership structure are available.

in the *Financial Post Surveys* for that year. (We use 1988 data here because free trade with the United States changed the corporate landscape subsequent to that. We return to these changes below.) We follow Canadian corporate governance laws and define a controlling shareholder as anyone with a stake that bestows 20 percent voting power or more. This is a restrictive definition of control by U.S. standards, where much smaller stakes are thought sufficient to allow control.

Only 53 of the largest 246 public Canadian firms are widely held by this definition. This figure rises to 67 if publicly traded subsidiaries, subsidiaries of subsidiaries, and so on of widely held firms are added. The average stake of the largest shareholder is about 50 percent.[3] This contrasts starkly

3. The degree of concentration of Canadian ownership is greatly understated because the other 254 firms in the top 500 list are privately held and so must be dropped from our sample for lack of data.

with the United States, where Demsetz and Lehn (1985) report that the combined holdings of the largest five shareholders average less than 25 percent.

We proceed by dissecting Canadian firm-level data to see whether our explanations apply to that country. Obviously, firm-level analyses in other countries are needed before reliable generalizations are warranted. We also recognize that this leaves the issue of causality open, as future researchers may consider other mechanisms than those that we have evaluated.

## 11.3 Inherited Wealth and Corporate Control

In the United States, firms whose boards are dominated by a controlling family are beginning to attract the attention of corporate-governance critics. Referring to family-dominated public companies, Jon Lukomnik, the deputy controller for pensions of New York City, commented: "When you look at really abusive companies, you tend to find them" ("Boards Cut Out of Family Trees" 1996). U.S. family firms recently targeted by shareholder rights activists include Ethyl Corporation, where chairman and CEO Bruce Gottwald's 17.7 percent stake brings directorships for his two sons, a brother, and a nephew. Archer Daniel Midlands, Paccar Inc., the *New York Times,* and the Gap have attracted similar attention ("Boards Cut Out of Family Trees" 1996).

Stulz (1988) and Shleifer and Vishny (1989) develop theoretical frameworks describing how corporate governance might suffer when U.S. firms are unable to throw off substandard but entrenched managers. In this section, we argue that such problems may be many times worse in other economies.

### 11.3.1 The Divergence of Interests in Control Pyramids

Outside the United States, moneyed families often leverage their wealth into control over corporate assets worth far more. La Porta, Lopez-de-Silanes, and Shleifer (1999) show that this is achieved primarily through the use of *control pyramids.* An example of a control pyramid is the group of firms controlled by the Canadian billionaires Edward and Peter Bronfman. They own Broncorp Inc., which controls HIL Corporation with a 19.6 percent equity stake. HIL owns 97 percent of Edper Resources, which owns 60 percent of Brascan Holdings, which owns 5.1 percent of Brascan, which owns 49.9 percent of Braspower Holdings, which owns 49.3 percent of Great Lakes Power Inc., which owns 100 percent of First Toronto Investments, which owns 25 percent of Trilon Holdings, which owns 64.5 percent of Trilon Financial, which owns 41.4 percent of Gentra, which owns 31.9 percent of Imperial Windsor Group (*Directory of Inter-Corporate Ownership,* various issues). The Bronfmans' actual equity stake in Imperial Windsor works out to 0.03 percent, yet they have full control of it and of all the other firms in the pyramid above and beside it. This is because they either own more than 50 percent of the stock at each stage or control more than 50 percent of the votes via supervoting shares, intercorporate cross-holdings, or other arrangements that reduce the minimum size of a control stake. This branch of the Bronfman family controls several hundred firms in this way (*Directory of Inter-Corporate Ownership* 1998).

More formally, a simplified control pyramid can be thought of as an arrangement where a wealthy family owns fraction $\alpha \in (0, 1)$ of firm $A$, which owns fraction $\alpha$ of firms $B_i$, which each own fraction $\alpha$ of firms $C_i$, and so on.

Such a control pyramid leverages a family's wealth, $\omega$, into control over corporate assets, $\wp$, worth many times more. For example, let firm A be worth \$1 million. It owns fraction $\alpha$ of each of the \$1 million firms $B_1$ and $B_2$. Firm $B_1$ then owns fraction $\alpha$ of the \$1 million firms $C_1$ and $C_2$, and firm $B_2$ owns $\alpha$ of $C_3$ and $C_4$. These can then own eight firms worth \$1 million each, and these in turn can own sixteen \$1 million firms. If one vote per share of stock is used, $\alpha$ must exceed 50 percent. If differential voting shares, intercorporate shareholdings, or other irregularities are allowed, $\alpha$ can be much lower, and the rate at which divergence of ownership from control grows with each additional layer is larger.

If fractional ownership $\alpha$ is required for control, the value of the assets under a family's control is $\wp$, and the family's wealth is $\omega$,

$$\wp = \Delta\omega, \tag{2}$$

where we define the *pyramid multiplier* to be

$$\Delta \equiv \frac{1}{\alpha^n}. \tag{3}$$

For example, if $\alpha$ is 1/3 and a family used a six-layer pyramid to control its actual physical assets, it can leverage \$1 billion of wealth into control over $3^6$ or \$729 billion in corporate assets.[4]

### 11.3.2 Billionaires' Objectives and Public Share Value

Pyramids generate a divergence of interests between controlling shareholders and other shareholders analogous to that noted by Jensen and Meckling (1976) between managers and shareholders, but more extreme. Jensen and Meckling showed that, if a manager who owns fraction $\alpha \in [0, 1]$ of an equity-financed firm's stock destroys \$1.00 worth of corporate assets to receive personal benefits worth $\gamma \in [0, 1]$, he is better off as long as $\gamma > \alpha$.

4. In practice, $\alpha$ may be different in each level of the pyramid and in each chain of control. A more general formula for the pyramid multiplier of the control chain $\{\alpha_{1j}, \alpha_{2j}, \ldots, \alpha_{nj}$ linking firm $j$ to the family firm $n$ levels above is $\Delta^j = [\Pi_{i=1}^{n} \alpha^{ij}]^{-1}$, and the analogue of eq. (2) is correspondingly more complicated.

In a pyramid, the divergence between control and actual ownership is potentially much worse than in Jensen and Meckling's example. The divergence is essentially compounded once for each pyramid level that separates the firm in question from the family firm that holds ultimate control. The family's welfare is advanced when it spends $1.00 of corporate wealth in a pyramid company it controls to gain $\gamma < 1$ in personal benefits if $\gamma > \alpha^n$. Again, differential voting shares, golden shares, and other devices allow control to be exercised with $\alpha << 50$ percent at each level, so the divergence of ownership from control rights can be even more extreme. Since $\alpha^n$ approaches zero as $n$ becomes large, value-destroying consumption of corporate resources becomes more attractive as the number of levels in the control pyramid rises.[5]

Examples of such consumption of corporate resources are abundant. Controlling families may confiscate corporate property for their personal use. They may interfere in corporate decision making to benefit themselves or their friends, to advance pet projects, or to push political goals. They may use transfer pricing to shift income from publicly traded firms they control to private firms they own outright, from firms low in control pyramids to firms near their apexes, or from firms they control via supervoting shares to firms in which they actually own a majority of the stock. Such transfer pricing can be accomplished via payments for intermediate goods, the private placement of one firm's securities with another, royalty payments for patent or brand-name use, captive insurance subsidiaries, or any number of other channels.

In some cases, the family patriarch may use corporate resources to advance a particular political or social view. For example, when the Wallenberg family's top professional manager, Percy Barnevik, told a *New York Times* reporter, "If we can't get value, we will sell out," indicating that weak Wallenberg firms might be sold, a surprised Peter Wallenberg clarified, "We would go to very great lengths to resuscitate a company. Whatever he might have said is still a matter of interpretation." In the same article, Anders Scharp, vice-chairman of the Wallenberg flagship, Investor's AP, quipped, "It's family values versus shareholder values" (Latour and Steinmetz 1998). Although Peter Wallenberg's views may reflect popular opinion in Sweden, this need not always be so. If the family patriarch uses corporate resources he controls, but does not fully own, to pursue an agenda with which shareholders do not agree, a misallocation of resources can result. The family patriarch does not bear the full economic costs of his agenda, but the shareholders and the society at large do.

The potential for such prima facie misallocation is a central concern of

5. For more formal and complete models of corporate pyramids, see Bebchuk and Zingales (chap. 2 in this volume), Bebchuk, Kraakman, and Triantis (chap. 10 in this volume), and Wolfenzohn (1998).

corporate-governance law outside the United States (see Daniels and Morck 1995). For example, Canadian corporate-governance law contains strict regulations about the disclosure of "related-party transactions" and about minority shareholders' rights. Officers and directors are expected to treat all shareholders equally, rather than simply safeguard the shareholders' presumably identical interests in value maximization, as in the United States. However, a recent study of Canadian corporate governance concluded that these protective measures are inadequate (see Daniels and Morck 1995).[6]

### 11.3.3 Entrenched Family Control

Most students of psychology agree that intelligence is, at best, only partially hereditary. Since entrepreneurial ability is presumably one dimension of intelligence, successive generations of heirs to a business entrepreneur's fortune should, on average, exhibit abilities that regress steadily toward the population mean. Entrenched family control, therefore, leads to an increased probability of mediocre management with each successive generation unless the family either delegates decision making to professional managers or is genetically very lucky.

Consistent with the argument that they value control, many wealthy families have difficulty accepting professional managers. In 1995, Stanley Heath resigned after only one year as CEO of Bata Inc., a multinational shoe store chain. The Czech-Canadian Bata family had hired him to usher in fundamental changes and then, according to the *Toronto Globe and Mail,* decided that they did not like the changes after all (Heinzl 1995). According to the *New York Times,* Swedish billionaire Marcus Wallenberg repeatedly denounced his son Peter as having "neither the intelligence nor the vision to head the family businesses" (Strom 1996, 12F). In 1982, near the end of his life, Marcus tried to position Volvo chairman Gyllenhammer, a professional manager, to take his place. Peter quietly bought shares in the relatively widely held Volvo until he had enough leverage over Gyllenhammer to force him out of the Wallenberg companies. Peter is now the undisputed patriarch of the Wallenberg business group, which remains a strong and important part of the Swedish economy.

This unwillingness to cede power to professional managers means that the question of succession can also adversely affect corporate governance. Prolonged internecine power struggles can paralyze family corporate

6. In a country where a few large shareholders control most corporations through pyramids, supervoting shares, or other means, there is little if any opportunity for managers to ignore the large shareholders' wishes. Shleifer and Vishny (1988) convincingly argue that large-shareholder oversight in the United States should prevent managers from pursuing their self-interest at the shareholders' expense. In many other economies, such a salutary view of large shareholders sounds naive or even disingenuous.

groups. For example, the Canadian McCain corporate group was maimed by a festering dispute between the ruling brothers, Wallace and Harrison, over whose son should succeed them (McLaughlin 1995a). In Ecuador, deceased banana billionaire "Lucho" Naboa's second wife, Mercedes, and his second son from his first marriage, Alvaro, fought an unseemly struggle for control of his corporate group. Apparently, someone even hired thugs to steal copies of the will hidden in New York.[7] Meanwhile, the family's firms drifted (De Cordoba 1995). Different families have attempted to avoid such problems in different ways. The Eaton family of Canada defused succession problems by bringing increasing numbers of Eatons into managerial positions with each successive generation. The family's flagship company is currently in bankruptcy. The Bronfman family has used a more Darwinian approach, letting contending heirs compete to be named *dauphin.* Having no immediate successor can be as big a problem as is too many possible successors. When patriarch Ted Rogers of Rogers Communications retired in 1994, his children Lisa, then twenty-seven, and Edward, twenty-six, were regarded as heirs apparent who would take control after another ten years or so of training. Interim managers were unable to exercise leadership in this situation, and Ted Rogers returned despite triple bypass and eye surgery (McLaughlin 1995b).

Many aging founders have difficulty even contemplating their retirement, let alone readying their corporate groups for professional managers or for the next generation of the family. Despite a public declaration of his intention to retire at sixty-five, Paul Desmarais, patriarch of Power Corporation, the key company of one of Canada's largest control pyramids, remains firmly in control. The *Financial Post* reports an anonymous possible successor as saying, "I don't know how to get rid of dad's old boys. They don't understand present competitive life, customer service, and just-in-time delivery. They're just sort of performing an activity, like having coffee every morning. But I can't do anything about it because dad won't let me fire them" (McLaughlin 1995a, 14–15).

All these examples are qualitatively similar to *entrenched management* in U.S. firms with insider ownership above a certain threshold, as modeled by Stulz (1988) and Shleifer and Vishny (1989). That is, the family-appointed managers of firms in control pyramids are not vulnerable to removal by public shareholders through hostile takeovers, proxy contests, or other mechanisms as only a minority of the stock of any individual firm is in public hands. The difference is that the entrenchment of these family dynasties in other countries is hereditary and affects the dozens or hundreds of companies in family-controlled pyramids.

7. Who hired the thugs is unclear, although the *Wall Street Journal* (De Cordoba 1995) reported that the police suspected a family power play.

### 11.3.4 Family Control and Firm Performance: The Worst of Both Worlds?

In the United States, many studies have found that divergence-of-interests problems, like those described in section 11.3.2, reduce shareholder value for very widely held firms while management-entrenchment problems, like those described in section 11.3.3, reduce shareholder value for relatively closely held firms (see, among many others, Stulz 1988; McConnell and Servaes 1990; and Morck et al. 1988). We have shown how pyramids can magnify the divergence of interests between controlling families and the public shareholders of pyramid companies. We have also argued that pyramids entrench hereditary management, regardless of competence, in more complete control over more corporate assets than is possible with the same family wealth in the United States.[8] Firms in pyramids are thus simultaneously potentially subject to the worst of both problems in terms of public-shareholder value.[9]

Of course, if the family provides superior management in firms it controls, this may negate all the problems outlined above. Khanna and Palepu (1999, chap. 9 in this volume) argue that skilled corporate management is scarce in India and that family corporate groups organized as pyramids are, on net, beneficial because they expand the scope to which the families' management skills are applied. This may be true in many cases, including the Bronfman, Wallenberg, and other corporate groups mentioned above.[10] Nonetheless, pyramids and the leverage that they introduce between ownership and control unquestionably create latitude for immense corporate-governance problems.

To investigate these issues, tables 11.4 and 11.5 compare the performance of Canadian firms according to the type of controlling shareholder they have. The categories of controlling shareholder that we consider are analogous to those covered in the previous section. Firms in pyramids are defined as having the same controlling shareholder as the firm at the pyramid's apex. We divide firms into the following categories: Firms with-

8. Control pyramids are essentially unknown in the United States. We suspect that this is because the United States imposes double taxation on virtually all dividends. In contrast, Canada and other countries with which we are familiar tax dividends paid to people, leaving most intercorporate dividends tax-free for the recipient firm. Clearly, pyramid control becomes prohibitively expensive when intercorporate dividends are taxed. Public finance and tax economists seem not to have appreciated the corporate-governance implications of dividend-taxation policies.

9. Note that some discussions of managerial entrenchment assume that managers gain pure utility from control. This assumption is not necessary. If rent-seeking power is proportional to assets controlled rather than wealth and rent seeking allows those with control to pursue their self-interest, managers and large shareholders should value control as a means for increasing their consumption.

10. Daniels, Morck, and Stangeland (1995) find that Bronfman pyramid firms performed no worse than other similar firms but appear to follow higher-risk strategies.

**Table 11.4** **Relation of Controlling Shareholder's Category to Performance of Large Canadian Firms, Based on 1984–89 Annual Reports Controlling for Firm Age and Size (industry benchmarks are 3-digit U.S. industry averages)**

| Controlling Shareholders' Categories Compared | Dependent Variable | | | | | | | | | | | | | | | |
|---|---|---|---|---|---|---|---|---|---|---|---|---|---|---|---|---|
| | Operating Income over Assets | | | | Operating Income over Sales | | | | Sales Growth | | | | Employees Growth | | | |
| | 1984–89 Mean | | 1984–89 Median | | 1984–89 Mean | | 1984–89 Median | | 1984–89 Mean | | 1984–89 Median | | 1984–89 Mean | | 1984–89 Median | |
| Heir minus business entrepreneur | −.0113 | −.0156 | −.0131 | −.0188 | **−.0299** | **−.0274** | **−.0346** | **−.0350** | **−.115** | **−.0794** | **−.0661** | −.0430 | **−.285** | −.0526 | **−.265** | **−.219** |
| | (.56) | (.32) | (.52) | (.26) | (.08) | (.13) | (.05) | (.07) | (.10) | (.12) | (.18) | (.54) | (.06) | (.85) | (.08) | (.05) |
| | [52] | [70] | [52] | [70] | [52] | [70] | [52] | [70] | [52] | [70] | [52] | [70] | [52] | [70] | [52] | [70] |
| Heir minus widely held | −.00915 | **−.0192** | −.00498 | −.0150 | **−.0547** | **−.0443** | **−.05820** | **−.0426** | **−.0756** | **−.0938** | **−.0663** | **−.0685** | −.0112 | .221 | .0478 | **.0622** |
| | (.56) | (.10) | (.76) | (.23) | (.01) | (.02) | (.01) | (.02) | (.11) | (.08) | (.09) | (.10) | (.88) | (.22) | (.43) | (.17) |
| | [74] | [101] | [74] | [101] | [74] | [101] | [74] | [101] | [74] | [101] | [74] | [101] | [74] | [101] | [74] | [101] |
| Heir minus all other domestic private-sector firms | −.00918 | **−.0241** | −.00223 | **−.0180** | **−.0354** | **−.0300** | **−.0342** | **−.0274** | −.0859 | −.0666 | **−.0525** | −.0330 | −.128 | .144 | −.0334 | −.0125 |
| | (.53) | (.05) | (.85) | (.08) | (.05) | (.05) | (.06) | (.07) | (.29) | (.33) | (.13) | (.27) | (.38) | (.24) | (.56) | (.80) |
| | [200] | [200] | [200] | [200] | [200] | [200] | [200] | [200] | [200] | [200] | [200] | [200] | [200] | [200] | [200] | [200] |
| Business entrepreneur minus widely held | −.00960 | −.00934 | −.00454 | −.00188 | **−.0332** | **−.0284** | **−.0317** | −.0193 | −.0101 | −.0454 | −.0378 | −.0600 | **.184** | **.180** | **.233** | **.247** |
| | (.55) | (.47) | (.78) | (.89) | (.16) | (.20) | (.20) | (.41) | (.89) | (.57) | (.44) | (.31) | (.12) | (.09) | (.03) | (.01) |
| | [68] | [83] | [68] | [83] | [68] | [83] | [68] | [83] | [68] | [83] | [68] | [83] | [68] | [83] | [68] | [83] |
| Business entrepreneur minus all other domestic private-sector firms | −.00611 | −.00805 | .00271 | .00161 | −.00935 | −.00040 | −.00128 | −.0112 | −.0101 | −.0104 | −.00813 | −.00962 | .147 | .141 | **.233** | **.225** |
| | (.71) | (.61) | (.84) | (.90) | (.64) | (.98) | (.95) | (.56) | (.91) | (.90) | (.83) | (.80) | (.37) | (.36) | (.00) | (.00) |
| | [200] | [200] | [200] | [200] | [200] | [200] | [200] | [200] | [200] | [200] | [200] | [200] | [200] | [200] | [200] | [200] |
| Pyramids included | No | Yes | No | Yes | No | Yes | No | Yes | No | Yes | No | Yes | No | Yes | No | Yes |

*Note:* The numbers shown are coefficients on dummy variables $\delta_i$ (one if the firm is in subsample 1, zero if it is in subsample 2) in ordinary least squares regressions of the form $p_i - \bar{p} = \beta_0 + \beta_1 \log(\text{sales}_i) + \beta_2 \log(\text{age}_i) + \beta_3\delta_i$ estimated across the relevant two subsamples. Boldface type indicates significance at the 10 percent level in a one-tailed $t$-test. Numbers in parentheses are two-tailed $t$-test probability levels. Numbers in brackets are sample sizes.

**Table 11.5** **Performance Differences for Large Canadian Firms by Controlling Shareholder Category, Performance Data from 1984–89 Annual Reports (benchmark for each Canadian firm is a U.S. firm matched by size, age, and 3-digit industry)**

| Controlling Shareholders' Categories Compared | Dependent Variable | | | | | | | | | | | | | | | |
|---|---|---|---|---|---|---|---|---|---|---|---|---|---|---|---|---|
| | Operating Income over Assets | | | | Operating Income over Sales | | | | Sales Growth | | | | Employees Growth | | | |
| | 1984–89 Mean | | 1984–89 Median | | 1984–89 Mean | | 1984–89 Median | | 1984–89 Mean | | 1984–89 Median | | 1984–89 Mean | | 1984–89 Median | |
| Heir minus business | **−.0737** | **−.0417** | **−.0690** | −.0319 | **−.0510** | **−.0888** | **−.0514** | **−.0901** | **−.117** | −.0556 | −.0879 | −.0195 | −.147 | .114 | −.126 | .0883 |
| entrepreneur | (.04) | (.12) | (.05) | (.24) | (.11) | (.02) | (.13) | (.02) | (.14) | (.37) | (.27) | (.67) | (.53) | (.21) | (.59) | (.29) |
| | [33] | [56] | [33] | [56] | [33] | [56] | [33] | [56] | [33] | [56] | [33] | [56] | [33] | [56] | [33] | [56] |
| Heir minus widely held | −.0531 | **−.0417** | −.0451 | −.0319 | **−.106** | **−.0888** | **−.115** | **−.0901** | −.0688 | −.0556 | −.0349 | −.0195 | .105 | .114 | .0951 | .0883 |
| | (.56) | (.10) | (.76) | (.23) | (.01) | (.02) | (.01) | (.02) | (.38) | (.37) | (.55) | (.67) | (.38) | (.21) | (.41) | (.29) |
| | [41] | [56] | [41] | [56] | [41] | [56] | [41] | [56] | [41] | [56] | [41] | [56] | [41] | [56] | [41] | [56] |
| Heir minus all other domestic | **−.0524** | **−.0392** | **−.0454** | **−.0364** | **−.0483** | **−.0477** | **−.0451** | **−.0462** | **−.0946** | −.0586 | −.0527 | −.0345 | .0150 | .0590 | .0117 | .0220 |
| private-sector firms | (.04) | (.06) | (.07) | (.09) | (.14) | (.09) | (.20) | (.12) | (.11) | (.24) | (.29) | (.42) | (.89) | (.52) | (.41) | (.80) |
| | [104] | [104] | [104] | [104] | [104] | [104] | [104] | [104] | [104] | [104] | [104] | [104] | [104] | [104] | [104] | [104] |
| Business entrepreneur minus | −.00770 | −.0184 | −.00194 | −.00597 | **−.0652** | **−.0779** | **−.0749** | **−.0813** | .0472 | .0349 | .0474 | .0490 | .0976 | .142 | .0995 | .131 |
| widely held | (.81) | (.49) | (.96) | (.83) | (.12) | (.05) | (.10) | (.05) | (.56) | (.61) | (.47) | (.36) | (.52) | (.25) | (.49) | (.27) |
| | [44] | [54] | [44] | [54] | [68] | [83] | [68] | [83] | [68] | [83] | [68] | [83] | [68] | [83] | [68] | [83] |
| Business entrepreneur minus | .00395 | .00124 | .00742 | .00421 | −.00967 | −.0106 | −.00586 | −.00887 | .0562 | .0590 | .0562 | .0531 | .113 | .122 | .118 | .116 |
| all other domestic private- | (.87) | (.96) | (.76) | (.85) | (.76) | (.72) | (.86) | (.78) | (.32) | (.27) | (.24) | (.24) | (.27) | (.21) | (.23) | (.21) |
| sector firms | [104] | [104] | [104] | [104] | [104] | [104] | [104] | [104] | [104] | [104] | [104] | [104] | [104] | [104] | [104] | [104] |
| Pyramids included | No | Yes | No | Yes | No | Yes | No | Yes | No | Yes | No | Yes | No | Yes | No | Yes |

*Note:* The numbers shown are coefficients on dummy variables $\delta_i$ (one if the firm is in subsample 1, zero if it is in subsample 2) in ordinary least squares regressions of the form $p_i - \bar{p} = \beta_0 + \beta_1 \log(\text{sales}_i) + \beta_2 \log(\text{age}_i) + \beta_3\delta_i$ estimated across the relevant two subsamples. Boldface type indicates significance at the 10 percent level in a one-tailed $t$-test. Numbers in parentheses are two-tailed $t$-test probability levels. Numbers in brackets are sample sizes.

out control blocks of 20 percent or more are called *widely held.* Firms controlled by descendants of their founders are called *heir controlled.* Firms controlled by their founders are called *business entrepreneur controlled.* In some comparisons, we use a category called *all other domestic private sector.* This group is different in each comparison and includes all private-sector firms in our full sample less the firms to which they are being compared. For example, in a comparison of heir-controlled firms and all other private-sector firms, the latter include all the firms listed in table 11.3 above for which data are available except heir-controlled firms, government-owned firms, and foreign-owned firms.

We use four alternative measures of firm performance: *return on assets, return on sales, real growth in total sales,* and *growth in number of employees.* Return on assets and return on sales are defined as income plus taxes plus interest plus depreciation over total assets and total sales, respectively. Data for these variables are from the *Report on Business* database. In analyses like these, controlling for industry differences is important. Unfortunately, many large Canadian firms have no comparable rivals within Canada. We therefore use two methods to control for industry norms: table 11.4 uses U.S. three-digit industry averages, constructed from Compustat data as proxies for Canadian industry benchmarks, while table 11.5 uses U.S. firms of approximately the same size and age as our Canadian firms and in the same three-digit industry.[11] Canadian corporate groups with consolidated balance sheets are compared to diversified U.S. conglomerates. Because the U.S. and Canadian economies are broadly similar in most dimensions except for ownership structure, such comparisons are legitimate. To smooth the performance indicators, we consider medians of each from 1984 through 1989. We define firm size as total 1988 sales and firm age as the number of years between the initial incorporation year and 1988, as listed in the *Financial Post* surveys or in corporate histories.

Table 11.4 shows the values and significance levels of dominant-shareholder-type dummies $\delta_i$ in regressions of performance, $p$, relative to U.S. industry average benchmarks, $\bar{p}$, and with controls for firm size and firm age. For example, in a test of heir-controlled firms versus self-made business-entrepreneur-controlled firms, $\delta_i$ is one if the dominant shareholder is an heir and zero if the dominant shareholder is an entrepreneur. The regression

$$(4) \qquad p - \bar{p} = \beta_0 + \beta_1 \log(\text{firm size}) + \beta_2 \log(\text{firm age}) + \beta_3 \delta$$

is then run across the two subsamples of firms, and the values of the coefficient $\beta_3$ are recorded in table 11.4 for each pair of subsamples. Table 11.5 contains the values and significance levels of the same regression coefficient, but the benchmark, $\bar{p}$, is the analogous performance measures

11. For details, see the data appendix.

for a U.S. firm in the same three-digit industry and of the same size and age as the Canadian firm in question.[12]

We can summarize the pattern findings in tables 11.4 and 11.5 as follows. Control by heirs is associated with lower returns on sales and assets and with growth that is less than or equal to that observed in other comparable firms.[13] In contrast, founder control is associated with earnings lower than those in widely held firms but higher than those in heir-controlled firms and with growth greater than or equal to that of widely held firms and that of other firms in general. The pattern of signs and significance levels is similar regardless of whether we include firms in control pyramids or consider only firms directly owned by the shareholders in question. This evidence is consistent with the hypothesis that widespread corporate control by heirs is, at least partly, responsible for the reduced economic growth of countries with large wealthholdings by heirs shown in table 11.2. It does not, however, substantiate our concern that control pyramids might worsen the damage.

## 11.4 Inherited Wealth and Capital Market Power

In some countries, control pyramids and other mechanisms give billionaire families control over substantial fractions of their country's capital assets. This could conceivably translate into monopoly and monopsony market power in their domestic capital markets.

### 11.4.1 Limited Sources of Capital for Entrepreneurs

An efficient microeconomic allocation of capital requires that the risk-adjusted cost of capital be the same for all firms. The legal, regulatory, and institutional structures of many countries arguably channel capital to certain firms and limit other firms' access to capital.

First, many countries' stock market regulations are such that entrepreneurs find equity initial public offerings (IPOs) unattractive sources of capital (La Porta et al. 1997). Private equity financing in the form of ven-

12. We continue to include age and size controls in table 11.5 because the relation between relative performance and ownership may be different for firms of different sizes and ages. In fact, the logarithm of firm age retains its significance in many of the regressions in table 11.5.

13. We need to be careful about our inference that heir-controlled firms have lower average returns on assets. Research-and-development (R&D) spending is a minus item in the calculation of after-tax operating income since it is part of general, sales, and administrative expenses, but it does not enter into the calculation of total assets since it is expensed rather than depreciated. A precise adjustment is difficult since the disclosure of R&D is optional under Canadian generally accepted accounting policy. However, only the numerator of the return-on-sales figures should be affected by this problem. As a rough check of whether R&D is biasing our results, we first estimated the relation of reported R&D to heir ownership. R&D is negatively correlated with heir ownership. If actual R&D mirrors reported numbers, this effect strengthens, rather than weakens, our return on sales-and-assets findings.

ture capital is primarily a U.S. phenomenon. Although other countries are attempting to foster venture capital financing, their scale remains limited (see "Adventures with Capital" 1997; "Finance and Economics" 1998). In Canada, the federal government has been providing generous tax incentives to create a venture capital industry controlled by labor unions.[14] In both Europe and Canada, government-run funds play large roles in the venture capital business, but these initiatives tend to confuse venture capital financing with subsidies to depressed regional economies (see Murray 1998; and Best and Mitra 1997).

Second, entrepreneurs' access to debt financing is often limited. Public-debt issues are unavailable to small, start-up firms. The junk bond industry in the United States changed this, starting in the 1980s, but it has yet to spread outside that country in any significant way (see Hagger 1997). Banks in most countries prefer to lend to large, established borrows. Although the large Canadian banks have recently begun to boast of their lending to small businesses, they still require substantial collateralizable assets—a rarity among entrepreneurial firms whose main asset is usually the intangible ideas of the entrepreneur (MacIntosh 1994). If billionaire families either control banks outright or influence them through political rent seeking more effectively than can entrepreneurs or the representatives of widely held firms' shareholders, a redirection of capital might occur.[15]

Third, government industrial policies in many countries direct capital toward large, established businesses. Plausibly, these firms are more able to lobby for subsidies. Their stability is also more likely to be the object of lobbying by organized labor. For example, Beason and Weinstein (1996) document that the (in)famous Japanese postwar industrial policy, by and large, subsidized unprofitable established industries. Also, until very recently, the Korean government had an explicit policy of orchestrating generous low-cost bank loans to large family-controlled *chaebol* corporate groups. The result was an average debt-to-equity ratio of 4.0 in 1996 and relentless capital expenditure growth by these firms. The same year, *chaebol* firms averaged a 1 percent return on equity.[16] A key part of the IMF's ongoing criticism of Asian "crony capitalism" is that established firms have too ready access to capital while new entrants cannot raise money locally.

Finally, firms in many countries have been prevented from obtaining foreign capital by restrictions on inward investment flows. Explicit policies to deter both foreign direct investment (FDI) and inward foreign portfolio investment were especially common in emerging markets (Kim and Singal

14. Management-expense ratios in these funds can reach 10 percent per year, and their voting structures lock in union control (see Austin 1996).

15. In sec. 11.6 below, we argue that such a differential investment in rent seeking might well exist.

16. For a detailed financial analysis of Korean public firms in the 1990s, see Kim, Kim, and Yi (1998).

1993). Interestingly, many of the countries in our sample with the highest heir-controlled wealth had explicit share classes or industry sectors that were unavailable to foreigners, ceilings on foreign shareholding, or mandatory long holding periods for foreign investors, at least until quite recently. These include Argentina, Chile, Colombia, Greece, Indonesia, Korea, Malaysia, the Philippines, and Thailand. Except for closed-end funds, Taiwan's stock market was closed until 1991, after which foreigners were allowed to invest up to a 10 percent ceiling. This was only raised to 15 percent in 1995. Even advanced countries have regulations hindering foreign portfolio investment. For example, Japanese firms could not issue bonds to foreigners until quite recently. Even Canada, under Pierre Trudeau, made local firms' access to FDI contingent on bureaucratic approval.

These distortions might lead to more aggressive use of capital by family pyramid firms than by other firms. The absence of a well-developed venture capital market impedes entrepreneurial firms but not established family firms. If billionaire families are better at lobbying for subsidies than entrepreneurs or representatives of the shareholders of widely held firms, a differential access to capital might also ensue. Also, if families are overly optimistic about their management abilities, the greater divergence of interests and entrenchment problems in pyramid firms (discussed in sec. 11.3 above) might allow them to overexpand more aggressively than would be prudent for a widely held firm. If the initial complement of large firms are members of family pyramids, barriers to capital inflow arguably lock in control by those firms, preventing entrepreneurial firms and widely held firms from rising to challenge them.

### 11.4.2 Limited Investment Opportunities for Savers

Economic efficiency also requires free competition for savers' money. Again, the legal, regulatory, and institutional structures of many countries severely restrict savers' portfolio choices, or did until very recently.

Given the prevalence of billionaire control, savers in many countries have little choice but to hold the stocks of billionaire-controlled companies in their portfolios. These problems afflict investors in most countries other than the United States and the United Kingdom. Even in Canada, only fifty-three of the top 500 firms are widely held (see table 11.3 above). Since these do not span all the industries in the Canadian economy, a diversified portfolio of large widely held Canadian firms is not possible.

The same lack of choice for savers applies to debt. Until recently, Japanese corporate bonds were unavailable to domestic investors in that country because regulations forced firms to use bank debt. Even now, only bonds in highly profitable large firms are available. In Europe, legal access to foreign corporate bonds developed only recently, although the Eurobond market may have provided informal access for wealthy savers. Bank savings in Europe are generally intermediated investments in larger established local firms, as banks in the main lend money to these firms or to governments. Many countries' industrial policies are also essentially schemes to channel bank and postal savings to chosen firms.

Finally, barriers against investing abroad have been ubiquitous throughout the world in recent decades and appear quite resilient to liberalization. To "manage" their exchange rates, "insulate" their macroeconomies from external influences, and prevent the "sterilization" of their monetary policies, many countries have instituted capital control measures that restrict domestic savers' freedom to invest outside their home markets. Foreign portfolio investment by residents was banned in Argentina from 1983 to 1990, until 1990 in Chile, and until 1994 in Greece. It remains tightly restricted in Korea (Kim and Singal 1993) and is illegal in Colombia and India. Other countries use regulatory hurdles or tax disincentives to discourage capital outflow. For example, Canada currently limits tax-free retirement savings accounts and pension funds to 20 percent foreign content.

These restrictions on savers' choices might allow large, existing firms to access capital at monopsony prices. Since family pyramid firms are all controlled by the same party (the family), they are better able to realize such market power than are collections of independent widely held firms, even if the individual firms are otherwise similar.

Of course, restrictions on savers' portfolio choices and on entrepreneurs' financing options can, and often do, exist simultaneously. Thus, capital markets can be subject to both monopoly and monopsony distortions simultaneously, the favored parties being the established large firms, many of which are controlled by local billionaire families.

### 11.4.3 Corporate Control and Capital Intensity

To test for differential access to capital, we look again at large Canadian firms. Canada's restrictions on the inflow and outflow of capital were relatively mild compared to those of many other countries. We are therefore using data from a country in which the likelihood of finding statistically significant results is relatively low.

We cannot estimate firm-level costs of capital because of the intricate web of intercorporate financial agreements typical in large family-controlled corporate groups. We can, however, ask whether large heir-controlled firms use labor less intensively relative to capital than do other comparable firms. If they do, this would be consistent with these firms having preferential access to capital. Our sample is again the set of large Canadian firms described in table 11.3 above.

We also examine labor-to-sales ratios, which is an indirect indicator of capital utilization. If a firm has a lower labor-to-sales ratio than other comparable firms, it is less labor intensive and is therefore plausibly more capital intensive than its peers. Of course, an extremely inefficient firm might have both higher labor-to-sales and higher capital-to-sales ratios than its peers, muddying inferences about labor-to-capital ratios. Despite this, and because accounting asset measures can be highly problematic, the labor-to-sales ratio may still be more informative, even though it is only indirectly related to the cost of capital.

The dependent variables in our regressions are thus labor-to-capital ratios and labor-to-sales ratios. As in tables 11.4 and 11.5, we use two methods of adjusting for industry, firm size, and firm age. First, we run regressions analogous to those in table 11.4, and, second, we use matched pairs analogous to the analysis in table 11.5.

Table 11.6 shows that large Canadian firms controlled by heirs have significantly lower labor intensity than entrepreneur-controlled firms, widely held firms, and other firms in general. These differences are most consistently significant when we include pyramid firms. In contrast, entrepreneur-controlled firms have higher labor intensity than heir-controlled firms, widely held firms, and other firms in general. These findings are consistent with heir-controlled firms having access to lower-cost capital and with pyramid control structures facilitating this access.[17] Recall that Canada's capital market distortions and barriers are relatively benign compared to those of many other countries. The fact that we find significant results in that country raises the possibility of more severe capital misallocation elsewhere and suggests that relatively low barriers to capital flow can be potent.

## 11.5 Inherited Wealth and Innovation

Not surprisingly, established firms have been shown not to be supportive of radical innovations (Betz 1993; see also Gompers and Lerner, chap. 1 in this volume). Indeed, entrenched managers, including heirs, plausibly have a vested interest in blocking innovation (Acs et al. 1995). This should be particularly so for entrenched billionaires as their wealth is due to existing capital, the value of which creative destruction destroys. We therefore conjecture that heir-controlled firms spend less on innovation than do other comparable firms. Moreover, in economies where heir control is extensive, economywide aggregate enterprise spending on R&D should be low.

Table 11.7 contains regressions analogous to those in tables 11.4 and 11.5 above but explaining R&D spending. These regressions are more problematic than those in tables 11.4–11.6 for several reasons. First, R&D has skewed distributions, bounded below at zero. We correct for this by using limited dependent variable regression techniques. Second, Canadian generally accepted accounting policy differs from U.S. accounting rules in

17. It is also consistent with other interpretations, however. For example, Hoshi, Kashyap, and Scharfstein (1990) argue that intercorporate transfers in Japanese corporate groups reduce firm default risk and therefore reduce group firms' costs of capital.

**Table 11.6** **Coefficients on Dummies for Controlling Shareholder Category in Regressions of Labor-to-Capital and Labor-to-Sales Ratios, 1984–89, Relative to Either U.S. Industry Averages (panels A and B) or Industry-, Age-, and Size-Matched U.S. Firms (panels C and D) (all regressions include the logarithms of firm age and sales as controls)**

| Controlling Shareholders' Categories Compared | Dependent Variable | | | | | | | | | | | | | | | |
|---|---|---|---|---|---|---|---|---|---|---|---|---|---|---|---|---|
| | A. Employees/Assets Relative to U.S. Industry | | | | B. Employees/Sales Relative to U.S. Industry | | | | C. Employees/Assets Relative to U.S. Matched Firms | | | | D. Employees/Sales Relative to U.S. Matched Firms | | | |
| | 1984–89 Mean | | 1984–89 Median | | 1984–89 Mean | | 1984–89 Median | | 1984–89 Mean | | 1984–89 Median | | 1984–89 Mean | | 1984–89 Median | |
| Heir minus business entrepreneur | −0.922 | −2.19 | −1.04 | −2.28 | **−2.34** | **−1.88** | **−2.65** | **−2.32** | −4.36 | **−10.9** | −3.85 | **−11.3** | **−4.30** | **−4.28** | **−4.78** | **−4.48** |
| | (.75) | (.38) | (.72) | (.35) | (.06) | (.08) | (.05) | (.04) | (.46) | (.15) | (.48) | (.14) | (.08) | (.13) | (.04) | (.11) |
| | [52] | [70] | [52] | [70] | [52] | [70] | [52] | [70] | [33] | [56] | [33] | [56] | [33] | [56] | [33] | [56] |
| Heir minus widely held | −1.42 | −1.28 | −1.67 | −0.503 | −1.00 | **−1.80** | −1.43 | **−1.72** | −0.846 | **−10.9** | −1.35 | **−11.3** | −1.47 | **−4.28** | −1.57 | **−4.48** |
| | (.58) | (.54) | (.52) | (.80) | (.47) | (.17) | (.32) | (.13) | (.75) | (.15) | (.59) | (.14) | (.40) | (.13) | (.36) | (.11) |
| | [74] | [101] | [74] | [101] | [74] | [101] | [74] | [101] | [41] | [56] | [41] | [56] | [41] | [56] | [41] | [56] |
| Heir minus all other domestic private-sector firms | −0.248 | −2.25 | −0.166 | −2.24 | −1.31 | **−1.36** | **−1.76** | **−1.68** | −2.04 | **−13.5** | −2.13 | **−13.7** | −2.20 | **−5.33** | −2.39 | **−5.56** |
| | (.93) | (.34) | (.97) | (.32) | (.24) | (.15) | (.08) | (.05) | (.78) | (.03) | (.78) | (.03) | (.38) | (.01) | (.34) | (.01) |
| | [200] | [200] | [200] | [200] | [200] | [200] | [200] | [200] | [104] | [104] | [104] | [104] | [104] | [104] | [104] | [104] |
| Business entrepreneur minus widely held | 0.587 | 0.108 | 1.39 | 1.20 | 0.662 | 0.308 | 0.966 | 0.361 | 2.77 | 2.60 | 2.45 | 2.24 | **2.59** | 1.79 | **3.04** | 1.87 |
| | (.85) | (.97) | (.63) | (.62) | (.69) | (.85) | (.56) | (.81) | (.53) | (.47) | (.56) | (.51) | (.14) | (.23) | (.08) | (.21) |
| | [68] | [83] | [68] | [83] | [68] | [83] | [68] | [83] | [44] | [54] | [44] | [54] | [44] | [54] | [44] | [54] |
| Entrepreneur minus all other domestic private-sector firms | −0.146 | −0.285 | 0.00429 | −0.126 | 0.683 | 0.686 | 1.11 | 1.06 | 4.94 | 4.56 | 4.58 | 4.16 | **3.57** | **3.23** | **3.73** | **4.16** |
| | (.96) | (.92) | (1.0) | (.96) | (.59) | (.57) | (.34) | (.33) | (.49) | (.50) | (.52) | (.53) | (.14) | (.15) | (.12) | (.15) |
| | [200] | [200] | [200] | [200] | [200] | [200] | [200] | [200] | [104] | [104] | [104] | [104] | [104] | [104] | [104] | [104] |
| Pyramids included | No | Yes | No | Yes | No | Yes | No | Yes | No | Yes | No | Yes | No | Yes | No | Yes |

*Note:* The numbers are coefficients on dummy variables $\delta_i$ (one if the firm is in subsample 1, zero if it is in subsample 2) in ordinary least squares regressions of the form $p_i - \bar{p} = \beta_0 + \beta_1 \log(\text{sales}_i) + \beta_2 \log(\text{age}_i) + \beta_3\delta_i$ where the dependent variable is either employees over assets or employees over sales and is adjusted for the U.S. industry mean in panels A and B and for the analogous ratio of industry-, age-, and size-matched U.S. firms in panels C and D. Regressions are estimated across the relevant two subsamples. Numbers in parentheses are two-tailed $t$-test probability levels. Numbers in brackets are sample sizes. Boldface indicates significance at the 10 percent level or better in a one-tailed $t$-test. The industry benchmark for panels A and B is U.S. industries, for panels C and D U.S. matched firms.

**Table 11.7** **Research-and-Development Activity for Large Canadian Firms, by Controlling Shareholder Category**

| | Dependent Variable | | | |
|---|---|---|---|---|
| Controlling Shareholders' Categories Compared | Reported R&D > 0 Dummy[a] (1) | Reported R&D/Sales 1984–89 Mean (2) | Relative Reported R&D Dummy[b] (3) | Relative Reported R&D/Sales 1984–89 Mean[c] (4) |
| Estimation technique | Logit | Tobit | Ordered logit | OLS |
| Industry benchmarks | None | None | U.S. matches | U.S. matches |
| Controls for | Size and age | Size and age | Size and age | Size and age |
| Heirs minus business entrepreneur | **−1.16** | −.0114 | 0.665 | −.000708 |
| | (.19) | (.24) | (.34) | (.78) |
| | [70] | [70] | [42] | [42] |
| Heirs minus widely held | **−1.43** | **−.0469** | **−1.34** | −.00115 |
| | (.03) | (.03) | (.06) | (.73) |
| | [101] | [101] | [56] | [56] |
| Heirs minus all other domestic private sector | **−1.518** | **−.0451** | **−0.704** | −.00104 |
| | (.02) | (.01) | (.17) | (.71) |
| | [200] | [200] | [104] | [104] |
| Business entrepreneur minus widely held | −0.246 | −.0175 | −0.743 | .00106 |
| | (.71) | (.38) | (.33) | (.79) |
| | [83] | [83] | [54] | [54] |
| Founders minus all other nongovernment | −0.218 | −.0145 | 0.183 | .00126 |
| | (.71) | (.42) | (.75) | (.67) |
| | [200] | [200] | [104] | [104] |

*Note:* Table entries are coefficients on dummy variables $\delta_i$ (one if the firm is in subsample 1, zero if it is in subsample 2). Regressions in cols. 1 and 2 are of the form $y_i - \beta_0 + \beta_1 \log(\text{sales}_i) + \beta_2 \log(\text{age}_i) + \beta_3\delta_i$, while subsequent columns are of the form $y_i - \bar{y}_i = \beta_0 + \beta_1 \log(\text{sales}_i) + \beta_2 \log(\text{age}_i) + \beta_3\delta_i$, where $\bar{y}_i$ is the value of $y$ for the matching U.S. firm. Numbers in parentheses are two-tailed $t$-test probability levels, numbers in brackets are sample sizes.

[a]Dummy is one for R&D > 0, zero otherwise.

[b]Dummy is two if the Canadian firm reports R&D but its U.S. match does not, one if both either do or do not report R&D, and zero if the Canadian firm reports no R&D but its U.S. match does.

[c]Dependent variable is the Canadian firm's R&D over sales minus that of its U.S. match.

that it lets companies freely choose whether to report their R&D. This makes R&D comparisons with U.S. firms difficult to interpret since Canadian firms may strategically report R&D spending. We industry adjust our Canadian firms' R&D spending by subtracting the R&D spending of an industry-, size-, and age-matched U.S. control firm. These adjustments are problematic because of intrinsic data problems, so we also report regressions with no industry adjustments. Unfortunately, adding industry dummies is not feasible given the sample sizes.

Column 1 in table 11.7 is a logistic regression of a dummy variable (one if the firm reports R&D and zero otherwise) on ownership type and our firm size and firm age controls. Column 2 displays coefficients from a Tobit regression of unadjusted R&D spending over sales on the same right-hand-side variables. We scale R&D by sales to avoid heteroskedasticity. Regressions 3 and 4 are analogous to regressions 1 and 2 but use matched U.S. firms to benchmark R&D spending. Regression 3 is an ordered logit where the dependent variable is two if the Canadian firm reports R&D but the U.S. match does not, one if both either do or do not report R&D, and zero if the match reports R&D but the Canadian firm does not. Regression 4 uses R&D over sales for the Canadian firm minus R&D over sales for the U.S. match and so can be estimated using OLS.

The results reported in table 11.7 are broadly consistent with the hypothesis that heir-controlled firms invest less in innovation than comparable entrepreneur-controlled and widely held firms. In contrast, Canadian entrepreneur-controlled firms and widely held firms invest roughly comparable amounts in innovation.

Our second conjecture is that economies in which heir control is extensive tend to have less private-sector spending on innovation. To test this, we correlate 1993 private-sector R&D spending, scaled by GDP, with billionaire-entrepreneur and billionaire-heir wealth, as in table 11.2 above, across countries. The first column of table 11.8 shows that enterprise R&D spending is negatively correlated with heir wealth ($p$-value = .13). Since richer countries plausibly have higher R&D spending, we consider a multiple regression of private-enterprise R&D that controls for per capita GDP. Heir wealth draws a negative and highly significant coefficient. Surprisingly, we also find that billionaire-entrepreneur wealth is negatively correlated with private-enterprise R&D spending ($p$-value = .16) and that the corresponding regression coefficient is negative and marginally significant ($p$-value = .10). We are unable to explain this result.

In summary, we find that Canadian heir-controlled firms indeed appear less innovative than other firms. A cross-country regression also shows that countries with extensive heir wealth have less aggregate private-sector spending on innovation. These findings are consistent with our conjecture that heirs favor the status quo.

**Table 11.8** **The Cross-Country Relation between Barriers to Entry, Enterprise R&D Investment, and Capital Ownership Structure**

| | Innovation Spending and Barrier to Entry Measures | | | | | |
|---|---|---|---|---|---|---|
| | Enterprise R&D Spending Scaled by GDP (1) | Height of FDI Barriers Index (2) | Height of Regulatory Barriers Index (3) | Extent of Government Intervention (4) | Height of Overall Tax Burden Index (5) | Height of Trade Barriers Index (6) |
| Simple correlation coefficients: | | | | | | |
| Business entrepreneur wealth over GDP, *B*/*Y* | −0.228 | −0.269 | −0.420 | −0.311 | −0.442 | −0.179 |
| | (.16) | (.07) | (.00) | (.04) | (.00) | (.24) |
| Inherited billionaire wealth over GDP, *H*/*Y* | −0.244 | 0.416 | −0.265 | 0.069 | −0.417 | −0.071 |
| | (.13) | (.00) | (.08) | (.65) | (.00) | (.64) |
| Multivariate regressions: | | | | | | |
| Intercept | 0.042 | 2.44 | 3.54 | 2.05 | 3.72 | 4.05 |
| | (.04) | (.00) | (.00) | (.00) | (.00) | (.00) |
| Log of per capital GDP, ln(*Y*/*L*) | 2.38 | −0.106 | −0.326 | 0.233 | 0.229 | −0.619 |
| | (.00) | (.10) | (.00) | (.03) | (.02) | (.00) |
| Business-entrepreneur billionaire wealth/GDP, *B*/*Y* | −0.31 | −0.08 | −0.086 | −0.112 | −0.118 | −0.051 |
| | (.10) | (.00) | (.00) | (.01) | (.00) | (.25) |
| Billionaire-heir wealth over GDP, *H*/*Y* | −0.18 | 0.054 | −0.018 | 0.021 | −0.053 | 0.001 |
| | (.05) | (.00) | (.22) | (.98) | (.01) | (.95) |
| $R^2$ | .49 | .36 | .50 | .22 | .39 | .50 |

*Note:* The maximal sample consists of the countries listed in table 11.1 above minus the United States and the United Kingdom. Numbers in parentheses are probability levels for two-tailed *t*-tests.

## 11.6 Inherited Wealth and Market Barriers

We have argued above that heir-controlled firms are relatively unprofitable but that the heirs who control them are entrenched. Their strong economic position is due to their heritage and their controlled firms' prominence as capital users and suppliers, not their abilities to manage or innovate. Given this, billionaire heirs are likely to see both innovation and openness as potential threats to the status quo, which favors them. We have shown above that heir control is associated with less innovation. In this section, we explore whether billionaire-heir control is also related to explicit barriers to entry protecting product and capital markets.

Control pyramids potentially create incentives for controlling families to invest in excess political lobbying. Pyramids let controlling families lobby using the resources of firms low in their pyramids, whose profitability is relatively unimportant to them. This means that the wealthy families can, in essence, use other people's money to lobby for policies that preserve their positions. For example, for the owner of a privately held firm to justify spending \$1.00 on lobbying, he (or his firm) must gain $\gamma \geq \$1.00$ in benefits. In contrast, the controlling shareholder in a pyramid $n$ levels high with control stakes of $\alpha$ at each level need gain benefits worth only $\gamma \geq \alpha^n$ to him (or the apex firm) if he uses \$1.00 of the resources of a firm at the base of the pyramid for lobbying. In general, the controlling shareholder of a such a pyramid would continue spending his controlled firms' resources on lobbying until his total private marginal rate of return equals $1/\Delta$, where $\Delta \equiv 1/\alpha^n$ is the *pyramid multiplier* defined in equation (3) above.

La Porta et al. (1998) show that countries with weaker political structures have less developed capital markets and speculate that this might be a deliberate policy to entrench the economic control of wealthy families and politicians. Anecdotal evidence consistent with wealthy families having considerable influence over national governments is also abundant. As reported in the *Toronto Globe and Mail,* Revenue Canada allowed the Bronfman family to move \$2 billion (Canadian) to the United States in 1991 without triggering capital gains taxes. When the auditor general reported that this "may have circumvented the intent of the tax code," he was attacked by the government finance committee for violating the Bronfmans' right to privacy (see "Auditor Was Wrong" 1996). Samuel Gordon, the former chairman of Del Monte Fruit, is reported to have said of the late Ecuadorian billionaire Luis "Lucho" Naboa, "If Lucho wanted a law passed, it passed. He could do things in Ecuador that I, as a multinational, couldn't" (see De Cordoba 1995). Most famously, Alfred Krupp (1812–87), heir to the Krupp steel and armaments businesses founded in 1811 by his father, Friedrich Krupp, is said to have quipped: "As pants the deer for cooling streams, so do I for regulation."

We can use our cross-country data to explain barriers to entry in local capital markets, both against foreigners obtaining local savings for investment abroad and against locals wanting to use foreign capital. Table 11.8 investigates whether countries in which inherited family wealth is large relative to GDP show evidence of such barriers, as measured by a set of country-level institutional structure variables.

Following Feldstein (1995), we use an index of the *height of FDI barriers* to measure the maintenance of capital market segmentation. We also consider the *height of regulatory barriers,* the *extent of government intervention,* and the *overall tax burden index* in each economy as general measures of impediments to market entry and capital flow. These variables are obtained from Holmes, Johnson, and Kirkpatrick (1997). They all take high values when the country in question is relatively difficult to enter and low values when entry is easy. Capital tends to avoid and flee heavy regulation, widespread government intervention, and high taxes, and the same policies reduce investment inflows. Barriers against capital outflows therefore often accompany such policies. We also include a measure of the height of trade barriers as a proxy for the general openness of the economy, as barriers to capital flow often accompany high trade barriers.

We first estimate simple correlation coefficients of these measures with our country-level ownership structure variables and then run regressions controlling for per capita GDP. We include the regressions because the country's openness to the world economy may depend on the level of its economic development, but we also include the simple correlations because economic growth, and therefore the level of economic development, may be endogenous.

Columns 2–6 of table 11.8 show that billionaire-heir wealth is greater when barriers to FDI are higher, consistent with these economies being subject to barriers to capital inflow. Our other barrier variables are uncorrelated with billionaire-heir wealth, except for tax burden, which has a negative sign.

In contrast, billionaire-entrepreneur wealth is strongly negatively correlated with FDI barrier height, regulatory barrier height, and extent of government intervention in the economy. Thus, billionaire-entrepreneur wealth is high when barriers to capital flow are low, and neither monopsony nor monopoly pricing in capital markets is likely.

Note that the height of general trade barriers in product markets is uncorrelated with billionaire-heir and billionaire-entrepreneur wealth. This is consistent with barriers around capital markets being more important than general, overall openness in this context.

In summary, heir control appears to be associated with higher investment-flow barriers but not necessarily with more government regulations, greater tax burdens, or trade barriers. In contrast, such barriers are lower in economies with more entrepreneur billionaire wealth.

## 11.7 Diagnosing a Canadian Disease?

Our query is about why economic growth is negatively related to a country's stock of inherited billionaire wealth and positively related to its self-made billionaire wealth. We propose four underlying explanatory factors. First, billionaire heirs are often entrenched, poor managers and have perverse incentives to engage in costly wealth shifting between firms they control. Poor governance causes heir-controlled firms to do poorly in the aggregate. Second, extensive old wealth distorts capital markets to favor these entrenched heir-controlled firms. Third, billionaire-heir-controlled firms spend less on innovation. Fourth, they also lobby to erect entry barriers.

Our four proposed explanations include both direct and indirect effects. The direct explanation is that billionaire heirs are entrenched, poor managers with perverse incentives. The indirect explanations are that billionaire-heir wealth distorts capital markets, lowers R&D, and creates pressure for entry barriers and that these distortions, in turn, lower economic growth. We have country-level variables that capture the latter two indirect channels—our enterprise R&D spending and entry-barrier variables from table 11.8—and we find cross-country evidence consistent with these channels.[18] If they are the primary channels operating, adding variables that directly capture these effects to the regressions of table 11.2 above should eliminate the heir- and entrepreneur-wealth variables. In contrast, if either the direct effect or the capital market distortion channel predominates, adding these same variables should not affect the coefficients or significance of the wealth-structure variables.

Table 11.9 displays regressions of the form

$$(5) \qquad \frac{\Delta Y}{Y} = \beta_0 + \beta_1 \ln\left(\frac{Y}{L}\right) + \beta_2 \frac{I}{K} + \beta_3 \ln(E) + \mathbf{a} \cdot \mathbf{P} + \mathbf{b} \cdot \mathbf{C} + \varepsilon,$$

where $Y$ is GDP, $L$ is population, $I$ is capital investment, and $E$ is average years of education. The vector **P** contains entry-barrier variables and spending on innovation. Different specifications in table 11.9 use different subsets of the elements of **P**. As before, the vector **C** contains our country-level capital ownership structure variables.

18. It is unclear how we may directly proxy for capital market distortions. Broadly, less distortion might lead to larger markets. But market capitalization also reflects economic development, which in turn affects growth. Moreover, market capitalization per se does not adequately capture the counterfactual benchmark required, i.e., what market capitalization would be if capital market distortions were absent. This benchmark is difficult to obtain—first, because of the endogenous relation between economic development and market capitalization and, second, because of the incomplete theoretical development of this area. We therefore leave these issues to future research.

**Table 11.9** **The Cross-Country Relation between Economic Growth and Capital Ownership Structure Controlling for Current per Capita Income, Capital Investment Rate, Level of Education, Enterprise R&D Investment, and Various Measures of Barriers to Entry**

| | (1) | (2) | (3) | (4) |
|---|---|---|---|---|
| Intercept | **7.39** | 2.72 | **7.88** | 4.99 |
| | **(.05)** | (.58) | (.02) | (.39) |
| Log of per capita GDP, ln( $Y/L$) | **−2.30** | **−2.28** | **−2.36** | **−2.40** |
| | (.00) | (.00) | (.00) | (.00) |
| Capital accumulation rate, $I/K$ | **0.197** | **0.154** | **0.241** | **0.188** |
| | (.00) | (.02) | (.00) | (.02) |
| Average total years of education, $E$ | **0.312** | **0.503** | **0.323** | **0.444** |
| | (.14) | (.05) | (.12) | (.09) |
| Extensive business regulations | **−1.00** | −0.503 | **−1.058** | −0.757 |
| | (.08) | (.47) | (.05) | (.34) |
| Height of trade barriers | −0.428 | −0.154 | . . . | . . . |
| | (.27) | (.74) | | |
| Height of FDI barriers | . . . | . . . | **−1.055** | −0.694 |
| | | | (.05) | (.44) |
| Enterprise R&D spending over GDP, $R\&D/Y$ | . . . | −0.039 | . . . | −0.013 |
| | | (.69) | | (.90) |
| Overall tax burden | −0.242 | 0.283 | −0.255 | 0.144 |
| | (.59) | (.64) | (.56) | (.81) |
| Business-entrepreneur billionaire wealth over GDP, $B/Y$ | **0.29** | **0.389** | 0.23 | 0.32 |
| | (.07) | (.03) | (.14) | (.12) |
| Billionaire-heir wealth over GDP, $H/Y$ | **−0.30** | **−0.28** | **−0.27** | **−0.263** |
| | (.03) | (.07) | (.04) | (.07) |
| $R^2$ | .579 | .578 | .603 | .587 |

*Note:* The sample consists of the countries listed in table 11.1 above minus the United States and the United Kingdom. When we include enterprise R&D spending (scaled by GDP, 1993 data from OECD's 1996 *Industrial Competitiveness Benchmarking Business Environments in the Global Economy*), we lose five countries owing to missing data: Austria, Belgium, Taiwan, South Africa, and Singapore.

Table 11.9 shows that *extensive regulation, trade barriers, FDI barriers,* and *high taxes* are all correlated with slower economic growth, but only regulations and FDI barriers are significant. If we substitute *extent of government intervention* for *extent of regulation,* the results are similar, but the intervention variable is uniformly less significant. Surprisingly, and (apparently) inconsistent with the endogenous-growth literature, spending on R&D does not have a significant relation with economic growth.

Billionaire-business-entrepreneur wealth is at best marginally significant in a one-tailed test once the height of barriers to capital flow is included. This is consistent with billionaire entrepreneurs adding to economic growth by lobbying government for economic openness. It is important to note that we cannot assign a direction of causality here: the openness of an economy could be due to lobbying by entrepreneurs, or openness to world capital markets could allow entrepreneurs to flourish and become billionaires. In either case, it appears that the association of entrepreneur wealth with economic growth is intimately connected to capital market openness and economic freedom in general.

In contrast, billionaire-heir wealth remains negatively correlated with economic growth after the barrier-to-entry variables listed are introduced. This is consistent with the linkage between heir wealth and slow economic growth operating through mechanisms other than barriers to entry and investment in innovation. It is evident from the results presented in table 11.9 that our primary observation of a negative correlation between billionaire-heir wealth and economic growth mainly reflects some combination of a direct negative relation due to heir control and an indirect linkage through capital market distortions. This does not rule out other links, most significantly, lobbying for barriers to capital flow.

Poorly performing, heir-controlled firms should be driven out of business in competitive economies. However, preferential access to capital and capital market entry barrier protection may provide heir-controlled firms with an offsetting advantage that allows them to survive. In short, widespread billionaire-heir control may lead to a locking in of the status quo and a permanently reduced rate of economic growth.

Again, a causal interpretation cannot be unambiguously based on cross-sectional regression results. A reverse causality interpretation of our table 11.2 and table 11.9 results is that high growth adds to entrepreneur wealth and diminishes heir wealth. If economic growth is typically lower in countries with more entry barriers (Edwards 1998), our results in table 11.8 follow. However, this interpretation begs the question, Why should high growth augment entrepreneur wealth but lower heir wealth? Growth through capital accumulation might enrich entrepreneurs, but why should it impoverish heirs? Growth through Schumpeterian creative destruction clearly does both, but this answer still leads to the question of why this process operates more rapidly in some economies than in others, which is the focus of this study.

We have argued that widespread inherited corporate control leads to a locking in of the status quo and a consequently reduced rate of economic growth. We rely heavily on Canadian firm-level data to support this argument, so a natural question arises as to its generalization. Are we describing a uniquely Canadian disease? Clearly, the negative cross-country relation between billionaire-heir wealth and economic growth may or may not reflect the same conditions elsewhere. More micro-level studies of other countries would be useful.

## 11.8 Liberalization: The Control and Treatment of the Canadian Disease?

We have argued that entry barriers and preferential access to capital allow heir control to survive and thus preserve uncompetitive firms. This implies that a sudden and unexpected regime shift that removes many of these advantages will affect heir-controlled firms more adversely than it will other firms. Moreover, if entrepreneurs have previously been held back by entry barriers and limited access to capital, entrepreneur-controlled firms should be affected more positively by these changes than should other firms. Therefore, in this section, we consider an event that suddenly and unexpectedly rendered Canada more open to foreign capital and less protected by entry barriers, the 1988 Canada-U.S. Free Trade Agreement (FTA). We conduct an event study using daily stock-price data and a comparison of accounting and ownership data before and after the FTA.

The FTA eliminated product market trade barriers over the ten years following ratification, according to a preset schedule. Chapter 16 of the FTA also provided for prospective national treatment of investors. This immediately barred future barriers to capital flow of any kind between the two countries, although certain discriminatory taxes and regulations were grandfathered. Chapter 16 unquestionably provoked the greatest outrage from the Canadian nationalist press.

There are several ways in which the FTA could conceivably have affected the relative standing of heir-controlled firms. First, heightened product market competition could have reduced the value of poorly managed firms. Second, a greater inflow of U.S. capital to Canadian entrepreneurs could reduce heir-controlled firms' market power over the supply capital. It could also create more competition for Canadian corporate assets that are not shielded from takeovers. Third, U.S. firms active in Canada might raise capital there, creating more competition for Canadian savings and eroding entrenched players' market power on that side of the capital market as well. Any or all of these would level the playing field between heirs and others.

The FTA is suitable for an event study because ratification was not expected. Canada had reached the final stages of negotiation of free trade agreements with the United States several times over the previous century and had always balked at the last minute. To establish a mandate for free trade, the Conservative prime minister, Brian Mulroney, had called a snap general election. The protectionist Liberal candidate, John Turner, was far ahead in the polls. Indeed, the best that a few late pre-election polls were predicting for the Tories was a draw and a consequent hung parliament or minority government. Neither boded well for the FTA, which required a

**Table 11.10** **Sequence of Events Leading up to the Canada-U.S. Free Trade Agreement Ratification by the Canadian Parliament**

| Event Date/First Trading Date | Event | Effect on Entrenched Firms |
|---|---|---|
| | *General background.* Canada has negotiated free trade with the United States several times over the past century but never ratified the result | Positive? |
| 4 Nov. 86/14 Apr. 86 | *Threat to deny fast-track authorization.* The U.S. Senate Finance Committee threatened to deny fast-track consideration of the FTA | Positive? |
| 23 Apr. 86/24 Apr. 86 | *Approval of fast-track procedure.* The Senate Finance Committee vote was tied; negotiations could begin | Negative? |
| 23 Sep. 87/24 Sep. 87 | *Negotiations were discontinued* | Positive? |
| 30 Sep. 87/1 Oct. 87 | *Negotiations might restart.* Discussions of the possibility of resuming negotiations announced at midnight, 30 September | Negative? |
| 2 Oct. 87/2 Oct. 87 | *Negotiations resume* | Negative? |
| 3 Oct. 87/5 Oct. 87 | *Agreement reached.* A trade accord was reached; for the first time, the media treats the possibility of free trade with the United States as a serious possibility | Negative |
| 26 Oct. 88/26 Oct. 88 | *Turner does well in televised pre-election debate.* Liberal opposition leader John Turner vows on national television to dismantle the FTA | Positive |
| 28 Oct. 88/28 Oct. 88 | *Turner declared clear winner of televised debate.* *Globe*-Environomics poll result released | Positive |
| 7 Nov. 88/7 Nov. 88 | *Liberal Party 10% ahead.* Gallup Poll results | Positive |
| 10 Nov. 88/10 Nov. 88 | *Tories and Liberals tied.* *Globe*-Environomics poll; a minority government or hung parliament might not be able to ratify the FTA | Negative? |
| 14 Nov. 88/14 Nov. 88 | *Tories and Liberals tied.* Gallup poll confirms the 10 November *Globe*-Environomics poll result | Negative? |
| 19 Nov. 88/21 Nov. 88 | *Surprise Tory majority government.* Prime Minister Mulroney's Tories win a second term with a surprise majority | Negative |

majority vote for ratification, as the third party in Parliament, the socialist New Democrats, was even more protectionist than the Liberals. Nonetheless, to the surprise of virtually everyone, a Conservative majority government was returned with a clear mandate to implement the Free Trade Agreement.[19] Table 11.10 lists the major events leading up to the Conservative election victory.

19. The increasing liberalization of the global economy should provide other opportunities for similar tests using data from other countries.

### 11.8.1 Stock-Price Reactions to the FTA

We first examine the stock-price reactions of firms classified according to types of dominant shareholders, as listed in table 11.3 above. We use the period from 10 through 21 November as our event window. The election was held on Saturday, 19 November, so 21 November is the first trading day following the Tory victory. On 10 November, the first polls showing a tie with the Liberals were published, and subsequent polls on 14 November confirmed a tie. These dates thus include the period from the first hint that the Liberals might not win through to the news of a Tory majority government.

Our methodology in this section is thus to construct cumulative abnormal returns (CAR) using daily firm-level stock returns $r_t$ as

$$\text{(6)} \qquad \text{CAR} = \sum_{t=11\text{ Nov.}}^{21\text{ Nov.}} (r_t - \bar{r}_{i,t}),$$

where $\bar{r}_{it}$ is the relevant Canadian industry index, constructed using three-digit SIC codes. We control for industry average stock-price movements, rather than market movements, because Thompson (1994, table 2, 13) finds evidence that industry indexes move on these dates in ways plausibly related to Canada's comparative advantage relative to the United States.[20] We also control for firm age and size. Thus, our regression is as follows:

$$\text{(7)} \qquad \text{CAR}_i = \beta_0 + \beta_1 \log(\text{age}_i) + \beta_2 \log(\text{sales}_i) + \beta_3 \delta_i,$$

where the dummy variable $\delta_i$ is one or zero according to the type of controlling shareholder, if any, the firm has.

Table 11.11 shows parameter estimates and significance levels for $\delta_i$ when various subsets of dominant owners are compared with each other and with widely held firms.

Heir-controlled companies appear most adversely affected, while firms controlled by business entrepreneurs appear to gain the most from the unexpected liberalization.[21] Intriguingly, the stock prices of heir-controlled

20. Industry benchmarking in a small open economy is problematic as many large Canadian firms have no similarly sized Canadian rivals. Clearly, in this instance, benchmarking with U.S. industry returns makes no sense, so we use Canadian industry averages. We recognize that our industry benchmarks are consequently noisy.

21. Khanna and Palepu (chap. 9 in this volume) find that economic liberalization in India is associated with a strengthening of family pyramid companies relative to other firms. Interestingly, greater capital market competition is not a part of India's current liberalization strategy. Note, however, that, when we drop Canadian pyramid member firms from our comparisons, as in the first and third columns of table 11.11, the significant point estimates move away from zero. Among freestanding firms only, entrepreneur-controlled firms' prices rise more relative to heir-controlled and other firms. This is consistent with intragroup transfers mitigating the positive and negative expected effects of liberalization on group firms.

**Table 11.11 Cumulative Abnormal Returns of Large Canadian Firms on the News That the Canada-U.S. Free Trade Agreement Would Be Ratified by the Canadian Parliament**

| Controlling Shareholders' Categories Compared | Mean Differences | | Mean Residual Differences Controlling for Firm Age & Size[a] | |
|---|---|---|---|---|
| | (1) | (2) | (3) | (4) |
| Heirs minus business entrepreneurs | **−.0993** | **−.0729** | **−.0765** | **−.0623** |
| | (.03) | (.04) | (.12) | (.10) |
| | [15] | [23] | [15] | [23] |
| Heirs minus widely held | .01347 | .0260 | .00034 | .0188 |
| | (.37) | (.26) | (.50) | (.33) |
| | [24] | [37] | [24] | [37] |
| Heirs minus all other private-sector firms | −.0317 | −.0068 | −.0316 | −.0098 |
| | (.22) | (.42) | (.23) | (.39) |
| | [61] | [61] | [61] | [61] |
| Business entrepreneurs minus widely held | **.1128** | **.0989** | **.1328** | **.1271** |
| | (.00) | (.04) | (.00) | (.02) |
| | [21] | [28] | [21] | [28] |
| Business entrepreneurs minus all other private-sector firms | **.0802** | **.0767** | **.0916** | **.0857** |
| | (.05) | (.05) | (.04) | (.04) |
| | [61] | [61] | [61] | [61] |
| Includes firms in pyramids | No | Yes | No | Yes |

*Note:* Categories are defined as in table 11.3 above. Subsamples are smaller because we do not have stock returns for all firms listed in that table. Numbers in parentheses are probability levels from *t*-tests. Numbers in brackets are sample sizes. Boldface type indicates significance in a one-tailed *t*-test at the 10 percent level. The cumulative abnormal return is for all trading days from 10 November, the date of the first poll questioning the Liberal lead, through to 21 November 1988, the first trading day after a surprise Conservative majority government was returned. Cumulative abnormal returns are returns minus the value-weighted returns of all other firms in the three-digit industry. Using equal weighting gives similar results.

[a]This panel contains coefficients and *p*-levels for $\delta$, a dummy variable set to one if the firm is in subsample 1 and zero if it is in subsample 2 in the ordinary least squares regression $CAR_i = \beta_0 + \beta_1 \log(\text{age}_i) + \beta_2 \log(\text{sales}_i) + \beta_3\delta_i$.

firms and widely held firms move in statistically indistinguishable ways. In contrast, stocks of business-entrepreneur-controlled firms rise relative to those of widely held firms. These findings are consistent with the hypotheses that heir-controlled firms are less able to meet increased product market competition and/or are less able to adapt to a more competitive capital market.

### 11.8.2 Changes in Capital Intensity

As mentioned above, chapter 16 of the FTA requires national treatment of investors from the United States. This encourages U.S. enterprises both to invest in Canada and to raise capital there, raising the general level of competition in Canadian capital markets. Heir-controlled firms should therefore lower their capital intensity as whatever capital market power they formerly enjoyed is eroded.

We return to our statistical analyses of industry-adjusted labor-to-sales ratios in table 11.6 above, but now we consider the post-FTA period from 1992 through 1996. Table 11.12 also shows the changes in these ratios from the pre-FTA (1984–89) period to this post-FTA period for various categories of firms surviving through 1996. Each entry in the first and third panels of table 11.12 is a regression coefficient of an ownership dummy for controlling shareholder type in a regression of (U.S.-industry-adjusted) labor over sales on that dummy and controls for the logarithms of firm age and size.[22] U.S. industry averages are the industry benchmark in panel A. U.S. firms the same size and age in the same industry serve in this capacity in panel C. In panels B and D, the dependent variables are the changes for each firm in the figures in panels A and C, respectively, from the 1980s.

A clear pattern emerges. Table 11.6 above shows that, in the 1980s, heir-controlled firms had lower labor intensity than did entrepreneur-controlled firms. Table 11.12 shows that, for heir-controlled firms that survived, these differences remain in the 1990s, although they have become less significant. Table 11.6 also shows entrepreneur-controlled firms having insignificantly higher labor intensity than widely held firms, while heir-controlled firms' labor intensity was significantly lower than that of widely held firms. After liberalization, this changes. Both heir-controlled and entrepreneur-controlled firms that survived became significantly more labor intensive than widely held firms. The coefficients are also all significantly different from those in the 1980s. Panels B and D show that surviving heir-controlled and entrepreneur-controlled firms both increased their labor intensity significantly more than widely held firms did. If our assumption that a low labor-to-sales ratio means high capital intensity is valid, widely held firms began using significantly more capital per worker after liberalization. This is consistent with widely held firms' access to capital improving.

### 11.8.3 Stronger Competition?

The FTA increased product market and capital market competition in Canada. This should have been most detrimental to the least-competitive Canadian firms and most advantageous to the best Canadian firms. Tables 11.13 and 11.14 repeat the analyses in tables 11.4 and 11.5 above and compare firm groups' returns and growth for the period 1992–96 to see whether the gaps in performance between firms controlled by different types of shareholders have widened. Heir-controlled firms continue to

22. Panel A of table 11.12 is analogous to table 11.4 in construction, while panel C is analogous to table 11.5.

**Table 11.12** **Coefficients on Dummies for Controlling-Shareholder Category in Regressions of Labor-to-Capital and Labor-to-Sales Ratios Controlling for Industry, Firm Size, and Firm Age (1992–96 in panels A and C; differences from 1984–89 and 1992–96 in panels B and D; panels A and B use measurements relative to U.S. industries; panels C and D use measurements relative to U.S. firms matched on industry, age, and size)**

| Controlling Shareholders' Categories Compared | Dependent Variable: A. Employees/Sales Relative to U.S. Industry | | | | B. Change in Employees/Sales Relative to U.S. Industry | | | | C. Employees/Sales Relative to U.S. Matched Firms | | | | D. Change in Employees/Sales Relative to U.S. Matched Firms | | | |
|---|---|---|---|---|---|---|---|---|---|---|---|---|---|---|---|---|
| | 1992–96 Mean | | 1992–96 Median | | 1992–96 Minus 1984–89 Mean | | 1992–96 Minus 1984–89 Median | | 1992–96 Mean | | 1992–96 Median | | 1992–96 Minus 1984–89 Mean | | 1992–96 Minus 1984–89 Median | |
| Heir minus business entrepreneur | −2.40 | −1.92 | **−2.63** | **−2.11** | 2.38 | 0.161 | 1.45 | 0.520 | **−3.50** | −0.846 | **−3.51** | −0.829 | 0.657 | .540 | 1.41 | .971 |
| | (.22) | (.24) | (.19) | (.20) | (.52) | (.93) | (.57) | (.81) | (.16) | (.41) | (.17) | (.42) | (.72) | (.65) | (.44) | (.45) |
| | [36] | [47] | [36] | [47] | [36] | [47] | [36] | [47] | [19] | [29] | [19] | [29] | [19] | [29] | [19] | [29] |
| Heir minus widely held | **2.37** | 1.08 | **2.34** | 1.12 | **3.43** | **3.47** | **3.86** | **3.14** | −0.37 | −0.85 | −0.35 | −0.83 | **2.29** | .540 | **2.62** | .971 |
| | (.15) | (.43) | (.17) | (.41) | (.10) | (.06) | (.11) | (.07) | (.79) | (.41) | (.80) | (.42) | (.05) | (.65) | (.06) | (.45) |
| | [43] | [60] | [43] | [60] | [43] | [60] | [43] | [60] | [21] | [29] | [21] | [29] | [21] | [29] | [21] | [29] |
| Heir minus all other domestic private-sector firms | 0.0521 | 0.287 | −0.079 | .202 | **1.98** | **1.67** | **2.49** | **2.02** | −1.45 | **−1.47** | −1.43 | **−1.47** | 1.91 | .276 | **2.38** | .703 |
| | (.96) | (.75) | (.94) | (.82) | (.14) | (.15) | (.05) | (.07) | (.27) | (.18) | (.29) | (.19) | (.23) | (.84) | (.12) | (.59) |
| | [124] | [124] | [124] | [124] | [124] | [124] | [124] | [124] | [57] | [57] | [57] | [57] | [57] | [57] | [57] | [57] |
| Business entrepreneur minus widely held | **4.66** | **3.31** | **4.82** | **3.46** | **3.47** | **3.76** | **3.13** | **2.69** | 2.42 | 1.62 | 2.46 | 1.63 | 0.765 | .863 | 0.312 | .738 |
| | (.00) | (.05) | (.00) | (.04) | (.07) | (.10) | (.11) | (.13) | (.23) | (.34) | (.23) | (.35) | (.59) | (.47) | (.82) | (.54) |
| | [38] | [45] | [38] | [45] | [38] | [45] | [38] | [45] | [25] | [29] | [25] | [29] | [25] | [29] | [25] | [29] |
| Entrepreneur minus all other domestic private-sector firms | **1.85** | **1.85** | **1.95** | **1.95** | 1.20 | 1.20 | 0.756 | 0.756 | **2.03** | **2.03** | **2.03** | **2.03** | 0.714 | .714 | 0.571 | .571 |
| | (.11) | (.11) | (.09) | (.09) | (.43) | (.43) | (.60) | (.60) | (.07) | (.07) | (.08) | (.08) | (.60) | (.60) | (.67) | (.67) |
| | [124] | [124] | [124] | [124] | [124] | [124] | [124] | [124] | [57] | [57] | [57] | [57] | [57] | [57] | [57] | [57] |
| Pyramids included | No | Yes | No | Yes | No | Yes | No | Yes | No | Yes | No | Yes | No | Yes | No | Yes |

*Note:* The numbers in panels A and C are coefficients on dummy variables $\delta_i$ (one if the firm is in subsample 1, zero if it is in subsample 2) in ordinary least squares regressions of the form $p_i - \overline{p} = \beta_0 + \beta_1 \log(\text{sales}_i) + \beta_2 \log(\text{age}_i) + \beta_3\delta_i$ where the dependent variable is either employees over assets or employees over sales and is relative to the U.S. industry mean in panel A and to the analogous ratio for a U.S. firm the same size and age in the same industry in panel C. Numbers in panels B and D are simple differences. Estimates are across the relevant two subsamples. Numbers in parentheses are two-tailed $t$-test probability levels. Numbers in brackets are sample sizes. Boldface type indicates significance at the 10 percent level in a one-tailed $t$-test.

**Table 11.13** **Relation of Controlling-Shareholder Category to Performance of Large Canadian Firms, 1992–96 Annual Reports, Controlling for Firm Age and Size (industry benchmarks are 3-digit U.S. industry averages)**

| Controlling Shareholders' Categories Compared | Dependent Variable | | | | | | | | | | | | | | | |
|---|---|---|---|---|---|---|---|---|---|---|---|---|---|---|---|---|
| | Operating Income over Assets | | | | Operating Income over Sales | | | | Sales Growth | | | | Employees Growth | | | |
| | 1992–96 Mean | | 1992–96 Median | | 1992–96 Mean | | 1992–96 Median | | 1992–96 Mean | | 1992–96 Median | | 1992–96 Mean | | 1992–96 Median | |
| Heir minus business entrepreneur | −.00423 | .00126 | −.00472 | .00069 | −.0134 | −.0125 | −.0111 | −.0086 | .00133 | .0309 | .0311 | .0461 | .0251 | .0261 | .0401 | .0375 |
| | (.84) | (.95) | (.83) | (.97) | (.47) | (.45) | (.59) | (.64) | (.98) | (.55) | (.50) | (.29) | (.75) | (.69) | (.61) | (.58) |
| | [38] | [49] | [38] | [49] | [38] | [49] | [38] | [49] | [36] | [46] | [36] | [46] | [33] | [43] | [33] | [43] |
| Heir minus widely held | **−.184** | −.115 | **−.182** | −.114 | **−.0674** | **−.0578** | **−.0668** | **−.0547** | −.0554 | −.0174 | −.0698 | −.0359 | −.00751 | −.0142 | .0146 | −.00233 |
| | (.19) | (.24) | (.19) | (.25) | (.16) | (.10) | (.16) | (.11) | (.38) | (.72) | (.26) | (.44) | (.92) | (.79) | (.84) | (.96) |
| | [44] | [60] | [44] | [60] | [44] | [60] | [44] | [60] | [44] | [58] | [44] | [58] | [37] | [51] | [37] | [51] |
| Heir minus all other domestic private-sector firms | −.0805 | **−.100** | −.0810 | **−.101** | **−.0643** | **−.0805** | **−.0626** | **−.0784** | −.00892 | .00899 | −.00579 | .00613 | .00255 | .00165 | .0191 | .0182 |
| | (.31) | (.15) | (.31) | (.14) | (.16) | (.04) | (.19) | (.06) | (.83) | (.80) | (.88) | (.86) | (.95) | (.96) | (.62) | (.59) |
| | [125] | [125] | [125] | [125] | [126] | [126] | [126] | [126] | [118] | [118] | [118] | [118] | [105] | [105] | [105] | [105] |
| Business entrepreneur minus widely held | −.187 | −.152 | −.185 | −.150 | −.0473 | −.0538 | −.0494 | −.0538 | −.0364 | −.0247 | −.0620 | −.0542 | .00366 | −.0181 | .0165 | −.00755 |
| | (.25) | (.28) | (.25) | (.29) | (.38) | (.27) | (.35) | (.26) | (.63) | (.72) | (.41) | (.43) | (.95) | (.74) | (.70) | (.86) |
| | [41] | [47] | [41] | [47] | [41] | [47] | [41] | [47] | [39] | [44] | [39] | [44] | [33] | [38] | [33] | [38] |
| Business entrepreneur minus all other domestic private-sector firms | −.0545 | −.0545 | −.055 | −.055 | −.0311 | −.0311 | −.0323 | −.0323 | −.0129 | −.0129 | −.0378 | −.0378 | −.0182 | −.0182 | −.0117 | −.0117 |
| | (.53) | (.53) | (.53) | (.53) | (.54) | (.54) | (.54) | (.54) | (.78) | (.78) | (.40) | (.40) | (.69) | (.69) | (.79) | (.79) |
| | [125] | [125] | [125] | [125] | [126] | [126] | [126] | [126] | [118] | [118] | [118] | [118] | [105] | [105] | [105] | [105] |
| Pyramids included | No | Yes | No | Yes | No | Yes | No | Yes | No | Yes | No | Yes | No | Yes | No | Yes |

*Note:* The numbers shown are coefficients on dummy variables $\delta_i$ (one if the firm is in subsample 1, zero if it is in subsample 2) in ordinary least squares regressions of the form $p_i - \bar{p} = \beta_0 + \beta_1 \log(\text{sales}_i) + \beta_2 \log(\text{age}_i) + \beta_3\delta_i$ estimated across the relevant two subsamples. Boldface type indicates significance at the 10 percent level in a one-tailed $t$-test. Numbers in parentheses are two-tailed $t$-test probability levels. Numbers in brackets are sample sizes.

**Table 11.14** **Relation of Controlling-Shareholder Category to Performance of Large Canadian Firms, 1992–96 Annual Reports, Controlling for Firm Age and Size (industry benchmarks are U.S. firms matched by size, age, and 3-digit industry)**

| Controlling Shareholders' Categories Compared | Dependent Variable | | | | | | | | | | | | | | | |
|---|---|---|---|---|---|---|---|---|---|---|---|---|---|---|---|---|
| | Operating Income over Assets | | | | Operating Income over Sales | | | | Sales Growth | | | | Employees Growth | | | |
| | 1992–96 Mean | | 1992–96 Median | | 1992–96 Mean | | 1992–96 Median | | 1992–96 Mean | | 1992–96 Median | | 1992–96 Mean | | 1992–96 Median | |
| Heir minus business entrepreneur | −.0214 | −.160 | −.0256 | −.162 | .0446 | −.0754 | .0435 | −.0680 | .0573 | .0879 | .0490 | .0445 | −.0590 | **−.1056** | −.0584 | **−.0862** |
| | (.71) | (.41) | (.66) | (.41) | (.36) | (.29) | (.39) | (.34) | (.69) | (.34) | (.73) | (.60) | (.58) | (.15) | (.60) | (.15) |
| | [21] | [30] | [21] | [30] | [21] | [30] | [21] | [30] | [21] | [29] | [21] | [29] | [18] | [25] | [18] | [25] |
| Heir minus widely held | **−.435** | −.160 | **−.441** | −.162 | **−.153** | −.0754 | **−.150** | −.0680 | .00103 | .0879 | −.0482 | .0445 | **−.159** | **−.106** | **−.121** | **−.0862** |
| | (.12) | (.41) | (.11) | (.41) | (.08) | (.29) | (.09) | (.34) | (.99) | (.34) | (.66) | (.60) | (.10) | (.15) | (.13) | (.15) |
| | [22] | [30] | [22] | [30] | [22] | [30] | [22] | [30] | [22] | [29] | [22] | [29] | [18] | [25] | [18] | [25] |
| Heir minus all other domestic private-sector firms | −.110 | −.0479 | −.113 | −.0499 | .0195 | .00409 | .0201 | .00715 | .0880 | **.105** | .0679 | .0688 | **−.114** | **−.104** | **−.113** | **−.0946** |
| | (.43) | (.69) | (.42) | (.68) | (.77) | (.94) | (.76) | (.90) | (.26) | (.11) | (.38) | (.29) | (.10) | (.07) | (.09) | (.09) |
| | [61] | [61] | [61] | [61] | [61] | [61] | [61] | [61] | [58] | [58] | [58] | [58] | [52] | [52] | [52] | [52] |
| Business entrepreneur minus widely held | **−.323** | −.200 | **−.323** | −.199 | **−.157** | **−.144** | **−.153** | **−.137** | .0112 | .0468 | −.0207 | .0138 | −.0285 | −.0102 | .0168 | .0232 |
| | (.19) | (.33) | (.19) | (.34) | (.06) | (.05) | (.06) | (.06) | (.86) | (.45) | (.78) | (.85) | (.70) | (.88) | (.80) | (.69) |
| | [26] | [30] | [26] | [30] | [26] | [30] | [26] | [30] | [26] | [29] | [26] | [29] | [23] | [26] | [23] | [26] |
| Business entrepreneur minus all other domestic private-sector firms | −.0221 | −.0221 | −.0150 | −.0150 | −.0286 | −.0286 | −.0234 | −.0234 | −.0245 | −.0245 | −.0370 | −.370 | .00105 | .00105 | .00359 | .00359 |
| | (.86) | (.86) | (.91) | (.91) | (.63) | (.63) | (.69) | (.69) | (.73) | (.73) | (.59) | (.59) | (.99) | (.99) | (.95) | (.95) |
| | [61] | [61] | [61] | [61] | [61] | [61] | [61] | [61] | [58] | [58] | [58] | [58] | [52] | [52] | [52] | [52] |
| Pyramids included | No | Yes | No | Yes | No | Yes | No | Yes | No | Yes | No | Yes | No | Yes | No | Yes |

*Note:* The numbers shown are coefficients on dummy variables $\delta_i$ (one if the firm is in subsample 1, zero if it is in subsample 2) in ordinary least squares regressions of the form $p_i - \bar{p} = \beta_0 + \beta_1 \log(\text{sales}_i) + \beta_2 \log(\text{age}_i) + \beta_3\delta_i$ estimated across the relevant two subsamples. Boldface type indicates significance at the 10 percent level in a one-tailed $t$-test. Numbers in parentheses are two-tailed $t$-test probability levels. Numbers in brackets are sample sizes.

perform worse than widely held firms and other firms in general, and the point estimate differences have widened. But the differences between heir-controlled and entrepreneur-controlled firms have narrowed, although entrepreneur-controlled firms continue to grow faster. Entrepreneur-controlled firms' earnings continue to be lower than those of widely held firms, and widely held firms' growth now matches that of entrepreneur-controlled firms.

In short, widely held firms appear to have benefited disproportionately as Canada became more integrated with U.S. product markets and capital markets. In contrast, heir-controlled firms continue to report slower growth and lower earnings than other firms, and they may actually be falling further behind.

### 11.8.4 The Staying Power of Concentrated Wealth

The implementation of the FTA also lets us look at transition rates between different ownership structures as competition grows. To do this, we first compare the ownership structures of our sample of large Canadian firms in 1988, immediately prior to the FTA, to those in 1994, the last year for which we have complete data.[23] This comparison is summarized in the transition matrix of table 11.15.

The fraction of firms that are either widely held or owned by a widely held parent increases from 27.24 percent (sixty-seven firms) in 1988 to 32.11 percent (seventy-nine firms) in 1996. Four of the eight firms that ceased to be heir controlled became widely held. Also, most firms whose founders left the scene become widely held. Of the twenty-seven firms classified as owned by business entrepreneurs, four became widely held, two ended up with a financial institution as a controlling shareholder, one went bankrupt, one was acquired by a foreign parent, and in only one firm was "control" passed on to an heir. In both cases, a $\chi^2$ goodness-of-fit test soundly rejects the hypothesis of random changes in ownership structure ($p$-level $< 5$ percent).[24] The proportion of widely held firms also rose because four of the five privatized state-owned enterprises in our sample of very large firms became widely held.[25]

23. Our 1994 ownership data are from the same sources as our 1988 data.

24. In the $\chi^2$ tests, we treat categories *i* (cooperatives) and *j* (labor controlled) as one category. We also collapse *c* (no controlling shareholder) and *f* (widely held Canadian parent) into a single category. Because heir-controlled firms cannot become "entrepreneur-controlled" firms, the number of categories into which heir-controlled firms can pass is one minus the number open to entrepreneur-controlled firms. The $\chi^2$-statistic is calculated as the sum of squares of observed minus expected transitions over the number of expected transitions. The $\chi^2$-statistic is calculated as the sum of squares of observed minus expected transitions over the number of expected transitions. The $\chi^2(6)$-statistic for the hypothesis that the transformations of heir-controlled firms follow a random pattern is 27.42, with a probability value less than 0.5 percent. The $\chi^2(7)$-statistics for changes of entrepreneur-controlled firms is 17.99, with a probability value less than 2.5 percent.

25. We obtain qualitatively identical results when we include firms without accounting data in the transition matrix reported in table 11.15.

**Table 11.15** **Transition Matrix for Large Canadian Firms Relating Controlling-Shareholder Description in 1988 to Controlling-Shareholder Description in 1994**

| 1994 Controlling-Shareholder Type | 1988 Controlling-Shareholder Type | | | | | | | | | | Changes into 1994 Category |
|---|---|---|---|---|---|---|---|---|---|---|---|
| | a | b | c | d | e | f | g | h | i | j | |
| a | **36** | 1 | | | | | | | | | 1 |
| b | | **18** | | | | | | | | | 0 |
| c | 4 | 4 | **47** | 2 | 1 | 5 | 3 | 4 | | | 23 |
| d | 2 | | | **19** | | | 1 | | | | 3 |
| e | | 2 | | 1 | **3** | 2 | 1 | | | 1 | 7 |
| f | | | 1 | 1 | | **6** | 1 | | | | 3 |
| g | | 1 | | | 1 | 1 | **42** | 1 | | | 4 |
| h | | | | | | | | **18** | | | 0 |
| i | 1 | | | | | | | | | | 1 |
| j | | | 1 | | | | | | | | 1 |
| Bankruptcy | | 1 | | 3 | 1 | | | | | | 5 |
| Acquired | | | 3 | 1 | | | 1 | | | | 5 |
| Unknown | 1 | | 1 | 2 | | | | | | | 4 |
| Total in category for 1988 | 44 | 27 | 53 | 29 | 6 | 14 | 49 | 23 | 0 | 1 | |

*Source:* Sample is firms in the 1988 *Financial Post* 500 for which accounting and ownership data are available.

*Note:* Definitions are as follows:
a = heir
b = business entrepreneur
c = no controlling shareholder (widely held)
d = other individual or family
e = investment fund
f = widely held Canadian parent firm
g = foreign parent firm
h = government
i = co-op
j = labor

### 11.8.5 A Cure?

We contend that the negative relation between heir control and economic growth is due to heirs often being entrenched, poor managers whose firms nonetheless survive because of their preferential access to capital and protection from competition. The liberalization stemming from the Canada-U.S. Free Trade Agreement arguably increased both product and capital market competition in Canada. Heir-controlled firms' inability to compete in this harsher environment is exposed in their negative stock-price reactions to the FTA. The value discount that outsiders attached to heir control rose. At the same time, heir-controlled firms capital-to-labor ratios converged to those of other firms, suggesting less preferential access to capital. Finally, in the years following the FTA, the firms of departing entrepreneurs tend to become widely held rather than heir controlled, again consistent with a large value discount connected with heir control. We suggest, therefore, that liberalization in international trade and capital flow may alleviate the Canadian disease by rendering product and capital markets more competitive and thereby raising the price that families must pay to maintain inherited corporate control. These findings can be interpreted as providing empirical support for the ideas set forth in Olson (1982) that trade liberalization has important beneficial effects related to dislodging entrenched special interest groups.

## 11.9 Conclusions

The central result of this paper is that the ownership structure of a country's capital matters. Economic growth depends, not just on the stock of physical capital, but also on who controls it. We find that entrenched family control of a nation's capital is correlated with lower rates of economic growth while billionaire entrepreneurs' control of capital is correlated with higher rates of economic growth.

We consider several explanations for this finding. First, old wealth may entrench poor management, and control pyramids may distort their incentives. Second, a sharply skewed wealth distribution may create market power in capital markets, causing inefficiency. Third, entrenched billionaires have a vested interest in preserving the value of old capital and thus in slowing creative destruction. Fourth, old money becomes entrenched through control of the political system and, most especially, by erecting barriers to capital mobility. In contrast, substantial self-made billionaires' wealth is observed where such forces are edentulous and creative destruction occurs.

Using micro-level data from Canada, we find evidence consistent with the first three explanations. Switching to cross-country data, we find supportive evidence for the third and fourth explanations. In an expanded regression analysis of cross-country differences in growth, we confirm that the positive relation between entrepreneur-controlled capital and economic growth is connected with lower entry barriers and openness. In contrast, the linkage between heir-controlled capital and lower economic growth is due, not just to higher inward foreign investment barriers, but also to entrenched heir control and capital market distortions arising from this.

We dub depressed growth associated with widespread corporate control by wealthy heirs the *Canadian disease.* It is characterized by one or more of the following symptoms: poor overall management quality, capital markets and institutions that channel money to large, established family firms, a dearth of innovation that locks in the status quo, and political rent seeking that deters entry. The term *Canadian disease* is appropriate because our empirical evidence relies heavily on Canadian data. We suspect that this malady is widespread globally and that it is especially deleterious in many developing economies. More work is clearly needed before this supposition can be confirmed.

We show that freer international trade and capital flow appear to level the playing field between heir-controlled, entrepreneur-controlled, and widely held Canadian firms. If our conjecture that entrenched family control is detrimental to an economy is correct, trade and capital flow liberalization may have important beneficial economic effects that are not captured by standard models of international trade and international finance.

## Data Appendix

### International Data

Our country-level sample begins with all countries having 1997 GDP greater than U.S.$1 billion. We drop postsocialist economies, such as China, the Czech Republic, Hungary, Poland, and Russia; economies subject to economic sanctions, such as Cuba, Iran, and Iraq; the oil sheikdoms Bahrein and Brunei; the tax havens Liechtenstein and Luxembourg; Ethiopia, Kuwait, and Lebanon, which are undergoing postwar reconstruction; Sri Lanka and the Democratic Republic of the Congo, which are currently experiencing civil war; and Bangladesh, Egypt, El Salvador, Ghana, Jordan, Kenya, New Zealand, Nigeria, Saudi Arabia, Syria, Tanzania, and the United Arab Emirates because of missing data. The final sample consists of Argentina, Australia, Austria, Belgium, Brazil, Canada, Chile, Colombia, Denmark, Ecuador, Finland, France, Germany, Greece, Hong Kong, Iceland, India, Indonesia, Ireland, Israel, Italy, Japan, Korea, Malaysia, Mexico, the Netherlands, Norway, Peru, the Philippines, Portugal, Singapore, South Africa, Spain, Sweden, Switzerland, Taiwan, Thailand, Turkey, the United Kingdom, the United States, and Venezuela. We exclude the United States and the United Kingdom from our sample on the grounds that their corporate ownership structures are highly atypical, in that their large listed companies are predominantly directly held by small shareholders (La Porta, Lopez-de-Silanes, and Shleifer 1999).

Data on billionaire wealth is from *Forbes* magazine's annual list of billionaires for 1993. We use *Forbes'* description of the billionaires to classify them as *heirs, entrepreneur-founders,* and *heir-entrepreneurs* (people who inherited huge fortunes but greatly increased them). We double-check in the 1994–97 issues of *Forbes* to verify the accuracy of our classification of each billionaire. (The 1997 *Forbes* explicitly classifies billionaires as self-made or not.) Members of billionaire political dynasties (obtained from *Forbes* 1997) are classified as heirs. Dropping them does not change the results. Ambiguous classifications by *Forbes* are cross-checked with *Who's Who.* If they are still ambiguous, these billionaires are assigned to a fourth, *probably heir* category. Including them and/or the heir-entrepreneurs in the heir category does not change the results.

Our GDP and population data are from the World Bank, with data for Taiwan obtained from the website of that country's government. Our data on investment rates and education (human capital) are from the World Bank Growth Data used by, for example, Barro and Lee (1996). The political economy variables are from Holmes, Johnson, and Kirkpatrick (1997).

Univariate statistics for these variables are shown in table 11A.1.

### Canadian Data

Our sample of large Canadian firms begins with the *Financial Post* 500, the largest 500 firms in 1988, ranked by sales as listed in the *Financial Post* magazine. Ownership and minimal financial data are available for 246 of these.

Ownership data are from the *Financial Post Survey of Industrials* and the *Financial Post Survey of Energy and Mining Companies.* These data are cross-checked against Statistics Canada's *Directory of Intercorporate Ownership* for 1989. Inconsistencies are resolved by checking proxy statements. For each firm, the total number of shareholder votes is calculated assuming that all warrants, convertibles, and stock options have been exercised. The total number of votes controlled by the largest shareholder is calculated in a similar way. This is divided by the total number of votes to obtain the largest shareholder's voting power. We define a firm as having a dominant shareholder if the largest single shareholder owns or controls

**Table 11A.1 Univariate Statistics for Country-Level Data**

| Variable | Mean | Standard Deviation | Minimum | Maximum |
|---|---|---|---|---|
| Economy characteristics: | | | | |
| Growth rate in GDP (%) | 4.11 | 2.50 | −0.233 | 9.03 |
| Per capita GDP (U.S.$ × 1,000) | 13.5 | 10.7 | 0.314 | 38.1 |
| Capital investment rate (%) | 22.3 | 6.20 | 12.9 | 36.7 |
| Average years of education | 6.82 | 2.18 | 3.05 | 10.4 |
| Economy capital ownership structure:[a] | | | | |
| Business-entrepreneur billionaire wealth over GDP | 1.47 | 3.35 | 0.000 | 19.3 |
| Billionaire-heir wealth over GDP | 1.96 | 3.23 | 0.000 | 15.8 |
| Political economy variables (1 = low, 5 = high): | | | | |
| Level of government intervention | 2.38 | 0.990 | 1.000 | 5.00 |
| Extent of regulations | 2.72 | 0.759 | 1.000 | 4.00 |
| Trade barrier height | 2.64 | 1.11 | 1.000 | 5.00 |
| FDI barrier height | 2.21 | 0.570 | 1.000 | 3.00 |
| Index of overall tax burden | 3.96 | 0.920 | 1.500 | 5.00 |
| Innovation rate variables: | | | | |
| Private-sector R&D over GDP | 0.406 | 0.517 | 0.000 | 1.88 |

*Note:* The sample is 39 countries, as listed in table 11.1, except for private-sector R&D over GDP, which is available for only 34 countries. Sample excludes the United Kingdom and the United States.

[a]Billions in wealth over trillions of GDP.

more than 20 percent of total voting rights. Where more than one shareholder is listed as having voting control over a trust, we assign each an equal proportion of the votes. Firms with no dominant shareholder are classified as widely held. The name of the largest shareholder among those with stakes exceeding 20 percent is determined. Information from corporate histories, proxies, the *Blue Book of Canadian Business,* and *Who's Who* allow us to determine the name of each firm's founder. If the founder and the current major dominant shareholder are the same, we call the firm *entrepreneur controlled.* If the current dominant shareholder has the same last name as the founder, we define the firm as *heir controlled.*

Financial data are from the *Toronto Globe and Mail*'s InfoGlobe database and are available for 200 of our firms. We compare these Canadian firms with U.S. industries and with U.S. firms matched by industry, sales, and age (see details below). U.S. financial data are from the Standard and Poor's Compustat database. We adjust fiscal year definitions of our Canadian firms to correspond to Compustat's convention that annual reports dated before 15 June of year $t$ are defined as year $t - 1$ data.

All Canadian dollar amounts are converted to U.S. dollars. Monthly exchange rates are noon averages from the *Bank of Canada Review* quarterly issues. Using the average of the twelve monthly averages ending with the month of the fiscal year end, Canadian figures are converted to U.S. dollars. Numbers for Canadian companies that report in U.S. dollars are not adjusted.

Industry classifications are made using the Standard Industrial Classification (SIC) codes system of Standard and Poor's Compustat database. U.S. rivals are defined as all U.S. firms belonging to the same industry (defined by three-digit SIC codes) as the Canadian firm. For each set of U.S. rivals, we construct an industry profit rate by adding up the total operating income of the firms and dividing this by the total of their sales. Many of our Canadian firms are not included in Compustat. For these, an industry classification was found in Dun and Bradstreet's *Canadian Directory.* Since the industry codes used by Dun and Bradstreet are not identical to those used by Compustat, a conversion table was worked out using firms listed in both. The first three industry codes (in declining importance by sales in that industry) from Dun and Bradstreet were used in deriving the conversion table. U.S. matched-pair firms are the U.S. firms in the same three-digit industry as the Canadian firm in question for which the sum of the absolute values of the percentage differences in sales and firm age is minimized.

Operating income is defined as earnings gross of depreciation, interest, and tax payments. This is scaled by either total assets or total sales. Sales growth is measured in U.S. dollars for Canadian and U.S. firms. To reduce distortions caused by extraordinary events or macroeconomic factors, we smooth our measure by taking the median of the industry-adjusted profit

Table 11A.2 Univariate Statistics for Canadian Firm-Level Data

| Variable | Mean | Standard Deviation | Minimum | Maximum |
|---|---|---|---|---|
| Operating income over assets, 1984–89: | | | | |
| Mean of annual observations | .0107 | .0728 | −.170 | 0.616 |
| Median of annual observations | .00686 | .0592 | −.179 | 0.180 |
| Operating income over sales, 1984–89: | | | | |
| Mean of annual observations | .0122 | .0887 | −.169 | 0.445 |
| Median of annual observations | .0101 | .0898 | −.198 | 0.501 |
| Growth in sales, 1984–89: | | | | |
| Mean of annual observations | .0931 | .412 | −.316 | 4.85 |
| Median of annual observations | .0297 | .178 | −.4367 | 1.40 |
| Growth in number of employees, 1984–89: | | | | |
| Mean of annual observations | .142 | .716 | −.742 | 8.40 |
| Median of annual observations | .0384 | .282 | −.742 | 2.35 |
| Date of first incorporation | 1945 | 33.3 | 1670 | 1987 |
| Total sales in billions of 1988 U.S. dollars | 1,111 | 2,167 | .0399 | 15.6 |
| % of votes controlled by largest shareholder with 20% or more | 46.1 | 29.8 | 0 | 100 |

*Source:* Sample is 200 firms, as in table 11.4. All mean and median variables are deviations from U.S. industry averages by three-digit SIC.

rates between 1984 and 1989 for each Canadian firm. The exchange rates at the beginning and the end of this period are almost identical at about $1.20 Canadian per U.S. dollar, despite swings in intermediate years. Since the median is usually calculated from six observations (an even number), after ordering the observations we define their median as the halfway point between the third and the fourth observations. We use the logarithm of total 1989 sales to measure firm size and the logarithm of the number of years since the firm's first incorporation date to measure firm age. This date is obtained from the *Blue Book of Canadian Business, Who's Who,* financial reports, and corporate histories.

Missing from this list of variables is a measure of stock market valuation. Many of the Canadian firms that we study have one or more classes of equity that do not trade publicly. It is not possible reliably to estimate variables such as *q*-ratios for these firms. Excluding these firms would result in a very unrepresentative picture of the Canadian economy. Also, valuing firms that are included in control pyramids can be problematic as shares in other firms constitute large fractions of their assets.

Univariate statistics for all our variables are given in table 11A.2.

## References

Acs, Zoltan J., Randall Morck, J. Myles Shaver, and Bernard Yeung. 1997. The internationalization of small and medium-sized enterprises: A policy perspective. *Small Business Economics* 9:2–7.

Adventures with capital. 1997. *Economist,* 25 January, 17–18.

Auditor was wrong on family trusts. 1996. *Toronto Globe and Mail* (electronic ed.), 19 September.

Austin, Richard E. 1996. Labour-sponsored venture funds. *Canadian Shareowner* 9, no. 4 (March/April): 9.

Barro, Robert, and Jong-Wha Lee. 1996. International measures of schooling years and schooling quality. *American Economic Review, Papers and Proceedings* 86, no. 2:218–23.

Beason, Richard, and David E. Weinstein. 1996. Growth, economies of scale, and targeting in Japan (1955–1990). *Review of Economics and Statistics* 78, no. 2 (May): 286–95.

Best, Andrea, and Devashis Mitra. 1997. The venture capital industry in Canada. *Journal of Small Business Management* 35, no. 2 (April): 105–10.

Betz, Frederick. 1993. *Strategic technology management.* New York: McGraw-Hill.

Birdsall, Nancy, David Ross, and Richard Sabot. 1995. Inequality and growth reconsidered: Lessons from East Asia. *World Bank Economic Review* 9, no. 3 (September): 477–508.

Boards Cut Out of Family Trees. 1996. *International Herald Tribune,* 2 February, 13, 17.

Daniels, Ronald J., and Randall Morck, eds. 1995. *Corporate decision making in Canada.* Calgary: Industry Canada/University of Calgary Press.

Daniels, Ronald J., Randall Morck, and David Stangeland. 1995. In high gear: A case study of the Hees-Edper corporate group. In *Corporate decision making in Canada,* ed. Ronald J. Daniels and Randall Morck. Calgary: Industry Canada/University of Calgary Press.

De Cordoba, Jose. 1995. Heirs battle over empire in Ecuador. *Wall Street Journal* (electronic ed.), 20 December.

Demsetz, Harold, and Kenneth Lehn. 1985. The structure of corporate ownership: Causes and consequences. *Journal of Political Economy* 93, no. 6 (December): 1155–77.

*Directory of inter-corporate ownership.* Various issues. Ottawa: Statistics Canada.

Edwards, Sebastian. 1998. Openness, productivity and growth: What do we really know? *Economic Journal* 108 (March): 383–98.

Feldstein, Martin. 1995. The effects of outbound foreign direct investment on the domestic capital stock. In *The effects of taxation on multinational corporations,* ed. Martin Feldstein, James R. Hines Jr., and R. Glenn Hubbard. Chicago: University of Chicago Press.

Finance and economics: Europe's great experiment. 1998. *Economist,* 13 June, 67–68.

Fishlow, Albert. 1996. Inequality, poverty, and growth: Where do we stand? *World Bank Research Observer: Annual Conference,* suppl., 25–39.

Hagger, Euan. 1997. Will Europe get its high yield market? *International Bond Investor,* April, 21–32.

Heinzl, John. 1995. Bata CEO quits after only a year, in shakeup at top. *Toronto Globe and Mail* (electronic ed.), 7 October.

Holmes, Kim, Bryan Johnson, and Melanie Kirkpatrick. 1997. *The 1997 index of economic freedom.* New York: *Wall Street Journal;* Washington, D.C.: Heritage Foundation.

Hoshi, Takeo, Anil Kashyap, and David Scharfstein. 1990. The role of banks in reducing the costs of financial distress in Japan. *Journal of Financial Economics* 27:67–88.

Jensen, Michael, and William Meckling. 1976. The theory of the firm: Managerial behavior, agency costs, and ownership structure. *Journal of Financial Economics* 3:305–60.

Khanna, Tarun, and Krishna Palepu. 1999. Policy shocks, market intermediaries, and corporate strategy: The evolution of business groups in Chile and India. *Journal of Economics and Management Strategy* 8, no. 2:271–310.

Kim, E. Han, Myeong Kyun Kim, and Jay K. Yi. 1998. Economic value-added of non-financial firms listed on the Korea stock exchange. Seoul: Korea Stock Exchange.

Kim, E. Han, and Vijay Singal. 1993. Mergers and market power: Evidence from the airline industry. *American Economic Review* 83, no. 3 (June): 549–69.

La Porta, Rafael, Florencio Lopez-de-Silanes, and Andrei Shleifer. 1999. Corporate ownership around the world. *Journal of Finance* 54, no. 2:471–517.

La Porta, Rafael, Florencio Lopez-de-Silanes, Andrei Shleifer, and Robert Vishny. 1997. Legal determinants of external finance. *Journal of Finance* 52, no. 3: 1131–50.

———. 1998. Law and finance. *Journal of Political Economy* 106, no. 6 (December): 1112–55.

Latour, Almar, and Greg Steinmetz. 1998. Investor AB chairman tries balancing family's values with shareholder values. *Wall Street Journal* (electronic ed.), 18 May.

MacIntosh, Jefferey G. 1994. Legal and institutional barriers to financing innovative enterprises in Canada. Discussion Paper no. 94-10. Kingston: Queen's University School of Policy Studies.

Mankiw, N. Gregory. 1995. The growth of nations. *Brookings Papers on Economic Activity,* no. 1:275–310.

McConnell, John J., and Henri Servaes. 1990. Additional evidence on equity ownership and corporate value. *Journal of Financial Economics* 27, no. 2:595–612.

McLaughlin, Gord. 1995a. In the name of the father and the son. *Financial Post,* 20 September, 14–15.

———. 1995b. What if he dies? *Financial Post,* 23 September, 14.

Morck, Randall, Andrei Shleifer, and Robert Vishny. 1988. Management ownership and corporate performance: An empirical analysis. *Journal of Financial Economics* 20 (January/March): 293–316.

Murray, Gordon C. 1998. A policy response to regional disparities in the supply of risk capital to new technology-based firms in the European Union: The European seed capital fund scheme. *Regional Studies* 32, no. 5 (July): 405–19.

Olson, Mancur. 1982. *The rise and decline of nations: Economic growth, stagflation, and social rigidities.* New Haven, Conn.: Yale University Press.

Shleifer, Andrei, and Robert Vishny. 1986. Large shareholders and corporate control. *Journal of Political Economy* 95:461–88.

———. 1989. Management entrenchment: The case of manager-specific investments. *Journal of Financial Economics* 25, no. 1 (November): 123–39.

Strom, Stephanie. 1996. In Sweden, a shy dynasty steps out. *New York Times* (electronic ed.), 12 May.

Stulz, René. 1988. On takeover resistance, managerial discretion, and shareholder wealth. *Journal of Financial Economics* 20, nos. 1/2 (January/March): 25–54.

Thompson, Aileen J. 1994. Trade liberalization, comparative advantage, and scale

economies: Stock market evidence from Canada. *Journal of International Economics* 37:1–27.
Wolfenzohn, Daniel. 1998. A theory of pyramidal ownership. University of Michigan, Department of Economics. Typescript.

## Comment David M. Levy

I have essentially one comment on the vastly instructive paper by Morck, Stangeland, and Yeung (MSY): Why do they constrain their analysis, both positive and normative, to the mean of a distribution? Of course, this query is not directed specifically to MSY but to the literature of which they are such distinguished exemplars.

### Why a Regression Mean?

The international data set used by MSY is of highly mixed quality. Ordinary least squares (OLS) regression estimates—a multiple-dimension generalization of a sample mean—are highly sensitive to contamination of high-quality data by data of a lesser quality. To shelter their technique from the hard facts of data quality, MSY restrict their international regressions to forty-one countries. Perhaps techniques more robust to violations of ideal conditions than OLS might reveal information from an extended data set.

What concerns me is that, in a context in which MSY attempt to find the effect of politically connected billionaires, their technique-driven exclusion of some countries may hide some enormously interesting questions of political stability. It can be argued, in particular, that central planning was a device by which the politically connected exploited others—and thus central planning created political billionaires in terms of consumption if not measured income (Levy 1990). Thus, the fact of the breakdown of the planned economies—justifying their exclusion from the regressions—is precisely the kind of evidence of the effect of politically connected wealth for which MSY are looking.

For an example of political wealth and political instability, consider MSY's table 11.1 "politician billionaire wealth" series. I find it most illuminating that the maximum of the series occurs with Indonesia! Newspaper accounts tell us that it was precisely the concern of the ruling family for its own well-being to the exclusion of other considerations that motivated the recent upheavals.

David M. Levy is associate professor of economics at George Mason University and a research associate of the Center for the Study of Public Choice.
Thanks are due to Andrew Farrant for error detection.

### Why Mean Income?

The dependent variable in MSY's cross-country regressions is per capita income. The justification for this is twofold: (*a*) the data are available, and (*b*) traditional economic utilitarianism uses mean income as a serviceable scalar metric of well-being. I think that there is really only one justification—economic utilitarianism tells us what data we ought to have collected.

The consequence of mean income as metric is that it makes no difference to whom the income goes. It makes no difference on this metric whether income is widely shared or concentrated in a few politically connected families. The reaction of many economists to this issue has been to renounce scalar metrics of well-being in favor of vectors, for example, to argue for a trade-off between "efficiency" and "equity" to take distributional issues into account.

Nonetheless, mean-based utilitarianism runs as deep as can be in modern economics. Consider what we teach our students about the efficiency of competition and monopoly. A competitive industry is more efficient than a single-price monopoly because the welfare triangle loss means that there is less income to divide between producer and consumer. Thus, a perfectly discriminating firm is as efficient as a competitive industry precisely because there is no welfare triangle loss (Robinson 1933). Distribution of income between producers and consumers is irrelevant to welfare judgments. But, again, this is a simple property of means.

Before utilitarianism was even named, a group of thinkers who moved seamlessly between economics and philosophy—Adam Smith, William Paley, and T. R. Malthus—argued that the well-being of the *majority* ought to be the metric by which we judge societies.[1] A utilitarianism recentered to consider median well-being has the enormous appeal of making explicit the link to political stability via the median-voter approach to democratic politics (Downs 1957).

As an illustration of how a median-based welfare evaluation might modify our results, consider how the evaluation of competition and monopoly would change. Let there be $N$ consumers but only $K$ firm owners, where $N/2 > K \geq 1$. Thus, the median member of society is a consumer, and, to find a social rank, we look only at the consumer's surplus. The ranking is obvious: competition, single-price monopoly, perfect discrimination. Thus, the social ranking of competition and single-price monopoly would remain unchanged, but the perfect discrimination case would move from a tie for first to dead last.

If MSY were to think about their model in terms of median income

1. Levy (1995) discusses Smith in this context; Hollander (1997, 830–31) discusses Malthus's median-based utilitarianism. Paley's majoritarianism is clear at Paley (1785, 61–67).

instead of mean income, the link between political stability—and thus what countries have nice enough to data with which to work!—and the underlying norm would seem to me to be more natural.

## Conclusion

Economists unsatisfied with the use of mean income as a scalar metric of social well-being sometimes propose adding considerations of "equity." If equity concerns are something that the political process addresses with a democratic procedure, then such equity considerations could be more closely approximated by considering the well-being of the median member of society.

## References

Downs, Anthony. 1957. *An economic theory of democracy.* New York: Harper & Row.

Hollander, Samuel. 1997. *The economics of Thomas Robert Malthus.* Toronto: University of Toronto Press.

Levy, David M. 1990. The bias in centrally planned prices. *Public Choice* 67: 213–36.

———. 1995. The partial spectator in the *Wealth of Nations:* A robust utilitarianism. *European Journal of the History of Economic Thought* 2:299–326.

Paley, William. 1785. *The principles of moral and political philosophy.* London.

Robinson, Joan. 1933. *The economics of imperfect competition.* London: Macmillan.

# Contributors

Lucian Arye Bebchuk
Harvard Law School
Harvard University
Cambridge, MA 02138

Robert D. Brown, FCA
Price Waterhouse Coopers
PO Box 82, Royal Trust Towers
Toronto-Dominion Centre
Toronto, Ontario M6K 1G8 Canada

Ronald J. Daniels
Faculty of Law
University of Toronto
78 Queen's Park
Toronto, Ontario M5S 2C5 Canada

Larry Y. Dann
Lundquist College of Business
University of Oregon
Eugene, OR 97403

Daniel Feenberg
National Bureau of Economic Research
1050 Massachusetts Avenue
Cambridge, MA 02138

Merritt B. Fox
University of Michigan Law School
Ann Arbor, MI 48109

Paul A. Gompers
Harvard Business School
Morgan Hall 483
Soldiers Field
Boston, MA 02163

Clifford G. Holderness
Finance Department
Fulton Hall 224C
Boston College
Chestnut Hill, MA 02467

Mark R. Huson
Faculty of Business
University of Alberta
Edmonton, Alberta T6G 2R6 Canada

Edward M. Iacobucci
Faculty of Law
University of Toronto
78 Queen's Park
Toronto, Ontario M5S 2C5 Canada

Marcel Kahan
New York University School of Law
40 Washington Square South
New York, NY 10012

Tarun Khanna
Harvard Business School
Morgan Hall 221
Boston, MA 02163

Reinier Kraakman
Harvard Law School
1575 Massachusetts Avenue
Cambridge, MA 02138

Josh Lerner
Harvard Business School
Morgan Hall 395
Boston, MA 02163

David M. Levy
James Buchanan Center
MSN 1D3
George Mason University
Fairfax, VA 22030

Paul G. Mahoney
University of Virginia School of Law
580 Massie Road
Charlottesville, VA 22903

Vikas Mehrotra
Faculty of Business
University of Alberta
Edmonton, Alberta T6G 2R6 Canada

Jack M. Mintz
Rotman School of Business
University of Toronto
150 St. George Street
Toronto, Ontario M5S 3E6 Canada

Randall Morck
Faculty of Business
University of Alberta
Edmonton, Alberta T6G 2R6 Canada

Krishna Palepu
Harvard Business School
Morgan Hall 419
Boston, MA 02163

Edward B. Rock
University of Pennsylvania Law School
3400 Chestnut Street
Philadelphia, PA 19104

Dennis P. Sheehan
Finance Department
College of Business
Penn State University
State College, PA 16802

David A. Stangeland
Department of Accounting and Finance
444 Drake Center
University of Manitoba
Winnipeg, Manitoba R3T 5V4 Canada

George G. Triantis
University of Chicago Law School
1111 East 60th Street
Chicago, IL 60637

Michael L. Wachter
University of Pennsylvania Law School
3400 Chestnut Street
Philadelphia, PA 19104

Michael S. Weisbach
University of Illinois
340 Commerce West
1206 South Sixth Street
Champaign, IL 61820

Thomas A. Wilson
Institute for Policy Analysis
University of Toronto
140 St. George Street
Toronto, Ontario M5S 3G6 Canada

Bernard Yeung
New York University
Stern School of Business
44 West 4th Street, Room 7/65
New York, NY 10012

Luigi Zingales
Graduate School of Business
The University of Chicago
1101 East 58th Street
Chicago, IL 60637

# Name Index

# Subject Index